Tax, Borrow and Spend:
Financing Federal Spending
in Canada,
1867–1990

The Carleton Library Series

A series of original works, new collections and reprints of source material relating to Canada, issued under the supervision of the Editorial Board, Carleton Library Series, Carleton University Press Inc., Ottawa, Canada.

Tax, Borrow and Spend: Financing Federal Spending in Canada, 1867–1990

by

W. Irwin Gillespie

Carleton University Press

Ottawa, Canada

1991

ISBN   0-88629-153-4 (paperback)
ISBN   0-88629-151-8 (casebound)

Printed and bound in Canada

Carleton Library Series 170

Canadian Cataloguing in Publication Data
 Gillespie, W. Irwin (William Irwin), 1937–
  Tax, borrow and spend: financing federal spending in Canada,
  1867–1990

ISBN 0-88629-153-4 (paperback)
ISBN 0-88629-151-8 (casebound)

1. Finance, Public–Canada–History.   2. Fiscal policy–Canada–History.
I. Title. II. Series.

HJ2449.G54 1991   336.71'09   C91-090359-X

Distributed by   Oxford University Press Canada,
        70 Wynford Drive,
        Don Mills, Ontario,
        Canada. M3C 1J9
        (416) 441-2941

Cover design: Y Graphic Design

Acknowledgements

Carleton University Press gratefully acknowledges the support extended
to its publishing programme by the Canada Council and the Ontario
Arts Council.

This book has been published with the help of a grant from the Social Science Federation of Canada, using funds provided by the Social
Sciences and Humanities Research Council of Canada.

For Anthea Foster

**Better to light one candle
than to curse the darkness.**

Table of Contents

List of Figures, Tables and Charts

Charts

Preface and Acknowledgments

From the dew of the few flakes that melt on our faces we cannot reconstruct the snowstorm.

(John Updike, "The Blessed Man of Boston,
My Grandmother's Thimble, and Fanning Island,"
in *Pigeon Feathers and Other Stories*, 1963, p. 157)

John Updike, in one of his earlier Olinger stories, used the above imagery to describe how limited is the reach of the aspiring novelist in illuminating the world around us. And yet the artist tries, through his or her craft, to reconstruct that snowstorm.

For the past twenty-seven years I have thought of the economist's craft as a similar, albeit less poetic, endeavour to understand the economy as a contribution to the illumination of the world around us. And although the observations of prices and quantities with which economists work may seem more lasting than melting snowflakes, understanding their meaning is no less challenging. The same can be said about the observations of taxes, borrowing and government expenditures with which public finance economists work in an attempt to understand the government sector within the overall economy. We are in the business of reconstructing snowstorms.

This book is about one such snowstorm, the financing of federal government spending in Canada from 1867 until 1990. My interest in embarking on this fiscal history of taxing and borrowing was stimulated by four separate lines of enquiry. Harvey Perry's classic two volume treatise on *Taxes, Tariffs and Subsidies* provides a richly detailed description of the making of Canada's tax policy and a sensitive treatment of some political constraints that influenced actual tax policy. Perry's study hints at several interesting hypotheses that could be examined within a comprehensive conceptual framework of revenue generation.

Georg Rich's seminal work on money and the Canadian business cycle prior to the first great war, *The Cross of Gold*, reminds us of the substantial reliance of Canada's early Dominion governments on deficit financing. The size and frequency of borrowing as a source of revenues to finance Dominion spending suggest the possibility that such deficit financing was not just a balancing item in the budget accounts. It might rather be the case that such borrowing might be a potential revenue source that is weighed against other potential revenue sources, such as the tariff and excise duties on alcohol and tobacco, when a government chooses its revenue mix to finance its spending. This possibility could only be examined within a comprehensive conceptual framework of revenue generation.

Some of my own work on evaluating fiscal policy within a stabilization framework after the second great war led me to conclude that the research questions I and other analysts were asking were possibly the wrong ones. Our findings, that federal fiscal policy performed poorly in terms of a stabilization objective, may indicate that what is required is a comprehensive positive model of federal budgetary behaviour that would allow us to discuss the factors determining and the constraints impinging upon actual tax, borrowing and expenditure policy.

Finally, my colleagues, Walter Hettich and Stanley Winer, arrived, via a different route, at the research decision to direct their attention to tax structure and, specifically, a positive model of tax structure. Our discussions during the early stages of the various projects were invaluable to me. We were convinced that interesting research questions, previously unasked or only partially addressed, could be posed within the context of a more comprehensive, positive framework of revenue structure. The core of our models has a similar genesis, while the questions asked and methods of garnering supporting evidence differ.

Some parts of the argument found in Chapters 2 and 9 are reprinted with the kind permission of: The Canadian Tax Foundation from, "The 1981 Federal Budget: Muddling Through or Purposeful Tax Reform?" (November–December 1983), 31 *Canadian Tax Journal*: 975– 1002; and the Institute of Public Administration of Canada from, "Tax Reform: The Battlefield, The Strategies, The Spoils" (Summer 1983), 26 *Canadian Public Administration*: 182–202.

The Social Sciences and Humanities Research Council and Carleton University have provided financial support at various stages of the study, for which I am very grateful. I am indebted to Else Brock, Barbara Guy, Patricia Nagy, Norma Rankin and Linda Saslove, who typed the earlier drafts of the manuscript. I am especially appreciative of the efforts of Charlotte Burba, Lalita Figueredo, Ginette Harte, Alex Howard, Rita Monaghan and Nonie Shickle, who were primarily responsible for typing the penultimate and final version of the book. Noel Gates, as copy-editor, and Pauline Adams and Christina Thiele of Carleton University Press, deserve special thanks for guiding me through the editorial process.

Students in my public finance classes and participants in the public economics workshop at Carleton University have provided critical and perceptive comments on earlier versions of the study. In addition, the critical comments and helpful suggestions of Richard Bird, Gino Bordignon, John Burrett, Robert Dimand, John Graham, Gordon Hawley, Walter Hettich, Jim Johnson, Alan Kerr, Baxter MacDonald, Allan Maslove, Robin Neill, Denis Normand, Harvey Perry, T.K. Rymes, Mac Urquhart, Bill Watson, Stan Winer and several anonymous referees have strengthened the manuscript. In addition, Walter Hettich and Stanley Winer kindly provided me with their data base for 1968–1985, created on the same basis as the data base for this study.

The research assistance of Chris Busutill, Linda Herron, Margaret MacDonald, Robert Rowe and Jody Shore has been extremely valuable at various stages in the study. In addition, Jim Feehan, who was my principal research assistant during the early stages of the investigation, not only carried out the many pedestrian tasks with unfailing thoroughness but contributed to the development of several of the hypotheses of the positive model of Chapter 2. He continued to serve as a helpful critic up to the penultimate draft of the manuscript. Frank Vermaeten, who was my principal assistant during the final revision of the book, not only helped in extending the analysis from 1968 through 1990 but was instrumental in the integration of the model of Chapter 2 with the fiscal history of the remainder of the book. The structure, form and content of the ideas in this book have been immeasurably strengthened by his perceptive contributions.

Finally, I am indebted to my friends, Gilles Paquet and Tom Rymes, the former for his insistence that the big questions, however intractable, are the only ones worth asking and the latter for his affirmation that the search for the answer, however protracted, challenging and revealing, provides its own reward. This book is my testament to those shared beliefs.

Chapter 1

Introduction

Don't tax you, don't tax me, tax that fellow behind the tree . . .
Don't tax me . . . .

(old Hungarian folk saying)

Aim and Scope of Study

This book tells the story of taxes, borrowing, and government spending. It illuminates and explains the fascinating tax and borrowing choices that Canadian federal governments have made in financing government spending from Confederation in 1867 through 1990.

Few influences are more pervasive than government in shaping the conduct of our day to day affairs, determining the quality of our lives, and nurturing our hopes and dreams for the future than government. Perhaps faith, or possibly belief in self, but no one escapes the touch of government.

The tax touch of government is felt each time we open a pay cheque to find that income tax, unemployment insurance premiums and Canada or Quebec pension plan premiums have been deducted before we get the chance to spend our earnings. The tax touch is felt, even if imbedded in the price of the goods, when we purchase appliances, furniture, carpets, food, sports equipment, cigarettes, beer, wine, scotch, a car, and a new home.

The spending touch of government is felt each time we use the roads to cycle, drive or ride to work or to shop. It is there each time we use the services of a doctor or a hospital. It was there to provide our schooling and our children's schooling. The spending touch is felt each time a mother receives a family allowance cheque, an unemployed worker receives an unemployment insurance benefit cheque and a citizen over sixty-five years of age receives an old age security pension.

What mechanism generates this pervasive taxing and spending influence? Is it an uncontrolled leviathan exploding outwards from some dimly remembered simple government past? Is it a random walk of no discernible direction or path which, at this time, happens to be "walking" everywhere? A glance ahead in this chapter to Chart 1-2 should be enough to increase the reader's scepticism about such possible explanations.

The answer may be as diverse across many countries as it is complex for each individual country. Yet in all democratic countries one key relationship is at the core of that engine — the relationship between citizen and elected government.

No relationship between two parties, with the possible exception of that between client and psychiatrist, is more fraught with love and hate than that between citizen and elected government. We love the government spending that benefits us directly; we hate the taxes that we are called upon to pay. We love the taxes that someone else is called upon to pay; we hate the government spending that provides benefits for others but does not seem to benefit us directly. We know that in order to persuade government to launch the desirable projects, beneficial programs and great public works that we value highly (and are prepared to pay for), we may have to accept and help pay for the misguided projects, wasteful programs and extravagant public works that others value much more highly than we do. We accept this but we grumble, we apply pressure, we try to persuade others and we threaten "to vote the scoundrels out of office".

Each politician must, in order to gain power, retain power and use power, persuade more citizens to vote for him or her than for the competing candidate. A political party, in order to gain power and become the government, must compete with other parties for the most support. Politicians and political parties offer political agendas or political platforms that they hope will secure more electoral support than the agendas of their competitors. Of all the elements that comprise a political agenda, it is the collection of taxes from citizens and the spending of those revenues by governments that are the most important and most contentious.

Politicians know that a proposed new spending program will win the support of the citizens most directly affected by the program and may even garner support from a few less directly involved. They also know that the additional tax revenues to finance the program will likely take away some support. On the balance of this net vote gain, and all other net vote gains or losses associated with the proposed political agenda, rests a politician's success or failure in gaining and retaining office.

Successful politicians need citizen support and fear its volatility. Citizens need elected politicians and fear their powers to tax and to spend. This tension in the relationship between the citizen and elected government helps to define, constrain and steer the pervasive taxing and spending influence that we observe.

These common elements within the mechanism that motivates and powers a government hold for democratic countries as disparate as Canada, the United States, Sweden, the United Kingdom, Israel and Japan. They have increasing relevance for such countries as the Soviet Union, Poland and Hungary. This makes it much more feasible to construct a generalized model of government taxing and spending behaviour.

Government spending has been extensively studied and modelled. The work of Alan Peacock and Jack Wiseman, entitled *The Growth of Public Expenditure in the United Kingdom*, and Richard Bird's *The Growth of Government Spending in Canada*, are two of the most important treatises on the spending side of the government's budget.[1]

This book focuses on the financing side of the government's budget — the taxing and borrowing behaviour of government. It will develop a theory of taxation and borrowing that accounts for and explains the level and type of tax and the amount of borrowing chosen by a government in order to finance spending. Initially, in order to make more manageable the task of analyzing the financing side of the budget, I assume that the level of government expenditures is fixed. Later in the book a partial attempt is made to integrate the two sides of the budget.

What our governments do and what we as citizens think they ought to do are two entirely separate issues. I believe that it is important to understand how governments operate, to explain the tax and borrowing choices that governments make in financing their spending, and ultimately to define what powers, steers and constrains governments. Such an understanding, to which I hope this book will make a contribution, may also aid us as citizens to shape and mould our governments as part of the search for the good society. I wholeheartedly subscribe to Richard Musgrave's creed, which holds that, "intelligent conduct of government requires an understanding of the economic relations involved; and the economist, by aiding in this understanding, may hope to contribute to a better society."[2]

Research Strategy

This book is the first part of a long term research inquiry that will eventually encompass the evolution of the financing policies of Canada's federal, provincial and municipal governments. The data and primary sources that are available to document such an evolution are very limited. These sources and their limitations are discussed in Appendix A.

The research strategy is geared to the objective of explaining and accounting for the level and type of tax and the amount of borrowing chosen by federal governments in Canada to finance the spending of the past one hundred and twenty-three years. A comprehensive conceptual model of revenue structure is developed in the following chapter and it will serve as a framework to guide the discussion in the remainder of the book.

The methodology of this study relies upon two important sources of information, a new data base on federal government spending, taxing and borrowing, from 1867 to 1990, and an analysis of the budget speech of each Minister of Finance during the same period. These sources of information will, when combined with the positive model of revenue structure of Chapter 2, allow us to understand the financing policies of Canada's federal governments.

The study provides a new data base for federal government expenditures, tax revenues by revenue source and deficit financing (borrowing). These new data are expressed as a percentage of national income in order to provide for the first time, annual estimates of the relative importance of federal government spending, taxing and borrowing and the national debt. These series are derived in Appendices B and C.

These data provide several important advantages over other existing series. First, the series on total expenditures and total revenues are as consistent as it is possible to make them for the one hundred and twenty-three year period. All spending and taxing items have been dealt with in a similar fashion for the entire period. Second, the data are comprehensive, including the total financing and spending of several accounts that are often treated separately from the budgetary accounts. For example, as part of the revenue totals, unemployment insurance taxes and old age security taxes are integrated into the accounts and provided as separate revenue sources. Third, an error in officially published public accounts data for expenditures during the 1929–1933 period has been corrected.

Fourth, a series on the deficit (surplus) derived from a comprehensive definition of federal government expenditure and revenue has been established for the first time, covering the entire period. The cumulative result of this series on the deficit (surplus) is a consistent measure of the national debt, annually, from 1868 to 1990. These series are important for this study. They will also be available for other uses as well.

The study uses, as a second important piece of information, an analysis of the budget speech of the Minister of Finance. The speech and its accompanying documentation articulate the Minister's interpretation of the weight of various factors that he or she took into account in formulating and presenting the tax, tariff, borrowing and expenditure policies of the government. The budget debate in Parliament provides an accompanying source, as opposition is crystallized around those issues which citizen-taxpayers are prepared to use against proposed changes in tax, tariff, borrowing and expenditure policies.

The government responds, and must be prepared to respond, throughout the required six-day parliamentary debate in a way that will convey to voters its view of the political package contained in the budget speech, and to convince them that this package best serves their interests. In a minority government situation the Minister of Finance and the government must be especially careful to articulate a budgetary policy that secures political support from some opposition members as well, but ultimately the source of such political support is the voters. In a majority government situation the Minister of Finance may have a slightly larger margin of manoeuvre, but must still take into account the political competition that will assure exposure of budgetary policies likely to serve as rallying points for political opposition, especially at election time.

The budget speech, accompanying documentation and parliamentary debate together constitute an important primary source that can illuminate the motivations of governments as they go about the business of financing their spending. The budget speech, as a political resolution of a complex of competing interests, is precisely the institutional instrument that might be expected to open a window on the politics of tax making and make it possible to refute or validate elements of the positive model of revenue structure.

Each budget speech was analyzed in terms of direct references, indirect inferences and broad fiscal stance and the consistency of these components with the various determinants of political costs developed in the next chapter. A quantitative summary of such references provided the basis for grouping determinants into three broad categories, those of major, modest and minor influence. The budget speeches were reviewed again in light of this broad categorization in order to confirm the broader fiscal stance and amend, if necessary, the ranking of the political factors.

This budget analysis serves as a major source of information for the discussion, in Chapters 3 and 4 below, of broad themes that have influenced one hundred and twenty-three years of fiscal history. The budget speeches are referenced by Finance Minister and date in Appendix E. Canadian federal election dates since Confederation are found in Appendix D.

A Preview of the Taxing, Borrowing and Spending Story 1867–1990

It has been a fascinating one hundred and twenty-three years of taxing, borrowing and spending for the federal government of Canada.

Chart 1-1

Major Revenue Sources, as a percentage of Total Financial Requirements (TFR), Canada, Selected Fiscal Years, 1868-1990.

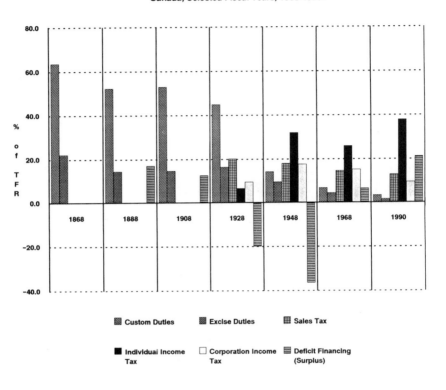

Source: Table B-3

Consider the dramatic changes in financing instruments. Chart 1-1 summarizes a rapid romp though the history of the major revenue sources chosen by Canadian federal governments. In 1868, 54 cents out of every dollar spent by the government was raised from the tariff, whereas excise duties, on alcohol and tobacco, and borrowing raised 21 and 13 cents respectively. By 1928, 45 cents out of every dollar spent was raised from the tariff and 13 cents from excise duties; three new taxes on manufacturers' sales, corporation profits and personal incomes accounted for 12, 11 and 8 cents respectively and an extra 12 cents was used to reduce the national debt. By 1990, 38 cents out of every dollar spent was raised by the personal income tax whereas borrowing raised 21 cents. The manufacturers' sales tax and corporation profits tax raised 13 and 10 cents, respectively, whereas the once mighty tariff and excise duties on alcohol and tobacco produced a trivial 3 and 2 cents respectively.

Consider, next, the interesting pattern of spending, taxing and borrowing, all viewed in relation to the size of the Canadian economy. Chart 1-2 traces in a more leisurely fashion three indicators, reflecting the total spending, total borrowing and total tax revenues chosen by Canadian federal governments. The spending indicator, total government expenditures as a percent of gross national product, is a widely used measure of government sector size. The borrowing indicator is deficit financing as a percent of gross national product. The tax indicator, total government tax revenues as a percent of gross national product, is the distance between the spending indicator and the borrowing indicator. In Chart 1-3 the tax indicator is provided separately.

These charts offer an interesting picture of the federal government's financing of its spending. The tax indicator was virtually constant until about 1914, at 6 per cent, then rose sharply through the end of the second great war before settling down to approximately 17 percent, around which there has been considerable variation. Within the total tax indicator are considerable variations in specific taxes that are not shown in Charts 1-2 or 1-3, but that will be demonstrated later. During a remarkably fecund period of tax births, 1917–1923, the personal income tax, the corporation income tax and the manufacturers' sales tax were introduced, and after seventy years of considerable variations in growth rates now account for the three most important tax sources in the family of revenue sources.

The total spending indicator, the tax indicator and the borrowing indicator all rose substantially during each of the two great wars and fell dramatically after the wars had ended. The federal public sector exhibited markedly similar wartime patterns, even though the increase in the tax indicator during the first great war lagged somewhat. The

Chart 1-2

**Federal Expenditures, Borrowing and Taxes,
as a percentage of GNP, Canada, 1870-1989.**

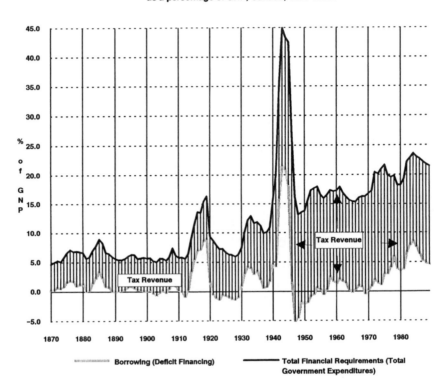

Source: Table C-3

two post-war periods reflected a no less remarkably consistent pattern of declining spending and taxing and of substantial surpluses which were used to reduce the federal debt.

The fiscal record demonstrates that Canadian federal governments regularly financed a significant part of their spending by borrowing. Even if we leave aside the first and second great war periods, when the borrowing indicator reached 8 and 22 per cent respectively, we find that deficit financing was actively pursued during the great depressions of the 1870s–1890s and the 1930s when it reached 4 percent each time. The 1970s–1980s are also characterized by substantial deficit financing, with the borrowing indicator increasing to a high of 9 percent in 1985. And these periods, as Chart 1-2 indicates, are just the peaks.

These observations summarize the highlights of the story of Canada's fiscal history. Up until now it has been a sadly neglected and badly reported story. Writers on taxation, with few exceptions, have, in general, not seen the evolution of the revenue structure in Canada as a topic worthy of analysis. I intend to describe, explain and account for this fiscal history. I intend to discuss how federal governments choose among their many tax sources and borrowing as they finance their total spending and to account for the birth, growth and death of taxes.

The remainder of the book is organized around these highlights of the fiscal history story, rather than within a chronological time frame. However, the reader should have no problem translating the following discussion into a chronological account of the evolution of the Canadian revenue structure through time, with the aid of Charts 1-2 and 1-3.

In Chapter 2, I develop the model that will guide the discussion throughout the book. The government, in this model, maximizes its chances of political survival by financing its spending in such a way as to minimize the political costs of raising its revenues from many potential revenue sources, including borrowing. The real determinants of those political costs are defined by fourteen hypotheses. The political equilibrium is established when a government has extended its utilization of each revenue source up to the point where marginal political costs are equalized. Exogenous shocks to the determinants of these political costs result in revenue structure changes and tax reforms that can be described by predictions of three crucial variables — the birth or death of a tax, the change in the tax rate and the change in the share of the tax in total financial requirements.

In Chapter 3, I discuss the extent to which several broad fiscal structure themes influenced the evolution of the federal revenue structure from Confederation in 1867 to the summer of 1917, a time when attracting immigrants and persuading the remaining colonies to join the Union were

Chart 1-3

Federal Tax Revenue, as a percentage of GNP, Canada, 1870-1989.

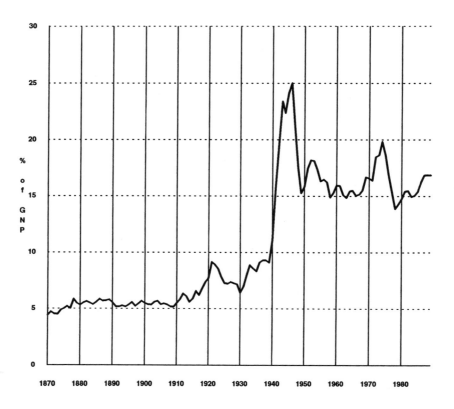

Source: Table C-3

important objectives of federal policy. The tariff, excise duties on alcohol and tobacco and deficit financing are the three most important revenue sources during this period. Federal governments revealed, through budget speeches of the Minister of Finance and parliamentary debates on budgetary issues, that they took into consideration some of the real determinants of political costs in shaping the revenue structure variation during this fifty year period. Further analysis of the quantitative record within the framework of the model helps to account for three interesting observations regarding this revenue structure variation through time — the relative constancy of the total taxes relative to gross national product (noted in Chart 1-3), the decision to eschew the creation of a direct tax on incomes and the active, vigorous reliance on borrowing to finance a substantial share of government spending.

Chapter 4 provides a broad overview of the fiscal structure themes that influenced the continuing evolution of the revenue structure from the summer of 1917 to 1990. The personal income tax, the corporation income tax and the general sales tax were created and grew to dominate the variation in, and the evolution of, the revenue structure during the following seventy-three years. Federal governments continued to reveal that they took into consideration several of the real determinants of political costs in creating the revenue structure that financed their spending during this period. Comparison of the two major periods shows that there was some reranking of the weights attached by Ministers of Finance to these determinants of political costs.

The remainder of the book is devoted to a detailed analysis of the birth, growth and death of taxes and the considerable shifts in the components of the revenue structure from 1917 through 1990. In Chapter 5 the births of the personal income tax, the corporation income tax and the sales tax are examined and explained within the conceptual framework of this study. These findings are contrasted with several widely held misconceptions about the births of these taxes, for example, the erroneous belief that the personal income tax was a "temporary" tax.

In Chapter 6 the financing of the sharp rise in spending during each of the two great wars is analyzed. The borrowing strategy that resulted in financing close to half of government expenditures by borrowing is explained. The taxing strategy that resulted in the tariff and the personal income tax, in the first and second great war respectively, providing the largest share of tax revenues is also analyzed and explained. These findings too are contrasted with the erroneous view in the literature that spending during the first great war was primarily financed by borrowing, while during the second great war it was primarily financed by taxing.

In Chapter 7 the financing of the sustained reductions in the national debt, after each of the two great wars through the generation of sizeable surpluses on the budget is analyzed. A post-war demand for debt reduction and strong opposition from taxpayers most affected by wartime taxes caused governments to reduce the debt and lower effective tax rates on specific revenue sources. The sources of funds for these reductions came from very large decreases in government spending, a new sales tax, increased tax rates on some revenue sources and revenue buoyancy produced by a rapidly growing economy. The key role played by the manufacturers' sales tax in reducing the national debt in each post-war period is highlighted. These findings demonstrate that Keynesian fiscal stabilization policy did not play a significant role in determining revenue structure changes after the second great war.

I analyze the financing of the modest rise in government spending during the great depression of the 1930s in Chapter 8. The borrowing and taxing choices of governments are described and analyzed. An especially important role is played by the manufacturers' sales tax. These findings undermine some further erroneous beliefs that the 1930s witnessed a "tax jungle" and that revenue structure policy was a haphazard and indiscriminate attack upon the taxpayer launched in a attempt to balance the budget.

In Chapter 9, I analyze and explain the financing of tax reform from 1963 through 1990. Benson's 1971 tax reforms, MacEachen's 1981–83 tax reforms and Wilson's 1988 tax reforms, each of which achieved a reduction in tax rates and a broadening of the bases for the personal income tax and the corporation income tax, were crafted with the aid of a consultative tax reform strategy. Turner's 1974 tax reform that indexed the personal income tax was achieved through a budget strategy. These findings cast doubt on several popular perceptions of these tax reforms, especially the mistaken notion that Finance Minister MacEachen's tax reform budget was a failure and a fiasco.

Chapter 10 explains the increases in deficit financing and the national debt relative to the size of the Canadian economy from about the middle of the 1970s to the present. The initial surge in debt creation was caused, not by profligate federal governments spending recklessly, but by Finance Ministers choosing to decrease tax rates of the three major taxes — the corporation income tax, the personal income tax and the manufacturers' sales tax. I discuss and explain the increasingly important role played by the sales tax during the 1980s, culminating in Finance Minister Wilson's tax reform that replaced the manufacturers' sales tax with the value-added Goods and Services Tax.

Chapter 11 concludes the Canadian taxing and borrowing story of the past one hundred and twenty-three years by summarizing the findings of the study. This entails a discussion of the major determinants of political costs that have shaped the evolution of the revenue structure over the entire period, as well as a drawing together of the various political mistakes that have caused Finance Ministers to amend or withdraw their tax proposals. The important conclusions concerning the vigorous and active use of borrowing and the birth, growth and death of taxes are highlighted. The book concludes with a speculative glimpse of the taxing and borrowing story through the year 2000.

Chapter 2

A Positive Model
of Revenue Structure

Time and again, the government has chosen the course that will either (a) lose the fewest number of votes in the next election or (b) gain the greatest possible number of votes in the next election. Other considerations need not apply.

(Erik Nielsen, *The House is not a Home*, p. 126)

In this chapter, after discussing the need for a comprehensive theory of revenue structure, I develop the model that is to serve as a guide throughout the remainder of the book. The conceptual framework is based on a government that maximizes its chances of political survival by financing any given level of spending in such a manner as to minimize the political costs of obtaining the revenues. A discussion of the determinants of those political costs results in fourteen hypotheses that can shed light on the political equilibrium of the model and the structure of revenues in such an equilibrium. Exogenous shocks to the determinants of political costs are analyzed to explain tax reforms and revenue structure changes through time. The model is compared with the seminal work of Walter Hettich and Stanley Winer. Finally, several reservations about the model are discussed.

The Need For a Theory of Revenue Structure

Writers on taxation have devoted much more time to telling us what taxes ought to be chosen by government than they have to explaining the choices that governments actually make with respect to taxes, tax rates and borrowing. The theory of taxation in the literature is largely the normative theory of taxation. The analyst begins with a preselected set of norms, such as equity, economic efficiency, administrative ease and certainty, and then analyzes each tax and the total tax structure with reference to these norms. If the tax structure compares badly with the set of norms the analyst recommends changes or "tax reforms" that will improve the tax system.

The norms of equity and economic efficiency are the benchmarks most often chosen by scholars for the analysis of taxes. Writers, from Adam

Smith to Paul Samuelson, have used these norms to build an imposing edifice called the economic theory of taxation.[1] The edifice has provided the basis for academic "tax reform" proposals during the past three centuries.[2] It has also provided support for the recommendations of royal commissions or committees on taxation. The two most illustrious of such bodies in Canada have been the Rowell-Sirois Royal Commission on Dominion-Provincial Relations in 1940 and the Carter Royal Commission on Taxation, 1967, both of which made extensive recommendations for reforming the tax systems in Canada.[3]

The normative framework within which most scholars, and royal commissions of this kind operate, prevents them from explaining the actual introduction of new taxes, the evolution of the tax system over time and the elimination of some taxes. In other words, there is no theory that elucidates what it is that motivates governments in their actual choice of taxes and tax systems.

Some writers have attempted to understand the forces shaping the tax and fiscal structure through time by interpreting them within a framework of social, economic and political change.[4] This broader, historical approach suggests several hypotheses that could account for particular tax structure changes within a temporal framework.

Richard Musgrave's "tax handles" hypothesis is developed from the possibility that revenue bases which facilitate collection and enforcement and minimize collusion between tax collector and taxpayers provide handles to which the revenue system can be attached with low political costs.[5] Countries at an early stage of economic development will tend to use indirect taxation since customs revenues and excise duties are easier to collect and to enforce than direct taxation, which requires well developed systems of record-keeping, skilled administrators and courts prepared to enforce fines. This hypothesis, at best, goes only part of the way to explain the evolution of tax structures through time.

Harvey Perry's classic treatise on *Taxes, Tariffs and Subsidies* presents illuminating suggestions about forces that might have affected and constrained the evolution of the tax structure in Canada.[6] The interplay of constraints such as the extent to which other levels of government are taxing the same revenue base, political preferences for different kinds of taxes, the cost of acquiring the right to impose certain taxes under the terms of the constitution, and the complexity of administration is described in detail. However, the discussion stops short of providing a comprehensive conceptual framework within which to analyze the emergence and growth of the Canadian tax structure through time.

Several writers have focused primarily on selected aspects of the political process within this broader, historical approach.[7] Walter Hettich's and Stanley Winer's seminal attempt to model formally the determination of the tax structure is especially useful.[8] These authors develop a model where, for a mature tax system, politicians minimize the political costs of extracting revenues from a variety of tax sources in order to finance a given level of government spending. They use the analysis to explain the variation in the share of income taxation among state jurisdictions in the United States. Their model, while more comprehensive than most, nevertheless does not include a complete conceptual framework and does not allow for the introduction of a new tax or the repeal of an existing tax.

With these few exceptions the theory of taxation in the literature is either the normative theory of taxation or the theory of the effect of a tax change or tax substitution on designated target variables, such as output, employment and the distribution of income.[9] However, a different, more comprehensive theory of taxation is needed in order to explain what we observe — governments choosing new taxes, increasing and decreasing tax rates on existing tax sources, occasionally repealing a tax and borrowing extensively.[10]

The structure of taxes is created by the process of a very political market place, where groups of politicians compete against each other for the votes of the electorate which will bestow the prize of political power. The exchanges of this political market place are public goods, transfers and subsidies, paid for with taxes and borrowed funds. In a federation such as Canada, the national political market, the several provincial political markets and the many local political markets are interconnected within a complex mosaic, the pattern of which seems to be constantly changing. This revenue structure mosaic reflects the outcome of a highly complex and competitive political process. To ignore this political process is to neglect the systematic, analytical examination of the structure of revenues, the causes of tax reform, the processes of tax reform and the potential limitations on tax reform proposals.

What is needed is a conceptual model of revenue structure in which politics is at the heart of the model, the structure of the revenue system is the equilibrium outcome of an active political market process, and tax changes or tax reforms are the results of shocks to that revenue structure mosaic. Such a model puts the focus on a theory of government choice among alternative revenue sources, including borrowing.

The positive model of fiscal structure would be capable of providing some insights into, and convincing explanations for, the fiscal structure decisions of governments that are embedded in the revenue structures of the past. In addition, the model would be capable of giving weights to the various factors determining political costs — costs which impinge so directly upon a government's revenue structure decisions.

This information should help tax reformers to prepare the way for implementing proposals to introduce new taxes or repeal old taxes. If some political costs can be lowered with little effort or demonstrated to be not as pervasive as politicians think they are then the chances for "tax reform" are enhanced. In this way a positive model of revenue structure could assist those of us who advise governments on the tax changes that ought to be made. Moreover, it may aid us as citizens in guiding and constraining our government's choices of revenue structures, this being one aspect of building a better society.

The following sections of this chapter develop a comprehensive positive model of revenue structure.

The Political Process and Revenue Structure

[One influence on the evolution of the Canadian tax structure is] the political factor . . . in the deeper and more realistic sense of politics as the art of the possible . . . Occasionally matters of taxation are the subject of an exercise in this political art.

(Perry, 1953:12)

The model takes as its starting point the obvious fact that taxes are introduced and tax rates are varied by governments through time. Thus decisions concerning taxes will usually be weighed in terms of the political benefits and political costs entailed.

A government provides goods, services, subsidies, transfer payments and political policies for its citizens. These government expenditures and political policies provide political benefits in the form of electoral victory, or of defeat if the expenditures and policies promised by the opposition party are more attractive to the voters. The government finances expenditures and political policies by taxing diverse sources of income, expenditure or wealth, by borrowing funds, by creating money and regulating the flow of credit, by coercion and by broad regulatory powers. Each potential revenue source which is drawn upon generates a political cost — the opposition of the voter whose revenue source is being taxed. The government, in the pursuit of electoral victory, attempts to maximize the political benefits from spending and minimize the political costs of financing the spending, achieving thereby a political equilibrium.

The political equilibrium is characterized by a structure of spending: some citizens receive few goods, services and transfers; others receive many, and the amount varies by specific expenditure. Some goods falling completely within the collective consumption category are available for consumption in equal amounts for all citizens. The political equilibrium also entails a structure of taxes: different revenue sources are taxed; for each revenue source, the base may or may not be comprehensive, and the tax rate may or may not be the same for all similarly situated citizens. For the purpose of this study I take the level and structure of government expenditures as given, albeit determined within the political framework, along with the structure of regulatory policies. The level of total expenditures then becomes the required level of total financing. It is this level of total financing which the government will strive to achieve in such a manner as to minimize the political costs of achieving it.

There is a powerful disincentive for a government to deviate from this cost-minimizing behaviour: the risk of being ejected from office by an aroused citizenry. Alternatively, we may speak of a "survival rule". To survive a government will minimize the total political costs of obtaining its required level of total financing. Different potential revenue sources — real property, imports, income, sales, — raise, for reasons to be examined below, very different degrees of political opposition and therefore entail different political costs.

It follows from the survival rule that a government will utilize each revenue source up to the point at which the marginal political cost is equal for all such sources. New taxes will be imposed on a potential revenue source when the political costs are less than they would be from increasing the tax rate on an existing revenue source. When the political opposition to an existing old tax increases, for whatever reason, as compared with the opposition to another old tax, the effective tax rate will be be lowered on the former and raised on the latter. When the political opposition to an existing old tax increases substantially as compared with the opposition to all other old taxes and to new taxes on potential revenue sources, the tax which the voters oppose so strongly will be repealed.

Within this conceptual framework total and marginal political costs constitute a powerful engine generating the motivations of politicians — and they are not directly observable. However, real factors that influence and determine these political costs are observable. I formulate below a number of hypotheses linking such real determinants to the political cost functions. The resultant structure of the revenue system is the equilibrium outcome of government behaviour responding to these changing political costs, and this revenue structure is directly observable. Thus, the predictions of the positive model are capable of being invalidated by reference to real data.

Three features of this conceptual framework may require further explanation. First, the model takes the total budget as the focus or outcome of a very political process but then proceeds to develop a theory of revenue structure, holding the structure and level of government expenditures constant. As we are seeking to explain the structure of revenues and changes in that structure, this is a reasonable approach to adopt. In addition, it makes the analytical task of examining fiscal structure more manageable. Most positive models of the public household have focused almost exclusively on the expenditure side of the budget, with the revenue side allowed for only indirectly through the budget constraint.[11] This one-sided approach has been a useful strategy in examining expenditures. I expect that it will prove to be an equally manageable approach to the development of a model for the purpose of examining the structure of revenues. This may involve some sacrifice in generality when the structure of the expenditure side of the budget decision has implications for revenue structure.

It does not, however, reduce the generality of analysis when the level of total government expenditures has implications for revenue structure. I develop below the situation in which an increase in total government expenditures results in a change in the structure of revenues. In an historical analysis, in which the level of total government expenditures can change dramatically, the possibility of allowing for such change on the structure of the revenue system is important. The approach of this study enables us to account for such changes.

Second, the model approaches the budget decision from a perspective that allows for citizens choosing a collective instrument — the government, its policies and its budget — to provide goods, services, subsidies and transfers that generate benefits, and to tax and to borrow in order to finance these benefits. At the same time the model allows for citizen opposition to the attempt by the government to raise such revenues. It may not be readily obvious why a citizen would both choose a vehicle to tax personal resources and oppose the taxes when they are applied. And in the small-number case, where taxing and spending decisions are seen to be simultaneously determined by or on behalf of a few individuals, opposition to any tax applied would be much less likely. However, in the large-number case, where the citizen perceives a separation between spending decisions and tax decisions, and the receipt of benefits is less obviously linked to actual taxes paid by each citizen, there is much more scope for active political opposition to particular taxes.[12] Most real world situations involve many thousands of citizens and the separation of expenditure from tax decisions is more likely to motivate individual citizens to engage in political or other activity.[13]

The third feature involves the political cost functions associated with each potential revenue source. At one level of analysis these political costs reflect expected vote loss to the governing party of increasing the tax take per dollar's worth of revenue base. I shall argue below that real observable factors determine the nature of these political cost functions. However the political costs themselves are perceived by, interpreted by, and acted upon by politicians. Thus the politicians in the model play a crucial role in translating these political costs from a "perceived view" of the political market place into an "actual view" of the same market place. Accordingly I interpret these political costs as "perceived" political cost functions; this allows one to account for some fiscal behaviour that seems designed to bring "perceived" political costs closer to "actual" political costs, rather than to respond simply to a change in actual costs.

Several terms need to be defined with greater precision. Revenue structure encompasses two aspects of the revenue system — the division of total revenues among different revenue sources, and structural features of particular taxes (i.e., definition of tax base, deductions, exemptions and credits, and the structure of tax rates). The effective tax rate is the revenue per dollar's worth of revenue base for a particular revenue source. There is an effective tax rate for each revenue source. Revenues from a particular revenue source result from multiplying the effective tax rate by the base of the particular revenue source. So long as the base of a particular potential revenue source is fixed, and I assume this for the time being, effective tax rate readily translates into revenues.

The survival rule can be reinterpreted in these terms: a government will utilize each revenue source up to the point where a dollar of extra revenue raised from each existing and potential revenue source involves equal political costs. Revenues for each tax source can be added together to produce total revenues. Tax reform is defined as a major change in government revenues in relation to national income, or as any large change in the structure of a revenue source or of the total revenue system. This could involve either a change in the comprehensiveness of the base of the revenue source or a large change in the effective tax rate for a revenue source (or the structure of effective rates for a given revenue source), or some combination thereof. It could also involve the taxation of a new revenue source for the first time.

Factors Influencing Political Costs

In the following discussion I examine the major factors that can influence and determine the nature of political cost functions of the many revenue sources that play a key role in the positive model of revenue structure. For the time being I hold the structural features of particular taxes constant (except the tax rate), especially the potential base associated with each revenue source.

Consider, first, economies of scale of organizing political opposition. These determine the relationship between political opposition and the effective tax rate on a given revenue source. Let us assume, by way of example, that a government is considering a new tax on a revenue source that hitherto has not been taxed. The introduction of a new tax produces an announcement effect which rallies political opposition of all sorts — within the legislature, in the press and among the citizens who are going to be taxed. The visibility of a proposed new revenue-raising activity can bring together opponents representing disparate views for purposes of organizing resistance. There are large, fixed start-up costs of organizing these political elements into an effective opposition to the proposed new tax.

The persistence of opposition to the tax depends on the effective tax rate. As this rate is increased by the government to meet a rise in total required financing, the perceived burden on each taxpayer grows; as the tax per dollar's worth of tax base for the particular revenue source increases, the taxpayer's perceived burden becomes greater and thus his or her potential opposition strengthens. Given the economies of scale in co-ordinating and organizing effective political opposition and distributing information about the probable effects of the tax on concerned groups, many more taxpayers will become involved in the "politics" of opposition as the tax rate increases. Hence, total political opposition grows at an increasing rate as the effective tax rate rises. Such political opposition translates directly into the total political costs facing a government — eventually total political costs grow at an increasing rate as the effective tax rate rises. Given the assumption that the size of the potential base for each revenue source remains fixed, it follows that the marginal political cost for each revenue source increases with the increase in the revenues extracted by the government from each revenue source. This conclusion may be reformulated as our first hypothesis (H-1):

H-1: Total political costs eventually rise at an increasing rate and marginal political costs increase as the effective tax rate is increased by a government.

This hypothesis is developed on the assumption that all other possible factors that determine political costs are held constant. Economies of scale in organizing political opposition and the resulting H-1 are advanced as one determinant of political costs, independent of any other possible determinants. The same approach is used in deriving the remaining determinants.

Consider next those factors which influence the level of the political cost functions — number of taxpayers, constitutional arrangements, tax preferences, vertical and horizontal tax competition, horizontal tax shifting and administrative costs of collection and compliance. The level of the political cost function includes the location of the intercept on the vertical axis of Figure 2-1 below (see page 34) and the extent to which the marginal political cost function is shifted up or down by a particular determinant.

Under certain circumstances there is a link between the fixed costs of introducing a new tax for the first time and the rate of increase of political costs as the effective tax rate is increased. The link is established by the number of taxpayers. Assume that there is a potential revenue source (corporation profits) which involves relatively few taxpayers (shareowners). The small number of shareowners, with the assistance and encouragement of an even smaller number of corporations, can initially organize an effective political opposition easily and at a low cost. Because of this initial low cost of organizing political opposition to a proposed corporation profits tax, the initial political opposition and initial political costs facing a government contemplating such a new tax are high. Of equal importance, because the initial fixed costs of organizing political opposition are low, there are some, but not extensive, economies of scale to exploit as additional taxpayers, burdened by any increase in the effective tax rate, join the original opposition. Thus, as the effective tax rate is increased by a government, political opposition and total political costs grow at a slowly increasing rate and marginal political costs increase gradually. This combination of factors results in a marginal political cost function with high initial costs and a very gradual rise in costs thereafter.

Assume now that there is a potential revenue source (consumption of imported goods) which involves many taxpayers (consumers of imports). At the outset these potential taxpayers cannot easily organize such large numbers. Because of this initial high cost of organizing political opposition to a proposed customs tariff on imports, the initial political opposition and initial political costs that face a government contemplating such a new tariff are low. However, the high initial organization costs provide ample scope for extensive economies of scale to be exploited as additional taxpayers, burdened by any increase in the effective tariff rate, join the original political opposition. Economies of scale are high and thus political opposition and total political costs grow at a rapidly increasing rate. This combination of factors results in a marginal political cost function with low costs at the outset and a rapid rise in costs thereafter.

The conclusions of these two paragraphs are reformulated as the second and third hypotheses (H-2 and H-3).

H-2:   Total political costs of introducing a new tax are negatively related to the number of taxpayers: as the number of taxpayers increases, the political costs of introducing a new tax fall.

H-3:   The slope of the marginal political cost function of a revenue source is positively related to the number of taxpayers: as the number of affected taxpayers increases, the slope of the marginal political cost function of the respective revenue source increases.[14]

The constitutional agreements can play a crucial role in determining political costs, especially during a country's formative years. In a federal system the initial terms of agreement allocating spending and taxing powers between the central and regional governments can have a profound effect on the costs of using different revenue sources to meet a particular government's required total financing. The sources of costs in this case are twofold — legal and design. If a government is prevented by the terms of the constitution from levying a tax on a particular revenue source — as the Canadian Provinces were prevented from imposing "indirect" taxes — there are additional resource costs involved in designing an indirect tax that qualifies as a legitimate tax in terms of the constitutional agreements, and there are legal and court costs involved in the inevitable challenge to this tax.

These additional costs have to be covered by an increase in revenues from some source, and they therefore generate political opposition. The court challenge itself will produce an announcement effect and encourage political opposition to the tax proposal which is more organized than usual. The additional costs increase the initial level of political opposition to the introduction of a new tax on a revenue source that appears to be prevented by the constitutional agreements.

The costs attributable to the agreements are in one sense unique. They exist only until one government in a federation has successfully redesigned a tax in such a way that it falls legally within the terms of the constitution. Thereafter they fall to zero for the first government and all governments similarly situated. These conclusions provide the fourth and fifth hypotheses.

H-4:   The political costs of introducing a new tax that would appear to be prevented by the constitution are higher than the political costs of introducing a new tax that is allowed by the constitution.

H-5:   Political costs associated with constitutional agreements fall to zero for all governments as soon as one government is successful in introducing a tax which had appeared to be prevented by the constitution.

In addition to constitutional agreements on taxing powers and spending allocations there may exist agreements embedded in the constitution or arrangements accepted by all members of the federation with respect to debt creation and money creation that limit, for some governments, their ability to use these revenue sources as a means of financing total expenditures. Debt creation and money creation are two sources of financing that, together with the many tax sources of financing, comprise the array of potential revenue sources available to a government. Within the conceptual framework developed here a government, to the extent that it has the constitutional right, will choose its mix of borrowing and money creation on the same basis as that on which it chooses its mix of taxes on incomes and taxes on sales — an assessment of the relative political costs.

Many constitutions assign the right to create money exclusively to the central government or its agent and prevent regional or local governments from drawing upon this potential revenue source. When local governments are constitutionally prevented from creating money as a revenue source, they will levy higher effective tax rates on other revenue sources, than those levied by local governments not so constitutionally limited.

Some constitutions permit regional or local governments to create debt only up to a legislated debt limit, and some prevent local governments from creating debt to finance current expenditures. When a constitutional and/or legal limitation exists, the political cost to a government is very high and therefore alternative revenue sources will be used more intensively: taxes per dollar's worth of revenue base will be higher. These conclusions provide the sixth hypothesis.

H-6:   For a given level of required total financing, a government within a constitutional framework that limits or prevents debt and/or money creation will impose higher effective tax rates on alternative revenue sources than would be levied by a government within a constitutional framework that does not limit or prevent debt and/or money creation.

The political cost function of money creation as a source of revenue is defined by Hypothesis H-1. In a simple Keynesian world with large quantities of unemployed resources the real cost of money creation is virtually zero: resources are eventually put to work, output rises and there is no inflation of prices. In a world of fully employed resources the cost of money creation is inflation of prices and incomes; if prices rise more rapidly than incomes then real incomes of some citizens fall and inflation has become, in effect, a tax on these citizens. The potential redistributive aspects of inflation, wherein the real incomes of some citizens rise, do not alter the impact of the inflation tax on those citizens who lose. In a growing economy it is money creation in excess of the natural rate of growth of output that results in this inflation tax, a tax which could then be analyzed within the context of this positive model of tax structure. The reduction in real incomes leads to political opposition of those affected in the same manner as any tax; total political costs rise at an increasing rate as the rate of money creation — the inflation tax — is increased.

The political cost function of debt creation as a source of revenue is defined by Hypothesis H-1. When a government finances an increase in spending by creating debt instead of introducing a new tax or increasing the effective tax rate on an existing revenue source it is foregoing a current tax revenue increase in favour of a future tax revenue increase. In the future taxes will be increased to pay back the debt. If citizens have a longer time horizon than one taxation year — and I assume that they do — then their political opposition to taxes on some revenue sources in the future will be taken into account by a government interested in minimizing total political costs of financing a given level of spending. In other words, relative political costs will influence a survival-seeking government in choosing among its current alternative revenue sources and among its current and future alternative revenue sources (which is the choice between current tax sources and current debt financing).

Debt financing entails one additional cost — the cost of borrowing the funds — that must be covered by increased future taxes on some revenue source. This interest cost results in increased political opposition that is associated with a comparison between debt creation and an increase in the effective tax rate on a current revenue source.

The political units that became the Canadian provinces and municipalities borrowed extensively before Confederation, and all governments continued to borrow after this event. Thus the question of introducing borrowing as a new revenue source into the revenue system does not arise. The only interesting question relates to the extent to which borrowing has been used by various levels of governments as a revenue source. Other things being equal, we would expect to find a government relying more on borrowing when interest rates are low than when interest rates are high. We would expect to find a government anxious to achieve and maintain a good credit standing among potential lenders since this credit rating will help in maintaining favourable (low) interest charges. This conclusion provides the seventh hypothesis.

H-7:   The political costs of borrowing when interest rates are low are less than they are when interest rates are high. These political cost curves are inversely related to the good credit standing of the nation.

Citizens may not be indifferent between two revenue sources, for each of which the tax per dollar's worth of tax base could be equal for a given taxpayer. This tax preference could arise because verification of one revenue source interferes more directly in the conduct of a citizen's affairs (say, a direct tax on incomes, compared with an indirect tax on imports). It could arise because one revenue source is judged by citizens to be the product of their own, meritorious efforts (say, labour income), whereas another revenue source is judged not to be the result of hard work (say, an inheritance, a gift or a lottery win). It could arise because one revenue source is judged by taxpayers to have unhealthy, immoral or sinful connotations[15] (expenditures on alcoholic beverages and tobacco products), whereas the connotations of another revenue source are seen as healthy, moral or meritorious (expenditures on milk, footwear and clothing for children and expenditures on charitable donations).

I define this phenomenon as tax preference, although strictly speaking it is a preference for or against the behaviour giving rise to the revenue source or to verification of that source. I expect these preferences to be reflected in weak and strong political opposition to a government contemplating the introduction of a new tax or an increase in the effective tax rate of an existing tax. If citizens have tax preferences for these or other valid reasons the differential political costs will impinge upon governments with a wish to survive.[16] The eighth hypothesis is now formulated.

H-8:   The political cost of introducing, maintaining or increasing a tax on a revenue source for which citizens have a tax preference will be lower than the political costs of introducing, maintaining or increasing a tax on a revenue source for which citizens do not have a tax preference.

Eventually three variants of the tax preference hypothesis will be identified in one hundred and twenty-three years of Canada's fiscal history. The "sin" tax variant hypothesizes that voters have a preference for taxes on sinful products, such as alcohol and tobacco products, as compared with other products that are not viewed in such an unfavourable light. Thus, taxes on alcohol and tobacco products are less politically costly than taxes on other products with a similar consumption expenditure base.

The "equity" tax variant hypothesizes that voters have a preference for taxes that are just, fair or equitable, as compared with those which are not. Thus, taxes on revenue sources that are regarded as fair are less politically costly than taxes on revenue sources that are considered unfair or inequitable. This is one circumstance where an hypothesis of the positive model of tax structure is consistent with a normative theory of tax structure in which the norm is fairness. The point here is that if voters believe that taxes ought to be fair, then they will have a preference for taxes which are and they will be less opposed, politically, to such taxes than to other taxes. Accordingly, governments will respond by utilizing fair sources of revenue more intensively than other sources.

The "stabilizing fiscal policy" tax variant hypothesizes that voters have a preference for taxes that stabilize incomes. Thus, taxes that stabilize income, either through built-in stabilization provisions or through discretionary policy, will carry lower political costs than taxes which do not stabilize income.

Vertical tax competition could be especially important in a federal system where there are several levels of government. In Canada, there are three — the Dominion (Federal), the provinces and the municipalities. A potential revenue source could be available for "occupancy" by all three governments; however, the Canadian municipalities are creatures of the Provinces, and so a province can restrict legally, if it so chooses, the potential revenue sources that are available to its municipalities. No such legal restriction can be imposed within the framework of relations between the provinces and the Dominion government, except the constitutional restrictions noted above.

A potential revenue source that can be occupied by several governments raises the possibility of vertical tax competition. The first government to tax the revenue source raises the political cost to a government at a different level which is introducing a tax on the same or similarly defined revenue source. The political costs facing the government which enters the field later are higher than for the first government for two main reasons: voter opposition and government opposition. There already exists some organized political opposition of voters to the tax of the first government. This political opposition can be mobilized with little extra effort against a government at a different level that decides to introduce a tax on the same revenue source.

In addition, the government that first taxed the source can be expected to oppose the proposed new tax as a threat to its future opportunities for revenue-raising. In a federation this government-to-government

opposition may be much more significant than citizen-to-government opposition. Certainly it can be mobilized quickly and with little additional
resource cost or effort on the part of the opposing government. The potential threat to the government already occupying the revenue source
will be a potential source of political opposition to the "newcomer" in
the field.

For both these reasons a potential revenue source that is already "occupied" by one government will have higher associated political costs for
a government at a different level within the federation. Once the field is
actually "occupied" by several governments, it follows that the political
costs to any one government of increasing the tax rate will be larger than
the political costs of increasing the tax rate of an "unoccupied" source.
The presumption throughout is that the taxpayer reacts to the effective
tax rate on a given revenue source. The jurisdictional source of the tax
burden — whether one, two or three different governments — does not
alter the amount of the taxpayer's opposition; it can influence the choice
of target against which hostility is directed. This conclusion provides
the ninth hypothesis.

H-9:   The political costs of introducing, maintaining or increasing a
         rate of tax on a revenue source that is already "occupied" by a
         government at a different level in the federation are higher than
         the political costs of introducing, maintaining or increasing a rate
         of tax on a revenue source that is not so "occupied".

Whereas vertical tax competition arises between taxes imposed on the
same or a similarly defined revenue source by different levels of government, horizontal tax competition concerns taxes imposed on the same
or a similarly defined revenue source by other governments at the same
political level. In other words it posits a national government which
considers the political costs of what other national governments are
doing, a provincial government which considers what other provinces
are doing and a municipal government which takes account of other
municipalities.[17]

If a government considers introducing a tax on a revenue source which
is not taxed in a neighbouring jurisdiction and if the revenue source has
some mobility, then there exist clear political costs. A tax on a mobile
source could encourage migration of the owner of the revenue source to
a neighbouring, non-taxing jurisdiction. This potential flight of a part of
the revenue base would entail a partial loss of a resource which would be
viewed as a cost by the government. This would inhibit the use of such a
tax, since the rate would have to be higher on the reduced revenue base.
For the very same reason a revenue source that is taxed in a neighbouring

jurisdiction offers less inducement to migration when a government taxes the source for the first time.

H-10: The political costs of introducing, maintaining or increasing a tax on a revenue source that is mobile and would not be taxed in a neighbouring jurisdiction are higher than the political costs of introducing, maintaining or increasing a tax on a mobile revenue source that would also be taxed in a neighbouring jurisdiction.[18]

Horizontal tax shifting involves the ability of residents of one political unit to shift a tax to residents of a different political unit at the same level within a federal system and to neighbouring political units in a different country. Horizontal tax shifting is one aspect of political costs that the economic literature has addressed: the ability to export taxes beyond the borders of the political unit.[19] A necessary condition for the success of this strategy is that the residents of the political unit to which the tax is exported by shifting do not retaliate against the original government in any cost-imposing manner. An expectation of retaliation on the part of the government introducing the tax would increase the political cost of the tax considerably. Given this extremely important condition, the political costs of a tax that can be shifted horizontally are less than the political costs of a tax that cannot be so shifted; other things being equal, one would expect to find a more extensive use of the former.

H-11: Given the absence of retaliation, the political cost of introducing, maintaining or increasing a tax which is capable of being shifted to residents of other political units is less than the political cost of introducing, maintaining or increasing a tax which is not capable of being shifted.

The costs of collection, compliance, and enforcement associated with tax revenues also influence the political cost functions. The administrative costs of collecting the tax on a revenue source have to be financed out of lower spending or extra revenues, both of which increase political opposition. Compliance costs fall directly on the taxpayer and for many revenue sources entail initially high start-up costs such as revised bookkeeping records and accounting expenses. Enforcement costs have to be financed by additional revenues drawn from taxpayers and thus eventually add to political opposition. These enforcement costs will tend to be higher, the greater the capacity of the taxpayer to shift away from the taxed activity to non-taxable alternatives. This conclusion provides the twelfth hypothesis.

H-12: The political costs of introducing, maintaining or increasing a
tax on a revenue source that entails higher costs of collection,
compliance and enforcement will be higher than the political costs
of introducing, maintaining or increasing a tax on a revenue source
for which the costs of collection, compliance and enforcement are
lower.[20]

This hypothesis contains the relationship between the number of taxpayers and the administrative costs of collection, compliance and enforcement. The reader is reminded of hypotheses H-2 and H-3 above,
which contain the relationship between the number of taxpayers and the
extent of economies of scale to organizing political opposition. These
hypotheses lead to a very different prediction about political costs than
does hypothesis 12. As noted above, each determinant is analysed for
the assumption that other things are equal.

Hypotheses 1 through 12 establish the determinants of the political
cost functions, with all structural features of taxes except the statutory
rates held constant. While still holding the defined base of each potential
revenue source constant I want to allow the base to vary in response to
changing economic conditions.

There are two situations in which revenue base changes occurring in
response to economic conditions, can be expected to influence political
cost functions and hence the structure of taxes in political equilibrium.
First, revenue sources with some base elasticity in a period of economic
growth result in an increase in total tax revenues, because, even though
the tax per dollar's worth of base has not changed the base has grown.
This allows a government to increase spending without the increase in
effective tax rates necessary for a constant base revenue source. Thus
the government could reduce effective tax rates or repeal a tax, thereby
enhancing its net political benefits. Either policy response provides benefits to politicians that do not accrue for a constant base tax (zero base
elasticity). One would expect governments to have a preference for such
elastic base revenue sources. This conclusion provides the thirteenth
hypothesis.

H-13: The political costs of introducing, maintaining or increasing a
tax on a revenue source, the base of which has some elasticity in
relation to national income, are smaller than those of introducing,
maintaining or increasing a tax on a revenue source, with no base
elasticity.

The second situation occurs when revenue sources with great base
variability in response to changing economic circumstances, produce un-
predictable changes in revenues and consequently occasional unplanned

deficits or surpluses.[21] Given the budget constraint, this shortfall in revenues must be made up, either by introducing a new tax, increasing the tax rate on an existing revenue base, creating new debt or creating additional money. These alternatives involve additional political costs and the added political embarrassment of resorting to "hastily conceived" instrument changes. The occasional large unplanned surplus may be no less of a political problem for a government than an unplanned deficit, since it may generate political pressure for reductions in effective tax rates from taxpayers who feel burdened and can point to the surpluses as "over-taxation". A government that realizes the short-run nature of these unplanned surpluses will nevertheless be hard pressed by its political opponents to cut taxes. One would expect governments to eschew revenue sources with extremely high base variability.[22] This conclusion provides the fourteenth hypothesis.

H-14: The political costs of introducing, maintaining or increasing a tax on a revenue source which is excessively volatile in relation to changes in national income are greater than the political costs of introducing, maintaining or increasing a tax on a relatively stable revenue source.

Hypotheses 13 and 14 link expected political costs to revenue base elasticity and volatility in relation to changes in national income. Within a conceptual framework where voters are viewed as weighing the expected benefits of public goods, subsidies and transfers against the expected costs of taxes now and in the immediate future, governments can be expected to choose the revenue mix that will minimize total political opposition both now and in the immediate future. Governments care about the future because voters do. Therefore revenue base elasticity, which has implications for future political equilibrium, could be an important determinant of relative political cost functions and the resultant structure of taxes.

There may well be other determinants of political costs. The model is general enough to permit the appropriate adaptations. One possible exception is the discretionary behaviour of bureaucrats. In the model developed here the marginal political cost functions associated with each potential revenue source play the key role in determining the structure of taxes and major changes in those political costs define tax reform. Bureaucrats have no special skill or knowledge or ability which they can use to shift the constraints which help determine the political cost functions. They may possess a comparative advantage in their knowledge of the cost of supplying public goods, but there is no reason to assume that they possess a similar comparative advantage in the knowledge of the cost of political opposition to different taxes, or that they can exploit that knowledge in any way so as to alter the structure of taxes in their favour.[23]

In the conceptual framework developed here the Minister of Finance screens tax proposals originating in the Department of Finance for their political acceptability. Those that pass his or her scrutiny and become a part of the actual tax structure are appropriately viewed as having been determined on political grounds: the survival rule is not neglected by successful Ministers of Finance! In my judgment, this model gives ample opportunity for creative ingenuity on the part of tax experts and senior tax advisors, constrained only by the political costs as perceived by the Minister of Finance.[24]

A summary of all 14 hypotheses is given in Table 2-1. On the following page, Figure 2-1 presents a diagrammatic interpretation of the shape of the political cost curve and also illustrates the effects of an exogenous shift in political costs.

Political Equilibrium and the Structure of Revenues

> I propose to find those revenues in ways that hurt least, and I propose to apply them to help people most in need.
>
> (Finance Minister John Turner, 1974:8)

The positive model developed here contains a government that attempts to meet its required revenue needs in such a manner as to minimize the total political costs of raising those revenues. There are political costs associated with each potential revenue source — the initial fixed costs when a tax is introduced for the first time, and any additional political costs that occur as the effective tax rate is increased to meet an increasing revenue requirement. A government, in order to minimize total political costs, takes the initial fixed costs into account and expands the use of each revenue source until marginal political costs are equal across revenue sources.

Political equilibrium and the composition of revenues is described in Figure 2-2 for a system that contains the three potential revenue sources of Figure 2-1. All three revenue sources exhibit economies of scale to the organization of political opposition, with total political costs increasing at a rising rate as the effective tax rates increase (hypothesis H-1). Given the assumption that the revenue bases are fixed, the effective tax rates readily translate into tax revenues, a, b and c, on the horizontal axes of both Figures.

It is assumed that revenue sources a, b and c have many, fewer and fewest taxpayers respectively (hypotheses H-2 and H-3), although this

TABLE 2-1

Hypotheses Summary of the Conceptual Framework

Shape of Political Cost Function

H-1: Total political costs eventually rise at an increasing rate and marginal political costs increase as the effective tax rate is increased by a government.

H-2: Total political costs of introducing a new tax are negatively related to the number of taxpayers: as the number of taxpayers increases, the political costs of introducing a new tax fall.

H-3: The slope of the marginal political cost function of a revenue source is positively related to the number of taxpayers: as the number of affected taxpayers increases, the slope of the marginal political cost function of the respective revenue source increases.

Constitutional Considerations

H-4: The political costs of introducing a new tax that would appear to be prevented by the constitution are higher than the political costs of introducing a new tax that is allowed by the constitution.

H-5: Political costs associated with constitutional agreements fall to zero for all governments as soon as one government is successful in introducing a tax which had appeared to be prevented by the constitution.

H-6: For a given level of required total financing, a government within a constitutional framework that limits or prevents debt and/or money creation will impose higher effective tax rates on alternative revenue sources than would be levied by a government within a constitutional framework that does not limit or prevent debt and/or money creation.

A Good Credit Standing

H-7: The political costs of borrowing when interest rates are low are less than they are when interest rates are high. These political costs are inversely related to the good credit standing of the nation.

Tax Preference

H-8: The political cost of introducing, maintaining or increasing a tax on a revenue source for which citizens have a tax preference will be lower than the political cost of introducing, maintaining or increasing a tax on a revenue source for which citizens do not have a tax preference. The three following variants will be identified — a preference for "sin" taxes (H-8a), "equitable" taxes (H-8b), and "stabilizing" taxes (H-8c).

Vertical Tax Competition

H-9: The political cost of introducing, maintaining or increasing a tax on a revenue source that is already "occupied" by a government at a different level in the federation are higher than the political costs of introducing, maintaining or increasing a tax on a revenue source that is not so "occupied".

Horizontal Tax Competition

H-10: The political costs of introducing, maintaining or increasing a tax on a revenue source that is mobile and would not be taxed in a neighbouring jurisdiction are higher than the political costs of introducing, maintaining or increasing a tax on a mobile revenue source that would also be taxed in a neighbouring jurisdiction.

Horizontal Tax Shifting (Tax Exporting)

H-11: Given the absence of retaliation, the political cost of introducing, maintaining or increasing a tax which is capable of being shifted to residents of other political units is less than the political cost of introducing, maintaining or increasing a tax which is not capable of being shifted.

Administrative Costs

H-12: The political costs of introducing, maintaining or increasing a tax on a revenue source that entails higher costs of collection, compliance and enforcement will be higher than the political costs of introducing, maintaining or increasing a tax on a revenue source for which the costs of collection, compliance and enforcement are lower.

Allowing The Revenue Base To Vary

H-13: The political costs of introducing, maintaining or increasing a tax on a revenue source, the base of which has some elasticity in relation to national income, are smaller than those of introducing, maintaining or increasing a tax on a revenue source with no base elasticity.

H-14: The political costs of introducing, maintaining or increasing a tax on a revenue source which is excessively volatile in relation to changes in national income are greater than the political costs of introducing, maintaining or increasing a tax on a relatively stable revenue source.

Figure 2 -1

Political Cost Curves of Different Revenue Sources

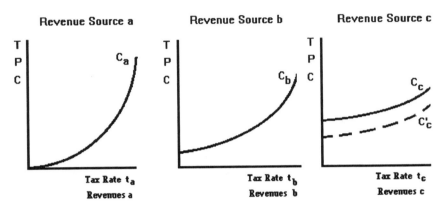

T P C : Total Political Costs: C_a, C_b and C_c.

Assumptions:
Revenue sources a, b and c exhibit, respectively, zero, moderate and high initial fixed political costs of introducing a tax. Each revenue source exhibits economies of scale to the organization of political opposition as the tax rate is increased. Therefore total political costs increase at an increasing rate. The base for each revenue source is fixed.

Exogenous Shocks:
A neighbouring state introduces a tax on its revenue source c. Consequently, the political costs of introducing and utilizing a tax on mobile revenue source c falls to $C_c{}'$. An independent change in any other determinant will also shift the total political cost curve for a revenue source.

assumption is not absolutely necessary to the analysis. For example, revenue source a, with many taxpayers and thus very high initial costs of organizing political opposition exhibits zero political costs to start with, but very extensive economies of scale and thus more rapidly rising total costs as the effective tax rate is increased. It is assumed, for illustrative purposes only, that for revenue sources a and b marginal political costs when a new tax is first introduced are initially zero, whereas for revenue source c marginal political costs when a new tax is first introduced are positive to start with.

The bottom diagram in Figure 2-2 depicts the crucial political equilibrium of the model, derived from the total cost curves of the three potential tax structures. $TC(1)$ is the total political cost of a tax structure consisting of the revenue source with zero fixed costs, revenue source a. $TC(2)$ is the total political cost of a tax structure that includes revenue sources a and b, utilized to the point where the marginal political costs of each tax are always equalized and including the initial fixed costs of revenue source b. $TC(3)$ is the total political cost of a three-tax structure.

Required total revenues are depicted along the horizontal axis. For required total revenues up to R_1, $TC(1) \leq TC(2) \leq TC(3)$; thus the government will choose to tax revenue source a only. For required revenues from R_1 to R_4, $TC(2) \leq TC(1)$ and $\leq TC(3)$; thus the government will introduce a new tax on revenue source b (initially incurring the high fixed costs) and adjust tax rates so that marginal political costs are equalized. This entails initially a reduction of the tax rate on revenue source a: at R_1 the slope of $TC(2)$ is less than the slope of $TC(1)$. The fall in the marginal political costs of revenue source a is achieved by a tax rate decrease. For required revenues beyond R_4, $TC(3) \leq TC(2) \leq TC(1)$; thus the government will choose to alter the tax structure again by introducing a new tax on revenue source c, and adjusting the tax rates on revenue sources a and b.

The top panel of three diagrams can be used to describe the changes in the composition of revenues, by revenue source, that accompany the major tax structure changes just described. A small budget, requiring total revenues of up to R_1 can be satisfied at minimum political costs by a tax structure of one tax on revenue source a, generating revenues up to a_3. At R_1 the existing tax structure and a new tax structure containing the two revenue sources a and b, minimize total political costs. If required revenues increase beyond R_1 total political costs will be minimized by introducing a new tax on revenue source b and equating the marginal political costs of both revenue sources. This necessitates a reduction in the effective tax rate on revenue source a such that revenues fall from

Figure 2 - 2

Political Equilibrium and the Composition of Revenues

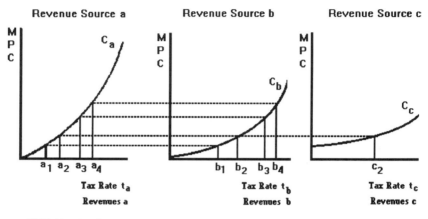

MPC: Marginal Political Cost

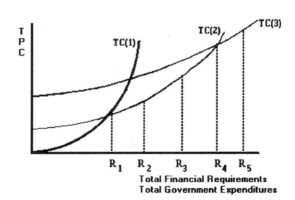

Total Financial Requirements
Total Government Expenditures

Three Tax Structures	Composition of Revenues
TC(1): one-tax structure (a)	at R_1 : $a_3 = a_1 + b_1$
TC(2): two-tax structure (a + b)	at R_3 : $a_3 + b_3$
TC(3): three-tax structure (a + b + c)	at R_4 : $a_4 + b_4 = a_2 + b_2 + c_2$

a_3 to a_1. The combined revenues of a_1 plus b_1 equal the total revenues from the old tax system at a_3.

A medium-sized budget, say one that requires total revenues between R_1 and R_4 can be satisfied at minimum political cost with this two-tax structure on revenue sources a and b. As required revenues increase from R_1 to R_3 the government will increase tax rates on both sources so as to equate marginal political costs. Required revenues of R_3 indicate a budget wherein the effective tax rate on revenue source a has risen to the level where it stood before the change from a one-tax to a two-tax system (at a_3). The slope of TC(2) at R_3 equals the slope of TC(1) at R_1.

At R_4 the existing two-tax structure (where $a_4 + b_4 = R_4$) and a new three-tax structure (where $a_2 + b_2 + c_2 = R_4$) both minimize total political costs. When required revenues increase beyond R_4 total political costs will be minimized by introducing a new tax on revenue source c and equating the marginal political costs of the three revenue sources. This necessitates a reduction in the effective tax rate on revenue sources a and b such that revenues fall from a_4 and b_4 to a_2 and b_2 respectively.

In summary, the positive model underlying Figure 2-2 can be used to demonstrate three propositions when a new tax or a new tax structure is introduced. First, given a small increase in total required financing, a new tax on a new revenue source will reduce the utilization of all existing taxed revenue sources (tax rates on existing sources will fall). Second, a new tax on a new revenue source will begin at some positive utilization rate, and will not grow continuously from a zero rate of utilization. Third, given a large enough increase in total required financing, a new tax on a new revenue source will be accompanied by increased utilization of all existing taxed sources (tax rates on existing sources will rise).[25]

Tax Reform and Revenue Structure Changes

> Reactions to new taxes conform to a clear pattern: shock, opposition, understanding and acceptance.
>
> (*The Times*, editorial, May 7, 1966)

The Causes of Tax Reform

When governments choose to increase spending, their decision necessitates an increase in total financial requirements. The increased revenue requirements may be substantial, as in the case of wartime spending, or may be a more modest increase in government spending from one year to the next. Given this need for increased revenues, two possibilities exist: (1) increasing tax rates on already existing revenue sources or (2) introducing a tax on a previously unexploited source and making consequential changes in rates on other revenue sources.

Consider the bottom diagram of Figure 2-2. The government is at budget size R_2 and now requires greater revenues, say R_3. The politically least costly way to raise these funds is to increase the tax rate on all existing taxes, such that sufficient revenue is raised and the marginal political cost of raising revenues is once again the same for all taxed sources. Given the variation in political costs of raising revenues on different revenue sources, it is not possible to predict whether the share of a particular tax in total financial requirements will increase. I call this a *balanced-budget rate restructuring*.

Now, consider a government at budget size R_3 that requires a much larger increase in revenues to budget size R_5. The shock is large enough to necessitate the introduction of a tax on a new revenue source. Thus, a previously unexploited revenue source is now taxed, and rates are once again set at the equilibrium level, where marginal political costs are identical for each revenue source. I call this a *balanced-budget tax reform*.

For both these balanced-budget changes, the government required different levels of revenues and responded accordingly. However, governments also respond to exogenous changes in political costs for the same level of total financial requirements. For example, a lowering of the corporate tax rate in the United States may make it politically costly to sustain the existing Canadian corporate tax rate because of the risk of 'capital flight'. This is an increase in horizontal tax competition, as in Hypothesis H-10. A change in a determinant of political costs underlying hypotheses H-1 through H-12 has the same general result. Given this exogenous shift in the political cost curve without an accompanying change in revenue requirements, the government can respond in two ways by: (1) a change in the mix of tax rates on existing revenue sources or (2) the introduction of a tax on a new revenue source with appropriate changes of tax rates on existing taxed sources.

Consider, first, a relatively small shock affecting political costs. To minimize political costs of raising the same level of revenue rates on existing taxed sources are changed until once again the marginal political costs are the same for each revenue source. There is no new tax, but the tax rate and tax share of the revenue source whose political costs have fallen will rise, while the tax rates and tax shares of the revenue sources whose political costs have remained constant will fall. I call this a *tax-substitution rate restructuring*.

Second, consider a large shock affecting political costs. For example, assume a government is collecting R_3 total revenues and a neighbouring province introduces a property tax. Horizontal tax competition reduces the political cost to other provinces of introducing a similar tax. In Figure 2-3, the property tax (revenue source c) has not been levied previously because the perceived political costs of taxing it have been very high for horizontal tax competition reasons. Now that a neighbouring government has introduced a tax on its revenue source c, horizontal tax competition declines, and with it the political costs of taxing source c. This results in a fall in the total political cost curve for a three-tax system, TC(3). If it shifts down far enough it will fall below the total political cost curve for a two-tax system at required total revenues of R_3. The new tax in the neighbouring jurisdiction results in a tax reform package which includes the introduction of a new tax on revenue source c, reduced effective tax rates on revenue sources a and b (such that the marginal political costs are equal for all three revenue sources) and reduced tax shares for revenue sources a and b along with an increased tax share for the new revenue source c. The difference from the previous case is that a shift in the political cost curve of a revenue source results in the introduction of a new tax, instead of a change in tax rates, because this is the politically least costly way to raise the given level of revenues. Rates on existing revenue sources are modified to satisfy the survival rule, that is, the marginal political costs of a dollar's worth of revenue are the same for each taxed source. I call this a *tax-substitution tax reform*.

A change in political cost curves through hypotheses H-1 to H-12 leads to two types of tax substitutions: in the first only rates are changed and in the second the number of taxed revenue sources change and rates are adjusted accordingly. However, the situation is more complex for exogenous shocks operating through hypotheses H-13 and H-14, in which the elasticity of revenues comes into play. The first twelve hypotheses of the model are developed for a fixed revenue base for each revenue source; consequently the tax rate translates directly into revenues, for each revenue source, along the horizontal axis in Figures 2-2 and 2-3. It follows that the predicted sign for changes in a tax rate and a tax share are identical for each revenue source.

Hypotheses H-13 and H-14 emphasize the effect of a change in the base of the revenue source and the political costs associated with taxing that source. For example, assume that at budget size R_3, with a two tax-structure, TC(2), a structural change in the economy results in the base elasticity of revenue source b increasing over that of to revenue source a. This enhanced revenue buoyancy of source b as compared with source a

Figure 2 - 3

Tax-Substitution Tax Reform

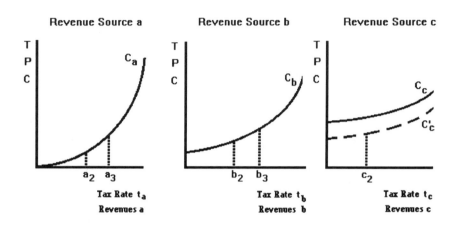

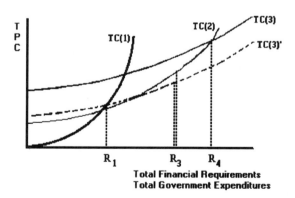

Total Financial Requirements
Total Government Expenditures

TPC: Total Political Costs: C_a, C_b, and C_c
Political Equilibrium:

Pre-reform, at R_3: two-tax structure, $a_3 + b_3$
TC(3)' replaces TC (3)
Post-reform, at R_3: three-tax structure $a_2 + b_2 + c_2$

would result in increased tax revenues for the given tax rate on source b and the given political costs of that source. To keep revenues constant, the tax rate on source b is decreased and this lowers the political costs of raising revenues from source b. The fall in the political costs of taxing source b relative to the political costs of taxing source a is the incentive which leads a government to utilize revenue source a less extensively (so that the tax rate on, and tax share of, a falls) and to tax revenue source b more extensively until marginal political costs are once more equal for both revenue sources. However, it is not possible to predict whether the associated increase in the tax rate on revenue source b will be less than, equal to or greater than the fall in the tax rate which will initially keep revenues and political costs constant. Thus, for the more revenue elastic base, b, the tax rate may fall, remain constant or rise, while the tax share must rise.

This discussion leads to predictions, based on the positive model of revenue structure, for three key variables: the introduction or repeal of a tax, the change in the tax rate and the change in the share of the tax in total financial requirements. These three variables are observable. In addition, the potential determinants of political costs are observable, even though the political costs themselves are not. It is therefore possible to refute predictions of the model.

The positive model developed here is a theory of government choice among alternative revenue sources made with a view to minimizing the total political costs of raising a given level of revenues. An exogenous change in a determinant of the political costs associated with one revenue source, all other factors held constant, will lead a government interested in survival to alter its tax policy and choose a different combination of revenue sources.

The nature of this positive model draws attention to the political equilibrium — the solution of the government's choice problem — and changes in this political equilibrium designed by a government in response to exogenous shocks. This focus is natural, and especially understandable when the observed change in revenue structure results in tax reform that entails new taxes or repeal of old taxes. In my judgment, it is also important to understand the process of change — the movement from one political equilibrium to another. For want of a better term, I define this process or movement as the evolution of revenue structure policy. The present study will cast some light on this evolution, as well as the choices at equilibrium.

An element that must be stressed is that the perceived political costs are not observable, although the determinants of those costs are potentially capable of being observed. In order to offer a menu of taxes that voters find the most palatable the government and opposition parties engage in various activities in an effort to interpret these political costs. Polling, surveys, political conventions, debates and "mainstreeting" are just some of the regular practices followed by political parties and politicians for the purpose of extracting information on the magnitude and depth of opposition to proposed taxes. For the most part, the government effects frequent adjustments at the margin of taxation, a slight increase here and a slight decrease there, in an effort to equate the marginal costs of taxation for each revenue source.

From time to time, however, the government gets a sense that more significant changes are required. Sometimes, these changes may be rendered necessary by major shifts in political cost curves resulting from exogenous shocks. For example, the United States may implement substantial tax changes which alter the pressures of horizontal tax competition in Canada. At other times it may be determined that large, discrete changes in tax rates and sources are an appropriate way of reducing total political costs. In both cases, substantial alterations of the tax structure are known as tax reform. If a government undertakes such tax reform, it attempts to do so in the way which is most satisfying politically. Throughout the evolution of the Canadian tax system, two strategies or processes of tax reform have emerged, each appropriate for a different set of circumstances.

The Strategies of Tax Reform

> New taxes are always disagreeable. Taxes generally — and this is admitted by everyone . . . are not very appetizing. Taxes are repulsive to most people.
> (Hon. Jacques Bureau, Minister of Customs and Excise, 1923b:924)

I define the strategy or process of tax reform as the method by which the changes in tax structure to accommodate a new political equilibrium are brought about. I discuss two very different processes — a consultative model and a budget model — which share some features in common, but basically are very different methods of effecting tax reform.

The tax reform generated within the conceptual framework is the result of major changes in real variables: economies of scale in organizing political opposition, innovation in tax collection, heightened taxing activity of provincial governments within a federal system, the reduction in taxes on, say, corporate profits in a neighbouring country, etc. The government of the day responds to these events. The events themselves carry political support. But because there are winners and may be losers in all tax structure changes the potential exists for considerable short-run political costs as well as political gains, depending upon the way in which the tax reforms are brought into effect. Moreover, governments may be uncertain about the extent of the political costs and political benefits involved in making some tax changes.[26] A government that underestimates the former and overestimates the latter runs the risk of failing to survive. It is in a government's interest to use whatever means are available to it for assessing the weight of the potential political costs and political benefits of any proposed major tax structure change. One example of such means is the process or strategy of tax reform.

The *consultative strategy* of tax reform is a method which actively builds in many opportunities for voter feedback as the views of the government are formed, step by painstaking step, into final legislation. The government, knowing there will be winners and there may be losers after any major tax change, uses the process of constant criticism and feedback to gauge the strength of opposition to and support for various proposed changes. The government knows that it is those with means at their disposal who will marshall their resources if they are threatened with a tax reform which would cause them substantial loss. The government also knows that an extensive consultative process carries with it the potential for benefit, as those who stand to gain are made aware of the fact and political opposition is reduced because of the "fair hearing" element of the political process. For these reasons a government considering major tax structure changes might be expected to adopt a process which, though lengthy and time-consuming, serves to guide politicians on the government's side of the House in ways of surviving voter rejection.

A stylized description of such a consultative process might be as follows. From an extensive menu of tax reform dishes the government prepares a sub-menu of choices and publishes it as a white paper for discussion. The government then calls for briefs and representations in response to the white paper, and may even conduct open meetings at which interested parties can comment, criticize, etc. The government next prepares a sub-sub-menu, designated as draft legislation, and submits it to Parliament for consideration. At this stage it may even be channelled to all-party standing or special committees of Parliament for study, review and comments. Recommendations of such committees may be accepted by the government when it is packaging its final legislation.[27]

The *budget strategy* of tax reform contrasts starkly with the consultative process. The latter encourages voter feedback, thrives on strong opposition and generates criticism which is used to mould the final form of the legislation that effects tax reform. The budget process discourages voter feedback, minimizes the time available to potential losers to marshall their resources in an all-out attack on the government's proposed legislation, and strives to translate initial proposals into final legislation with as little modification as possible.

One would expect that a government would choose the budget process in preference to the consultative process when: (i) it is certain about the number of persons who will gain or lose when the package of legislative proposals is adopted; (ii) the winners are clearly and easily identified and, in terms of political support, exceed the losers; (iii) the losers, although identifiable and possibly commanding considerable resources, are located in very different sectors of the economy and have few, if any, links before the proposals were adopted. This latter condition increases the cost to the losers of organizing a unified attack on the proposal; separate attacks are relatively ineffective and can be described by the government as narrow and oriented to the protestors' self-interest — which they decidedly are! In these circumstances, a government can ignore the costs and benefits of a lengthy consultative process, and choose a short, sharp debate instead.

A stylized description of the budget process might be as follows. From an extensive menu of tax reform dishes the government chooses a sub-menu of proposals and introduces it for the first time as part of the budget speech. The formal legislation follows shortly after, and while there may be technical adjustments that lead to some divergence between initial proposals and final legislation these are few and far between. The choice of the budget process over the consultative process dictates that voter feedback, special interest group criticism and political opposition is noted but receives neither encouragement, acknowledgement or response. From the government's viewpoint the cost of enduring a short, sharp, critical battle is well worth the benefits of winning the war — namely, the achievement of a desired change in the tax structure.

Up to this point, I have portrayed the politician as playing a passive role within a political market place where there are other politicians competing for the voters' allegiance. Political costs are parametric, politicians undertake activities to interpret the underlying signals of the curves representing these costs and then offer a package of tax changes most suitable to these constraints. Practices such as polling, political conventions and a consultative strategy of tax reform were discussed as methods of extracting this information and the budgetary process is viewed as one of minimizing the costs of implementing tax reform. Similarly, politicians undertake various methods of advertising and other promotional activities in the hope of enhancing the palatability of a tax change.

It is possible that a government would not only respond to changes in relative political costs in choosing its equilibrium revenue structure but would also initiate efforts to alter the relative political costs while choosing its equilibrium revenue structure. The vehicle is the Minister of Finance's budget speech, which can be devoted to persuasion, exhortation and cajolery, as well as the revelation of factors taken into account in formulating budgetary policy. For example, the attitudes of voters to "sin" taxes, H-8a, may be especially sensitive to such attempts at persuasion. Whether this possibility has had any significant impact on Canada's evolving revenue structure during the past is not clear. If politicians can significantly alter the tastes of voters, then like the consumer model in the Galbraithian world where producers create tastes more than they cater to the wants of consumers, the model breaks down and loses its predictive power.[28]

For the consumer model, the jury is still out on the question as to whether tastes are parametric to the firm. For our positive model of taxation the government's preferences, as articulated by the Minister of Finance, are filtered through numerous groups of individuals, ranging from voters with their diverse interests and rankings of relative benefits and costs of both public expenditures and taxes to elected politicians and cabinet. In such a model the perception of 'changing tastes' may be more of a conceptual problem than it is in the application of the consumer model to households or groups that comprise more than one individual. This would make it more difficult to model and formally test those circumstances in which the observed government action is the resolution of internal conflicts among very different competing interests. It is a reservation that should be kept in mind in the pages that follow and it is hoped it will be satisfactorily reconciled in the concluding chapter.

Efforts to interpret and minimize political costs have been considered — but what of a government which fails to take the appropriate steps? Governments may make "political mistakes" in their choices and "miss" in a very tangible way the actual political equilibrium that is meant to assure their survival. In a democratic system political competition from the "alternative government(s)" in waiting will ensure that these "political mistakes" are visible and publicized. This political competition will be aided and abetted by a free press, investigative journalism and, from time to time, the odd curious academic.

This present study will attempt to accommodate and detect such mistakes and analyze the role they play within the evolution of revenue structure policy. First, the government might so misread the relative political costs associated with a major tax change as to fail to win sufficient electoral support to ensure survival and lose an election. Secondly, the government might misperceive the relative political costs of a major tax change, and, in response to strong public opposition to the budget proposals of the Minister of Finance, alter those proposals. In fact, a government that does respond to continuing and determined public opposition and alter its budget proposals is behaving in a manner consistent with the framework of this study. Such a government is reflecting its perceived inability to mould voters' tastes with respect to alternative tax revenue sources. In this way an examination of the pathological budget proposals may lend considerable support to the thesis when it is applied to healthy budget proposals.

Political Equilibrium and the Hettich-Winer Model

The positive model underlying this study owes a considerable intellectual debt to the stimulating and innovative work of Walter Hettichs and Stanley Winers on a positive model of tax structure.[29] The centrepiece of both models is constituted by a government adjusting the structure of taxes in such a way that, at the margin, the political costs of all actual and potential revenue bases are equal: the objective being to minimize total political costs of a given budget size. There are, however, a number of significant differences between the two models that should be kept in mind. First of all, the Hettich-Winer model does not allow for the introduction of a new tax on a previously untaxed revenue source. It is restricted to "analysis of tax systems in which changes in the size of the public sector do not include the introduction of major new taxes or the disappearance of old ones, and where relatively small adjustments in the composition of revenues will be the rule".[30]

The present study intends to describe, explain and understand the introduction of new taxes and the occasional elimination of an old tax during one hundred and twenty-three years of Canadian fiscal history. Therefore tax births and tax deaths must be built into the conceptual model and any resulting discrete changes in the composition of revenues must be allowed for in the research strategy.

In the second place, the empirical estimation procedure led Hettich and Winer to restrict the initial model to five hypotheses related to the political cost functions: opposition to effective tax rates via horizontal tax shifting, costs of organizing political opposition, the scale effect of a changing public sector size, horizontal tax competition and tax base volatility. The model in this study also includes: relative number of taxpayers, constitutional agreements, good credit standing of the nation, tax preferences, vertical tax competition, collection compliance and enforcement costs[31] and revenue base elasticity. Again, given the broader historical context of which the positive model of this study will have to take account, it is necessary to launch the investigation within a much broader framework.

Conclusions

> income taxes . . . taxes on goods and services and corporate profits taxes
> [have to be] efficient, fair and flexible sources of revenue, causing as little
> harm and irritation as possible for each dollar we must derive from them.
>
> (Finance Minister Abbott, 1949a:11)

In this chapter I have developed the model that will guide the discussion and analysis throughout the rest of the book. The government in this model maximizes its chances of political survival by financing its spending in such a way as to minimize the political costs of raising its revenues from many potential revenue sources, including borrowing. The real determinants of those political costs are defined by fourteen hypotheses. The political equilibrium is established when a government has extended its utilization of each revenue source up to the point where marginal political costs are equalized. Exogenous shocks affecting the determinants of these political costs result in revenue structure changes and tax reforms that can be described by predictions in three crucial variables: the introduction or repeal of a tax, the change in the tax rate and the change in the share of the tax in total financial requirements.

The model of government choice developed here is analogous to the standard consumer theory model of individual choice, where tastes are assumed to be parametric. Readers who see the model in this study as a deterministic approach to the government's choice problem will realize that it is the same conceptual difficulty as that which confronts those who are uneasy with the standard economic theory of consumer choice.[32] Several additional reservations may come to the reader's mind throughout the remainder of the book. It is hoped to deal with these effectively in the concluding chapter.

Chapter 3

Attracting People and Building the Union:
Dominion Revenue Policy 1867–1917

. . . all taxation . . . is a loss *per se* . . . it is the sacred duty of the government to take only from the people what is necessary to the proper discharge of the public service; and that taxation in any other mode, is simply in one shape or another, legalized robbery.

(The Honourable Sir Richard Cartwright, Minister of Finance, *Budget Speech*, 1878, p. 22)

Taxation is the only gateway to progress and in a country . . . [the way a political collectivity enjoys great public works] is through the gateway of taxation.

(The Honourable George E. Foster, Minister of Finance, *Budget Speech*, 1889, pp. 19, 20)

Introduction

The political and economic union of New Brunswick, Nova Scotia and the Province of Canada (Upper and Lower Canada) in 1867 created a federal system of government capable of responding to internal difficulties and meeting external threats. This extended free-trade area with enhanced interprovincial transportation systems would increase domestic prosperity and encourage international trade at a time when the United States and the United Kingdom were imposing hostile trade policies. The political union that accommodated regional and local differences among provinces with a strong central government would not only promote westward expansion at a time of aggressive behaviour on the part of the United States, but would also establish a stronger credit standing (badly damaged by very large colonial debts) in order to attract the capital to finance westward territorial expansion.

Under the terms of Confederation the new Dominion government had extensive legislative responsibilities, especially in the areas of development and transportation, and unrestricted taxing powers.[1] It took over the existing debts of the former colonies, most of which had been incurred for establishing transportation systems. It also assumed exclusive right to indirect taxation — the lucrative customs and excise duties which had provided the major source of tax revenues for the colonies.

The provinces were restricted to direct taxes and licences. The new Dominion government was required to pay to the provinces a statutory subsidy of 80 cents per person — Canada's first unconditional transfer payments. These transfer payments were the most important source of provincial revenues for many years to come.

At Confederation the new central government had dominion over just 3.5 million Canadians in four provinces, and it was not yet a nation "A mari usque ad mare". Successive central governments tackled the job of nation-building with vigour. The transportation network was continued. The Intercolonial Railway, linking the Maritimes with the St. Lawrence Valley, was completed. Canals were deepened and improved. And after British Columbia entered Confederation in 1871 the Dominion government was committed to the building of a Pacific railway. The opening up of the West required settlers and immigration was encouraged. Other colonies, experiencing substantially increased debt charges associated with railway building, were eventually lured into the Union — Manitoba in 1870, British Columbia in 1871 and Prince Edward Island in 1873 and the Provinces of Alberta and Saskatchewan were created out of the Northwest Territories in 1905.

The financial settlement of Confederation was continually adjusted: in response to Nova Scotia's threat to withdraw from the Union, on the entry of each new province into the union and in response to special internal problems in individual provinces which have enlivened the evolution of federal-provincial relations ever since.

The two most important themes of national policy, luring immigrants and building the Dominion of Canada, influenced Ministers of Finance in the way they shaped the structure of revenues in order to finance Dominion spending. To meet these objectives Finance Ministers exercised two major revenue policy choices. The first of these concerned the broad division of revenue sources between debt issue and taxation. The second had to do with the type of or mix of taxes, reflected in the decision *not* to use the potential revenue source of direct taxation (income taxes) and in the decision to exempt from tax, or to tax at lower rates, some items of expenditure which were in principle subject to the tariff and excise duties.

The decision to borrow was constrained by the credit standing of the Dominion and the higher interest cost resulting from a fall in credit standing. The choice of the tax mix and associated tax rates was determined primarily by horizontal and vertical tax competition and influenced to some extent by administration costs, a tax preference for "sin" taxes and a minor tax preference for equitable taxes. These considerations helped to fashion and shape the variation in revenue structure during those first fifty years.

In this chapter I examine these two revenue policy choices — the borrowing versus taxing choice and the choice of the tax mix — and discuss the contribution of the important determinants affecting the decisions of Ministers of Finance as they financed Dominion spending from 1867–1917. The analysis of budget speeches of the Ministers of Finance reveals how acutely aware these people were of the scrutiny of the public and the opposition in Parliament. They crafted revenue policies that are consistent with what would be predicted within the conceptual framework of this study. An examination of the quantitative evidence from the new data base on federal government spending, taxing and borrowing developed for this study supports the broad picture that emerges from the budget speech analysis.

The major findings are drawn together in a concluding section which summarizes both the major themes determining the evolution of the revenue structure and the quantitative evidence for the evolution of that revenue structure over the first fifty years of Canada's fiscal history. Finally, these results are contrasted with the findings of the existing literature.

Luring Immigrants and Colonies

As was noted in the introduction, the two themes which dominated all others in the revenue policy discussions of the budget speeches during the period 1867–1917 were attracting people and building the union. Revenue policies that interfered with or inhibited the achievement of these objectives were seen as being politically difficult or impossible. These high political costs of interfering with the Dominion's population policy and union-building policy affected (1) the major division of revenue sources between debt issue and indirect taxation (the tariff and excise duties on alcoholic beverages and tobacco products), and (2) the choice of tax mix, ranging from the decision *not* to use the potential revenue source of direct taxation, to the choice of some items of expenditure which were taxed at reduced rates or exempted from taxation. Each of these major aspects of fiscal structure is examined in detail below.

To Borrow or to Tax: That is the Question

This was first major revenue policy choice of Dominion governments as they pursued the goals of luring immigrants and building the union.

There seems to be no issue discussed more frequently by virtually every Minister of Finance than the ability of the Dominion government to issue new debt at low interest charges in order to finance expenditures and thus permit a low rate of indirect taxation. The latter was seen as being a crucial factor in encouraging immigration into, and discouraging emigration out of, the Dominion. Dominion governments feared losing potential immigrants, as well as those immigrants who were newly settled in Canada, to the United States. Thus the principle applied to numerous tax rate changes was that they should not exceed the tax levels in the United States. Competition for these mobile human resources, not to mention the capital with which these immigrants (be they farmers or businessmen) arrived, was fierce. Consequently, all Dominion governments were determined to keep tax rates low.

The desire to keep indirect tax rates low led to a government demand for debt issue in order to finance Dominion expenditures, both of a capital and current nature. The Dominion government's strong demand for debt finance resulted in a search for low interest rates and a concern to preserve the 'good credit standing' of the Dominion. In turn, this desire to maintain a good credit rating, in order to have access to international capital funds at low interest rates, constrained the government's borrowing power. The revenue policy problem of Dominion governments involved the choice between incurring additional debt, if it could be lodged without seriously damaging the credit ratings, and imposing additional high indirect taxation, with the associated political costs of discouraging immigration and encouraging emigration.

Low tax rates were seen as increasing the future potential revenue bases of the Dominion. Being low in relation to those of the United States, they would attract immigrants and their capital to Canada, thus expanding the future potential revenue bases of the latter country. This expansion would enhance the capacity to pay off the debt, incurred in the immediate present in order to meet total financial requirements, and moreover, to pay it off with effective tax rates which would be lower.

This trade-off between additional debt issue and additional taxation as means of financing the spending plans of the government is consistent with the conceptual framework of this study. Given a political cost function for financing through debt and for indirect taxation, the government will draw upon each of these potential revenue sources up to the point where an extra dollar of revenue incurs the same additional political cost. The determinant of the political cost of an extra dollar of debt issue is the reduced credit standing of the Dominion and the associated higher interest charge (hypothesis H-7, the interest cost of the debt). The determinant of the political cost of an extra dollar of taxation is the reduced net immigration flow (hypothesis H-10, horizontal tax competition). Horizontal tax competition emerges very early as a crucial influence on revenue structure and, as we shall see, maintains its dominant role for one hundred and twenty-three years.

That early Dominion governments perceived this choice so directly is evident from many budget speeches and budget debates in Parliament. The governments were keenly aware of certain constraints on revenue raising, as can be seen from the 1876 and 1878 budget speeches of the Liberal Minister of Finance, the Honourable Sir Richard Cartwright. In 1876 Sir Richard noted that:

> The power of any Government to impose taxation is subject to stringent restrictions, and in no place to more stringent ones than in Canada. [There are] three important limitations — the financial, the political, and the geographic circumstances of the Dominion.
>
> (Cartwright, 1876:27)

He expanded upon these limitations. A tariff high enough to be protective would decrease consumption and increase smuggling, thus decreasing customs revenues and endangering the finances of the country. Any taxation imposed unequally upon the provinces of the country would disrupt the union and raise serious political problems. And the geographic proximity to the United States made it imperative to adjust excise duties and customs rates in order to remain competitive with respect to attracting and keeping immigrants. The financial difficulties at that time — falling revenues due to a trade recession — were met by issuing new debt.

A similar argument was made in 1878, when Sir Richard deferred any decision on levying additional taxes to cover the deficit and borrowed more extensively on international markets:

> . . . the power of imposing fresh taxation is limited within comparatively narrow bounds . . . there are considerable dangers incident to any largely increased measure of taxation. . . .
>
> (Cartwright, 1878:24)

He discussed again the financial, political and geographical limits on further taxation.

Dominion governments during the first fifty years of Confederation stressed the necessity for a young, growing country to have ready access to capital markets in order to finance extensive "public works". The Honourable William S. Fielding asserted in the strongest terms the case for deficit financing of the young Dominion's necessary expenditures:

I do not think any Minister of Finance of this country should be expected
to show often a reduction of the public debt. In a new country like Canada
with a great many public works requiring to be assisted with many demands on the treasury, it would not be surprising that each year we would
not only be obliged to spend our ordinary revenue but to incur some debt
in order to carry on our great public works.

. . . there have been only four years [since 1867] in which the Dominion
was able to provide for all its expenditures and have a balance herewith
to reduce the debt. . . . However, while I call attention to these reductions
. . . I do not hesitate to say that *as a rule, a Minister of Finance will not*
be able to show reductions of the public debt, and it will be no discredit to
him if he is not able to do so.

(Fielding, 1903:8, emphasis added)

This theme, that "increasing the public debt . . . ought to be the normal condition in a young country like [Canada]" was subsequently emphasized and reiterated for a number of years.[2] Dominion governments,
upholding the arguments for deficit financing of public works and also
the financing of some ordinary expenditures, established the case for,
and actively practised, the use of borrowing, as a regular revenue source
along with customs duties and excise duties.
Some Ministers of Finance extolled the virtues of achieving an "equilibrium in the finances" between tax revenues and ordinary expenditures,
excluding from this consideration government expenditures on canals,
railways and other infrastructure. Even this preference was tempered by
an awareness that higher taxes could decrease consumption, increase
smuggling or encourage emigration.[3] In consequence some additional
borrowing was undertaken to cover ordinary expenditures.[4]
A low rate of indirect taxation was clearly seen as a means of attracting and keeping immigrants. In 1868 the government rejected re-
taliatory restrictive tariffs against the United States in order not to discourage immigration.[5] Comparisons of the tax burdens of Canada and
the United States and/or Australia were often made, as a means of announcing the lower tax levels in Canada to potential immigrants and
disgruntled voters.[6] In 1873, the Minister of Finance lauded low indirect
taxation and debt financing of the transportation and communications
system over the coming ten years as a stimulus to population growth,
which would generate increasing revenues for the Dominion with no increase in tax rates.[7] In 1910, Fielding applauded the low rate of customs
taxation and argued that debt financing in the past had allowed population growth, thereby lightening the debt burden in the present and
the future.[8] The lumber interests were treated as "lightly as possible [in
1881 tariff changes because] . . . it drives people out of the country".[9]

The constant search for low interest rates on debt lodged in London and the maintenance of a good credit standing for this purpose, emerged in almost every budget speech, often in colourful language.[10] The Honourable R.J. Cartwright, two years into Liberal rule in 1875, boasted of loans "obtained on better terms than any of equal amount for the past *twenty* years".[11] Three years later he was claiming success in maintaining "our credit standing . . . [but] . . . our escape was a narrow one".[12] Later, Cartwright, now in opposition, took his anti-government campaign to the mother country and the Conservative Minister of Finance expressed concern because:

> the credit and reputation of Canada . . . contribute greatly to our prestige and our prosperity. . . . The time of the attack was a particularly opportune one for an enemy to have winged his arrow to a vital point in Canadian reputation and Canadian Credit . . . the money market was particularly sensitive.
>
> (Foster, 1892:7)

Three years later, the Minister of Finance exuded satisfaction at extracting debt money, in the midst of a trade depression, from London "vaults which would not be tempted out of its hiding or hoarding place, except by the very best securities and consequently affording the best test of the condition of the securities of a country".[13] The Minister was especially proud of obtaining funds at 3 1/6 percent while the United States had to pay 3 3/4 percent for its loan. The Honourable Thomas White assured members of the House in 1913 that, "it may be affirmed without question that this amount of indebtedness is not only not excessive but exceptionally reasonable in amount for a country with the territory, resources wealth and development of Canada".[14]

This examination reveals that Ministers of Finance were aware of the relative political costs of additional borrowing compared with additional taxation. They shaped their revenue policies in response to the interest costs of borrowing associated with a given credit standing of the Dominion and horizontal tax competition, especially with the United States. These determinants of revenue structure within the conceptual framework of Chapter 2 (hypotheses H-7 and H-10, respectively) carried substantial weight for Dominion governments intent on attracting immigrants and opening up the West.

These governments were also intent on attracting the remaining colonies into the union, and discouraging disgruntled provinces from leaving. Revenue policy was framed with this objective in mind: low indirect taxation and use of debt issue were instruments that could entice such new entrants into Confederation. This concern of the Dominion government for the effect of its tax policies on potential new entrants reflects the core of ideas underlying vertical tax competition. With the Dominion of Canada still not completed, the federal government was especially sensitive to financing policies that would facilitate and not inhibit the completion process. Its behaviour was consistent with what would be predicted within the positive model of Chapter 2. The Honourable John Rose put the issue directly in his second budget:

> We feel that the duty of the present hour is to consolidate the union. . . .
> We feel that every new measure of taxation is liable to be misinterpreted
> and misunderstood in Nova Scotia, and that until the union is firmly estab-
> lished, until those who are not yet entirely reconciled to it have become
> so, our policy ought to be one of forbearance and conciliation towards
> them . . . there is a desire . . . a magnanimous and generous desire to deal
> tenderly, and kindly, and considerately, with every interest which affects
> the peculiar position and well-being of the Maritime Provinces.
>
> (Rose, 1868:15 and 30–31)

Sir Leonard Tilley was later to express objections to increased tariff rates which might "break up Confederation by imposing unequal taxation; it would dissever this admirable superstructure which we are all proud of . . .".[15]

In 1885, Tilley was careful to be conciliatory towards a potential colonial entrant:

> it may be in the interest of this country to make arrangements with the
> government of that colony that in return for a reduction on flour or other
> products of Canada we will reduce or remove the duty on fish imported
> from Newfoundland
>
> (Tilley, 1885:8)

Newfoundland was also very much on the mind of the Honourable William S. Fielding when, in 1905, the issue of British imports that first passed through that colony before arriving in Canada arose:

> . . . and having regard to our desires to have the most friendly relations
> with our sister colony and hope that some day she may see fit to join her
> fortunes with ours.
>
> (Fielding, 1905:35)

The Finance Minister decided to treat such imports as direct British imports, subject to the preferential tariff.

In short, an additional factor shaping the revenue policies of Ministers of Finance was vertical tax competition with the provinces and potential new Provinces. This determinant of revenue structure which influenced the level of indirect taxes also affected the decision not to introduce an income tax, a policy choice to which we now turn.

Tax Individual Incomes? Never!

> I would like to see the man who could be elected in any constituency on a policy of direct taxation.
>
>   (The Honourable George E. Foster, Minister of Finance,
>   *Budget Speech*, 1893, p. 40)

The second major revenue policy choice of Dominion governments as they pursued the twin objectives of luring immigrants and building the union was the particular mix of tax sources, reflected primarily in the policy decision *not* to tax incomes and to rely almost exclusively on the tariff and excise duties. The municipalities of Ontario had been levying a direct tax on income long before Confederation. British Columbia levied the first provincial income tax in 1876 and Prince Edward Island followed suit in 1894. Thus the revenue source, income, was already "occupied" to varying degrees across the union. The Dominion government expressed concern that an added direct tax on top of the tax burden already carried by taxpayers — especially in Ontario — would raise several serious political difficulties.

First, the direct tax burden might become sufficiently high to encourage emigration to the United States. References were made to relative tax burdens between the two countries as an important political constraint. The economic loss of people and their resources to the United States would reduce the revenue bases available for taxation, necessitating higher tax rates or reduced government spending. Thus the potential economic cost of this horizontal tax competition would be reflected directly into higher political costs for the government.[16]

Second, with the Dominion government competing with the provinces for the same revenue source, the provinces would find it politically costly to introduce and/or raise their direct tax rates. This competition for the same revenue source might lead to increased provincial demands for a constitutional amendment that would allow the provinces to apply indirect taxes legally. In fact, the Liberals argued that the abuse of direct taxation by municipal bodies called for a constitutional amendment that would remove the right of the municipalities to levy direct taxes while granting the provinces and their municipalities a new right to apply indirect taxation. This constitutional reform was expected to be politically unpopular with the provinces already *in* the union (which wanted the right to impose indirect taxation but did not want their municipalities to give up the direct taxation revenue source) and to discourage potential entrants from joining the union. In the course of time this constitutional reform argument came to stand for an acknowledged, high cost alternative.

The high political costs of introducing a new tax on incomes were perceived by the Dominion government to be (1) reduction of the future tax base because of the emigration of discouraged residents, (2) non-expansion of the future tax base because of the refusal of other colonies to enter the union, and (3) increased demand for costly constitutional amendments because of competition between different levels of government. In short, horizontal tax competition with the United States, vertical tax competition among the Dominion, the provinces and the municipalities and the Confederation agreements (hypotheses H-10, H-9 and H-4, respectively) emerge as contributing determinants of one important feature of Dominion tax structure: the absence of a direct tax on incomes.

The Liberals first drew attention to municipal direct taxation in 1874 and, given the expected effect of high taxation on immigration flows, decided against introducing a direct tax:

> . . . in imposing fresh taxes upon the people we must bear in mind that a greater proportion of them, especially in Ontario, labour under heavy local taxation . . . . . . I do not think that much more taxation could be safely resorted to; nor do I think that we ought to resort to any great amount of direct taxation
>
> (Cartwright, 1874:19 and 41)

This concern for attracting immigrants was still in evidence in the early first world war budgets. The Honourable Thomas White, in his 1916 budget speech, stressed that, "Canada is a country inviting immigration and we must be careful not to create the impression that it is likely to become a country of heavy individual taxation".[17] A year later Mr. White, after rejecting an income tax, in part[18] because some Canadians "are already taxed now upon their incomes by municipalities and provinces", proceeded to plead that members of the house,

> in considering taxation measures for the period following the war keep in view the desirability of a flow of settlers and capital to Canada not being retarded through fear on their part of heavy federal taxation
>
> (White, 1917:8)

The vertical tax competition for direct taxes on incomes emerged as an issue as early as the 1874 budget speech quoted above. The verbal response of the two political parties differed, although their actual tax structure policy was the same: no income tax was introduced. The Liberals surveyed the "occupied" direct tax field and called for a constitutional reform removing the right of municipalities to tax incomes:

> I have always looked upon it as a very objectionable principle to allow
> this House, the local Legislatures, and the municipal bodies to have the
> power of imposing almost any amount of taxes we may severally see fit . . .
> I consider it would be highly expedient to have a revision of the system,
> in order to see whether we cannot devise some mode of re-distributing
> this power . . . . When any question arises between direct and indirect
> taxation, it will be well to remember that six millions are already levied
> by direct taxation for local purposes in [Ontario]
>
> (Cartwright, 1874:20)

The Honourable Sir Richard Cartwright's budget speech of 1878 developed this theme further:

> No one can have looked peacefully at the vast increases . . . in the amount
> of our municipal taxation, particularly in towns and cities without being
> aware that there is a very considerable risk that the almost unlimited
> power of direct taxation which has been granted to these bodies, will be
> grievously abused . . . city population are especially unfit to be entrusted
> with such very large powers. . . .
>
> I feel that it would be far truer in principle and far more conducive
> to their interests if they were confined to taxing certain subjects strictly
> selected . . . instead of, at present, allowing them to tax all kinds of
> property. . . . There is an urgent need that the power granted to those
> municipal bodies should be rigidly restricted. . . .
>
> . . . to push the economy further [in the direction of imposing direct
> taxation], unless indeed we submit to very important *alterations in our
> present constitutional system* would be both difficult and of doubtful expediency.
>
> (Cartwright, 1878:14, 15, and 19, emphasis added)

The Minister of Finance did not introduce a direct tax on incomes.

The difficulties alluded to were political, attributable in part by municipal occupancy of the field: the political costs, given municipal occupancy, were too high, compared with the cost of alternative courses of action. The Liberal government did not move to negotiate a constitutional alteration in municipal taxing powers; either the costs were too high or the time too short — the 1878 election did not return the Liberals to office! The lower cost revenue source was debt issue in the London market.

The Conservatives, mindful of the political difficulties of applying direct taxation, made no attempt to do so, and used the Liberals' willingness to tax incomes as a constant reminder to voters of the "crushing burdens" they would experience under a Liberal government. The Honourable A.W. McLean, in 1886, drew attention to the Liberals' criticism of paying statutory subsidies to the provinces and to their suggestion:

that the provinces should be taught to resort to direct taxation in order to raise the revenues they require. . . . But until that time comes and until the honourable gentlemen can persuade the country to accept that doctrine and resort to direct taxation for local purposes we shall have to provide in our estimates for provincial subsidies under the B.N.A. Act.

(McLean, 1886:30)

The Liberal policy of reciprocity or free trade with the United States was presented by Conservative Finance Ministers as one that would require direct taxation to make up the lost revenues. Reciprocity, cried Sir Charles Tupper, when he was Minister of Finance, would involve "enormous direct taxation that would crush the people of this country".[19] Three years later Finance Minister Foster predicted,

a practical necessity stronger than the fates of old which sat relentless above the will of men and gods, which will drive them upon direct taxation in spite of themselves if once [the Liberals] adopt unrestricted reciprocity.

(Foster, 1891:27)[20]

The Minister could not resist a jibe at his political foe, the Honourable Sir Richard Cartwright, who, it was claimed, "has stated over and over again that nothing but the incomprehensible stupidity of the people of Canada prevents them from adopting direct taxation".[21] Sir Richard objected, and no doubt Finance Minister Foster had taken some political license with his predecessor's words, but the substantive conclusion on which both politicians seemed to agree was that the "people of Canada" objected to direct taxation. Two years later the Honourable George Foster emphasized this point when he claimed he "would like to see the man who could be elected in any constituency on a policy of direct taxation".[22]

With the expenditure requirements of the first great war, new sources of revenues were a matter of concern in every budget speech. The Minister of Finance resisted the move into the income tax field. In 1915 double occupancy of the direct tax field was cited as the main reason[23] for not imposing a Dominion income tax:

At present under legislation existing in certain of the provinces income is subject to taxation by municipalities and in two instances by the province themselves. . . . My chief objection, however, to an income tax is the fact that several provinces are also likely to be obliged to resort to measures for raising additional revenue and I am of the view that the Dominion should not enter upon the domain to which they are confined to a greater degree than is necessary in the national interest.

(White, 1915:16 and 17)

In 1917, the concern not to impose an additional income tax on top of the municipal and provincial income taxes was expressed as the main reason, along with the fear of inhibiting a flow of settlers, for not introducing a Dominion income tax.[24]

The foregoing discussion reveals that Ministers were aware of the political costs of direct taxation as compared with those of indirect taxation and chose not to introduce an income tax because of considerations related to horizontal and vertical tax competition and the Confederation agreements. These tax policy decisions helped to shape the evolving revenue structure and assisted in attracting immigrants and building the Dominion.

With an Eye on the United States Tax on Tea

The revenue policy choice reflected in the mix of tax sources included avoidance of a tax on incomes and the selection of some items of consumption to be taxed (through an import levy or excise duty) at reduced rates or to be exempted from taxation entirely. These decisions, too, are reflections of population policy and efforts at union-building. Taxes on specific items of consumption expenditure were monitored closely by the Minister of Finance in order to keep them below the tax rates imposed by the government of the United States. Articles of general consumption that were of interest to settlers, such as tea or sugar, always had a rate of taxation well below the United States levels. The concern about possible emigration and discouragement of new settlers is clear evidence of the government's objective of attracting people and building the union. Both objectives underlie hypothesis H-10 (horizontal tax competition).

Sir Francis Hincks, in 1872, stressed the importance of remaining competitive with the United States with respect to duties on tea:

> I do not hesitate, however, to state that if the duties on tea are taken off in the U.S., we must make some re-adjustment in our tariff, and in the face of free importation of tea from the U.S. we should have to abandon a revenue of something like a million, which we now derive from this source.
>
> (Hincks, 1872:11)

Sir Leonard Tilley made the same point in 1883 when he reduced the duty on tobacco:

> . . . owing to the fact that the United States have reduced the excise duty on tobacco and snuff . . . . the government deems it an absolute necessity, for many reasons — though there are other articles on which they would rather relieve the people from taxation — to reduce our own duty on tobacco made from foreign leaf . . . . and Canadian leaf.
>
> (Tilley, 1883:29)

Such statements serve to confirm the observations already made about government objectives during the fifty-year period. The most significant determinants of the revenue structure are the interest costs of borrowing, horizontal tax competition with the United States and vertical tax competition among the three levels of government.

In addition, there are several modest determinants of tax policy — a concern for the costs of collection, compliance and enforcement and a tax preference for taxes on tobacco and spirits — and one minor determinant — a tax preference for sharing tax burdens equitably. I discuss each of these factors next.

Avoiding Smugglers and Con Men

The Dominion's tax structure policy hardly seems a likely hiding place for smugglers and con men. However, the costs of collection, compliance and enforcement emerge as a minor determinant of the tax structure; and smuggling and fraud emerge as two major contributing factors to those costs.

The Honourable William S. Fielding's comments in the 1899 budget speech are typical expressions of the concern that if some tax or customs duty rate was set too high it would encourage smuggling, reduce consumption and so decrease revenues derived from the article taxed:

> It is always possible, especially with an article of that character [tobacco] to place your duty at such a figure that you encourage smuggling to an enormous extent, and so obtain no increase in revenue.
>
> (Fielding, 1899:13)

The possibility that these costs of compliance would influence private sector behaviour and cost the government lost revenues served as a constraint on tax policy throughout the period.[25]

Ad valorem excise and customs duties encouraged con men to fabricate invoices for purposes of cheating the revenue man. Dominion governments responded to this challenge by switching from ad valorem taxes to specific taxes. The Honourable George E. Foster described one such tax switch in 1894 in rather colourfull language:

> Specific duties in some respects, are absolutely necessary to guard against frauds of valuation: in other respects they are useful in indicating the consumption of a higher and healthier, and better grade of article. Every customs-house officer, of course, delights in specific duties; they are not complex, and the importers of the country find it easy to make their calculations under them.
>
> (Foster, 1984:20)

As a result of the perception that costs of collection, compliance and enforcement were reduced by the imposition of specific duties the latter came, in many cases, to replace duties levied.[26]

It is also of passing interest to note that the government acknowledged in the 1886 budget speech that a switch from an ad valorem to a specific excise duty, during a period when prices were falling (as in 1884–1886), would retard and possibly halt the decline in government revenues.[27] This raises the possibility that the "fraud" argument masked a somewhat different aspect of ad valorem duties, namely, their political cost. When prices are falling, it will be necessary to revise these duties upward from time to time in order to maintain government revenues. Thus, ad valorem duties are more costly, in political terms, than specific duties, the real value of which rise as prices fall.[28]

The Joy of Taxing Sin!

The wages of sin in the form of a levy of $50 on each of 69 women of doubtful character were used to defray part of the cost of two [fire] engines bought in 1898. In 1908 a hydrant system was installed.

(in response to fires in Dawson, during the Klondike Gold Rush)[29]

Sin taxes have taken many forms in Canada, as the above quotation suggests. Perhaps no aspect of Canadian tax policy is more instructive than the extent to which governments have been prepared to exploit the people's feeling of guilt about the use of tobacco and spirits by fashioning taxes that minimize political costs. Given the old notion that tobacco and spirits are, in some sense, sinful or evil, and the more recent, sanitized perception that they are unhealthy, voters — users and non-users alike — will display a relatively low level of opposition to any increase in the effective tax rate on the consumption of such items. This attitude produces a political cost function which is lower than would be the case for a different item of consumption with a comparable potential revenue base. The tax preference for "sin" taxes is one of the variants of hypothesis H-8, derived in Chapter 2.

The difference in relative political costs is independent of the price elasticity of demand for the taxed article. The potential revenue bases are held constant for all hypotheses except H-13 and H-14. A consumption good with an inelastic price demand will result in a larger potential revenue base than a consumption good with an elastic price demand, and thus the former will generate higher revenues at a given tax rate, or given revenues at a lower tax rate, than would be the case with the latter. It follows that, as a general rule, price-inelastic goods will entail lower political costs than price-elastic goods. This proposition is, in any case, accurately captured by hypothesis H-1.

The argument here is that, for consumption goods of a *given* price inelasticity (with identical potential revenue bases), one of which is widely judged to be sinful, it will be less costly, politically, to tax the consumption of that good. The price elasticity of demand for food, broadly defined, is inelastic; so, it is believed, is the price elasticity of demand for alcoholic beverages and tobacco. Food products have, for the most part, never been taxed, or have been taxed very lightly in Canada. Alcoholic beverages and tobacco have always been taxed, and taxed heavily. This observation is consistent with the existence of a tax preference for taxes on sin that lowers the political costs of taxing sinful behaviour in comparison with the political costs of taxing non-sinful or meritorious behaviour.

One would expect governments to take advantage of this tax preference with regard to spirits and tobacco by taxing such consumption bases more intensively. To the extent that citizens, wavering in their belief in the sinful or unhealthy nature of these activities, can be persuaded that the use of such items is voluntary, and a luxury, rather than compulsory and a necessity, governments can actively reinforce the tax preference for such levies.

Canada's Dominion governments drew upon these strands of belief in formulating one structural aspect of their tax policy. The Minister of Finance would divide total taxation into voluntary and involuntary taxation and claim that the level of "real" taxation was lower in Canada than it was perceived to be because only involuntary taxation should be taken into account. Sir Leonard Tilley, in the budget speech of 1882 drew the first link between luxuries and voluntary taxation when he noted the voluntary increase in taxation, "I say voluntary because the increases of last year, $778,000, was paid in luxuries such as wines, spirits, silks and satins".[30]

Sir George Foster strengthened the link between voluntary taxation and liquor and tobacco in 1889:

> Taxation, then, may be of two kinds — voluntary, and what you may call involuntary taxation. What I mean by it is this: I, for my part, do not use tobacco and intoxicating liquor. . . . My case, which is the case of hundreds of thousands, I think millions of people in this country. . . .
>
> If not millions now, it will be by and by, at no very distant period when my pleasant friend, who is looking upon me, comes to think as I do, and as so many others of the people of this country. . . .

> But out of this 28 million odd dollars that was paid into the coffers of this country, $8,084,780 was for tobacco and liquors alone. . . . *Now this is voluntary taxation.*
>
> (Foster, 1889:14, emphasis added)

He built upon this theme, with almost evangelical devotion, in his 1893 budget speech:

> What [the farmer] ought to drink, according to my opinion, are free [of taxes]. His water, tea and coffee are free. If he desires to drink anything stronger — which is optional with himself — it is a luxury he takes, and he has to pay for it, and *we will have a tax on that so long as Canada is a country. . . .*
>
> . . . of [the $36 million in taxation taken from people] $10 million is for liquors and tobacco, and no man would get up in this House or any other Anglo-Saxon House of Parliament and ask that these articles should be free. *So long as revenue is needed a revenue will be raised upon them.* They are not necessities but luxuries, and the man who buys them buys them with the knowledge that he is paying into the revenue, and when he does, it is a voluntary and not an involuntary tax.
>
> (Foster, 1893:29, emphasis added)[31]

Excise duties on spirits and tobacco were popular sources of revenues for Ministers of Finance, who judged they met virtually no voter opposition or, as the temperance movement developed during the 1880s and 1890s, came to view these taxes as politically very popular.[32]

Robin Hood as a Baby

The notion that tax burdens should be shared fairly or equitably has a long history in Canada. A distinction is often made between horizontal equity and vertical equity, where the former refers to equal treatment of equals and the latter refers to some different tax treatment of unequals.[33] Vertical equity is often referred to as a characteristic that facilitates redistribution from high income to low income families, in much the same way as that literary redistributor, Robin Hood, took from the rich and gave to the poor.

It has already been noted, in the discussion of taxing tobacco and spirits, that the preference for a tax on voluntary luxuries such as tobacco, alcohol, jewellery, satins and silks was considered quite appropriate. The theme that luxuries should be taxed heavily and necessities lightly — a crude form of vertical equity — was put succinctly by Sir George Foster in his 1889 budget speech:

> . . . we all argue that luxuries should pay the most [tax], and that necessary and staple articles should either pay less or pay nothing at all. . . .

> . . . [these tariff arrangements bring] the incidence of taxation where it should rest most heavily, upon the man who buys luxuries and has expensive tastes and is willing to gratify them, and least heavily upon the farmer.
>
> (Foster, 1889:15 and 17)

The same theme, treated fully or partially, emerged in several other budget speeches.[34] In a broader context, discussions of tax burdens on the rich man and the poor man in several earlier budget speeches revealed a strong preference for higher taxes on the rich man.[35]

With regard to the slighter emphasis on horizontal equity it was noted above that the government, in 1876 and 1878, was keenly aware of the political dangers of any unequal taxation across the provinces of the union — an inferred desire for geographic horizontal equity.[36] It should be emphasized that the perceived potential consequences of failure to achieve such horizontal equity were very grave: the disruption of the union. In 1893 Finance Minister Foster professed the desire that "all classes should bear proportionately equal burdens".[37]

Two years earlier this minister had argued the case for a broadly based item of consumption as an equitable tax:

> *Sugar* is one of the best articles possible for distributing the taxation, *the rich and poor use it largely in proportion to their means*, it is diffused through every section of the country . . . and there is possibly no article upon which a part of the revenue of the country can be more equitably placed.
>
> . . . we look to a different source for raising the $1,500,000, a source from which we think it can be raised most easily, with the least burden upon the great masses of the people . . . . [a] one cent per pound addition on *malt*.
>
> (Foster, 1891:10 and 11, emphasis added)

This argument could be interpreted as a desire to achieve horizontal equity through a tax on items of widespread consumption, sugar and beer;[38] but it could also be construed as a preference for some vertical equity, since the tax burden would be borne by the rich and poor "in proportion to their means". On either interpretation the speech presents an *a priori* superficial case for a tax preference for equitable taxes — the political costs of equitable taxes are lower than other potential revenue sources.

Except in the 1891 budget speech, no case is made for taxing articles of widespread consumption, and the arguments for not taxing (or at least not raising the tax rate on) staples have already been noted: it seems that the tax preference for equitable taxation had only a minor influence on tax structure. To the extent that it did, it took the form of taxing perceived luxuries or voluntarily consumed goods at a higher rate than necessities or broadly based items of consumption, some of which might not be taxed at all. In short, horizontal equity played a small role, but vertical equity was somewhat more important during the early years of the Dominion.

Finally, the theme of the protective tariff versus the revenue tariff permeates many budget speeches, especially after the introduction of the National Policy of 1879. The tariff represented a major contribution to the total financing needs of the Dominion, even before 1879 and, in fact, when power was in the hands of the Liberals (the free traders, who favoured reciprocity with the United States). In addition, the tariff could be used to provide significant protection to domestic industry. Domestic manufacturers stood to gain the most from this policy, while regions of the country which imported many goods stood to lose. Thus the protective tariff of the National Policy carried political costs in the Maritime provinces and, later, in the West, which had to be weighed against the benefits for particular manufacturers.

Financing Dominion Spending, 1867–1917

I have examined the broad themes of Dominion revenue structure policy, as conveyed by Ministers of Finance through their budget speeches. I now turn to the empirical record during the first fifty years of Confederation.

Dominion spending relative to the size of the economy was remarkably stable during most of the initial fifty-year fiscal history. This spending indicator varied between just 5 and 9 percent from 1870 to 1913.[39] The rise to 9 percent occurred during the 1880s, when national income was falling and the Dominion embarked on one of its "great public works" — the building of the Canadian Pacific Railway. Chart 1-2 in Chapter 1 records the spending variation, including the wartime spending surge which increased the public sector size to 14 percent by 1917. This stability of Dominion spending, relative to the size of the economy, masks years when the level fell as well as years when it rose.[40]

Spending was financed from three major Confederation revenue sources: customs duties, excise duties on alcoholic beverages and tobacco products, and borrowing (deficit financing).[41] Chart 3-1 traces the revenues for these sources, relative to national income, from 1870 through 1917, and Chart 3-2 traces them as a percentage of total financial requirements from 1868 through 1917. The tariff was the single most important revenue-raiser throughout the period (except in 1885 and the war years), financing between 40–66 percent of total spending. Excise duties accounted for 10–22 percent and deficit financing, although exhibiting greater variability, accounted for 10 percent regularly, and occasionally represented as much as 40 percent of total spending.

The variation in customs duties revenues from the tariff is consistent with what might be called a trade cycle effect.[42] When national income is rising the customs duties revenue base is increasing as well. Therefore, other things being equal, the political cost function of customs duties falls in relation to the political cost functions of other revenue sources, and this leads governments to increase the relative utilization of the customs duties revenue source. The reverse takes place when there is a decrease in national income and in the base of the tariff revenues. This observation is consistent with the conceptual framework of Chapter 2, and specifically with the revenue buoyancy hypothesis and the predicted revenue structure changes in response to variations in the revenue bases.

This tariff revenue buoyancy effect of the trade cycle is not the complete explanation of the changing importance of the tariff within the total financial requirements supporting the spending plans of Dominion governments.[43] The effective tariff rate was increased and decreased regularly during the fifty year period. The discussion, in the earlier sections of this chapter, of the major themes of revenue structure policy has demonstrated that governments were determined to keep indirect tariff rates low in order to encourage immigration. Finance Ministers altered tariff rates when such action would assist them in achieving their objectives.

The variation in revenues from excise duties on alcohol and tobacco during the first fifty years is much smaller than the wide swings in the tariff or deficit financing. This relative steadiness is consistent with the regular references of Finance Ministers to alcohol and tobacco products as a source of revenues. The heightened passion for such "sin" taxes, stimulated by the temperance movement during the 1880s and 1890s, is reflected in the enhanced significance of such tax revenues during the 1885–1900 period. This is reflected in both the tax indicator measure of Chart 3-1 and the revenue shares measure of Chart 3-2.

Dominion revenues from the tariff, excise duties and the other taxes noted in Appendix Tables B-2 and B-3 were, in total, approximately 5.5 percent of gross national product from 1870 through 1913, a period ending just before the war (see Chapter 1, Chart 1-3). The stability in the total tax indicator is consistent with Finance Ministers' continually expressed desire to keep indirect taxes low in order to attract immigrants and coax the other colonies into the union. These objectives provided the context for a demand for deficit financing, to serve as an integral component of the governments' total financial requirements.

Chart 3-1

Confederation Revenue Sources, as a percentage of GNP, Canada, 1870-1917.

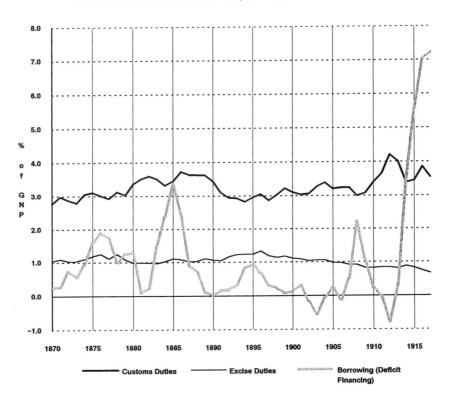

Source: Table C-3

Chart 3-2

**Confederation Revenue Sources,
as a percentage of Total Financial Requirements (TFR),
Canada, Fiscal 1868-1917.**

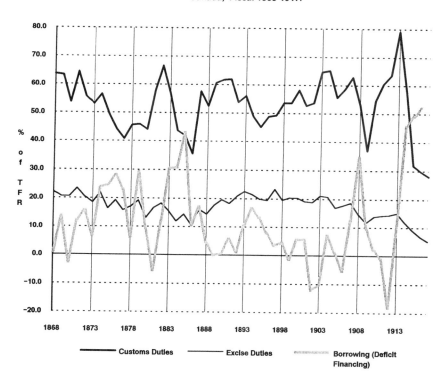

Source: Table B-3

The Dominion governments borrowed, both domestically and from foreign sources, in order to finance their spending. The domestic sources were government and post office savings banks and, to a minor extent, the chartered banks. The foreign sources were primarily bond issues floated in the London money market and, to a lesser extent, British banks. Domestic borrowing was important up to the mid-1880s, after which foreign borrowing became the major source of financing the deficit.[44]

Charts 3-1 and 3-2 trace the variability of the revenue obtained through borrowing, both in relation to the size of the economy and as a share of total financial requirements. Deficit financing was a significant, and at times, substantial source of revenues for Dominion governments as they carried out their spending plans.

The largest deficits were not incurred to finance the largest increases in total government spending from one year to the next. Four of the largest increases in total financial requirements were accompanied by deficit financing that accounted for a moderate (11–14%) share of the total (1870, 1872, 1883 and 1914). The three war years (1915, 1916 and 1917) did combine large increases, from year to year, in total financial requirements with deficit financing that accounted for a substantial (46–52%) share of total financing; but this can be explained by the special policy considerations of war finance, to which I return in Chapter 6. The year 1875 was the only one to record a large share (24%) of the total financial requirements met by deficit financing simultaneously with a large (24%) increase in total financial requirements over those of the preceding year.

On the other hand, there were eight years in which deficit financing accounted for a substantial share (23–43%) of total financial requirements and yet the change in financial requirements from one year to the next was a moderate increase or decrease (1876–1878, 1880, 1884–1886, and 1909). During these years the percentage share of customs revenues was not much above 40 and excise revenues ranged from 13–18 percent. In short, the overall record supports the conclusion that Dominion governments consistently and actively utilized deficit financing through borrowing as a regular source of revenue to finance expenditures. In addition, the relative importance of borrowing, as compared to customs and excise duties, is consistent with the positive model underlying this study: at times borrowing was pursued vigorously, which suggests that the relative political costs of the various revenue sources could have influenced the government's decisions.

Decreasing the public debt was not a policy goal at any time during the period covered. Debt issue was a source of revenue, actively pursued along with customs duties and excise duties. The data are consistent with a government policy that increased the public debt, especially for the purpose of carrying out the "great works" of the young Dominion. Even the six years of debt reduction are merely an aberration from this policy of debt expansion.[45] It is reasonable to suppose that, given the level of planned government spending, a buoyant economy resulted in increases in customs revenues which were larger than expected and so permitted an unexpectedly large reduction in borrowing, sufficient to retire some of the outstanding debt. The data bear out this supposition (see Chart 3-2) in that each year of surplus on government accounts is a year of substantial increase in customs duties revenues (1871, 1900 and 1913) or in customs duties revenues combined with either special receipts (1882 and 1903) or miscellaneous revenues (1904).

This evidence of a deliberate policy of deficit financing and, consequently, increasing the public debt, complements the most forceful articulation of that policy, found in the budget speeches of Finance Minister Fielding which were delivered in 1903, 1904, 1905, 1906, 1909 and 1911. These have been discussed in an earlier section of this chapter. It is worth noting that Fielding defended with passion a policy of increasing the public debt during years in which he was able to reduce it due to surpluses in the accounts!

Conclusions:
Tax Lightly, Borrow Cheaply and Spend

> . . . increasing the public debt . . . ought to be the normal condition in a young country like Canada.
>
> (Fielding, 1904:15)

This analysis of the first fifty years of Dominion revenue policy, viewed in terms of the comprehensive positive model of revenue structure, leads to the following conclusions. First, three determinants of political costs outweighed all others in shaping the structure of revenues: the good credit standing of the Dominion (and hence the cost of borrowing money), horizontal tax competition and vertical tax competition. Dominion governments pursued an active policy of extensive borrowing and debt enlargement, in order to keep taxes low and to engage in spending on "great public works". Low taxes were seen as necessary in order to encourage immigration and discourage emigration, and to minimize the incentive to avoid taxes through smuggling. With borrowing regularly accounting for up to 10 percent, and not infrequently a larger proportion of total financial requirements, the good credit standing of the country and the cost of borrowing money were factors of critical importance to revenue structure policy.

Considerations of horizontal tax competition not only shaped indirect taxes — the tariff and the excise duties — so as to encourage immigration and discourage emigration, but also led Dominion governments to avoid imposing a direct tax on incomes throughout the first fifty years. Moreover, considerations of vertical tax competition, with municipal governments and eventually two provinces taxing incomes, reinforced the reluctance of Dominion governments reluctance to introduce such a tax when additional revenues were needed to cover spending commitments.

Second, the elasticity of the base to which the tariff was applied was an important determinant of the structure of revenues. When trade was expanding the tariff base grew and customs revenues automatically expanded to account for a larger part of total financial requirements. When trade was contracting the converse was true. Dominion governments also enacted many changes in the rate and structure of the tariff that are consistent with the conceptual framework of this study.

Third, the cost of collection, compliance, and enforcement, and a tax preference for taxes on spirits and tobacco were determinants of political costs that exercised a modest influence on the structure of the Dominion revenue system. The possibility that high tax rates on some items of consumption would encourage smuggling and thus increase the costs of compliance served as a constraint on both tariff and excise duty policies. The greater scope for fraud offered by ad valorem duties, as compared with excise duties, led to a switch from the former to the latter, with a consequent decrease in collection costs. Dominion governments used to their advantage any determinant that would lower the political cost of raising revenues from a particular source: it was acceptable to play on the sense of guilt occasioned by the consumption of alcoholic beverages or by smoking and if it was useful to foster a belief that taxes on spirits, tobacco, silks and satins were "voluntary" then some Finance Ministers were ready to spread the word.

Finally, there were several determinants of political costs that may have contributed in a minor way to shaping the revenue structure. Some concern regarding the political costs of reopening the Confederation agreements reinforced the decision not to introduce a direct tax on incomes. A degree of preference for vertical equity formed the basis for higher tax rates on luxury consumption items, and a less significant preference for horizontal equity, especially as between provinces, emerged occasionally.

This explanation of the evolution of the Dominion revenue structure during the first fifty years after Confederation differs from the conclusions in the existing literature. In large part, as I noted earlier, researchers have virtually ignored the role of the budget — and especially the revenue side of the budget — during Canada's early development. Moreover, when attention has been devoted to the financing side of the budget, the result has usually been a partial examination of the tariff and not a comprehensive analysis of the entire revenue structure.[46]

The literature has devoted some attention to two characteristics of the tariff that have an impact on the revenue-raising objectives of the government: the volatility of revenues from customs duties and the contrast between the revenue-raising and protectionist dimensions of the tariff. Harvey Perry refers to the tariff as a "fairweather friend among revenue sources . . . [producing] prolifically in good, and abysmally in poor, times".[47] Georg Rich notes that tariff revenues "regularly peaked with the reference cycle", and, in linking them to cyclical influences and discussing a discretionary role for government spending, implies that all resultant deficits were a passive function of the base elasticity of the tariff and of spending decisions.[48] I have concluded that, while base elasticity was an important determinant of the structure of government revenues, governments actively pursued a policy of substantial deficit financing in order to keep tariff and excise duty rates low.

Rich discusses an additional policy thrust that is consistent with the comprehensive approach of this study. He argues that the dramatic decline of domestic borrowing, as compared with foreign borrowing, during the 1868–1914 period was associated with a substantial fall in foreign interest rates in relation to domestic rates and therefore reflected a "desire to minimize the interest burden of the public debt".[49] It is reasonable to suppose that a government interested in keeping the interest burden of a given public debt as low as possible would also be interested in minimizing the burden of additional public debt relative to the cost of additional tax revenues, and that such a desire would find expression in a policy of discretionary deficit financing. Such a result is precisely what is found in this study.

The second characteristic of the tariff noted in the literature is the contrast between its function as a revenue-raiser and its use as a protectionist device.[50] Harvey Perry is careful to draw attention to the strong demand for protection coming from the manufacturing interests of Ontario and Quebec, and the equally strong sentiment in favour of lower tariffs in the Maritime Provinces, the latter acting as a constraint on the former.[51] Perry's analysis of the diverse political factors influencing the tariff is consistent with the broad approach adopted in this study, which encompasses all revenue sources.

I have extended this analysis by using a comprehensive positive model of revenue structure, in order to demonstrate the relative contribution of the major political costs in shaping the revenue structure of the Dominion government from 1867–1917. In addition, I have demonstrated that the government actively pursued a policy of substantial borrowing in order to keep tariff rates and excise duties low. Harvey Perry interprets Finance Minister Foster's 1895 budget speech, which announced that taxes would not be increased to cover the deficit, as an "interesting deviation from the rigid 'balanced-budget' philosophy of public finance".[52] I interpret it as consistent with the budget speeches of all Ministers of Finance which, while paying occasional lip-service to balancing current expenditures, reflected the decisions of governments to borrow when it suited their purposes not to increase the tariff, excise duties or other taxes.

This initial fifty-year period of Canadian fiscal history begins with Finance Minister Rose's budget of December 7, 1867 and ends with Finance Minister White's budget of April 24, 1917. Dominion governments, in seeking to attract immigrants, open up the West and build the union, financed their spending through revenue policy choices that entailed substantial borrowing, extensive reliance on indirect taxes (the tariff and excise duties), levied at low rates, and rejection of a direct tax on incomes. The resultant revenue structure, and its fifty year evolution, was heavily influenced by the good credit standing of the Dominion (and the associated interest charges), horizontal tax competition, especially with the United States, and vertical tax competition among the Dominion, the provinces and municipalities. Factors of lesser importance were revenue base elasticity, administration costs, a preference for sin taxes and a minor preference for equitable taxes.

Three months after Sir Thomas White's 1917 budget the Dominion government was to introduce a direct tax on incomes, and three years later it would introduce a general sales tax. These revenue policy choices would have profound effects on the evolution of the revenue structure throughout the next seventy-three years. Borrowing would continue to be a substantial revenue source. Revenues from the tariff would gyrate considerably, before withering away in importance, while excise duties would simply wither gradually. The evolution of the revenue structure after 1917 would come to be heavily influenced by a preference for equitable taxation, while the good credit standing of the Dominion, horizontal and vertical tax competition and administrative costs would continue to be contributing factors. The remainder of this study is devoted to an examination of these revenue policy choices and their effects on the further evolution of the tax structure.

Chapter 4

An Overview of
Dominion Revenue Policy
1918–1990

Introduction

Between 1917 and 1920 the Dominion government introduced three major new taxes, in rapid succession; and these revenue sources — the personal income tax, the corporation income tax and the sales tax — came to play an increasingly important role in the financing of government spending from 1918–1990. Of all the changes that occurred in this period, it was the introduction and growth of these taxes that had by far the most profound impact on the shape of the Canadian tax structure. The growing weight of these three major new revenue sources, in proportion to the size of the economy, can be clearly seen in Chart 4-1, whereas the declining significance of two of the original three Confederation revenue sources from 1918 to the present is demonstrated in Chart 4-2. The other new revenue sources are displayed in Chart 4-3.

In this chapter I discuss the extent to which several broad fiscal structure themes influence the evolution of the revenue structure, a process that includes the displacement of the old Confederation taxes by the new income and sales taxes. The approach is similar to the analysis of Chapter 3; the discussion is structured around the relative weights of the various political costs that Ministers of Finance took into account in creating the revenue structure which has been characteristic of the last seventy-three years.

Chapter 5 discusses the birth of the three major new taxes that played such an important role during the years to come. Chapter 6 analyzes the financing of the two great wars. Chapter 7 examines the financing of debt reduction that occurred after the two great wars, and Chapter 8 deals with the financing of the great depression. The subject of Chapters 9 and 10 is the financing of tax reform during the last twenty-five years.

Throughout the seventy-three year period there has been one fundamental influence guiding Ministers of Finance: concern with a just, fair and equitable tax system. It was this recurring consideration that

Chart 4-1

Major New Revenue Sources, as a percentage of GNP, Canada, 1915-1989.

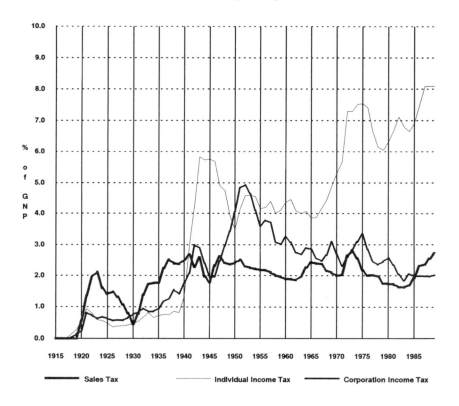

Source: Table C-3

Chart 4-2

Confederation Revenue Sources, as a percentage of GNP, Canada, 1915-1989.

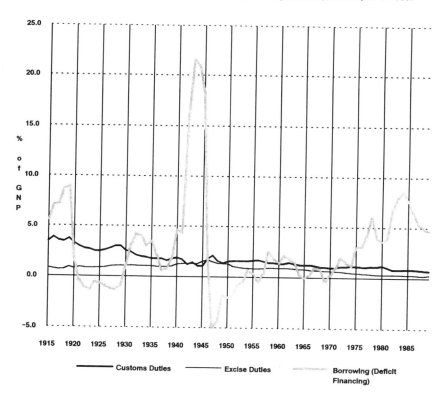

Source: Table C-3

Chart 4-3

Other Revenue Sources, as a percentage of GNP, Canada, 1915-1989.

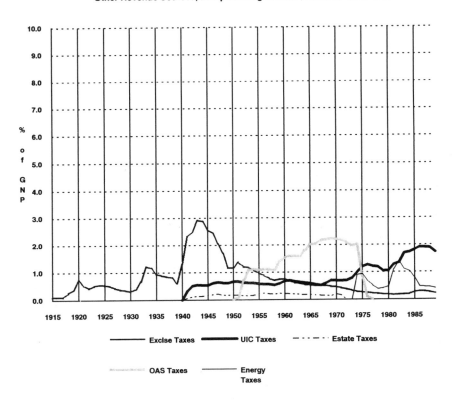

Source: Table C-3

was the primary motive for the gradual restructuring of the tax system. It was not the only influence, but it was the most important one. More modest themes are also present, such as the good credit standing of the Dominion, vertical tax competition among the several levels of government, horizontal tax competition and the administrative cost of collecting taxes. Other factors, of minor importance, base elasticity, a tax preference for fiscal stabilization policy and a tax preference for "sin" taxes helped to fashion the variation in revenue structure.

These themes will be examined in detail in this chapter and integrated with the positive model developed in Chapter 2. An understanding of the way in which they emerged should help to clarify for the reader the analysis and discussion of specific sub-periods in the following chapters.

Robin Hood Grows Up

We have seen that, in the period 1867–1917, legislators expressed limited interest in the fairness of the tax system. However, as interest in a just, fair or equitable tax system revealed itself as the most important theme shaping the (now more complex) revenue system during the 1918–1990 period, Robin Hood grew from a frail child into a robust adult.

The political costs of equitable taxation as discussed in hypothesis H-8b are relatively lower than those of unfair or inequitable taxation. The emergence of the equity motif manifested itself through three distinct phases. First came introduction and development of the income tax during the first great war; there followed the massive tax changes at the beginning of the second great war, and finally there were the formal tax reform efforts of the post second war period. The equity theme, although most evident during these stages of development of the tax system recurs through budget speeches of the last seventy-three years.

On Introducing the Income Tax

Resistance to the introduction of an income tax, due particularly to concerns about horizontal tax competition with the United States and vertical tax competition among the Dominion, the provinces and the municipalities, remained strong until after the budget of April 1917. However, by the summer of 1917 equity in taxation was very much on the mind of the Finance Minister. Sir Thomas White stressed the vertical equity dimensions of the income tax he introduced in these words:

> We have thought it advisable to adopt the principle of graduated tax
> . . . when we reach the higher salaries I regard it as *just and proper
> sentiment that the rate of taxation should increase as the scale of income
> increases.* . . .

> . . . by reason of the compulsory provisions of that measure [calling up of another 100,000 men] there exists a just and proper sentiment that *those who have substantial incomes should contribute substantially* to our growing expenses of the war.
>
>   (White, 1917b:3762 and 3769, emphasis added)[1]

The opposition, some members of whom had been urging an income tax upon the government for some time, concurred, and praise for the justness and fairness of the tax was readily forthcoming:[2]

> . . . the *income tax*, which of all taxation measures, *is the most natural and the fairest*. According to the best authorities, such as Adam Smith and Thiers, the income tax is the least objectionable of all systems of taxation, because it makes no distinction as between the taxpayers.
>
>   (Mr. Lemieux, in White, 1917b:3776, emphasis added)

Sir Thomas' next budget speech once again stressed equity in taxation, but also presented a fine contrast between desirable principles for the basis of a tax structure and the necessity of choice in difficult circumstances. Sir Thomas argued that:

> . . . no system of taxation should be in force which has a repressive effect on production and trade, hampers enterprise, or breeds discontent among our people, but none should be avoided which is essential to provide the revenue required and that will *distribute the incidence of taxation as equitably as conditions and experience dictate*. . . . in the trying circumstances and conditions which confront us it is a difficult task to provide any general scheme of taxation which shall completely fall within the rules I have just outlined. *We are confronted by conditions, not theories.*
>
>   (White, 1918:17–18, emphasis added)

I return in Chapter 5 to the considerations of vertical equity that were present at the birth of the income tax.

On Expanding The Income Tax

At the beginning of the second great war, "equitable" revenue sources had to be expanded to meet the financial requirements of defence spending. Concern with justice and equity was expressed with particular emphasis by Finance Minister Ilsley in his first war budget of 1939. He rejected financing the war through inflation in the strongest possible terms. He held that an inflation tax is the:

> . . . most unfair and inequitable of all methods of diverting labour and materials to [war materials purchases . . . it is] taxation of a most unjust type . . . [and] . . . throws a grossly unfair proportion of the burden upon

the person of small or medium income. . . . It represents a complete violation of the principle of taxation in accordance with ability to pay.

(Ilsley, 1939b:4)

The Minister, in deciding to finance the war heavily on a pay-as-you-go basis through higher taxation, adds further weight to the equity motif by arguing that the proposed new taxes "will be in conformity with our fundamental aim of providing for equality of sacrifice on the basis of ability to pay".[3]

Ralston, in 1940, specifically chose to increase the income tax rather than the sales tax because of the fairness of the former:

> [The incidence of the income tax] . . . approximates ability to pay. We realize that increases in indirect taxes disguise the burdens imposed by war but they are much more likely to distribute these burdens harshly and unfairly.

(Ralston, 1940:14)

This point was reiterated in Ilsley's 1941 budget speech (p. 13), and the fairness of the progressive income tax was constantly referred to throughout the war budgets.[4]

I return to the way in which vertical equity considerations supported the expansion of the income tax in Chapter 6.

On Reforming the Income and Sales Taxes

Following the Report of the Royal Commission On Taxation in 1967 and the White Paper on *Proposals For Tax Reform* in 1969, both of which stressed the need for an equitable tax system, the Minister of Finance, the Honourable E.J. Benson, guided through the House of Commons a tax reform, which had equity as its central objective. The Minister opened his 1971 tax reform budget with a classic definition of horizontal and vertical equity:

> A tax system must distribute the tax burden in an equitable manner, based upon ability to pay . . . it must not only be fair, it must be seen to be fair.
>
> . . . fairness in taxation implies two principles. First, it means that people in similar circumstances should accept similar shares of the tax load. Secondly, it means that people with higher incomes should be expected to pay in taxes a larger share of their incomes than persons with lower incomes.

(Benson, 1971a:3)

He concluded in the same vein:

> [Tax reform] will enable us to raise in a much fairer way the taxes we need to make Canada function. It will be more equitable not only between the various sectors of our society but also within these groups.
>
> (Benson, 1971a:38)

A decade later Finance Minister MacEachen made another attempt to reform the income tax system. His 1980 budget speech, with its emphasis on fairness, anticipated the tax reform budget to follow:

> I am particularly concerned to ensure that the tax system is fair and seen to be fair. . . . I made it clear on other occasions that the concept of sharing seems to be close to the distinctive fibre of the Canadian tradition. I do not believe the state can be the only agency by which sharing is effected or compelled.
>
> (MacEachen, 1980:15, 20)

In November 1981, the Minister stressed that a major:

> . . . theme of this budget is equity. *I dedicate myself and this government in this and succeeding years to maintaining a fundamental sense of fairness in our society.* As evidence of that dedication, I am proposing a major overhaul of the personal tax system.
>
> (MacEachen, 1981:2, emphasis added)

He concluded his budget on the same note, emphasizing that:

> The whole process will be much easier if everyone feels he is being treated fairly. That is why I have put so much emphasis on restraint with equity.
>
> (MacEachen, 1981:10)

Most recently, Finance Minister Wilson introduced his White Paper, *Tax Reform 1987*, with repeated emphasis on the goal of fairness in the tax system:

> We have an opportunity to build a new tax system that will be fairer and more progressive . . . this package . . . reflects basic principles of good and fair taxation . . . *Canadians want personal income taxes to be lower. They will be. We will have both lower rates and a fairer system. . . .*
> A fair and effective sales tax is an essential part of the overall balance of Canada's tax system. . . . *The new sales tax will be fairer for low- and middle-income Canadians.* It will be accompanied by important changes in the personal income tax system to achieve this goal.
>
> (Wilson, 1987:3, 4, 8, emphasis added)

The proposed reforms of the personal income tax, the corporation profits tax and the general sales tax were designed to achieve, among other objectives, greater fairness in the tax system. The Minister, in concluding his white paper, wrapped himself in the cloak of a vigorous Robin Hood:

> Some are being asked to pay a greater share through a reduction in tax [expenditures] . . . In making these decisions, I have considered carefully the key goals of greater fairness and competitiveness.
>
> . . . in the final analysis, *this package will be judged on whether we have given to* our senior citizens more peace of mind and security; *to those in greatest need, a fairer and reduced tax burden.* . . .
>
> (Wilson, 1987b:11, emphasis added)

The budget that introduced the tax proposals echoed this theme of equity,

> . . . we need a tax system that is fairer for individual Canadians. . . . To make the system fairer we are converting personal exemptions and many deduction to tax credits. . . .
>
> (Wilson, 1988:3)

The theme of equity or fairness in the tax system, permeated the budgetary policy of Ministers of Finance throughout the entire period. Successive Finance Ministers, Drayton and Robb in the 1920s, Rhodes and Dunning in the 1930s, Ralston, Ilsley and Abbott in the 1940s, Harris and Fleming in the 1950s, Gordon and Benson in the 1960s, Benson, Turner, Chrétien and Crosbie in the 1970s and MacEachen and Wilson in the 1980s, all emphasized a tax preference for equity and fairness as a consideration in shaping the tax structure.[5]

Modest Themes

While equity has been the most influential element in shaping the evolution of the revenue structure during the last seventy-three years, significant, although more modest themes also continued during this period. Revenue policy choices still reflected considerations of the major division between debt issue and taxation, horizontal tax competition, vertical tax competition and administrative costs.

To Borrow Or To Tax: Still An Important Questions

The trade-off between the use of higher tax rates and larger debt issue continued to play an important role throughout the time in which new taxes were being born and growing to maturity. Political concern focused on any tax rate increases that might be "too high", because they might stimulate increased emigration of people and their capital, or induce a significant reduction in the work effort of labourers and farmers.

Awareness of the need to preserve the good credit standing of the Dominion and to search out low interest rates on the public debt seemed to be a requisite characteristic of most Finance Ministers. The perceived constraints on additional revenue raising, either by taxing or borrowing, permeated most of their policy pronouncements.

In this section I trace through three interrelated aspects of the revenue policy decision to choose further debt issue or further tax increases to finance government spending. The first aspect is defined by the perceived political costs associated with further debt issue (the good credit standing of the Dominion) ranked against the perceived political costs associated with higher taxes (reduced work effort, reduced immigration and increased emigration). The second aspect represents the perception, by Ministers of Finance, of an increasing national debt as a blessing or a burden. This possibility is discussed in greater detail in Chapter 7. The third aspect is an expression of the search for low interest charges on the debt issued by the government.

Sir Thomas White introduced the Dominion's income tax in 1917 with a keen awareness of the painful choice between further borrowing and a new tax:

> In view of the expenditure involved, and in order to maintain the credit of the Dominion, it is necessary that we should adopt further taxation measures. . . .
> . . . the time has arrived when we must resort to this measure of direct taxation. I am confident . . . that the people of Canada . . . will . . . cheerfully accept the burden and the sacrifice of this additional taxation.
> (White, 1917b:3760 and 3761)

Several years later the Honourable William Fielding, on the Liberal side, emphasized the same painful choice in his budget proposals to increase rates:

> . . . it is quite certain that if we do not adopt some other method of taxation we should be adding enormously to the public debt . . . that is a course to be guarded against. So we are proposing some new rates of taxation.
> (Fielding, 1922:25)

Unfortunately for Fielding, when the government is in a minority situation the results of painful choices are apt to be felt quickly and personally. The sixty-five Progressives, first elected in the 1921 election, held the balance of power and used it to oppose Fielding's tax proposals with vigour. The Finance Minister listened, and as he introduced a package of revised tax proposals, argued that:

Every interest that is touched feels injured, and comes and complains that it has been particularly singled out when it has not. However, *we are doing the best we can to modify cases and meet some of these objections.* . . . Now we have had representations . . . from numerous large and powerful deputations representing each interest, and we have had oceans of correspondence, and we have had the benefit of a long debate in the House. *It would be strange*, therefore, *if*, out of all these things *we did not learn something and find ground upon which to make some changes.*

(Fielding, 1922:47, emphasis added)

The amended budget proposals reduced the proposed tax rate increases on confectionery, soft drinks, ale, beer and porter, cigarettes, raw beet sugar, raw leaf tobacco, and automobiles, added exemptions under the sales tax and an upper limit on the stamp tax on cheques.[6] It is reasonable to conclude that the "ground" found for making such extensive changes in the Finance Minister's original tax proposals, was located within the strong opposition of affected groups, articulated by the Progressive Party. The Minister acknowledged that "in the budget . . . we have carried taxation about as far as we think the country can stand it".[7]

The budget, as amended, increased the public debt more and tax revenues less than had originally been planned. This is the first of several "political mistakes" that will occur as Ministers of Finance choose the revenue structure for financing government spending throughout the period.

In 1923 the Finance Minister was applying the painful lessons he had learned in 1922. Responding to the call of some critics for higher taxes to balance expenditures, Fielding identified the heavy tax burdens of Canadians as a constraint and said:

. . . we may have to add some little amount to the public debt even yet, rather than introduce new forms of taxation.

(Fielding, 1923:5)

He actually added $50 million to the public debt.

By the latter half of the 1920s a buoyant economy was stimulating government revenues and permitting reductions in both the national debt and some tax rates. The government was being pressed to reduce the debt even faster. The Minister of Finance, in 1928, responded:

. . . I submit that until Canada is nearer pre-war rate of taxation, annual reduction of taxes is as important as reduction of debt. Our policy is to reduce both.

(Robb, 1928:9)

Nowhere is the trade-off between higher tax rates and larger debt issue as means of financing additional expenditures, more cogently put than in Mr. Ilsley's first war budget of 1939. With respect to the possibility of complete pay-as-you-go financing of the war, he argued it:

> . . . would become so disruptive in character as inevitably to produce disorganization and public discontent . . . [and would encounter] psychological reactions to taxation. . . . It is by a reasonable balancing of these various considerations that *we have to decide how much to tax and how much to borrow.* . . .
>
> (Ilsley, 1939b:4, emphasis added)

Moreover, he rejected the notion that complete pay-as-you-go financing of the first world war would have been appropriate:

> . . . [the] weight of taxation sufficient to pay for the whole cost of the [first] war would have been too revolutionary. . . . The sudden introduction of *such taxation measures would have been too drastic to be either economically or politically practicable.*
>
> (Ilsley, 1939b:5, emphasis added)

Throughout the second great war the government pushed against the upper political limit to which taxes could be increased. Ilsley's refundable tax proposal of the 1943 budget encountered such strong opposition that he withdrew it in 1944 (I return to this proposal in Chapter 6).[8]

The budgets of the years immediately following the second great war contained significant reductions in income taxes. Finance Minister Abbott, cut taxes during two successive years, and after considering the possibility of a substantial reduction in the national debt and the economic inadvisability of decreasing taxes during an inflationary period, argued that:

> . . . even after the substantial reductions made in the last two budgets, the present levels of personal income taxes are regarded as excessive by a large proportion of the public . . . those who must bear them are not ready to support income taxes on the present scale.
>
> (Abbott, 1947:11)

He cut personal income taxes for the third year in a row and made a further cut in 1949 because he had come to believe:

> . . . that most of the Canadian people would support and even welcome an enlarged measure of tax reduction this year . . . most Canadians . . . have shown that they prefer to pay taxes in forms other than higher income taxes. . . . The trouble is, we just don't like [the income tax], or at least we don't like too much of it.
>
> (Abbott, 1949:10–11)

In short, through good times and bad, through peace and war, the Dominion government, independently of its political colouring, revealed itself to be continually weighing off the political risks and political benefits of taxing against those of borrowing.[9]

By the end of the first great war Finance Ministers had abandoned the view accepted during the first fifty years after Confederation that an increase in the national debt was a normal course of events. The objectives of balancing the total budget (defined to include ordinary expenditures, capital expenditures, special and relief expenditures) and reducing the national debt became the focal point of considerable debate.

Finance Minister Drayton, saddled with an enlarged national debt after the war, was the first Finance Minister since Confederation to call for a reduction of the national debt in a budget speech:

> The duty today is to not only carry on . . . without any additions to the debt but . . . to promote measures which will reduce [it].
>
> (Drayton, 1920:2)

Fielding, who did more than any other Minister of Finance to convince Parliament and the electorate, in the first decade of the twentieth century, that an increasing national debt was a natural condition for a young, growing country, returned to office in 1922 with a radically different message:

> If we cannot reduce our debt, we should at all events make strenuous effort to guard against increasing it. We should endeavour to balance our budget, that is to pay all classes of our expenditure.
>
> (Fielding, 1922:7)[10]

The national debt was reduced, and the remainder of the 1920s witnessed several happy Finance Ministers taking credit for past successes and announcing further reductions.[11] I return to these policy choices in Chapter 7.

The great depression brought debt reductions, combined with tax rate reductions to an end, but not the desire to balance the budget. Dominion expenditures on relief increased, but so did tax rates, as Finance Ministers sought to close the gap between revenues and expenditures, an objective that was seen as fundamentally necessary to the economy's recovery. Finance Minister Rhodes, after announcing tax increases of about $55 million, argued that these sacrifices had to be made in order to:

> . . . fully meet our financial requirements, balance our budget and preserve our national credit in the eyes of an observant financial world. . . . Furthermore the preservation of our national credit is an indispensable prerequisite to the return of prosperity.
>
> (Rhodes, 1932:32)[12]

The second great war brought about another large increase in the national debt, with pressures to reduce it in the post-war period. We noted earlier that major tax cuts were highlights of the first few budget speeches, but as budgetary surpluses began to emerge, Abbott argued, in 1948, that the good times might not always continue:

> We should, therefore, be putting away what we can now for a rainy day. In our case, we put it away by paying off debt.
>
> (Abbott, 1948:10)

The Minister took pleasure in announcing, over the next few years, surpluses and debt reduction as a positive policy achievement.[13]

Finance Ministers of the late 1950s, 1960s and 1970s, with few exceptions, presided over deficits that were financed by borrowing. The Honourable John Crosbie, during his short-lived tenure as Minister of Finance was, in 1979, the first to sound a note of concern about the growing national debt and to build those concerns into his proposals:

> At present, federal government expenditures exceed revenues by 25% . . . Because of these deficits our interest rates have increased excessively, private borrowers have been crowded out of the domestic market for funds and our Canadian dollar has depreciated. . . . The fundamental objectives of our fiscal plan is to bring about a steady reduction in our deficits.
>
> (Crosbie, 1979:3)[14]

The Liberals returned to office in 1980 with a similar desire to reduce the size of deficits and slow down the growth of the national debt, but the deep recession of 1981–82, with automatically falling revenues and increasing expenditures, rendered the magnitude of the task more daunting.[15] During the remainder of the 1980s, deficit reduction and greater control over national debt growth rates have emerged as two major concerns of Ministers of Finance, as they have sought to change the division of financing between debt issue and tax financing of federal government spending.[16] I return to this development in Chapter 10.

Given the importance of borrowing for revenue-raising purposes, it is not surprising that almost every Minister of Finance has been sensitive to the credit standing of the country and has attempted to secure the lowest interest charges. With regard to the latter, the policy of the government was succinctly put by Rhodes in 1933:

> The policy of this government is to keep the interest charges on the public debt as low as possible by maintaining such financial policies as will enable us to raise new funds and convert maturing loans on the most economical basis.
>
> (Rhodes, 1933:5)

Given the continuity of this policy throughout the entire period, these could have been the words of any Finance Minister.[17]

Joint Occupancy of the Marriage Bed

Vertical tax competition emerged as one of the strongest factors influencing the Dominion revenue structure during the initial fifty-year period: Dominion governments were keenly sensitive to provincial and municipal occupancy of tax fields, especially the income tax. This observation conforms to hypothesis H-9 of Chapter 2. During the next seventy-three years vertical tax competition played a more modest role.

With the introduction of the Dominion income tax in 1917, a major hurdle for the government was overcome, and vertical tax competition ceased to be of any real importance, at least until the late 1930s. Sir Thomas White mentioned his longstanding opposition to an income tax, based in part upon concern for provincial and municipal tax sources, as he introduced the Dominion's new income tax:

> . . . the provinces and the municipalities are *confined* to direct taxation, and I have not regarded it as expedient . . . that the Dominion should *invade* the field to which the provinces are solely confined for the raising of their revenue.
>
> (White, 1917b:3760, emphasis added)

But he then proceeded to invade this very same field to which the provinces and municipalities were confined, thereby setting in motion significant changes in the structure of the Dominion revenue system.

In the depth of the Great Depression, Finance Minister Rhodes, after introducing an array of tax increases argued,

> . . . higher rates of taxation could not reasonably be imposed, bearing in mind not only the depleted incomes out of which the tax must be paid but also the fact that in some provinces the same incomes will be subjected to further levies for provincial and/or municipal purposes.
>
> (Rhodes, 1933:22)

The emphasis on the total (Dominion, provincial and municipal) tax burden had been noted previously as an inhibition on further tax rate increases.[18] However, within the context of budgets that did increase taxes, the argument was hardly an unqualified one.[19] In 1937 Finance Minister Dunning announced the creation of a Royal Commission to investigate the revenue-raising abilities, responsibilities, and powers of the provinces and the Dominion government, with a view to recommending changes.[20]

The second great war and the post-war period witnessed the reemergence of vertical tax competition as an important influence on the Dominion's revenue structure. The Dominion's heavy demand for revenues during the war, and the heavy demands of all governments throughout the post-war period, heightened intergovernmental conflict and included the creation of an interesting array of institutional arrangements, intended to limit the conflict over joint occupancy of some tax fields.

The Dominion government's concern that combined Dominion and provincial taxes were too "high" for the taxpayer was reflected in the words of Ilsley, introducing the wartime tax arrangement proposals:

> But these [war-necessitated] tax increases, if taken together with the existing provincial rates, would result in too heavy a burden and it is proposed therefore as a temporary expedient for the duration of the war only, to ask the provinces to vacate these two [income] tax fields.
>
> (Ilsley, 1941:11)

Similar concerns, and arrangements for compensating the provinces for the loss of revenues, were made in connection with gasoline taxes and taxes on alcoholic beverages.[21]

The government entered the estate tax field permanently in 1942 and the Minister of Finance emphasized the extent to which he felt circumscribed in his actions by the structure of existing provincial occupancy of the field.

> Some of the provincial legislatures have exploited this field to a greater degree than others, but on the whole . . . *they have not fully occupied it* . . . there is room for an additional and independent dominion tax at moderate rates . . .
> . . . the provinces have . . . *left relatively more room for us in the lower and middle ranges than at the top.* Consequently our tax cannot be quite as progressive on the very large estates as I would otherwise suggest.
>
> (Ilsley, 1941:16, emphasis added)

During the post-war period the government withdrew from several tax fields occupied by the provinces (gasoline tax, tax on consumption of electricity, tax on amusements, pari-mutuel bets and tax on transfer of securities), while at the same time it "hoped" that, "so far as possible, provincial taxing authorities will refrain from stepping in".[22] Finance Minister Gordon, in 1965, was still expressing the hope that, after his tax cut for voters, the "provincial governments [would not] move to raise their income taxes to take advantage of our action".[23]

This dependence of both provincial governments and the Dominion government on the same taxpayers, and in many cases the same revenue sources, lies at the heart of the Dominion-Provincial tax-sharing arrangements that occupied so much of the time of the post-war governments and influenced the evolving tax structure of that period. To a certain extent the Finance Minister's budget speech became an instrument in the Dominion government's negotiating position; and a fundamental principle of that position was the view that, without some form of agreement, fiscal chaos would follow.

Ilsley was most emphatic on the potential for future mischief in his 1946 budget speech. New fiscal arrangements, to replace the wartime tax arrangements, had to be made,

> to enable the provinces to meet their requirements without a *free-for-all scramble* to exploit the major tax sources . . . [without a new agreement] . . . several provinces are going to be faced with a difficult budget problem and a *chaotic tax situation is likely to arise* . . .
>
> . . . Financial pressure on the less favoured provinces will give rise to *increasingly arbitrary and discriminatory taxation*. . . merely in order to obtain additional provincial revenue *which of course would mean loss of revenue to the dominion*. . . . Moreover *the arbitrary and discriminatory provincial taxes* would come on top of dominion taxes.
>
> (Ilsely, 1946:9, 12, emphasis added)

It was left to Finance Minister Abbott to praise the tax rental arrangements, as they were eventually worked out, as helping to eliminate the "evils of duplication and conflict in the fields of direct progressive taxation".[24] A later set of tax rental agreements were praised as having

> . . . vastly lessened the risk that in times of economic difficulty . . . the provinces [would be led] *to a competitive scramble* to impose new and higher taxes.
>
> (Abbott, 1949a:6, emphasis added)

Finance Minister Harris praised the new set of 1956 arrangements and all earlier tax rental arrangements as being "a great advance over the pre-war fiscal chaos".[25] Finance Minister Benson introduced his 1971 tax reform budget with the express wish that the federal and provincial tax systems be "capable of being harmonized [in order to] avoid a tax jungle".[26]

By the early 1960s, the tax rental system had formally given way to a tax abatement system, in accordance with which the federal government lowered its tax rates and the provinces were required to introduce their own income taxes at rates of their own choosing. The federal government agreed to collect the provincial taxes provided that the tax bases were identical to the federal tax bases.[27] The emphasis on potential fiscal chaos ceased to be a major component of the federal government's negotiating position, as expressed in the budget speech, and was replaced by a concern to retain a substantial part of shared revenues for fiscal stabilization purposes, and to link the benefits of spending more directly with the pain of being taxed. Finance Ministers Gordon and Benson made this point clear in their 1963 and 1969 budgets, respectively:

> . . . no federal government can ignore the problems of federal finance in seeking to lighten the burdens upon provincial treasuries. . . . Most people will agree . . . that if the federal government were to give up a major part of its present revenue sources, even in exchange for compensating expenditure adjustments, its ability to exert an influence through fiscal policy over the level of economic activity in Canada would be weakened.
>
> (Gordon, 1963:7)

> The problems of joint occupancy of tax fields by the federal and provincial governments have continued to be a subject of vigorous debate . . . the federal government cannot go on abating its taxes in order to provide painless revenue for the provinces.
>
> (Benson, 1969:9)

These points continued to emerge in later budgets. In fact, provincial initiative in tax policy, which had been decried as arbitrary and chaotic during the early post-war period, was actually encouraged in later budgets, as federal Finance Minsters adopted the view that each level of government should be responsible for financing its own spending.[28]

Still Casting an Eye South

During the 1867–1917 period, the desire to attract immigrants and their capital operated as one of the four most important determinants of Dominion revenue structure policy. Horizontal tax competition, as articulated in hypothesis H-10 was a persistent theme of revenue policy choices of Finance Ministers. During the next seventy-three years horizontal tax competition played a more modest, but still substantial, role.

The introduction of the income tax was the occasion for the government's concern over net immigration flows to emerge. This is not surprising, given that, in 1917, this was one of the reasons Finance Minister White had given for hesitating to introduce such a tax:

> Canada has been and will continue . . . to be a country inviting immigration . . . we should not be known to the outside world as a country of heavy individual taxation.
> . . . the territories of [the United States and Canada] adjoin, and there is a continual flow of population over the border. . . . I think it would be undesirable, except for the gravest reason of national necessity, that our income tax should be substantially heavier than that in force in the United States.
>
> (White, 1917b:3761)

Maintaining an attractive country for immigrants and their capital was emphasized throughout debate on the Bill.[29] The Minister acknowledged that his income tax proposal was devised to take account of a measure before the United States Congress that would propose a "very much heavier degree of taxation" than existed at the time in the United States, and he emphasized that the Canadian income taxation could not be significantly heavier than in the United States.[30]

In 1919, tax rates on corporations and individuals were raised because further increases in comparable rates in the United States allowed such an adjustment.[31] However, the Minister refused the option of increasing tax rates further because:

> Canada is a country inviting immigration for settlement and capital and business enterprise for investment and development. We must be careful that our taxation of income and profits is not such as to place a barrier against either . . . carried beyond a reasonable point [income and profits taxation] can only defeat its purposes, with consequences detrimental to capital, labour and the community as a whole.
>
> (White, 1919:30–31)

A scant year later Sir Henry Drayton, who took over from Sir Thomas White as Minister of Finance, added an additional surtax of five percent to individual and corporation incomes, but in the same breath assured the House:

> That our measures of taxation must in view of our geographic situation have regard to United States legislation is a *principle* that has found general acceptance. *I do not desire to question it.* But revenue is urgently required and a difference of 5 percent in these . . . taxes will not deter immigration and the investment of outside capital. . . .
>
> (Drayton, 1920:24, emphasis added)

In 1923 the Minister opened his budget speech with an expression of reluctance to "add to the [tax] burdens" of the people of Canada, and closed it with an acknowledgment that emigration was a short-run concern to the government:

> We are so near to the United States, and it is so easy for our people to cross the border, that *when things are somewhat dull over here, and high wages are offered in the United States, there would naturally be such an exodus as there has been during the recent months.* But this I believe is only a temporary condition. . . .
>
> (Fielding, 1923:5 and 21, emphasis added)

By 1928, the Minister of Finance was enthusiastically noting the return home of Canadians and the inflow of "desirable types of immigrants" and ascribing it to the past budget and tax policies of his government.[32]

In 1931, falling revenues once more led a Finance Minister to increase tax rates. However, Finance Minister Bennett took comfort in the fact that the Canadian rate on corporate income was still less than the rate in the United States and the Canadian rate schedule for individual incomes was "a little, but not much, greater than the rate prevailing in the United States".[33]

Towards the end of the 1940s, when Finance Minister Abbott cut taxes from their high wartime level, he cited as a possible concern ". . . risk of serious drain of Canadian personnel to the south", and tailored the tax cuts to middle-income professionals who might consider moving to the United States, the United Kingdom or Australia.[34] He took pains to provide comparisons between Canadian and American tax rates that demonstrated Canadian rates were lower for many income brackets.[35]

The Honourable Walter Gordon, Finance Minister of a minority Liberal government, tangled with horizontal tax competition in 1963, when he proposed taxing non-resident takeovers of Canadian companies and increasing the rate of withholding tax on dividends paid to non-residents in cases where the paying company had less than twenty-five percent Canadian ownership.[36] The reaction from businesses, the market, the media and the opposition parties was almost instantaneous, and hostile enough to be termed virulent. The proposed takeover tax was withdrawn by the Finance Minister almost immediately in the face of such strong opposition. The proposed differential withholding tax was withdrawn in the next budget, following pressing and continuing strong opposition.[37]

In this way the possibility of a flight of mobile capital was forcefully brought to the attention of the Minister of Finance. By 1964 he had become no less aware of the possibility of an outflow of individuals; and he devoted some time to a comparison of personal income tax rates in Canada and the United States, by way of demonstrating that rates were higher in the latter country over many income brackets.[38] By 1965, Finance Minister Gordon was asserting, after another international tax rate comparison, that there was "no inducement to move to the United States or continue to live there".[39] A year later, Gordon's successor, Mitchell Sharp, was rejecting a possible corporate income tax rate increase because:

> . . . we must also keep in mind that the corporate income tax in Canada cannot get seriously out of line with that in the United States.
>
> (Sharp, 1966b:11336)

The Royal Commission on Taxation in 1967 formulated its proposals for the maximum rates of personal and corporation income tax, and the

inclusion of capital gains in income for taxation purposes, in full awareness of the comparable tax structure in the United States. The White
Paper on Tax Reform in 1969, and the Tax Reform Legislation in 1971,
continued to emphasize the impact of taxation on mobile capital and
labour. Finance Minister Benson introduced the capital gains proposal,
arguing that "Our system will be similar to that of the United States,
which also includes half of capital gains in incomes",[40] and spoke with
enthusiasm of the corporate income tax changes:

> This progressive reduction will bring the general corporate tax rate in
> Canada to a level below that in the United States, . . . and will contribute
> in an important way to making Canada a most attractive place in which
> to invest, grow and prosper.
>
> (Benson, 1971a:12)[41]

Finance Minister Turner's restructuring of the corporate tax system,
with the intention of encouraging investment in manufacturing and processing, was also a response to tax developments in these sectors elsewhere, especially the United States:

> This radical revision of the corporate tax system as it affects manufactur-
> ing and processors will require us to forego revenue . . . but these should
> not be regarded so much as a cost to the federal treasury as a major in-
> vestment by the nation that over time will repay itself in terms of creating
> jobs for our workers and increasing prosperity for all Canadians.
>
> (Turner, 1972:9)[42]

Finance Minister Chrétien, echoing his predecessors of a century earlier, released a study that compared the tax systems of Canada and the
United States, and argued that:

> This study destroys a myth. It shows conclusively that the Canadian
> personal tax system compares most favourably with that of the United
> States. I have also found that our business taxes are fully competitive.
>
> (Chrétien, 1978b:11)[43]

Almost a decade later, as soon as the United States had implemented
a tax reform that involved reductions in the personal and corporation
income tax rates and elimination of or restrictions on, tax expenditures,
Finance Minister Wilson moved, with considerable speed, to introduce
similar proposals in Canada. He argued that:

> The jobs of many Canadians depend on a corporate income tax system
> that is competitive with other countries, particularly the United States.

> Tax reform will improve the overall competitive position of Canadian business and industry. . . . *To maintain a competitive tax system, corporate tax rates will be reduced.*
>
> (Wilson, 1987b:6, emphasis added)

The theme of a competitive tax structure runs through all the debates on tax reform.[44] It is only a slight exaggeration to state that, if one idea has united Finance Ministers from Rose in 1868 to Wilson in 1990, it has been horizontal tax competition, especially with the United States.

Tax Collectors Experiment; Taxpayers Avoid

The administrative costs of collection, enforcement and compliance continued to play a modest role in determining tax structure during the period 1918–1990. However, the sources of such costs virtually cease to be con men and smugglers, and become instead the administrative cost of collection and the perfectly legal tax avoidance routes selected by taxpayers seeking to minimize their income tax payments.

Finance Minister Rhodes demonstrated in 1935 his determination to rout out smugglers, whom he saw as a threat to his tax revenues from alcoholic spirits. He reduced significantly the excise duties on spirits in order to bring the tax rates in line with those in the United States:

> . . . drastic action is necessary . . . [in order to eliminate] illicit sales which would otherwise continue as a constant menace to our revenues. [We intend to] stamp out the smuggling trade.
>
> (Rhodes, 1935:28)

Finance Minister Abbott faced the same problem when he increased the tax on cigarettes in his 1951 budget. A year later he expressed his disappointment with the ensuing increase in revenues, which he attributed to:

> . . . considerable increase in the importation of American cigarettes, both legal and illegal, although in my opinion the volume of smuggling has been greatly exaggerated . . . we seem to have reached a point of diminishing returns.
>
> (Abbott, 1952:15)

The Minister decided he had to reduce the tax rate to its 1951 level "due to avoidance and smuggling from the United States".[45]

But the government's major concern throughout this period was not smuggling, but the administrative costs of the income tax and legitimate avoidance techniques employed in response to it.[46] This concern was articulated when the tax was originally introduced:

> . . . the cost of administration of an income tax measure will be quite substantial . . . if the cost of administration of a tax is disproportionately

heavy, it is not a good tax. I do not say that the cost of administration of such an income tax as I shall propose today will be unduly heavy. . . .

(White, 1917b:3760–3761)

Several years later, concerns over lengthy administrative delays in collecting income tax revenues led Finance Minister Drayton to introduce self-assessment. The Minister noted that:

[Incomes and business profits taxes] are not collected with desirable dispatch and . . . there is reason for vexatious delays [time for taxation officer to check all possible information on taxpayer's income sources; exhaustive inquiry into a company for purposes of business profits tax; personal income in many cases depends on determination of business profits first]. The result is delay, loss of interest, and added difficulty in finally collecting the tax. Delay is inseparable from the business profits tax. The situation can, however, be materially improved in so far as the ordinary income tax is concerned. . . .

A Bill will be introduced making each taxpayer in the first instance his own assessor.

(Drayton, 1920:24)

The next set of administrative improvements, from the tax collector's point of view, occurred during the early years of the second great war. The national defence tax was introduced and collected, "As far as it is administratively practicable . . . at source", through deductions from employers.[47] Taxpayers were urged to adopt voluntarily an instalment plan for paying their income taxes.[48] When Ilsley combined the income tax and national defence tax in 1942 he acknowledged that very few taxpayers voluntarily chose to pay taxes by instalment, and he therefore decided to collect the new tax, "as far as possible by deduction at source, or where that is impracticable, by a compulsory instalment plan".[49] These moves had the important benefit, from the government's viewpoint, of assuring a reasonably steady and certain flow of tax dollars throughout the entire year at a low administrative cost. In other words, they eased the government's cash flow problems, but did not substantially increase tax revenues.

Concerns over administrative costs were cited as reasons for simplifying tax collection, rejecting, initially, an exemption for charitable contributions to "hospitals and higher education institutions", strengthening the penalty provisions under the Income Tax Act, deleting the estate tax on small estates, introducing the $100 standard deduction for charitable donations without production of receipts, rejecting an excess profits tax, and removing an awkward exemption under the federal sales tax.[50]

The potential for tax avoidance influenced the decision to introduce a gift tax at the same time as a surtax on investment income was introduced:

[the gift tax] will operate as a deterrent to transfers of property by gift, . . . which would have the effect of reducing personal income to lower brackets and thus securing income tax assessments at rates lower than would otherwise be applicable . . . [this should] put our income tax structure on a more secure foundation.

(Rhodes, 1935:27)

The Minister of Finance made further changes to the gift tax in 1938, in order "to discourage still further the making of gifts for tax avoidance purposes".[51] When Ilsley introduced the estate tax in 1941, he made additional changes to the gift tax in order to reduce taxpayers' attempts to avoid the tax.[52] Tax avoidance, through reduced work effort, was clearly an aspect which this minister took into account when he rejected complete pay-as-you-go financing of the second war. He was concerned about the:

. . . psychological reactions to taxation . . . we must recognize that when diversion by means of taxation rather than borrowing is carried too far, the average citizen begins to feel that there is no use in his working for any additional income, and therefore he does not put his best effort into his work, with the result that efficiency and production fall off.

(Ilsley, 1939b:4)

Two later finance ministers, Crosbie for the Conservatives and MacEachen for the Liberals, relied on the administrative attractiveness of an ad valorem tax and an indexed specific tax during a period of inflation to convert the federal sales taxes on gasoline and diesel fuel in 1979 and on alcohol and tobacco in 1980, respectively. The Honourable Mr. MacEachen put the case succinctly:

. . . it has been customary for excise taxes on alcoholic beverages and tobacco products to be levied as a specific amount per unit of the product rather than on an ad valorem basis. I recognize that *when changes are made periodically to specific taxes to maintain their real value, the process can be disruptive* and I am particularity sensitive to the changes in the weight of taxation as between the various products. Accordingly, I am proposing that these levies be automatically adjusted each quarter to reflect changes in the price indexes for these commodities.

(MacEachen, 1980:16, emphasis added)

We can probably assume that "disruptive" tax changes are perceived as being politically costly. However, by 1985 inflation rates had dropped considerably and Finance Minister Wilson was prepared to incur such disruptions as he de-indexed the excise taxes on alcoholic beverages and tobacco products and returned to periodic adjustments, especially substantial in the case of tobacco products.[53]

Minor Melodies

Three minor themes are woven through the broad pattern of the years 1918–1990: base elasticity, a preference for fiscal stabilization policy and a preference for sin taxes. These themes reflect hypothesis H-13 and two variants of hypothesis H-8.

The Honourable William Fielding, in 1923, became the first Finance Minister to pin his hopes on an expansion in business activity as a source of more tax revenues rather than introduce painful new taxes:

> The people of Canada are pretty heavily taxed today; between Dominion, provincial and municipal taxation, the burdens of the people are very great, and I am reluctant to add to those burdens. I do not want at present to yield to the temptation of opening up new fields of taxation . . . bear patiently . . . in the hope that *the betterment* which, we believe is at hand, *will enable us to bear the burdens* without opening up these new fields of taxation.
>
> (Fielding, 1923:5, emphasis added)

The Minister's hopes were high enough for him to propose a "considerable" reduction in custom and excise duties, in the expectation that income tax and sales tax revenues would automatically increase:

> I am hopeful that the reduction in taxation . . . will not seriously affect the revenue. We are looking forward to an increased volume of business to a sufficient extent to give us results equal to our present system of taxation.
>
> (Fielding, 1923:7)

By 1926, hope had become reality and Finance Minister Robb was able to report that "Happily our financial and commercial position now enable us to make a very substantial reduction in the income taxes".[54]

The economic downturn, already underway in 1930, deepened rapidly and brought in its wake falling tax revenues. Bennett underscored this negative characteristic of taxes, especially the sales tax, in the first Conservative budget of the 1930s:

> *No tax more quickly reflected the declining commodity prices than did the sales tax.* The shrinkage in the volume of business transactions, coupled with the decrease in values, made it apparent . . . that with business shrinking and sales contracting, the sales tax could not be depended upon to produce revenue to the same degree as in the previous year.
>
> (Bennett, 1931:6, emphasis added)

The Minister responded to these falling revenues by trying to increase tax rates on corporation income, individual incomes, and goods subject to customs or excise duties and the sales tax (we return to this budget later). For the next two years the trade shrinkage "both in volume and

value" and "the decline in business activity and commodity prices" led
to falling tax revenues and government fiscal action to raise rates on the
major tax sources.[55]

At the time of the 1934 budget the Minister of Finance was obviously
pleased at the prospect of a turnaround in business activity:

> . . . with higher prices and expanding volume of business the outlook for
> revenues in the current fiscal year is distinctly favourable . . . it seems rea-
> sonably clear that we can anticipate a greatly improved budget position
> without adding to the existing rates of taxation.
>
> (Rhodes, 1934:24)

Similar appreciation of the positive base elasticity of tax revenues was
expressed in each of the budget speeches of the next few years.[56] Finance
Minister Dunning noted approvingly the increase in tax revenues during
the 1936–37 fiscal year and went on to say:

> . . . while taxpayers may greet this news with mixed feelings, I think it will
> be generally accepted as a striking tribute to the recuperative powers of
> the Canadian economy and a convincing confirmation of the reality of the
> economic recovery . . . essentially, expanding government revenues reflect
> and confirm the increase in national income.
>
> (Dunning, 1938:13)

In much the same vein, Finance Minister Abbott expressed pleasure
at the buoyancy of revenues and the growth of the economy after the
second great war, and he underlined the role of revenue elasticity in an
expanding economy:

> . . . our revenues now are very sensitive to any change in business condi-
> tions . . . [our favourable situation now] . . . is due in a very large part to
> the generally favourable economic circumstances upon which our revenues
> so greatly depend.
>
> (Abbott, 1947:19)

This theme was repeated continually throughout the post-war period, in
which governments clearly assumed some revenue elasticity as the basis
for their plans to generate needed tax revenues at given tax rates.[57]

The second minor theme that influenced the evolution of the revenue
structure during this period was a tax preference for stabilization policy.
The Canadian government was one of the first to embrace officially fiscal
and monetary stabilization policy in order to maintain high levels of
employment and to restrain inflation.[58] This was a theme that emerged
in the years immediately following the second world war and had not
been officially articulated before the 1930s. To the extent that voters
might hold the government responsible for the state of the economy, it

is reasonable to suppose that the government would want to articulate policy aimed at maintaining economic growth without inflation. This fiscal stabilization policy can be analyzed as a tax preference of the government, in much the same way as we analyzed a preference for equity in the tax system or a preference for sin taxes within the positive model of revenue structure.

Finance Minister Ilsley stated the economic problems of the economy and the appropriate fiscal policy response in the first budget speech he delivered after the war:

> We must resist this pressure towards higher prices and keep the increases within reasonable limits. . . .
> . . . If only immediate economic conditions were involved, one could make a case for *temporary higher taxes* in order to curb the excess of spending . . . that is tending to pull prices up.
>
> (Ilsley, 1946:7, 8, emphasis added)

Considerations of a non-economic nature moved the Minister to cut personal taxes and corporate income taxes. He acknowledged that:

> . . . we recognize that such [tax] *reductions* at this time may possibly increase some of our difficulties during the period of shortages and inflationary pressures.
>
> (Ilsley, 1946:9, emphasis added)

Two years later Finance Minister Abbott, while praising the surpluses of recent years, noted that:

> Had we not geared our tax system to produce such a surplus . . . prices would have risen more rapidly.
>
> (Abbott, 1948:6)

The Minister could hardly have forgotten that the budgets of 1946 and 1947 reduced taxes, thereby reducing the surpluses that he held up for public approval as factors that had dampened prices. Untroubled by such thoughts, he proceeded to argue that:

> . . . we should deliberately budget, as a matter of policy, for substantial surpluses in [inflationary] times like these. Only that way can we hold inflationary forces in check.
>
> (Abbott, 1948:10)

The fiscal measures he steered through Parliament were a set of tax cuts that further reduced the surplus.

It will be seen, therefore, that the 1946 and 1948 budgets articulated an appropriate fiscal stabilization policy, and then proceeded to implement a different tax policy. Budget policy in 1947, 1949, 1957 and 1965 was similar.[59] Economic conditions revealed inflationary pressures that called for tax increases; actual policy led to tax decreases. Several such budgets preceded an election.[60]

The budget speeches of 1958 and 1960 described a set of economic circumstances — a slackening of economic growth and rising unemployment — that called for an expansionary fiscal policy. Nevertheless, Finance Minister Fleming did not embark upon any such course: he emphasized that the deficits had become large enough to cause business some concern, and initiated no significant tax changes in 1958 and increased taxes in 1960. Once again, fiscal stabilization policy was mentioned, but was not the decisive factor when it came to implementing actual tax policy. Other determinants of revenue structure policy clearly outweighed a tax preference for stabilization policy when revenue policy choices were being made.

However, this post-war period did witness some budgets in which the articulated fiscal policy coincided with the actual tax policies announced by the government. Harris' 1955 budget presented the case, with clarity and directness, for a set of policies that would achieve a balanced budget at full employment:

> I propose to recommend to the house a tax policy and a tax structure that would produce a balanced budget under conditions which represent a high level of output and employment.
>
> (Harris, 1955:10)

The Minister then cut taxes in order to stimulate employment and income to a full employment level, without generating excessive pressure on prices. Abbott's anti-inflation budgets of the early 1950s and Fleming's expansionary budgets of the early 1960s also contained appropriate stabilization tax policy initiatives.[61]

To sum up, few post-war budget speeches failed to devote some time to discussing the state of the economy and the appropriate fiscal stabilization policy for managing the economy. In practice, however, actual tax policy changes were consistent with the appropriate fiscal policy only some of the time.

The qualitative analysis of budget speeches suggests that a tax preference for fiscal stabilization policy exercised only a minor influence on the shaping of the revenue structure policy of the time.[62] I return to this aspect of revenue policy choices in Chapter 7. Other determinants of political costs, ranging from a strong preference for equity to horizontal tax competition with the United States, were more important.

The last minor theme to influence the evolution of the revenue structure during the seventy-year period was a tax preference for sin taxes. The fervour with which earlier Finance Ministers taxed alcoholic spirits, tobacco and luxury articles waned considerably after 1917. Sir Henry Drayton, for the Conservatives, did express some indignation at post-war consumption of luxuries,

> . . . extravagant and luxurious expenditure ought to be checked. . . . Extravagant buying should stop. With this end in view, it is proposed to levy on certain articles excise taxes.
>
> (Drayton, 1920:20–21)

In light of his proclaimed desire to generate additional tax revenue and issue less new debt, he was not likely to be very upset if consumers continued to spend money voluntarily on goods that now provided a 10 percent luxury tax for the government.[63]

The Honourable William Fielding, for the Liberals, acknowledged the attractiveness of spirits and tobacco as a source of revenues for the taxman:

> Ministers of Finance always *look upon tobacco and cigarettes as easy marks* . . . there was a time when whisky bore this burden but additional revenue is no longer possible from this source.
>
> (Fielding, 1923:9, emphasis added)

He was, however, forced to rescind an increased duty of $1.50 per thousand on cigarettes because of the ease of smuggling "along the boundary line", which had led to a decrease in consumption and in the revenues from the cigarette levy.[64] Fielding must have thought that he was doubly afflicted: the Progressives had forced major changes in his 1922 tax proposals, and the smugglers had now blunted the revenue effect of some of the measures which had been adopted.

Ministers of Finance continued to rely on taxes on spirits and cigarettes, and especially during the second great war and the Korean conflict these sources together with taxes on luxuries were regularly drawn upon.[65] However, the old-time fervour had vanished, and the relative importance of the revenues from the sin taxes declined considerably.[66]

Conclusions:
Tax, Borrow and Spend

The structure of revenues chosen to finance the spending of the federal government during the past seventy-three years has undergone profound changes. The dominant role played by the personal income tax, the corporation income tax and the sales tax is highlighted in Chart 4-4. This chart traces the considerable variation in the share of each of these three taxes as a percentage of total financial requirements, and it underlines the importance of the personal income tax, especially during the last twenty-five years.

The declining importance of two of the three Confederation revenue sources is highlighted in Chart 4-5. This chart, while tracing out some variability in the share of tariff revenues and excise duties as a percentage of total financial requirements up to the second great war, documents the virtual waning away of these pillars of the tax system in the post-war period. This chart highlights the great variability of the deficit financing share, with the surpluses of fiscal 1921–1930 and fiscal 1947–1954 available to reduce the debt.

The changing role of the other new revenue sources — excise taxes, unemployment insurance taxes, estate taxes, old age security taxes and energy taxes — is highlighted in Chart 4-6. These taxes are discussed in later chapters.

Dominion revenue policy from 1918 through 1990, analyzed within the conceptual framework of the comprehensive positive model of revenue structure, leads to the following conclusions.[67] First, one determinant of political costs outweighed all others in shaping the structure of revenues: a preference for equity in taxation. This preference for a system based on ability to pay was evident in the introduction of income taxes during the first great war, the substantial expansion of the base and increase in the rates of the income tax during the second great war, and the tax reform efforts of the last twenty-five years. Finance Ministers, in formulating their tax policies, responded to perceptions of the personal income tax as progressive and the sales tax as regressive, especially, though not exclusively, during the second great war.

Second, the good credit standing of the Dominion, vertical tax competition, horizontal tax competition and the costs of collection, compliance and enforcement all exercised a modest influence on the revenue structure. A good credit standing (and hence, low cost of borrowing) continued to be an important input into the trade-off between further debt issue and additional taxes, even though Dominion governments did voice an interest in reducing the size of the national debt and balancing the total budget in the years immediately following the two great wars and during the 1980s.

Vertical tax competition played a modest but significant role, especially after the second great war when innovative tax sharing arrangements between the Dominion and provincial governments resulted from the inevitable conflict of joint occupancy of several important tax bases. Horizontal tax competition received approximately the same degree of attention. Ministers of Finance repeatedly expressed concern over the potential loss of capital and persons in response to tax changes elsewhere

Chart 4-4

**Major New Revenue Sources,
as a percentage of Total Financial Requirements (TFR),
Canada, Fiscal 1915-1990.**

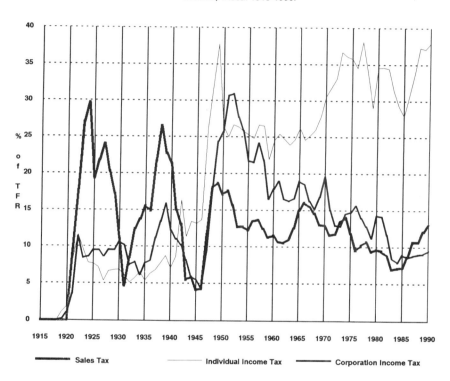

Source: Table B-3

Chart 4-5

**Confederation Revenue Sources,
as a percentage of Total Financial Requirements (TFR).
Canada, Fiscal 1915-1990.**

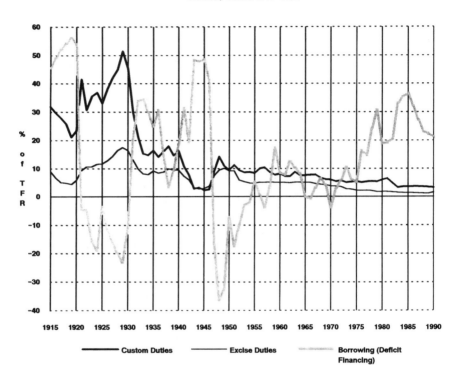

Source: Table B-3

Chart 4-6

Other Revenue Sources, as a percentage of Total Financial Requirements (TFR), Canada, Fiscal 1915-1990.

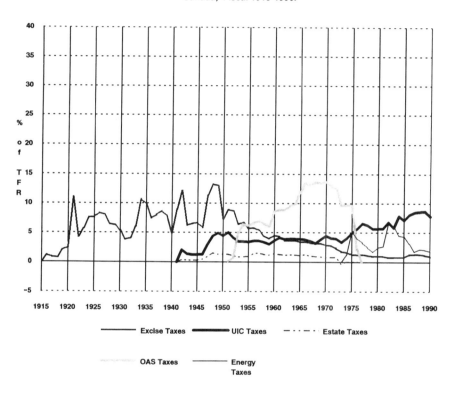

Source: Table B-3

— especially in the United States — or proposed tax changes in Canada.

The costs of collection, compliance and enforcement continued to exercise some influence on the revenue structure. Smuggling had become less of a threat to the revenues of finance ministers, while administrative experimentation with income tax collection and concern over tax avoidance emerged as significant aspects of tax policy.

Third, base elasticity, a preference for fiscal stabilization policy and a tax preference for sin taxes were all factors that contributed in a minor way to shaping the evolution of the revenue structure.

In this chapter I have developed the case for a particular ranking of the determinants of revenue structure during the period. The set of conclusions, based on the qualitative analysis of budget speeches, is tentative, and calls for an analysis of the more "time specific" segments of the evolution of the revenue structure.

It is therefore at this point that we begin the detailed story of the birth, growth and death of specific taxes in the period 1917–1990. The first part of our narrative deals with a phase of fiscal history which was remarkable for the number of new taxes that made their first appearance.

Chapter 5

Expansion of the Revenue Family: The Fecund Years: 1915–1923

Introduction

The eight years covered by this chapter deserves special attention for two reasons. First, it was the most productive period in our taxation history. Taxes were born, grew and died, at a speed unparalleled at any other time. But what is still more important is that these fecund years were responsible for the births of the income taxes and the sales tax. The personal income tax, the corporation income tax and the manufacturers' sales tax became preferred fiscal instruments in the succeeding years and eventually superseded all other taxes, totally changing the Canadian revenue structure.[1]

The chapter begins with a quick preview of the expansion of the revenue structure family from 1915 to 1923 and follows with a discussion of the war budgets until the summer of 1917. The birth of personal and corporation income taxes is then analyzed and income tax developments in the United States are compared with budgetary policy in Canada. The examination of war budgets continues and the birth of the general sales tax in the spring of 1920 is analyzed. The concluding section summarizes the major findings and contrasts them with several widely held misconceptions in the literature and the popular press.

The Fecund Years: A Preview

During [the war] period . . . the winning of the war required raising large sums of money in the easiest possible way and with the least interference with the public or with business methods.

(Sir Henry Drayton, Minister of Finance,
Budget Speech, May 18, 1920, p. 1)

Our only desire . . . is to try and raise money and raise it in a manner that will be as little objectionable as possible to the public at large.

(Hon. William Fielding, Minister of Finance,
House of Commons Debates, March 1923, p. 919)

These two quotations succinctly capture tax structure policy of successive governments throughout the fecund years. Total tax revenues had been more or less constant at 5.5 percent of gross national product for the previous 47 years, but with the coming of the war they rose sharply and amounted to 9 percent by 1921.[2]

From the budget of 1915 until 1920, expenditure needs and revenue requirements increased dramatically, for the most part in order to finance war and war-related activities. Dominion expenditures, which had taken 46 years to reach a level of $160 millions in fiscal 1914, had more than doubled by fiscal 1916 and more than guadrupled by fiscal 1920.[3] This major increase in total financial requirements was the most important determinant fuelling the revenue structure changes throughout the war period.

These increased expenditures "required raising large sums of money in the easiest possible way" and in a manner that was as little "objectionable as possible to the public at large". Sir Henry Drayton, the Honourable William Fielding and the other finance ministers of the period tapped a variety of new revenue sources to carry out their objectives.[4]

A special ad valorem customs duty was born in 1915 and died a prolonged death, extending over 1919 and 1920. A large collection of indirect taxes (later to be known as excise taxes) was also born in 1915. An excess profits tax was born in 1916 and died in 1920. The personal income tax and corporation income tax were both born in the summer of 1917, and grew, as we all know, into the healthy adults we observe today. A bundle of luxury excise taxes was born in 1918 and died in the years 1919–1920. The general sales tax was born in 1920 and grew into a robust adult.

These changes in revenue sources and revenue structure are reflected in Chart 5-1. Although the immediate revenues from the income taxes and the sales tax are small during the fecund years, a glance ahead to 1990, reveals the profound impact these taxes have had on the structure of our revenue system.

In the present chapter I use the conceptual framework of Chapter 2 as a guide to account for the birth of the new taxes during the fecund period. In later chapters I use the model as a guide to explain and understand the continuing evolution of the revenue structure.

The 1915–1917 War Budgets

The Minister of Finance, the honourable Thomas White, in his 1915 budget speech drew attention to the tariff "as the chief source and mainstay of our revenue" and proposed, "as our main revenue measure", a special

Chart 5-1

**Major Revenue Sources During the Fecund Years and Beyond,
as a percentage of Total Financial Requirements (TFR),
Canada, Fiscal 1915, 1918, 1921, 1923 and 1990.**

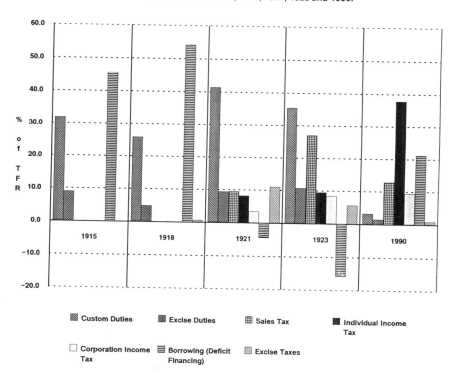

Source: Table B-3

ad valorem customs duty of seven and a half percent on the general and intermediate tariff and five percent on the British Preferential Tariff.[5] A second, "auxiliary means of raising revenue" introduced in the budget was a package of various indirect or excise taxes that became known as the War Revenue Act revenues, of which the burden was expected to fall, "upon those . . . best able to sustain it".[6] With the introduction of these two measures, the Minister acknowledged that:

> At the outbreak of the war it would have been premature to have brought forward measures which to-day *have been long foreseen by public opinion to be necessary and indeed inevitable.* It would also have been most inopportune and inexpedient by reason of the *profound dislocation and disorganization of business caused by the war* . . .
>
> (White, 1915:18, emphasis added)

A growing public awareness that the war was not going to be over quickly and that war expenditures were going to be higher than first expected was most likely conducive to the greater public acceptance of new taxes and substantially higher tax rates. A new tax, or a significantly higher tax rate on an existing revenue source that is anticipated as necessary and inevitable, generates less political opposition than one not so anticipated. A large increase in war expenditures, necessitating an equally large increase in total financial requirements, would be capable of triggering balanced budget tax reform of the revenue structure within the conceptual framework of the model.[7] A tax imposed when business uncertainty and dislocation is modest is apt to generate more revenues and less business opposition than one imposed during a time of initial major disorganization. For both these reasons the tax measures of the 1915 budget were consistent with lower political costs than would have been incurred during the early stages of the war.

Finance Minister White expanded his search for additional revenues in his 1916 budget speech. Having earlier ruled out the imposition of an income tax for horizontal and vertical tax competition and administrative costs reasons, he turned to an excess profits tax as the fairest since, "persons, firms, and corporations whose profits have been 'above the average' and 'of abnormal character' might well be called upon to contribute a share to the carrying on of the war".[8] The business profits war tax was initially introduced at rates of twenty-five percent of net profits in excess of seven percent of capital for corporations and in excess of ten percent of capital for persons, firms and partnerships (with a capital exemption of $50,000 and retroactive to the outbreak of war in August, 1914).

The April 1917 budget speech resisted pressure for an income tax and increased the effective tax rates under the business profits war tax. The

Minister argued, in effect, that considerations of vertical and horizontal tax competition and administrative costs precluded the introduction of a direct tax on incomes. However, this was to be the last time that a budget speech reflected this position.

Several months later the unwanted income tax was born. Sir Thomas White was later to acknowledge that it had been voluntarily conceived approximately nine months before he delivered his April 1917 budget speech.[9]

Abandoning a Policy of 50 Years: Birth of an Income Tax

> It is manifest to me . . . that the time has arrived when we must resort to this measure of direct taxation. . . . I regard it as just and proper that the rate of taxation should increase as the scale of income increases. . . . I am confident that the people of Canada . . . will *cheerfully accept the burden and the sacrifice of this additional taxation.*
>
> (White, 1917b:3761, 3762; emphasis added)

On July 25, 1917 the Minister reversed his longstanding position and introduced an income tax on personal and corporation incomes. He argued that financial requirements, boosted by the conscription measure which had been passed the previous day, were continuing to rise. In addition, the Minister relied upon justice and fairness as he linked conscription and the sacrifice required from those who were enjoying substantially higher incomes due to the war.[10] He detected,

> . . . in this House and in the country . . . a very just sentiment that those who are in the enjoyment of substantial incomes should substantially and directly contribute to the growing war expenditure.
>
> (White, 1917b:3760)

Well before the outbreak of the war Dominion governments had been facing strong pressure, especially from western farmers and farmers' organizations, for a graduated tax on incomes to replace part or all of the revenues from the tariff. Even before to the 1911 election, which Laurier lost on the issue of free trade with the United States, farm organizations in both Ontario and the West had pressed their opposition to tariffs and emphasized their willingness to submit to direct taxation as an alternative source of revenues.[11] *The Grain Growers' Guide* was the most persistent and activist of the various farmers' lobby groups that demanded reduction of the tariff and the institution of a graduated tax on income. Its campaign accelerated in June, 1914, when its editorial asked,

> Now, *is there any reason under high heaven why an income tax should not be introduced in Canada?* . . . The average man pays the tariff tax mainly on food and clothing. . . . The class of rich shareholders can only be reached by an income tax and it is high time that they were compelled to take up their proper share of the national burdens . . . the income tax in Canada is a necessary prelude to any chance of a permanent reduction in the tariff and *the sooner the leaders of progress begin to advocate its institution the better for their hope of eventual political success.*
>
> (*The Grain Growers' Guide*,
> June 24, 1914, pp. 769–770, emphasis added)

This pressure had increased, as war-related government spending generated high incomes and profits for some individuals and businesses. The "increasing disparity in wealth" provided the focus for public protest and calls for more taxes on the wealthy.[12] The decision to impose conscription generated additional opposition from farmers, labourers and their representative organizations. Many trade unions reacted by calling for a conscription of wealth before a conscription of men.[13] Farmers' organizations promoted the same theme, with detailed proposals for a graduated tax on incomes and low exemption levels.[14]

In the House some Liberal opposition members had been calling for a graduated tax on incomes over an exempted level since the outbreak of the war. Mr. M. Clark had called for a "good fat tax on incomes", in 1914 and 1915, as the best means of taxing according to ability-to-pay.[15] The plea for a "just and equitable scheme" of graduated income taxation had continued in the 1916 and 1917 budget debates.[16] In the 1917 debate, just two months before the introduction of the income tax, Mr. Graham had argued eloquently that:

> We speak of conscription of men, but there is another duty which the government ought to undertake and that is *the conscription* of wealth, in order that the two may go hand in hand for the carrying on of this great war . . . I again urge that one available source of taxation which should be reached is the *incomes of these men of wealth, which under the present taxation are not taxed at all.*
>
> (Mr. Graham, *House of Commons Debates*,
> May 22, 1917:1631, emphasis added)

The Minister's new tax proposals were greeted with enthusiasm by those Liberals who had been championing the income tax for some time. Mr. F.B. Carvell's support reflected their mood when he noted that he "knew nothing as fair and just upon everybody as an income tax".[17] The strong demand by farmers and labourers for a progressive income tax was acknowledged as a motivating factor in the government's decision when the Income Tax Bill was introduced in the Senate.

This tax is unquestionably the outcome of public opinion as represented by the most numerous class of citizens — a class which, in all probability, will have to contribute very little to the taxation provided for in the Bill.
(Sir James Lougheed, government leader in the Senate,
Debates of the Senate of Canada, August 29, 1917:720)

Sir Thomas also reiterated his longstanding concerns over possible migration of men and capital to the United States in response to high Canadian tax rates. However, he now felt that the proposed higher income tax rates contained in a new Bill before the U.S. Congress would make it possible to have a direct tax on incomes in Canada without deleterious effects on current and expected future immigration.[18] In short, proposed changes in income tax rates in the United States reduced the political costs associated with horizontal tax competition.

It may be useful to note some of the similarities and differences between the reincarnation[19] of the income tax in the United States and its birth in Canada. In the United States agrarian support for an income tax grew during the 1880s, culminating in official support of the Populist party, and eventually of the Democratic party, for a graduated tax on income "as a replacement for tariffs and excise taxes".[20] An amendment to an 1894 Wilson tariff bill that would have introduced an income tax was ruled unconstitutional by the Supreme Court in 1895. Congress eventually passed a constitutional amendment in 1909 introducing an income tax, and a sufficient number of states had passed the amendment to permit the reincarnation of the income tax in 1913.[21] From a modest beginning, with a very large exemption and a maximum rate of 7 per cent, the income tax had expanded dramatically within four years and now accounted for "close to 60 per cent of all revenue, [its] maximum rate [being] 77 percent".[22]

Three observations are pertinent. First, support by farmers and farmers' organizations for a graduated income tax to replace customs duties was similar in both countries, although it emerged much earlier in the United States. Second, there was little concern in the United States that income taxes would discourage immigration and encourage emigration to Canada, whereas there is ample testimony that Canadian governments were extremely sensitive to any expected effects of an income tax on the migration of people and capital.[23] Horizontal tax competition was not a significant determinant of tax structure in a large country like the United States, but it was a significant determinant of tax structure in a country like Canada, which was small in terms of population. These circumstances may partly account for the determination of Sir Thomas White not to introduce an income tax until tax rates in the United States were high enough to discourage any flight of men and capital out of Canada.

The rebirth and growth of the United States income tax may have been a necessary condition for the later birth in Canada of a similar income tax.

Third, the growth of income tax revenues in the United States, more rapid than in Canada, may also be linked to horizontal tax competition differences in the two countries. In the United States the share of income tax revenues in total tax revenues reached 60 per cent just four years after introduction of the tax. This was the setting south of the border when Sir Thomas introduced the income tax in 1917; four years later the share of income tax revenues in total Canadian tax revenues was a mere 12 per cent.[24] It is reasonable to hypothesize that the political costs associated with horizontal tax competition in Canada continued to play some role in curbing the growth of the Canadian income tax, even after it was introduced.[25]

Sir Thomas also reiterated his long-standing concerns about the administrative costs of a new income tax. Fortunately, the proposed higher tax rates in the bill before the United States Congress allowed the Canadian tax rates to be set much higher than had originally been intended, so that they generated more revenue for a given administrative cost. Consequently per unit collection costs had fallen, making it more attractive to introduce the tax in the summer of 1917 than it had been previously.[26]

In summary, three changes in determinants of political cost functions accounted for the government's policy reversal. A strong preference for a graduated tax on incomes — a "conscription of wealth" to match the conscription of men during a time of war — was becoming evident in the country as well as in the House: the desire for vertical equity was increasing. The marginal political cost represented by emigration was lowered considerably by higher income tax rates in the United States: horizontal tax competition with the United States had lessened. The marginal political cost per dollar's worth of revenue, of administering an income tax, was lowered considerably: costs of collection, compliance and enforcement fell. These changes were sufficient, when coupled with a war-related increase in revenue requirements, to cause the government to choose to introduce an income tax on personal and corporation incomes.

The corporation income tax was imposed at a rate of four percent of profits but it was payable only if it exceeded the business profits war tax. For the personal income tax a normal rate was four percent, and to this was added a graduated supertax that ranged from 2 percent on an income of $6000 to 25 percent on an income of $100,000 and over. Personal exemptions of $3000 and $1500, for married persons and single individuals respectively, were allowed only in respect of the normal tax.

This first income tax was a tiny baby indeed, according to one estimate it affected no more than one percent of the total population.[27]

The 1918–1919 War Budgets

The acting Minister of Finance, the Honourable A.K. MacLean, continued the search for additional revenues in the 1918 budget by increasing the effective rates on some of the special war revenue excises, the business profits war tax, the personal income tax and the corporation income tax. The acting Minister admonished the nation that "we must learn to dispense with luxuries", and introduced a modest package of luxury excise taxes, of which the most important commodity covered was the automobile.[28]

Sir Thomas White's 1919 budget speech was notable for the fact that, for the first time since the outbreak of the war, a major tax was reduced. He pointed out that war-related expenditures, such as demobilization and veterans' pensions, must continue but sounded a warning note of caution in calling upon the House to:

> . . . bear specially in mind the anxieties and burdens of the general public at a time of dislocation, unrest and high prices, and endeavour to *wisely bridge over this period* by giving such *measure of relief* as may be practicable. . . . [The increased cost of living during the war] . . . is causing *hardship to a large proportion of our population*, especially those of limited means and slender incomes.
>
> (White, 1919:20, emphasis added)

The relief came in the form of reductions in the customs war duty, by repeal of the 5 percent rate on the British Preferential Tariff, and extension of exemptions for goods such as, coffee, tea, soda ash and several other commodities subject to the 7.5 percent rate and ordinary customs duties. These tariff reductions would have a once-and-for all effect, bringing down prices on a large range of consumption goods and intermediate inputs. Organized labour and western farmers' groups, whose opposition to the tariff had intensified during the war, would view this proposal favourably.[29]

On the other hand, the Minister increased substantially the effective tax rates on personal incomes and corporation incomes. The substantial increase in the progressiveness of the personal income tax reflects an enhanced concern with vertical equity, the taxation of those with high incomes who were best able to bear the burden of the tax. The debates in the House make this point clear. Sir Herbert Ames, for example, approved of the 1918 increases, arguing:

> I know that the people are ready and willing to bear their fair share of
> the war taxation, and the widening of the base of taxation suggested this
> afternoon will meet, I think, and should meet, with universal approval.
>   (Ames, *House of Commons Debates*, April 30, 1918:1291–1292)[30]

Mr. F.F. Pardee reflected the mood of many Liberal opposition members
when he responded to the 1919 income tax rate increases in the following
terms:

> I am delighted that [the income tax rate] has been increased in some de-
> gree to what it ought to be, but it is not high enough yet . . . I see no
> reason why we should not go on taxing the big fellow very much higher
> than he is taxed under the present proposals.
>   (F.F. Pardee, *House of Commons Debates*, June 17, 1919:3545)[31]

A year later Finance Minister Drayton was to attribute the 1919 decision to increase personal income tax rates to concern over horizontal tax
competition with the United States.[32] The net effect of the 1919 budget was to reduce consumption-based taxes and increase income-based
taxes.[33]

A Quick, Easy Delivery:
Birth of a General Sales Tax

> In our sales tax operations *we wanted money and we wanted it badly.*
>   (Sir Henry Drayton, *House of Commons Debates*,
>   1923:919, emphasis added)

Sir Henry Drayton's budget speech of May 1920 repealed the remaining
war customs duty, and reduced the war profits business tax rates. The
war customs duty had been blamed for contributing to the "high cost of
living" and criticized because of an "incidence [that] works and maintains
inconsistencies".[34] The business profits war tax had also been blamed for
the high cost of living, its collection and administration were considered
to be inequitable and it was seen as an encouragement to business inef-
ficiency; it was continued for one more year, but at reduced rates and
with increased exemptions.[35] The Minister allowed it to expire at the
end of 1920, arguing that excess profits would be small anyway and that
the tax "works harm . . . in an ordinary period and . . . especially in a
period of business depression".[36]
    Sir Henry increased both the personal income and the corporation
income tax rates. This was the first occasion on which Canadian income
tax rates were above those in the United States. The Minister confidently

asserted that the 5 percent surtax on individual and corporation taxes would "not deter immigration and the investment of outside capital".[37]

Sir Henry took a swing at "luxurious expenditure" and "extravagant buying" and called for a halt to such behaviour. He hoped to assist consumers in curbing their tastes by increasing and expanding the luxury excises.[38] Most of the latter were extremely short-lived, as the Minister repealed them on December 18 of the same year.

Finally, with no elaboration except "the necessities of increased revenues", Sir Henry introduced the first Dominion general sales tax. This tax, originally proposed at 1 percent on sales of manufacturers, wholesalers, jobbers and importers, was revised one month later and converted into a two-stage turnover tax. The tax rate was initially set at one percent on sales of manufacturers to wholesalers and wholesalers to retailers (or consumers), and two percent on sales of manufacturers directly to retailers (or consumers). A similar rate structure applied to sales of importers.

The new sales tax, unlike the new income taxes of 1917, arrived without warning. No budget speech prior to 1920 had even mentioned a sales tax as a potential revenue source. No budget debate since the outbreak of war had revealed any Liberal opposition members ready and willing to champion a "conscription of sales", whereas some of them had been only too eager to call for a "conscription of wealth". No organized pressure group was actively calling for such a tax, a striking difference from the situation prevailing with respect to the income tax; farmers' associations and organized labour had been calling for a graduated income tax long before 1917. Finally, no similar type of tax existed in the United States.

The need for increased revenues, coupled with a concern for the magnitude of the debt, was advanced as the major justification for the new tax. Sir Henry Drayton, three years later, acknowledged the urgent need for increased revenues (in the words quoted at the beginning of this section).[39] Sir Henry introduced his 1920 budget expressing concern for the "pyramid of debt" which had accumulated during the war and saw it as his "duty . . . to promote measures which will reduce [the national debt]".[40] Preoccupation with debt reduction was to emerge in budget speeches throughout the 1920s. I return to this point in Chapter 7.

The Minister's need for additional revenues to finance debt reduction was a genuine concern, and could serve as an explanation for the birth of a new tax in 1920. Lest it be forgotten, however, part of the need for additional revenue was created by the Minister's own policy decision to repeal the 7.5 percent war customs duty. The foregone war customs duty revenues of $30 million were replaced with a sales tax that generated $37 millions during its first fiscal year.[41] The government, in repealing the war customs duty, was reducing a major source of irritation for farmers, and especially western farmers whose political importance was increasing significantly at this time.[42] The general tariff structure was still in place.

The government, by introducing a broadly based tax at a low rate on domestic and imported consumption goods (with exemptions), could diffuse the opposition across many unorganized consumers. This behaviour is consistent with hypothesis H-2 of Chapter 2 according to which a large number of collection points reduces the political costs of taxing a particular revenue source. From the fact that the 1920 budget debate virtually ignored the sales tax proposals we might conclude that the strategy was successful. However, by the time the 1921 budget debate, when the sales tax rates on imports were set higher than the rates on domestic goods, the similarities between the customs tariff and the sales tax were being seized upon by eager opposition members.[43]

In summary, the newly born general sales tax was mothered by fiscal need and fathered by a political shift from a revenue source with a high political cost to a source for which it was lower.

One other aspect of the birth of the sales tax is noteworthy. The form in which it was actually adopted one month after the budget — a two-stage turnover tax — was preferred by the government on administrative cost grounds compared to the three-stage turnover tax, which represented traditional practice. One year later, Sir Henry Drayton argued that a three-stage turnover tax had been rejected because of the costs of collection and compliance at the retail level,

> In practical administration, though, . . . it has been established that books are not kept in many retail stores. The cost of administration would be unduly great and difficulties of collection many.
>
> (Drayton, 1921:15)[44]

The government continued to reject suggestions for a three-stage turnover tax on administrative grounds, and the conversion of the tax into a one-stage manufacturers' sales tax on January 1, 1924, was, once again, in part, attributable to the cost of administering a form of sales tax at the retail level. The form of the tax, having been selected during 1920–1923 on grounds related to the cost of collection, remained unchanged until January 1, 1991.[45]

By the end of 1923 the surviving new taxes — the personal income tax, the corporation income tax and the manufacturers' sales tax — along with the old revenue sources — the tariff, excise duties on alcoholic beverages and tobacco and deficit financing — formed the family of Dominion revenue sources that would persist. The second great war would witness another flurry of births and deaths, and the tariff and excise duties would age gracefully, but the membership in the Dominion revenue structure family was basically fixed by January 1, 1924.

Conclusions:
Healthy Tax Births

The taxes that were born in the period 1915–1923, and survived into later years — the personal income tax, the corporation income tax and the manufacturers' sales tax — were the offspring of fiscal need and changing relative political costs. Their births are consistent with the balanced budget tax reform of the revenue structure that we discussed in Chapter 2. Because the fiscal need that gave rise to their creation is associated with the dramatic increases in Dominion spending attributable to war and defence-related post-war activity, it is important to note the differences between this explanation and several others in the literature.

First, the explanation differs from the displacement hypothesis, which argues that a divergence between a tolerable level of taxation and the demand for a higher level of government expenditures would be reduced during crises, such as wars and great depressions, thereby resulting in higher levels of both taxation and expenditures. The higher taxation levels would probably result in new taxes.[46] I have argued here that, except for political mistakes, governments in pursuit of survival will attempt to balance the political costs of raising revenues from diverse revenue sources to finance their spending. There will be no divergence between tolerable taxation and demand for government expenditures during peacetime.[47] The large increase in the demand for government spending was sufficient to create new taxes.

Our explanation also differs from the hypothesis of crisis-induced tax reform. Richard Bird argues that, because of the great political difficulty of instituting major tax reforms, such changes would "usually take place only in times of acute fiscal crisis, such as wars or depressions".[48] Malcolm Gillis holds the view that, because the manufacturers' sales tax was "created in response to fiscal crisis . . . worthwhile reform may be possible only in the presence of clear fiscal crisis".[49] When attention is focused on the "fiscal crisis" as a cause of major tax reform it is diverted away from the substantive causes or changes that have rendered, or could render, the "politically difficult" politically possible.

I have argued here that, while fiscal need must be present to mother a tax, the father of the new levy must be a shift in relative political costs; both factors were present at these three particular births. The income tax was born as a response to an increased demand for fairness in the tax system and only after income tax rates in the United States had become high enough to discourage mobile Canadian capital and labour from fleeing to those greener pastures. The general sales tax was born at the time when the government was killing off the war customs duties and thus reducing revenues, in response to strong political opposition to the tariff. These changes in relative political costs of taxing diverse revenue sources are of a critical importance equal to the fiscal need necessitated by increased war-related expenditures or the emergence of a demand to reduce the national debt.[50]

The birth of direct taxes on personal and corporation income has been interpreted by economists and historians as "a temporary measure to help finance the cost of World War I".[51] This mistaken view of the personal income tax as a temporary tax is continually being recycled by the popular press.[52]

Only Harvey Perry and Richard Krever have considered factors other than fiscal need as leading to the introduction of income taxes, and Perry's discussion at least casts doubts on the "temporary" nature of the tax. Perry stresses the role of strong public pressures, especially from western farmers, for direct income taxation as a partial substitute for the much-hated tariff.[53] Krever argues that the introduction of the income taxes was a "purely political act, part of a desperate attempt by the government of the day" to convince those Liberals who supported conscription and a new tax on income to join the Conservatives in a Union government prior to the crucial fall election of 1917.[54] The income tax by itself proved inadequate to seduce these wavering Liberals away from their party. Instead, a "series of much more direct and blatant political bills" was required to lure them into a Union team which, on December 13, 1917, defeated the Liberals by shutting them out of the west.[55] The new cabinet included three former Liberal champions of the income tax.[56]

These two studies are consistent with the general approach embodied in the positive model used in this book which emphasizes three dimensions, not fully developed in the earlier works. First, a comprehensive view is taken of government choosing among its various revenue sources (actual and potential) in such a way as to maximize its chances of electoral survival. The conceptual framework of Chapter 2 assumes that a government will always act in a "purely political" manner when framing its tax policy. It may make political mistakes in crafting its revenue structure, but that is a separate issue.

Krever argues that the events of 1914–1917 were unusual and that the behaviour of the Conservatives was a dramatic and unique attempt to retain power. I argue that the events were unique but the behaviour of the government of the day was not. It used all possible instruments of governing — new taxes, franchise manipulation and special exemptions for certain groups — to minimize the political costs of financing its spending and to remain in office. My approach is built on the premise that governments will continue to pursue these aims in war and in peace.

Second, I argue that, besides an increased demand for a graduated income tax, there were two factors that eventually led the government of the day to reverse its longstanding opposition to the tax — the risk that labour and capital would emigrate to the United States was reduced, as income tax rates in that country were increased during the war, and the administrative costs, per dollar's worth of tax revenue were lessened. Krever's focus on the admittedly important role of pressure from western farmers led to a neglect of the role played by changes in other determinants of the government's tax structure policy; and it was the changes in these three determinants combined that led to the changes in relative political cost functions which fathered the birth of the personal income and the corporation income tax.

Third, the income tax was not introduced as a temporary tax, and was not so regarded by Sir Thomas White and the government to which he belonged. Sir Thomas chose his words carefully in this regard, but at no time throughout the extensive parliamentary debate committed his government to repealing the tax after the war:

> I have placed no time limit upon this taxation measure; but I do suggest
> . . . that after the war is over this taxation measure should be deliberately
> reviewed. . . . by the Minister of Finance and the Government of the day,
> with the view of judging whether it is suitable to the conditions which
> then prevail.
>
> (Sir Thomas White, 1917b:3765)

Sir James Lougheed, the government leader in the Senate, introduced the bill to the Senate with the caution that the tax would not necessarily end after the war because the time might have come "to augment the revenues of the country by this particular form of taxation".[57]

Moreover, the continued utilization and expansion of the income tax in the United States permanently reduced the political costs that were associated with mobile people and capital and the high initial costs of administering the tax in Canada. These were the two factors that Sir Thomas had repeatedly referred to as inhibiting the introduction of a direct tax on incomes.

Most important of all, the income tax was not perceived to be temporary by those same Liberal supporters — Maclean, Guthrie and Carvell — who were finally enticed into the Union government, and eventually into the cabinet, and who were accurately reflecting the demands of their farmer constituents. Western farmers saw the progressive income tax as a preferred alternative to the tariff. The Dominion tax structure, from mid-1917 on, began to reflect this political preference.

Carvell reflected the mood which underlay the preference when he greeted the introduction of the tax with great fervour,

> I hope the income tax has become an institution in Canada, and that it will remain for all time. . . . *It will never be abolished, because the good sense of the people of Canada will see it is kept in effect for all time.*
> (Hon. Mr. Carvell in White 1917b:3770, emphasis added)

The birth of the general sales tax in 1920 has been interpreted as a post-war fiscal measure necessary to finance continued expenditures of a war-related nature and to assist in paying down the sizeable debt that had accumulated during the war.[58] My interpretation accepts this view that fiscal need engendered the sales tax baby. However, equally important was the father of the new offspring: a shift from a revenue source with high political costs (wartime customs duty and the tariff) to a new revenue source for which it was expected that political costs would be lower. The Minister reduced and eventually repealed the wartime customs duty, thereby creating part of the need for new revenues. The sales tax would affect in a minor way many consumers who were not well organized to oppose such a tax, and the broad coverage of the tax, even with the exemptions, held out the promise of a very productive source of revenue. I have, moreover, noted that the expected high costs of collecting a tax on sales at the retail level deterred the Dominion government from adopting the three-stage turnover tax which was, at that time, traditional.

Chapter 6

Financing War

Taxes and loans are not exactions from the people by a government. They are weapons which the people through their elected representatives and the free methods of democracy have fashioned for their own use and their common purpose.

(Honourable J.L. Ilsley, Minister of Finance,
Budget Speech, 1943, p. 1)

Introduction

Dominion spending increased sharply during each of the two great wars, and produced an equally sharp increase in total financial requirements.[1] Chart 1-2 in Chapter 1 indicates the extent to which government expenditures increased. During the first great war total expenditures more than doubled, rising from 6 percent of gross national product in 1913 to 16 percent in 1919. The increase in government spending was even more dramatic during the second great war when total expenditures soared from 11 percent of gross national product in 1939 to 45 percent in 1943.[2]

Although taxes were expanded, both at the margin and on the number of revenue sources, it was borrowing that became the primary source of government revenue during both wars. Chart 6-1 provides a snapshot of the variations in the shares of total revenue represented by the major revenue sources in selected years during each war period. A glance at this chart is sufficient to reveal the extent to which deficit financing carried the bulk of the burden of war finance. In addition, the chart displays a marked difference in the most important tax sources during the two war periods.[3]

The present chapter begins with an analysis of the borrowing strategy employed by two different governments (a Conservative-Union government and a Liberal government) to finance nearly half of government expenditures during the first and second war period respectively. A three-part hypothesis is then developed to account for the taxing strategy of these governments. Analysis of budgetary policy and tax choices reveals a pattern of revenue shares and tax rates that is consistent with this three-part hypothesis and fits into the conceptual framework of this

Chart 6-1

**Major Revenue Sources During the Two Great Wars,
as a percentage of Total Financial Requirements (TFR),
Canada, Fiscal 1915, 1917, 1920, and 1941, 1943, 1946.**

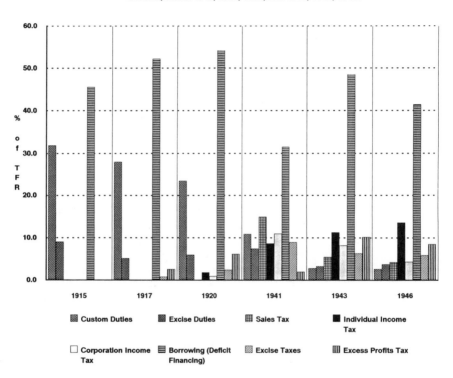

Source: Table B-3

study. The concluding section summarizes the major findings of the chapter and contrasts them with the literature.

The Borrowing Strategy

I cannot too strongly state . . . the imperative duty of our own people to loan to the Government.

(Hon. A.K. MacLean, Minister of Finance, *Budget Speech*, 1918, pp. 16–17)

. . . the turning of [war] bonds or certificates into cash . . . at this time is a betrayal of our obligation to the men who are risking their lives and dying in the great battle for world freedom.

(Hon. J.L. Ilsley, Minister of Finance, *Budget Speech*, 1944, p. 4)

The government of the day borrowed slightly more than half its total financial requirements during the first war period; its counterpart during the second great war borrowed slightly less than half. The remarkable similarities in borrowing during both war periods suggest that the political costs of drawing upon deficit financing fell in relation to those of other actual and potential revenue sources. This difference in political costs at the margin would have provided the incentive for governments to utilize the borrowing revenue source much more extensively, until political costs were once again equal at the margin and a political equilibrium was re-established.

The existence of a state of wartime emergency creates a context in which political costs may change considerably. While one group of citizens is fighting overseas, another can be called upon to "do their patriotic duty" and pay higher taxes, lend funds to the state at a rate below the market rate of interest and volunteer their services; and this should come as no surprise.

The government is providing an important public good for its citizens through its war effort and the greatly increased expenditures occasioned by that effort. Provided that there is substantial support for the war effort there will be also a substantial increased willingness to pay for increased war-related spending.[4] Finance Minister Ilsley reflected this causal force when he argued, "Taxes and loans are not exactions from the people by a government. They are weapons which the people . . . have fashioned for their own use and their common purpose".[5]

Great wars display other characteristics besides the increased demand for war-related government spending; one of them is a reduction of horizontal tax competition. Other governments too are increasing tax rates and introducing new taxes, and are thereby reducing the incentive to migrate in response to differential tax burdens. Moreover, some of the additional taxes required to finance the war-related spending may be considered temporary, and therefore may not have the same impact on potentially mobile capital and labour.

Finally, many citizens at home will feel an "obligation to the men who are risking their lives and dying in the great battle for world freedom".[6] This feeling, reinforced by the wartime finance ministers, will increase the willingness of some people to sacrifice consumption and saving and finance the increased war-related government spending.

Given the increased demand for defence spending in wartime and an increased willingness to finance such expenditure, why did Dominion governments rely primarily on deficit financing in preference to one or more of the other available, or potentially by available, tax sources? I hypothesize that there are two major reasons why the political cost curve of deficit financing fell relative to the political cost curves of the various tax sources during a major war. First, Dominion governments were pulled toward increased deficit financing because bond purchases were on a voluntary basis and therefore the political costs of raising a dollar's worth of revenue at the margin by this means fell relatively to the marginal political costs of the various compulsory tax sources. Secondly, governments were pushed towards increased borrowing because, as total financial requirements rose rapidly during wartime, the opposition and resistance of many citizens to yet higher tax rates or to new taxes, increased significantly. Such voter resistance increased the political costs of raising a dollar's worth of revenue from additional taxes and borrowing became a more attractive option.

Consider more closely the pull factor. Moral suasion can be used to exhort the people to "do their patriotic duty" and to lend more money to the state or pay higher taxes. One would expect, however, that exhortations to behave patriotically to be more effective with respect to a revenue source which is the result of voluntary action by citizens — lending funds to the state — than a revenue source which is the result of compulsory action by the state — paying a new tax on, say, income.[7]

If some citizens are more patriotically inclined than others — with or without the exhortations of ministers of finance — they will offer less political opposition to parting with funds to help finance the war than they would offer to similar action in peacetime. War bonds and victory loans allow a government to tap this potential revenue source, since these patriotic citizens voluntarily reveal their preferences. An increase in taxes, or a new tax, draws revenues from all citizens with a given revenue source, patriotic and non-patriotic alike; on average, therefore, the political opposition will be higher than in the case of deficit financing.

To the extent that war causes some citizens to become more patriotic than others, governments will exploit the difference and expand their use of borrowing, in preference to taxing.

Finance ministers were aware of this pull factor and encouraged it during each war period. They repeatedly used moral suasion to exhort Canadians to be industrious and thrifty and to buy government bonds. Maclean's 1918 budget plea displayed the characteristic tone of government persuasion during the first great war:

> . . . the people of Canada must loan to the Government the money to [finance the war]. That is, they must, year after year, purchase Victory Bonds . . . I cannot too strongly state the imperative necessity of the Government borrowing from our own people, and the *imperative duty of our own people to loan to the Government* . . . I say we can do better, and in very fact we must.
>
> (Maclean, 1918:16–17, emphasis added)[8]

Canadians did buy bonds; they bought lots of bonds. Finance Minister White was pleasantly surprised in 1915, when his first domestic bond issue "was most enthusiastically and patriotically received by the people of Canada, with the result that it was more than doubly subscribed".[9] He proceeded to tap that source of loanable funds extensively, both during and immediately after the first great war.[10]

This apparent ease of raising revenues to fight the war, with some left over for domestic non-war expenditures, including railway deficits, was a crucial factor in the government's overall revenue policy during the first great war period. White's post-war book, *The Story of Canada's War Finance*, was almost entirely devoted to the enormous success of the war and victory loans as the major new source of financing during the difficult war period. More neutral commentators have also acknowledged the very important role of the these domestic bond issues in war financing.[11] Such observations strengthen the thesis that the government pursued a politically logical course of action in regard to the major thrust of its revenue structure policy: extensive reliance on deficit financing and borrowing from the Canadian public.

Ilsley's 1943 and 1944 budget exhortations emphasized the government's determination to tap domestic saving during the second great war:

> Sales or redemptions [of war savings bonds and war savings certificates] to get dollars to buy things that are not essential have not (sic) legitimate reason. We must not only increase our voluntary savings and lend them to our country through the purchase of victory loan bonds and war savings certificates; we must also continue to hold these securities at least until

after the war . . . I repeat what I said in the budget last year, "*Let us compete with our neighbours, in saving, not spending.*"

(Ilsley, 1943:25, emphasis added)

Unnecessary spending, financed by the turning of bonds or certificates into cash . . . at this time is *betrayal of our obligation to the men who are risking their lives and dying in the great battle for world freedom.*

(Ilsley, 1944:4, emphasis added)

Each war budget speech stressed the need for Canadians at home to save and to lend the funds to the government as part of their patriotic duty.[12] And towards the end of the conflict — as can be seen from the above quotations — Canadians were being virtually shamed into not redeeming their bonds or certificates.

The government was engaged in a battle on two fronts — in the European theatre and on the financial front in Canada; not surprisingly, it was prepared to utilize psychological instruments as part of its battle on the home front. Nothing could be clearer in its intention than Ilsley's 1943 ringing declaration of the value of taxes and borrowing, quoted at the beginning of this chapter. The borrowing weapon was the important one. It provided by far the largest single source of financing of the government's requirements during the second great war period.

If the lure of "patriotically available"[13] loanable funds may be termed the pull factor inducing governments to pursue deficit financing extensively during both war periods, then the "political unacceptability" of new taxes and higher tax rates can be regarded as the push factor. Let us examine this push factor more closely. The substantial increase in war-related government spending is viewed as necessary by citizen and government alike. It is also seen as temporary, even though it is of unknown duration.

If a government attempted to finance most or all of its emergency wartime expenditure through taxation it would have to introduce sharp increases in effective tax rates (and new taxes) during the war, and sharp decreases in tax rates after the war. Such major variations in rates can increase uncertainty and exacerbate disincentive effects. As a result the political costs of taxing various revenue sources at the margin may increase substantially. Moreover, during wartime there is a strong desire to minimize any unwarranted disincentive effects that might inhibit the economy from achieving its productive maximum.

A government can use deficit financing to prevent extreme fluctuations in effective tax rates, both during and after the war. In so doing, it is helping to minimize distortions and disincentive effects during the war, and it is responding to citizen resistance to higher tax rates in such a way as to lower political costs throughout the combined war and immediate post-war period.

Given that voters and government alike expect the wartime emergency spending to be temporary, the government will be pushed to borrow more intensively during the war and pay off some of the debt during the post-war period. A corollary of this choice is that the post-war reduction in tax rates will be rather modest, and repeal of "temporary" wartime taxes will be delayed; in this way budgetary surpluses will be generated that can be used to reduce the national debt. This budgetary behaviour is consistent with the conceptual framework of Chapter 2.[14]

Finance ministers have been aware of the push factor. During the first great war Finance Minister White repeatedly expressed concern over the "practical" limits to further taxation.[15] Acting Finance Minister Ilsley, in his first war budget speech of September 1939, argued with respect to financing during the first great war, that,

> . . . the imposition of a weight of *taxation sufficient to pay for the whole cost of the War was too revolutionary a step to take.* . . . The sudden introduction of such taxing measures (income and profit taxation) on the scale required was *too drastic to be either politically or economically practical.*
>
> (Ilsley, 1939b:4–5, emphasis added)

The Royal Commission on Dominion-Provincial Relations was sufficiently impressed by this argument to adopt it verbatim in its 1940 Report[16] and other commentators picked up the theme.[17]

The Honourable Mr. Ilsley, having argued that financing of the first great war exclusively through taxation would have been too revolutionary an act, proceeded to apply the same reasoning to his attempt to finance government spending during the second great war. Total financing of the war through taxation,

> . . . would become so disruptive in character as inevitably to produce disorganization and public discontent . . . [such a policy would encounter] *psychological reactions to taxation.* . . . *there is a limit to the taxes that can be imposed without producing inefficiency, a lack of enterprise, and serious discontent.* . . . what we cannot meet by taxation we shall finance by means of borrowing from the Canadian public at rates as low as possible.
>
> (Ilsley, 1939b:4–5 emphasis added)

The potential "discontent", in response to very high tax levels continued to form a part of the background governing the financing policy throughout the second great war.[18]

The pull and push factors determined the broad overall financing strategies of the Dominion governments. Tax sources would be utilized, but not beyond the point where public discontent would disrupt the war effort or pose a threat to the government of the day. Deficit financing would be used extensively at low political cost. The results are clear in Chart 6-1. For both war periods deficit financing assumed the largest single share of financing total government spending — slightly more than half during the first war and slightly less than half during the second.

In Search of the Taxing Strategy

Revenue sources other than deficit financing, display greater variation as between the two war periods. During the first war, customs duties provided the largest proportion of tax revenue although their contribution to total financial requirements, fell from 58 to 23 percent, followed by excise duties and excess profits tax, which came far behind in second and third place, respectively. Revenues from excise tax, personal income tax and corporation income tax were all trivial contributors to total financial requirements.

The pattern is more varied and complex for the second war period. The most important tax revenue share was that of personal income tax, which, as a proportion of total financial requirements, doubled from 7 to 14 percent. The excess profits tax and excise taxes came close behind in second and third place, averaging about 7-8 percent.[19] The remaining four major taxes all declined in relative importance as the war period progressed.[20] The corporation income tax and sales taxes represented the next most important tax shares, and the original fundamental components of the Dominion tax structure, customs duties and excise duties, were the least important revenue-raisers of all.

These significant differences in tax structure can be explained with the aid of a three-part hypothesis: the belief that an old tax is a good tax, the emergence of a potential revenue source that had very low political costs and an increased demand for equity in the tax system. The first war period opened with a small family of existing major taxes — customs duties and excise duties — and these taxes provided the bulk of tax revenues throughout the war period. The second war period opened with a large family of tax sources — customs duties, excise duties, sales tax, excise taxes, personal income tax and corporation income tax — and all sources were utilized, each to a lesser extent than customs duties had been during the earlier war period.

The adage, "an old tax is a good tax", is consistent with a major part of the tax strategy of each government during the two war periods. It is, moreover, a popularization of one aspect of the positive model of this study: the fixed political costs of introducing a tax having already been absorbed at the time of introduction, there remain only the marginal political costs of increasing the effective tax rate for a given tax base. Adjustment costs of introducing a new tax can be quite substantial. During both war periods, political concern over disruption of the war effort translated into political sensitivity to public discontent and negative reaction to taxes. Given the higher initial fixed costs of new taxes, governments were doubly hesitant to introduce such taxes.

But the "old tax is a good tax" hypothesis was not the only element in the taxing strategy of the two periods. When the political costs of a potential revenue source, at the margin, fell relative to the political costs of existing tax sources, governments appear to have moved with the satisfaction of a child eyeing a succulent sweet. An excess profits tax, of differing format, was introduced during each war period and accounted for an important share of total financing. The tax was the third most important source of tax revenues during the first war period (and, in fact, the only significant source of revenue among the new taxes introduced during that time) and it constituted the second most important source of tax revenues during the second war period. Abnormally large profits and windfall gains that occurred during wartime were viewed as rewards to the lucky few who owned parts of the productivity machinery of war, at a time when many were sacrificing their lives to operate the machinery of war in the battlefield.

Governments observed a new potential tax revenue source, extraordinarily high profits. Voters observed a few owners gaining large benefits from the war, whereas other people were worse off. The owners of industry would probably reject such a view. However, the view that abnormally large profits were unfair created widespread support for, indeed demand for, taxes on such gains.[21] From a finance minister's perspective the political costs of taxing such high profits fell drastically, compared to the costs of all other sources. And the finance ministers of the day acted so as to take advantage of such a changed situation.

The third element in the taxing strategy of governments during these two periods was not unrelated to the second, in that it was a quest for equity: its goal was to spread the tax burden equitably over all and ensure that each paid his or her fair share. This admixture of horizontal and vertical equity preferences emerged in numerous decisions, and especially with respect to the wide array of taxes, levies and special charges that become known as excise taxes. Their importance as revenue-raisers during the first period was trivial, but during the second period excise taxes

ranked closely with the excess profits tax as the third most important
source of tax revenues.

In summary, three major elements formed the taxing strategy of Dominion governments during the two great war periods. Application of
the principle "an old tax is a good tax" constrained tax structure policy
and forced it to extract the bulk of tax revenues from the existing tax
structures at the beginning of each period. Low political costs of potential revenue sources, taxation of which was strongly demanded by the
public, led to the introduction and significant utilization of excess profits
taxes. Finally, a heightened tax preference for fairness in the tax system, at a time when some citizens were being called upon to make great
sacrifices on the battlefield resulted in tax structure changes to achieve
fairness: a vast array of excise taxes. These excise taxes complemented
the equity thrust of the personal income tax which was introduced at a
late date in the first war, but served as the major instrument of equity
during the second great war.

Tax Choices During Wartime

The budget speeches of the wartime Ministers of Finance and the observed budgetary behaviour of the government of the day support each of
the three components of the taxing strategy. In this section I document
each element of the strategy for the two great wars.

The family of taxes existing at the beginning of each war circumscribed the wartime tax policy. I noted earlier the importance that
Finance Minister White attached to the tariff, as the "mainstay" of the
revenue system, when in 1915 he introduced his most important revenue-
raiser — the customs war duty. In 1921 he was still stressing the value
of the increase in customs duties at the beginning of the war, on the
grounds that it had been "of utmost value to Canada in maintaining
general prosperity and financial stability during the war and the period
succeeding the armistice".[22] This old tax source, the tariff, did in fact
provide the largest tax share of total tax financing throughout the war.

The family of old taxes was much larger on the eve of the second great
war than it had been when the first great war began; consequently, the
government had a wider choice when deciding which taxes would be
utilized more intensively. All existing revenue sources were utilized to a
greater degree than before. Customs duties played a role through the war
exchange tax, ostensibly introduced to conserve U.S. dollar reserves, but
in practical terms a customs duty on imports from non-Empire countries. The tax generated about $85 million annually, although in the
year it was introduced (1940) it proved to be the largest source of the

increased revenues planned by the government for the remainder of the fiscal year.[23]

Excise duties on spirits, beer, wines and cigarettes were increased in the first war budget and were further increased several times during the period. The sales tax rate was not changed from 8 percent, but exemptions were reduced in almost every budget. The removal of the exemption for building materials was the most substantial wartime change, netting an additional $15 million. The corporation income tax rate was increased from 15 to 18 percent in the 1939 budget and then remained constant throughout the duration of the war. The tax rate on income of non-residents was raised from 5 to 15 percent in the 1941 budget. None of these changes significantly increased the weight of such taxes throughout the war.[24]

The personal income tax, however emerged as the "mainstay" of the revenue system. The personal income was an old tax with two characteristics that appealed to the policy makers as they sought to give concrete form to their oft-stated pay-as-you-go policy of financing the war. First, the revenue source, personal income, provided a broad base and ample scope for extracting large sums of money. Secondly, the tax could be so manipulated as to achieve equitable taxation based on ability to pay. This latter objective was not pursued on grounds of social principle alone. It would be more exact to say that it formed an integral part of the government's strategy, aimed at lowering the political costs of opposition to the tax by convincing taxpayers that they were all sharing the sacrifices of the war and doing so in proportion to their command over resources.

The expected rise in incomes, in large part due to the demands of war, was the lure that attracted finance ministers to the use of the personal income tax as the major vehicle of tax financing during the second great war. On the eve of the war, however, it applied to just five percent of working Canadians.[25] The tax would have to be extended down the income scale to cover middle-income and low-income recipients if it was to deliver its potential yield. Finance Minister Ralston made this clear in his 1940 budget speech:

> It would be popular, if it were practicable and possible, to pay the stupendous costs of war by imposing taxes only on those earning higher incomes. The stubborn fact is there is not enough income in the so-called higher brackets to produce more than a small fraction of the necessary revenue . . . it is clear that *we cannot go far to meet the costs of the war simply by taking large incomes, or even those of moderate size.*
>
> (Ralston, 1940:14, emphasis added)

This said, Ralston lowered exemptions and raised the graduated schedule of tax rates, and he introduced a new flat rate tax on total income, called a national defence tax, "to supplement the graduated income tax".[26] This national defence tax had lower exemption levels than the personal income tax and was collected at source — the first income tax to be so collected. Rates for both taxes were raised substantially in the 1941 budget.[27] The two taxes were merged into one graduated personal income tax collected at source, and the structure of tax rates was raised again in the 1942 budget.[28]

In three years the personal income tax had become a fully developed revenue source. By 1943 marginal tax rates had risen to levels that were probably inconceivable prior to the war and are astronomical from the vantage point of 1990. A worker with taxable income between $2000 and $3000 shouldered an increase in his or her marginal tax rate from 5 percent in 1938 to 49 percent in 1943. Persons with taxable income between $10,000 and $15,000 were subjected to an increase from 13.7 percent to 64 percent, and for wealthy individuals with taxable incomes between $100,000 and $200,000 the increase was from 49.4 percent to 98 percent, over the same period.[29] By 1943 over 50 percent of the work force was paying personal income tax and those with incomes under $5000 accounted for over half of the income tax revenues.[30]

The refundable tax feature of the 1942 budget offers an interesting example of a novel experiment that encountered substantial and sustained political opposition, resulting in Finance Minister Ilsley's repeal of the provision in 1944. The Minister of Finance, borrowing an idea from Lord Keynes' proposal for compulsory saving during wartime in order to achieve an increase in real earnings after the war, introduced a refundable tax as part of the very large tax rate increases of the 1942 budget.[31] Ilsley introduced the refundable tax or "minimum savings requirement" as an equity measure, to alleviate the burden of taxes on "those with incomes in the lowest brackets subject to tax". The refundable portion of the tax would be returned to the taxpayer "within a specified period after the war, with accrued interest at 2 percent". An allowance was made for "certain types of savings under existing contracts to be counted as part of the minimum savings requirements".[32]

Finance Minister Ilsley was not able to persuade many Canadians to see the laudable features of this refundable tax. The Minister, in his 1943 budget, defended the refunding condition passionately against:

> . . . those who mistakenly attach little importance to the refunding feature. . . . I have repeatedly stated and now wish to reiterate that within a reasonable time after the tax liability for 1942 is established and discharged, *the taxpayer will receive a receipt or certificate covering the re-*

fundable portion of the tax which will be just as binding an obligation of the Dominion as a victory bond or a war savings certificate . . . The refunding of this tax to those entitled to it is one of the most certain acts of any post-war government that I can imagine . . . *It would be political suicide for any government, however radical or however reactionary, to default on an obligation due to the mass of the wage-earners of the country.*

(Ilsley, 1943:17, emphasis added)

Opposition to the tax continued and the mass of wage-earners remained unconvinced. A year later Finance Minister Ilsley acknowledged defeat and, as part of an attempt "to do away with misunderstandings", withdrew the refundable tax:

. . . *many taxpayers apparently do not make any distinction in their minds between refundable and non-refundable* taxes but regard them as simply taxes. . . . *The refundable feature of our income tax provided simply a method of borrowing* . . . it embodied a principle of fairness which I regret to relinquish. Nevertheless, if this particular method of borrowing . . . has the one fault of discouraging production . . . or creates hardship among those income groups whose incomes leave little room for adjustment, then another method of borrowing must be found . . .
I have been forced to the conclusion that it would be desirable . . . *to discontinue the refundable feature of the income tax.*

(Ilsley 1944:9, 10 emphasis added)

It would seem, then, that taxpayers responded to compulsory taxes and compulsory savings (called refundable taxes) in a similar fashion. Productive activity was discouraged and opposition to higher tax (compulsory savings) rates rose. The repeal of the refundable tax, effective June 30, 1944, meant that personal income tax rates fell before the war was over, in response to widespread taxpayer resistance.

The government did, in fact, refund the tax in March 1948 and March 1949.[33]

The rapid enlargement of the scope and rate structure of the personal income tax, from 1940 through 1943, was facilitated by the government's efforts to convince voters of the superiority of the tax on grounds of fairness and equality of sacrifice from all Canadians. Finance Minister Ralston established the case for regarding an income tax as fairer than indirect taxes in his critically important 1940 budget speech:

We realize that increases in indirect taxes disguise the burdens imposed by the war but they are much more likely to distribute these burdens harshly and unfairly . . . we are striving . . . to deal with the situation . . . by a direct call on our citizens graded according to their means and responsibilities. We believe that a *straightforward contribution to the common cause will be loyally accepted and paid* as a small price for the preservation of our liberties . . . therefore [we have] decided to submit *not an increase in the sales tax but heavy increases in the direct tax on individual incomes.*

(Ralston, 1940:14, emphasis added)

This argument, with slight variation, was utilized each time effective tax rates on personal incomes were increased.[34] The Minister of Finance revealed that he was choosing, on grounds of universal equity and fairness in taxation, to utilize more fully the income tax base, as compared with the manufacturers' sales tax base. Given the pressing fiscal need for additional revenues, the demand for equity must have increased significantly during wartime to cause the government to forego any increase in the sales tax rate during the war.

Two additional considerations encouraged the government to renounce further increases in the manufacturers' sales tax rate. Finance Minister Ilsley argued in his 1942 budget speech that an increase in the sales tax rate that would increase consumer prices could disrupt the wartime price control program.[35] In addition, to the extent that any sales tax increase might lead to an increase in the prices of the machinery and equipment of war, required government spending would rise, necessitating the raising of additional revenues.[36]

In the broader context, the government declared that it was committed to preventing the inequitable distribution of the burden of war financing through inflation, some of which had occurred during the first great war.[37] In as much as this kind of income redistribution had led to clashes among interest groups during the earlier period, the government would wish to prevent the repetition of such a situation. If taxpayers could be convinced that the war financing program would ensure fairness and equality of sacrifice the potential for conflict would be reduced and difficulties for the government would be avoided. Ilsley stressed, in his first war budget speech in 1939, that inflation financing of a war was unfair, inequitable and "taxation of a most unjust type".[38] He reaffirmed in 1943 that the government was determined

. . . to continue to reserve to parliament the right to distribute the financial and economic sacrifices of the war by its taxation measures rather than to have them distributed by the haphazard forces of changing prices and incomes.

(Ilsley, 1943:2)

The Finance Minister's last war budget, which laid the groundwork for the transition to peacetime and emphasized the crucial role that the personal income tax would continue to play in the post-war period, continued to stress the importance of an "equitable distribution of income tax rates".[39] Ilsley took some satisfaction from his rejection of inflationary finance in the interests of all taxpayers.[40]

The personal income tax had indeed grown into a major revenue-raiser for the government. An old tax with a new tax folded into it (the national defence tax), it emerged as the mainstay of the federal tax structure after the war.

Next, consider the introduction of those new taxes that had very low political costs at the margin. That Finance Minister White in 1916 perceived above average or abnormal profits would be a popular source of additional tax revenues is evident from his introduction and extension of the excess profits tax.[41] His enthusiasm for the tax had waned by 1921, but he left no room for doubt that public acceptability was a major factor in the creation of the tax. He argued, in *The Story of Canada's War Finance*, that

> . . . profits became in many instances abnormal and such as to invite public criticism . . . A Business Profits Tax is justifiable during a prolonged war, because . . . *public opinion is offended at the sight of abnormal profits in a period of great suffering and deprivation.*
> (White, 1921:32–33, emphasis added)

This new tax source quickly became the third most important tax component of total financing during the first war period.

During the second great war period the excess profits tax was the first tax change announced by the government. Acting Finance Minister Ilsley introduced it by arguing as follows

> . . . under war-time conditions, when important sacrifices are being asked from the humblest citizen, and when human lives are at stake, no government can justify the making of profits that are excessive or unreasonable.
> (Ilsley, 1939b:6)

There was government concern over devising a format for the tax that would be equitable among different kinds of businesses (and it took two years to settle on a form that would generate sufficient revenues), but there was no hesitation about exploiting a revenue source for which there was widespread support.[42] This tax source came to represent the second most important tax share of total financing during the second war period.

Finance Minister Ilsley acknowledged in 1945 that the excess profits tax had "commanded overwhelming support as an important and necessary instrument of war finance".[43] Such support is equivalent to very low political opposition. The political costs of taxing the excess profits fell substantially relatively to the political costs of taxing other revenue sources. Within the conceptual framework of the positive model of Chapter 2 change of this kind led governments to utilize much more intensively an excess profits tax as part of their package of tax structure changes aimed at financing a higher level of spending during wartime.

Federal estate taxes were introduced by the government in its 1941 budget. The tax was an important part of the overall strategy of fairness in taxation, even though it did not raise more than a small amount of revenues during the war, or thereafter.

One spending and taxing change that commenced in 1941 was unrelated to wartime financing, but would play an important role in the evolution of social policy after the war's end — the creation of the unemployment insurance fund. The unemployment insurance taxes would eventually grow to account for close to 9 percent of total financial requirements.[44]

The third element in the wartime taxing strategy was the effort to achieve equity by spreading the tax burden fairly through the proliferation of excise taxes on many commodities. This strategy was pursued more vigorously during the second great war than during the first.

There was some concern on the government side for fairness in commodity taxation during the first war.[45] Finance Minister White relied primarily on the customs war duty of the 1915, budget with an "auxiliary" means of taxation — an extensive package of excise taxes and stamps on various commodities and services. These excises were introduced in order to cover most of the purchases made by all consumers and specifically to cast the taxman's net over "those best able to bear the burden".[46] The package was enlarged several times during the war period but the revenues raised never accounted for more than a trivial share of total financing.

The policy thrust represented by excise taxes, and its quantitative outcome, were markedly different during the second war period in which excise taxes were almost on a par with the excess profits tax revenues as the third most important tax revenue source of the government. In addition to fairness and ability to pay, the government cited as a reason for its use of excises the need to restrict demand for certain commodities, release resources used in their production, and to extract a revenue from consumers who made "unnecessary" expenditures. The overall result was an increase in excise tax revenues from sources associated with low political costs, during a war time crisis.

Besides increasing excise taxes on alcoholic beverages and tobacco products the government introduced new excise taxes on such commodities and services as gasoline, transportation and communications and amusements. These consumption taxes were very productive of revenue, whereas the very high rates on automobiles, electrical appliances, cameras, jewellery and luggage reduced domestic consumption dramatically and produced little additional revenue.[47]

Each war budget introduced some new excises or increased the rate on existing excise taxes; but perhaps it was the 1941 budget speech that defined most clearly the context for wartime excise taxation policy. Finance Minister Ilsley noted that the excise taxes were levied on expenditures that were

> . . . overt evidence of the existence of surplus income . . . We need the revenue. We need to hold down the consumption of non-essential goods and services. . .
>
> . . . when the need for revenue is great and when the need for concentrating our energies on the successful prosecution of the war is so vitally necessary, we must have recourse to taxes which if not good taxes are better than the others which we have rejected, but no one need pay all of them. If people choose to avoid some of these taxes by saving rather than spending, I shall be satisfied.
>
> (Ilsley, 1941:19 and 21)

A similar, though muted, argument accompanied the package of excise tax changes of the 1940, 1942 and 1943 budgets. Given the substantial increase in excise tax revenues during the war period it must be concluded that not all persons did, in fact, avoid such spending.

Conclusions:
Borrow, Tax and Spend

The foregoing discussion leads to four major conclusions on the financing of government spending during the two great wars. First, in each war period borrowing was the single most important source of finance for total government spending, and the relative contribution of borrowing, compared with taxation, was similar. Second, the tariff was the most important tax source of the first war, whereas the personal income tax occupied this position during the second war. Third, the emergence of a new revenue source with low political costs, namely, excess profits, led wartime governments to obtain a substantial part of their tax financing from this source. Finally, the various revenue structure changes during the two war periods can be explained by changes in relative political cost functions at a time when total government spending was growing dramatically.

These findings differ from the generally accepted interpretation of Canada's financing of expenditures during the two wars. It is widely believed that, during the second great war, the government relied very heavily on taxation to finance spending, and during the first, on borrowing.[48] Perry's otherwise perceptive discussion of government financing during the two war periods includes a table summarizing tax financing as a share of total expenditure during the second war, but does not provide such a table for the first, and inadvertently creates an impression that the tax share in the former was much higher than in the latter.[49] Les MacDonald argues that "The financing of the Second World War differed markedly from that of the first, in that approximately half the expenditures were paid for out of wartime taxation".[50] This study demonstrates that Canada relied very heavily on borrowing during both war periods and that the mix of taxation and borrowing during the two periods was similar, though not identical.

The role reversals of the tariff and the personal income tax during the two war periods has been noted by other writers.[51] The principle that an "old tax is a good tax" underlies, implicitly if not explicitly, the regret expressed at the absence of an income tax during the first war and appreciation of the growth potential of the income tax that did exist on the eve of the second war.[52] The strong thrust for equity conveyed through the income tax and through the packages of special excise taxes of both war periods has also been noted elsewhere in the literature.[53]

The introduction and use of excess profits taxes during each war period receives a different interpretation in the previous literature from that which is offered by this chapter. It is the general belief that "abnormally" high profits during wartime justified governments in taxing most of them away.[54] Morton and Granʳ ̄stein argue that the 1916 business war profits tax was designed "lesʳ for revenue than to demonstrate government indignation at profiteering".[55]

I acknowledge the disapprobation with which such abnormally high profits were viewed, except, of course, by those voters who were reaping the profits, but prefer to extend the argument by drawing the obvious conclusion regarding political costs of raising revenues. Governments, when faced with a fall in the political costs of taxing abnormal profits, compared with other revenue sources, can be expected to introduce, and exploit fully, a tax of some sort on such profits. That is precisely what happened in the periods under consideration. The rapid and full utilization of the new taxes turned them into a very significant contribution to total financing during each war period. They were the third most important source of tax revenues during the first war period and the second most important tax source during the second (see Chart 6-1).

The final conclusion, formulated in terms of the positive model of revenue structure used in this study, emphasizes changes in relative political costs, some of which are linked to the special circumstances of war, as explaining the changing revenue structure of the two war periods. The dramatic increases in war-related government spending generated a demand for increased revenues. A heightened sense of patriotism (fostered in part by exhortations of finance ministers) served as a pull factor; increasing taxpayer resistance to ever higher tax rates constituted a push factor that greatly reduced the political costs of borrowing, as compared with those of taxation and led governments to increase their borrowings, as compared with tax financing, during wartime.

The initially high fixed political costs of introducing a major new tax compared with the cost of existing taxes, encourages governments to rely primarily on the old taxes to finance a surge in spending — even during wartime. However, when a potential new tax source has strong public support and low political costs, which during wartime is the case with extraordinary profits, a new tax on that source will be introduced quickly and exploited fully.

War, with its heavy costs in human life, strengthens concern with the need for fair and equitable sharing of the financial burdens. This increased demand for equity lowers the political costs of equitable taxation and (with additional encouragement from eager Finance Ministers) leads governments to introduce and extend taxes linked to ability to pay.

It is only within a comprehensive model of revenue structure that all these changes in relative political costs can be integrated to explain the changing revenue structure during wartime in Canada. The model of Chapter 2 allows us to understand the impact of exogenous changes, and endogenous factors which found expression in the exhortations of Ministers of Finance, on the revenue structure changes of the two war periods.

It is interesting to note that many writers comment in passing on the importance of "politics", "political acceptability", "public psychology" or similar concepts, as factors in shaping taxation and borrowing policies during the two war periods.[56] Parkinson argues that, during wartime, "public finance — or the larger problem of war economics — is as much a problem of politics as it is of economics".[57] Stikeman notes that fundamental "tax logic in war time" requires taxing incomes and profits beyond a bare minimum "as much as circumstances require and public psychology permits".[58] McIvor, while acknowledging that the actions of the Minister of Finance "will be modified . . . by considerations of political expediency and public acceptability", clearly disapproves of such voter constraints and supports "war-time propaganda . . . [to educate] the public to accept and support . . . the economic programme which . . . [is] essential to the most effective prosecution of the war".[59] Perry discusses the crucial role of the "limits" to taxation during wartime, all of such limits involving responses of the citizens being taxed in order to finance the war. He argues that there is a

> ... major difference between [the use of taxation] in peace and war ... under peacetime conditions it is employed primarily to fill the public purse, while in wartime its primary use is to empty the private purse.
>
> (Perry, 1955:332)

The comprehensive model of revenue structure used in this study makes it possible to focus upon the fundamental role of political factors (political costs) in determining the revenue structure in peacetime and wartime alike. The nation may be at peace or at war; taxation is still used to "empty the private purse" in order to free resources for the government's spending programs — whether the latter apply to schools, railway subsidies, rifles or tanks. Voters whose private purses are being dipped into or emptied will respond in peacetime and wartime *in some manner*. It is their reaction, characterized by the political cost curves of the positive model underlying this study, that is the basic component of the notion of an equilibrium revenue structure. That the equilibrium revenue structure may change — possibly dramatically — during wartime, is perfectly consistent with the notion that change is generated by the reactions and responses of the voters being taxed.

The same considerations exist in peacetime.

Chapter 7

Financing Post-War Debt Reduction

Introduction

At the end of each of the great wars Dominion governments generated sizeable and persistent surpluses on their budgetary accounts. In fact, the fiscal years 1921–1930 and 1947–1954 are the only two periods over the one hundred and twenty-three years that have elapsed since Confederation in which the Canadian government has incurred a surplus for more than two consecutive years.[1] The uniqueness of these immediate post-war years is demonstrated in Charts 1-2 of Chapter 1 and 4-5 of Chapter 4 where the surpluses are measured relative to the size of the economy and as a share of total financial requirements respectively. The few remaining surpluses are insignificant.

After each great war the persistent, sizeable surpluses allowed the national debt to be reduced by substantial amounts. Chart 7-1 traces the debt relative to the size of the economy, from 1870 through 1989, and will serve best to orient the reader to the existence and positioning of the five "waves" of debt creation during Canada's fiscal history. The two most dramatic escalations and descents of the national debt occurred during and immediately after the two great wars.

The peaks and troughs of these five waves of debt creation have been isolated in Chart 7-2. The debt-to-GNP ratio declines each time surpluses allow the retirement of some of the national debt. However, it should be noted that the ratio also declines when the economy grows more rapidly than the growth in the national debt. It follows that, even when the nominal size of the national debt grows (through deficit financing) the debt may actually decline in relation to GNP. This factor contributed substantially to each of the four debt wave reductions. It remains to be seen if, and how, the latest debt peak is reduced (but that is getting ahead of the story).

Dominion spending decreased drastically after each of the two great wars.[2] We noted earlier, in Chart 1-2, the extent to which total government expenditures, relative to the size of the economy, plummeted, especially after the second great war. Towards the latter part of each post-war period Dominion spending rose — modestly through fiscal 1930 and strongly through fiscal 1954. These changes in government spending

Chart 7-1

**Federal Borrowing and National Debt, as a percentage of GNP,
Canada, 1870-1989.**

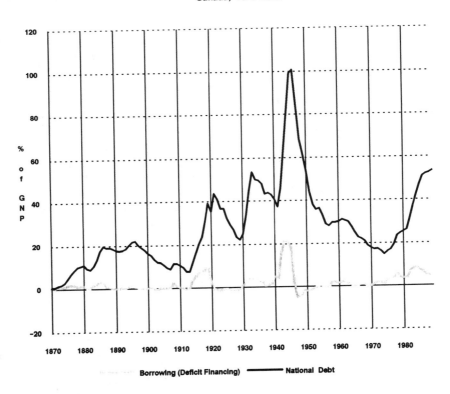

Source: Table C-3

influenced, in part, the pursuit of debt reduction during each of the two post-war periods.

Total Dominion tax revenues increased immediately after each war, especially the first, before declining modestly. From the mid-point of each post-war period onwards total tax revenues rose.[3] We saw earlier, in Chart 1-3, the extent to which total tax revenues, relative to the size of the economy, fell gradually throughout the first post-war period and decreased sharply immediately after the second great war, before increasing during the latter half of the second post-war period.

This changing total tax revenue pattern is the result of three separate forces. First, Dominion governments chose, after each war, to reduce tax rates on some revenue sources as soon as hostilities ceased. Second, these governments chose to introduce a new sales tax immediately following the first great war and increase its rates during the following years. During the second post-war period the Canadian government increased tax rates on many of its revenue sources. Finally, the growth of national income following the two great wars contributed to the automatic increase in government tax revenues. This growth was uneven during the two periods, especially during and after the recession of 1921 and the Korean war period of 1950–52.[4]

Chart 7-3 presents the changes in the shares of major revenue sources as percentages of total financial requirements for selected years during the unique periods of significant surpluses in the government's accounts. While all taxes contributed to funds available as surplus for debt reduction, the big contributors differed during the two periods. Customs duties and sales tax revenues, especially the latter, were the main sources of the available surpluses during the first post-war period, whereas the personal income tax and the corporation income tax were the major sources after the second great war.[5] In part, this difference reflects the government's reliance upon the tax structure existing at the end of each war period, and the importance which income taxes had acquired by 1946. But this is not the whole story: the sales tax had only been introduced in 1920 and its rapid rise in importance during the first post-war period (second only to customs duties revenues), will be examined later.

Given the regularity with which Canada's Dominion governments created debt to finance their spending, the post-war periods of debt reduction stand out as exceptional. It remains to analyze more closely the tax choices that governments made as part of the process of generating surpluses. What motivated politicians to choose "painful" taxation in order to reduce the national debt? The present chapter attempts to account for such "uncharacteristic" government behaviour.

Chart 7-2

National Debt Peaks and Troughs, as a percentage of GNP, Canada, 1870-1989.

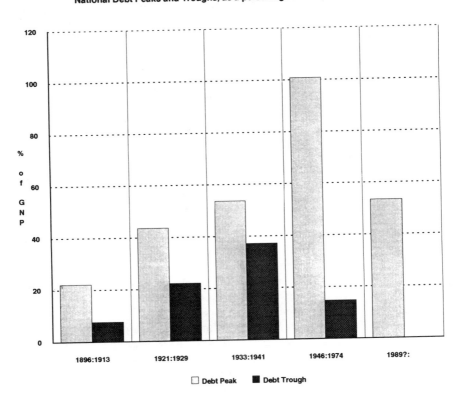

Source: Table C-3

Chart 7-3

Major Revenue Sources After the Two Great Wars, as a percentage of Total Financial Requirements (TFR), Canada, Fiscal 1921, 1924, 1929 and 1947 , 1949 , 1951.

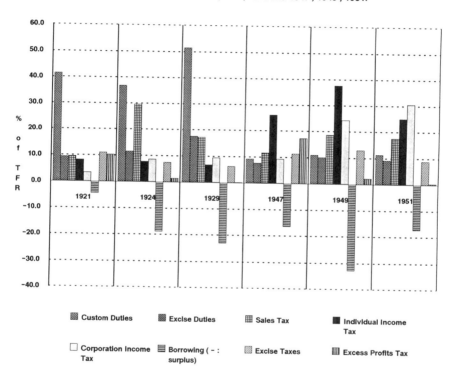

| Custom Duties | Excise Duties | Sales Tax | Individual Income Tax |
| Corporation Income Tax | Borrowing (- : surplus) | Excise Taxes | Excess Profits Tax |

Source: Table B-3

The argument will proceed in two stages. First, I develop a five-part hypothesis to account for government debt reduction strategies and tax choices during the two post-war periods. Second, I draw upon the available evidence to support this hypothesis. The major conclusions are summarized in a final section.

In Search of the Taxing Strategy

The foregoing section describes two extraordinary periods in Canada's fiscal history. After each war a demand for debt reduction emerged and persisted for an extended period of time. Two separate political forces created this demand. The wartime increase in patriotism, that was reinforced by the exhortations of wartime Finance Ministers, was reversed in the post-war periods. Patriotic holders of war bonds, victory bonds or war savings certificates, were likely to redeem them as soon as the war was over. I noted in the previous chapter the anxious attempts of wartime Finance Ministers, to persuade such debt-holders to retain their holdings. With the cessation of hostilities many debt-holders no longer had a "patriotic" reason to hold war bonds paying a lower rate of interest than alternative instruments. They cashed in their bonds. Given the substantial increase in wartime borrowing by the government, there was a large potential demand for debt redemption from the bondholders themselves.

There is a second potential source of demand for debt reduction. It must first be acknowledged that such a demand carries a price: an increase in taxes or a decrease in benefits from some government spending, or a combination of both. It is therefore not clear why any voter, other than the patriotic holders of war bonds, would voice such a demand.

However, a voter might well demand a public sector capable of responding to, and managing, instability in the economy and crises of a political or economic nature. Such a collective consumption good, like national defence and environmental protection, would be provided by the public sector, financed by revenues extracted from voters.[6] For the most part, therefore, such a public good would be provided as part of the total expenditures of the government in question, financed by revenues raised from the various revenue sources — including borrowing — that facilitate the minimization of total political costs.

Suppose, however, that a voter believes that at some "magnitude" the public debt itself poses a threat to stability in the economy and to the government's ability to respond to, and manage, instability or other crises. For example, the larger the debt is in relation to national income, the more difficult and costly it is to issue still more debt in order to finance stabilization policy initiatives for the purpose of managing a prolonged recession. The larger are the interest payments on the national debt as a fraction of total government expenditures, the more difficult it is for a government to effect the emergency or extraordinary expenditures that would enable it to handle a crisis without decreasing other essential government services.

The "magnitude" at which this perceived threat is believed to occur may be some absolute dollar level, or some relative level (the public debt in relation to national income), or even some high rate of increase in the public debt. Such a voter will be prepared to support financially a reduction in the debt. As the "magnitude" of the debt increases more voters may come to believe in the perceived threat, and eventually this conviction will stimulate a demand for debt reduction so large that a government will ignore it at its own peril.

Dominion government expenditures during the two great wars were financed heavily by borrowing, with a consequent rapid increase in the magnitude of the debt.[7] After the wars, those voters who perceived the public debt itself as a threat to stability demanded debt reduction, and were prepared to incur the cost of financing it. These attitudes of voters and bondholders constituted a force favouring debt reduction that was an important element in the respective governments' taxing strategy during the two post-war periods.

The second element of the tax strategy, especially during the early years of the post-war periods, consisted of a reduction in tax rates on those revenue sources that had been used most extensively to finance the war effort. The "old tax is a good tax" principle had served to raise effective tariff rates and greatly increase effective income tax rates during the first and the second great war respectively. Those very increases provided increasing opposition towards the end of each war period and created a potential demand for tax reduction on the part of the voters most affected. This demand provided the political incentive for post-war governments to lower tax rates significantly on some revenue sources. With the cessation of hostilities, the relative political costs of taxing these revenue sources, as compared with other revenue sources, were sufficiently high for governments to respond with major tax rate reductions.

Debt reduction and tax reduction comprise the first two elements of the taxing strategy of post-war governments. The political response to the competing demands for such action can be viewed as a "use of funds", whereby available revenues were used to reduce the federal debt and to lessen the tax burdens on those voters whose revenue sources had been taxed most heavily during the two wars. The remaining three elements of the taxing strategy concern the "sources of funds" that post-war governments drew upon in order to respond to the conflicting demands of the voters.

There was a large reduction in post-war government spending, as the war machine was rapidly dismantled. This reduction in war- and defence-related expenditures, especially during the early post-war years, made available substantial revenues that could be used to redeem the debt, or to reduce tax rates or finance increased spending on peacetime public expenditures. With the exception of veterans' pensions and, after the second great war, the introduction of family allowance payments and federally financed education, revenues were devoted to debt reduction and tax reduction. The observed behaviour of the early post-war governments is consistent with the absence of any major increase in voter demand for new peacetime government spending projects.[8]

The second source of funds in the taxing strategy of post-war governments was the introduction of a new tax and increases in effective tax rates on existing revenue sources. The government introduced a sales tax in 1920, at the same time as it was reducing effective tariff rates. Towards the latter part of the second post-war period the government raised tax rates on most revenue sources — including the manufacturers' sales tax. The Korean war, and defence-related expenditures during fiscal 1950–52 influenced the government's taxing strategy, and I return to this point later in the chapter. Nevertheless, it is noteworthy that governments during the two post-war periods chose a sales tax to help fund a reduction in the debt. These governments' sales tax policies constitute an element in taxing strategy that warrants further analysis.

The third source of funds utilized for this strategy, especially during the latter half of each post-war period, was the revenue buoyancy of a rapidly growing economy. The potential increase in revenues due to economic growth is a passive response of the existing tax structures that can be used to redeem the debt, to reduce effective tax rates or to finance increased peacetime spending. In the middle and late 1920s tax rates on many revenue sources were reduced and the debt was reduced. During the early 1950s tax rates were increased, government spending increased and the debt was reduced.

In summary, I hypothesize that five major elements formed the taxing strategy during the two post-war periods. A strong demand for debt reduction, one of the legacies of the wars, led governments to extract budgetary surpluses and pay off some of the debt. Vocal opposition to high wartime taxes led these governments to reduce effective tax rates considerably on those very revenue sources. The revenues that provided the source for these reductions came from large decreases in wartime government expenditures, a new sales tax and increased tax rates on some revenue sources and revenue buoyancy due to a growing economy.

Tax Choices During the Post-War Periods

There is evidence to support this five-part hypothesis concerning taxing strategy. The following discussion is based on the actions of governments of the day with respect to tax structure changes, the presentation of tax structure policy by the Minister of Finance and the parliamentary debates surrounding the budget speech.

The Demand for Debt Reduction

The persistent, sizeable budgetary surpluses during the two post-war periods suggest that debt reduction was not an unexpected or random result, but rather the outcome of active policy choices made by governments. The demand for debt reduction became a strongly articulated objective of governments during the 1920s, and constituted a reversal of the observed debt policy of both political parties from 1867 through the end of the first great war. Sir Henry Drayton became the first Canadian Minister of Finance to advocate and pursue a policy of debt reduction. He worried about the "pyramid of debt" and saw it as his "duty . . . to promote measures which will reduce the national debt".[9] Fielding returned as Finance Minister in the Liberal government of 1922, devoted to making "strenuous efforts to guard against increasing" the debt.[10] Throughout the 1920s, budget speeches reiterated the desire to reduce the debt; and as large surpluses were allocated to the achievement of this purpose, Finance Ministers took special care to claim credit for the happy outcome.[11]

Before the first great war, Finance Ministers regarded an increase in the national debt as a natural, normal phenomenon for a young country. Fielding, one of the few Finance Ministers to preside over some reductions in the national debt during the first fifty years of the Dominion, even hastened to assure Parliament that such reductions were not to be expected in the normal course of events. After the first war, debt reduction became a policy objective and budgetary policy was fashioned, in part, to achieve it; moreover, surpluses were generated and the debt was reduced.

The demand for debt reduction re-emerged at the end of the second war, as various Ministers of Finance formulated a policy thrust designed to "extinguish our deficit as rapidly as possible", to "reduce the national debt in good times" and to apply the surplus to "paying off the debt".[12] Finance Minister Abbott continued to express great pleasure, using his surpluses to reduce the national debt over the next few years.[13] This declared government policy could have been the result of an increased demand for debt reduction. In a qualitative analysis it is difficult to be more precise. However, the rapid rate of debt expansion during each great war, whether it is expressed in absolute levels or proportionately to the size of the economy as demonstrated in Charts 7-1 and 7-2, lends provisional support to the explanation.[14]

The Demand for Tax Reduction

Effective rates were reduced on the major tax revenue sources immediately after each great war. There were major reductions in tariff rates in 1920, 1922 and 1924, especially during the latter two years, on farm implements and some other primary industry implements and tools.[15] In other words, tariff rates were reduced at a time when governments were asserting the necessity of reducing the level of the national debt. Moreover, the tariff reductions of 1922 and 1924 resembled selective tax cuts from the general levels of the tariff aimed at satisfying opposition groups who might inflict significant political penalties: primarily western farmers who demanded free trade, especially in agricultural implements and machinery.

That the government chose selective tax cuts rather than reductions in the general level of the tariff suggests a desire to reduce political costs associated with particular groups, while maintaining substantial revenues from the tariff which could be used to effect some debt reduction. The minority Liberal government was at that time attempting to gain the support of the Progressives and to "woo the West".[16] The sharp recession of 1920–21, and the substantial tariff cuts of 1924, explain most of the two declines in the share of total revenues accounted for by customs duties revenues in fiscal 1922 and fiscal 1925.[17]

Immediately after the second war the Minister of Finance moved quickly to ease the tax burdens on personal and corporate incomes. The October 1945 and June 1946 budgets introduced major reductions in personal income tax rates and excess profits tax rates, at a time when the budget was still in a substantial deficit position.[18] The surpluses of 1947–1949 permitted the national debt to be reduced; but the major tax reductions of the 1947 and 1949 budgets, and the more modest tax reductions of the 1948 budget, reduced the size of the potential surpluses.

That tax reduction was preferred to debt reduction in the early part of the second post-war period was emphasized in Ilsley's earliest peacetime budget:

> Faced with the present fact of a very large deficit . . . and with the prospect
> of declining expenditures, it may well seem prudent to maintain our rev-

enues, reduce our borrowings and extinguish our deficit as rapidly as possible . . . but there are other considerations which claim attention.

(Ilsley, 1945:5)

These "other considerations" included the high level of personal income taxes, and Ilsley reduced such taxes by 16 per cent. In 1946 he reduced personal and corporation income taxes, while acknowledging that such action might aggravate inflationary tendencies already existing in the economy.[19] In 1947, Finance Minister Abbott emphasized still more strongly the importance of tax reductions, as he argued,

> From some points of view it can be strongly argued that under the prevailing . . . conditions we should concentrate upon the maximum reduction of the national debt . . . It is a sensible and far-sighted policy to reduce the national debt in good times . . . [but] even after the substantial reductions made in the last two budgets, *the present level of personal income taxes is regarded as excessive by a large proportion of the public.*
>
> (Abbott, 1947:11, emphasis added)

In this year, he effected another major reduction in personal income taxes. His 1948 budget introduced modest tax reductions at a time when inflationary pressures were still acknowledged as a problem.[20]

The Reduction in Government Spending

Of the three elements of the taxing strategy that provided the sources of funds for debt and tax reduction in the post-war periods, the most straightforward and self-explanatory is the reduction in government expenditures related to the fighting of the war. However, the nature of the expenditures that were cut by a substantial amount may have helped substantially to create widespread political agreement on the observed reduction in the debt. A demand for debt reduction by voters who perceived the "magnitude" of the debt as a threat to the ability of government to respond to future crises would lead a government to respond by paying off some of the debt. A government that knew it could cut defence expenditures, because the need for them had fallen, would encounter much less political opposition than, say, a peacetime government attempting to respond to a demand for debt reduction, while facing conflicting voter preferences with respect to cuts in government programs or projects.

Widespread political agreement of the kind referred to above may be a factor explaining why sustained debt reduction has only occurred in the aftermath of war. There may have been other times in Canada's fiscal history when a strong voter demand for debt reduction existed, accompanied, however, by little or no agreement as to how the costs should be distributed. By way of anticipation (see Chapter 10) it may be remarked that lack of such a political agreement seems to be restraining the finance ministers of the 1980s and the 1990s from reducing the annual amount of deficit financing, much less reducing the size of the debt.

Tax Rate Increases

A new tax, and increases in many tax rates, during the two post-war periods provided another major source of funds for debt reduction and the lowering of tases on other revenue sources. A noteworthy feature of the tax policy of that time is the introduction of a general sales tax in 1920, followed by rapid increase in its rate to 6 percent by fiscal 1924, which brought its share of total financial requirements to 30 percent (second only to customs duties revenues at 37 percent).[21]

The two-stage sales tax was introduced in 1920 with very little critical opposition. The opposition's concerns, with the exception of some mention of pyramiding, were centred on opposing the extensive package of luxury excise taxes which were introduced at the same time.[22] On the other hand, the increase in sales tax rates in the 1921 budget generated a sustained attack in Parliament, directed especially to the vertical equity aspects of the tax. Mr. McMaster reflected the critical tone of this attack when he argued:

> One of the first maxims of taxation is that the taxes should be determined by the ability of the taxpayer; they should be ability taxes, rather than consumption taxes. Now this [sales tax] is a consumption tax . . . you are placing this tax most heavily on precisely those people who should not be called upon to bear it.
> (McMaster, *House of Commons Debates*, May 10, 1921:3169–3170)[23]

The tax was also criticized for its alleged pyramiding effect and its similarities to "high protection in disguise".[24]

By the time of the 1922 budget the Liberals had replaced the Conservatives, but a new party, the Progressives, held the balance of power in the House. Fielding returned to his old post as Minister of Finance and increased the sales tax rates by 50 percent, asserting, as he pointed to the very substantial expected revenues of $90–100 million, that "no matter what custom duty you might have at the present time, you would need to have a sales tax".[25] In the budget debate that followed, the tax increases came under heavy attack. Concern over the regressive features of the tax was expressed persistently and forcefully. Mr. Crerar, of the Progressive Party, reflected the concerns of many members when he argued:

> A sales tax is unsound for the reason that it does not bear fairly upon those who have to pay it . . . the person who has the smallest income and is least able to pay this tax has to pay a share altogether out of proportion to his ability . . . In that respect the tax is unfair.
>
> (Crerar, *House of Commons Debates*, June 5, 1922:2462)

J.S. Woodsworth, who called the sales tax, "inherently vicious in principle", reflected the outrage that some members of Parliament and their constituent voters felt at the imposition of the tax.[26]

The sales tax rate increases were also criticized for being too large. Some Conservative critics found this a useful, if self-serving argument, since their party had first introduced the tax. But these critics were not alone; there emerges from the budget debate a strong sense of opposition to the size of the rate increase, even though the need to find additional revenues was acknowledged.[27]

Two months before the next budget H.H. Stevens called for a select committee to investigate the "difficulties of administration and collection" of the sales tax; his proposal formed part of a lengthy speech on the existing administrative problems of the tax and a conversion of the tax into a single-stage levy.[28] The debate that ensued seemed unique, for there was agreement on all sides of the House that the most urgent taxation problem was to raise more money "in a manner that will be as little objectionable as possible to the public at large",[29] and that there did exist administrative difficulties with the sales tax and inequities as between various different kinds of businesses. There was no discussion of the regressive features of the tax, although the former minister, Sir Henry Drayton, criticized the government for setting the rates too high.[30] The benefits of "fiscal illusion" embedded in the sales tax were not however, lost on Mr. Stevens, as he noted,

> . . . the general public prefer to pay a tax that does not appear under their noses specified as a tax. . . . I think everyone who has had any experience with it at all will admit that. Now, I know that a great many pseudo-economists who are very anxious to stir up discord will tell the consumers that this mysterious imposition of a tax in an intangible and undefined form has some criminal or some immoral taint about it. That, I think is a fallacy.
>
> (Stevens, *House of Commons Debates*, March 7, 1923:918)[31]

Finance Minister Fielding responded sympathetically to the complaints about administrative difficulties and inequities across business, but downplayed the vocal opposition to the tax as a temporary phenomenon:

> Taxation is not popular. New taxation is particularly objectionable. If your taxation has been in force for a number of years, . . . the people get accustomed to it and *cease to complain about it, but new taxes always bring forth a new cry against them*, and that is the situation regarding the sales tax.
>
> (Fielding, *ibid*:919, emphasis added)

This is a variant of the principle, "an old tax is a good tax".

The Minister's budget speech of May 11, 1923 did accept a one-stage manufacturers' sales tax at a uniform rate of 6 percent, effective January 1, 1924.[32] In this way, one source of concern, the administrative difficulties of the sales tax, was addressed. In the debate that followed the tax rate was again criticized as being too high and burdensome, and concerns over pyramiding of the tax and its regressive nature, were expressed.[33] The Minister continued to defend the sales tax rate increases as necessary to forestall further debt increases:

> I simply declare that the right thing to do . . . was to increase taxation in some form or other to meet [our obligations]. We increased the sales tax. If we had been willing to . . . allow the whole burden to be added to the public debt, we need not have increased the sales tax. But we did increase it, and we did so for good reasons.
>
> (Fielding, *House of Commons Debates*, May 23, 1923:3078)

The substantial rate increases were very productive of revenues. The strength of the tax during these first few years can be seen in Charts 4-1 and 4-4 in Chapter 4. Sales tax revenues, in relation to national income rise rapidly until 1924. As as a percent of total financial requirements they increase sharply, to account for 29 percent of total financial requirements by 1924. The rate increases were also productive of increasing political opposition within Parliament. Successive governments responded to charges of regressivity by expanding exemptions under the tax, but the high rate continued to generate opposition. It is more than likely that by 1924 the political costs of sales tax revenue had increased much more than expected and the tax structure was out of political equilibrium.

No new tax or increase in effective tax rates occurred immediately after the end of the second great war. However, during fiscal 1950–1952, with government expenditures increasing significantly because of the defence-related spending associated with the Korean war, tax rates on a wide selection of revenue sources were raised.[34] The 1950 budget increased excise duties on spirits and excise taxes, and raised the corporation income tax rate by 5 percent.[35] The 1951 budget increased excise duties on cigarettes and excise taxes, introduced a 20 percent defence surcharge on personal and corporate income taxes, and, for the first time since 1936, increased the manufacturers' sales tax rate from 8 to 10 percent.[36]

The 1952 budget increased the effective tax rate on personal and corporate incomes by means of the new old age security taxes. The old age security taxes were introduced as part of the funding of the universal old age security pensions, a new federal expenditure program that began in 1952. The OAS taxes are shown separately, as one of the other revenue sources in Charts 4-3 and 4-6 of Chapter 4, although they comprise in effect revenues from the personal income tax, the corporation income tax and the manufacturers' sales tax.[37]

Given the determination with which the government had reduced taxes on persons and corporations during the immediate post-war years, it seems all the more significant that the legislated tax rate increases of 1950–52 not only generated sufficient revenues to cover the increased expenditures related to the Korean war, but also generated surpluses that would be devoted to reducing the debt. In this respect, Canada's Korean war expenditures were 100 per cent financed by tax revenues, while the national debt continued to be reduced.

The Korean war period was therefore a time in which the government was determined to finance the additional war-related expenditures through additional tax revenues and to increase tax rates when necessary:

> Two of the principles enunciated [in Mr. Ilsley's war budget of 1939] are particularly apposite today. The first is that a "pay-as-you-go" policy should be followed to the limits of political and administrative practicability. The second is that to choose or to wander into inflationary methods of financing would be the most unjust of all methods of distributing the cost of any sharp increase in government expenditures . . . *Present conditions . . . call for . . . a prompt and effective anti-inflationary program . . . we* as a government *must fully and amply cover the whole of our expenditure by taxation* and other budgetary revenue . . . To plan to do less than this would be both irresponsible and a fraud on the public.
> (Abbott, 1950b:419, 420, emphasis added)

The Minister responded to the situation by increasing the taxes referred to previously. He continued with across-the-board increases in many tax rates in 1951 and 1952.

Among the many tax rates increased during the 1950–1952 period was the manufacturers' sales tax. The government's sales tax policy had remained virtually unchanged since the tax rate increase to 8 percent in 1936. It is true that major exemptions were allowed and then discontinued during the second great war, only to be reinstated in the immediate post-war period.[38] However, throughout that entire period, finance ministers refrained from increasing the sales tax rate, and made a virtue of their restraint, arguing that such increases would have been a hidden regressive burden.[39] In the context of the wartime thrust for fair and equitable taxes, the manufacturers' sales tax was the only major revenue sources that was not drawn upon for additional funds during the second great war.

On the other hand, it was drawn upon during the Korean war period. Finance Minister Abbott prepared the way for viewing it in a more favourable light by arguing in his second 1950 budget speech that,

> I should point out . . . that our present sales tax, particularly with its almost total exemption of food, fuel and building materials, does not deserve many of the criticisms that have been levelled against it.
>
> (Abbott, 1950b:423)

By 1951 the Minister had strengthened the tone of his argument:

> . . . contrary to the frequent assertions, the sales tax does not strike a higher proportion of expenditures of the low income group . . . To say that our sales tax is a harsh regressive tax simply is not true . . . *the fair thing at this time is to increase the sales tax.*
>
> (Abbott, 1951:16, emphasis added)

He proceeded to raise the rate from 8 to 10 percent.

Abbott overturned the sales tax policy of his predecessors, Ralston and Ilsley, by arguing it was a fair tax. He increased the rate to finance, in part, war-related expenditure increases, whereas his predecessors had carefully avoided such action when facing very much larger war-related expenditures. The absence of price controls during the Korean war period removed one constraint that had inhibited his predecessor during the second great war. The presence of a debt reduction objective during the Korean war period imposed a constraint that had not concerned his predecessors. These changes may have been sufficient to spur him to utilize the manufactures' sales tax revenue source more intensively.

The strengthened role of the sales tax is observed in Charts 4-1 and 4-4 in Chapter 4. The sales tax indicator — sales tax revenues relative to the size of the economy — rises during the early 1950s to regain its position of the mid-to-late 1930s. The revenue share indicator rises sharply from 4 percent of total financial requirements to its post-war high of 18 percent.

The sales tax rate increase helped to generate the surpluses that were used to reduce the debt in a time of 100 per cent pay-as-you-go war financing. It can therefore be concluded that the sales tax policy that facilitated debt reduction during fiscal 1950–52 was similar in its thrust to the sales tax policy of 1920–23, for this policy too accommodated substantial debt reduction.

Income Growth and Revenue Buoyancy

The third source of funds, and the final element in the five-part taxing strategy of governments after each great war was the revenue buoyancy of a rapidly growing economy. That the ministers of finance planned to take account of that revenue buoyancy is clear from the policy thrust of their budget speeches. That they responded by decreasing tax rates during the late 1920s and increasing tax rates during the early 1950s reflects differing structural and political circumstances during the two periods.

The economic environment that faced budget makers changed substantially during the 1920s. The early part of the period, even after the sharp recession of 1920–21, was one of sluggish growth and low revenue buoyancy. Thus governments could not rely upon the tendency of tax revenues from existing sources to rise automatically through time.[40] By 1923 the Minister of Finance was "hopeful" that increased business activity would generate sufficient revenues to offset proposed tax reductions.[41] This hope became reality and finance ministers came to rely upon continued economic expansion and buoyant tax revenues throughout the remainder of the 1920s.[42] The economic expansion did in fact continue unabated in this period, with real per capita income increasing by about one third.[43]

With employment, incomes, consumption and trade increasing, the respective bases of these revenue sources were increasing, thus generating automatic increases in government revenues. Selective tariff rate cuts, as we noted previously, were provided for agricultural implements and some other primary production machinery in 1926, 1928, 1929 and 1930. Some excise taxes were repealed or reduced. The personal income tax rate and the corporation profits tax rate were reduced in the 1926, 1927 and 1928 budgets. Finally, the manufacturers' sales tax rate was reduced in 1924, 1927, 1928, 1929 and 1930.[44]

The major tariff rate reductions, and especially the substantial selective tariff cuts on inputs used by farmers, represented a policy that had continued throughout the 1920s. The minority Liberal government had lost seats in the House by the time Finance Minister Robb presented his April 1926 budget. The announced tariff reductions were intended to accomodate farmers' opposition to tariffs and to take account of the presence in the House of members of the Progressive Party, who pressed those views vigorously.[45] Budget debates of the time reflected strong opposition to tariffs or taxes on the farmer and support for reductions or exemptions on inputs or consumption goods used by the farmers.[46]

Reductions and/or elimination of the special wartime excise taxes and the luxury excises also constituted a tax structure policy that had continued throughout most of the 1920s. As general revenue buoyancy came to characterize the latter part of the decade, Finance Minister James Robb took pleasure in announcing the move to "abolish nuisance taxes" completely.[47]

The personal and corporation tax rate reductions were the first since the introduction of the two taxes in the summer of 1917. The personal income tax had generated complaints and criticisms during the early 1920s, but no major change in rate structure or exemptions was introduced.[48] The 1926 budget had to gain support of the Progessives and pave the way for an election expected in the near future. The substantial increase in exemptions removed many low-income taxpayers from the tax rolls and was intended to appeal to Labour and Progressive members of Parliament. The reduction would moderate the opposition to the tax by middle-income taxpayers. Finally, the inclusion of dividends in the definition of income for tax purposes, while unwelcome news for wealthy taxpayers, would appeal to the Progressives (I return to this feature of the tax changes in Chapter 8 below).

It is worth noting that this early package of tax changes enacted at a time of increased revenue buoyancy, broadened revenue bases while increasing exemptions and reducing tax rates. The Prime Minister intended that the budget be politically attractive in a minority situation, and popular among the electorate.[49] The budget did in fact win the support of the Progressives, and the Liberals were returned with a majority government in the election of September 14, 1926.

The personal and corporation income tax reductions of 1926, 1927 and 1928, coupled with the growing incomes of the time, resulted in direct taxes just maintaining a constant share in financing total requirements: approximately 7 percent for personal income taxes and 10 percent for corporation profits taxes.[50] The personal income tax was still restricted to higher-income taxpayers and therefore its actual revenue base was modest, even though it was growing because of economic growth in the economy.

As previously mentioned, governments had during the early 1920s, increased the sales tax rate rapidly from 1 to 6 percent and sales tax revenues had risen to 30 percent of total financial requirements by fiscal 1924. By January 1, 1924 the two-stage turnover tax had been reformed into a one-stage manufacturers' sales tax. The budget of April 10, 1924 for the first time, reduced the sales tax rate.[51]

This reduction in the sales tax rate, from 6 to 5 percent, and the increase in exemptions under the tax was, along with the tariff concessions discussed above, part of the Prime Minister's plan to attract the support of the Progressive and Labour members of Parliament, most of whom had been highly critical of the sales tax increases of the early 1920s.[52] These structural changes, announced well in advance of an expected 1925 election, may be interpreted as the behaviour of a minority government responding to increasing political opposition to a particular tax.

The political context of 1924–1926 established the inital structural changes in the sales tax. The revenue buoyancy of the latter part of the decade facilitated further reductions in the tax rate. In 1927 Finance Minister Robb articulated a policy aimed at reducing the tax rate gradually:

> . . . the proper method of reducing this sales tax — and I agree with my honourable friends that as fast as possible the sales tax should be taken off — is to take it off gradually so that it will do no harm to anyone . . . Everyone admits that the sales tax adds to the cost of each commodity, and with the sentiment that as quickly as possible we should get rid of the tax. We on this side of the House are in accord. That has been the policy of this government: we have been gradually reducing the sales tax.
>
> (Robb, *House of Commons Debates*, 1927:758 and 1290)

The tax rate reductions of 1927, 1928, 1929 and 1930 brought the rate down to one percent.[53] The dramatic decline in the importance of the sales tax in financing the government's spending is observed in Charts 4-1 and 4-4, referred to earlier. This was the only major tax source for which the revenue share declined by such a significant amount during the last half of the 1920s.

The continuously increasing share of excise duty revenues in total financial requirements reflected revenue buoyancy, as the economy expanded during the 1920s and boosted the revenue bases of the sin taxes. The relatively low political costs of taxing alcohol and tobacco products accounts for the rise in the share as the base expanded.[54] The government did not reduce excise duties.

The selective tariff cuts noted above were more than offset by an expansion in the base associated with growing world trade, which actually increased the share of customs duties revenues in total financial requirements.[55] The storm clouds of the great depression which were gathering by the end of 1929, had already begun to dampen this fair-weather revenue source by fiscal 1930. Up to this latter year the tariff's sensitivity to international prices, and the economic expansion that gathered potent force during the second half of the 1920s, returned the tariff to its overwhelming pre-eminence as a revenue-raiser (last observed in fiscal 1914).

The economic environment that faced budget makers immediately after the second great war was much more favourable than it had been after the first.[56] Income, consumption and trade grew, and with them the revenue bases of the various taxes automatically expanded, generating an increase in tax revenues.

Rapid economic growth and revenue buoyancy were an acknowledged part of the economic context within which finance ministers crafted their budgets and planned for surpluses during the post-war period. Finance Minister Abbott stated these conditions most forcefully in his 1947 budget:

> . . . our revenues now are very sensitive to any change in business conditions . . . [our] favourable situation [the existence of a surplus] . . . is due in a very large part to the generally favourable economic circumstances upon which our revenues so greatly depend.
>
> (Abbott, 1947:19)

This theme of great buoyancy of revenues was continued throughout the post-war budgets.[57]

The economy grew in real terms throughout the period, except in the year 1954. This rapid growth, coupled with the positive elasticity of government revenues, generated a large part of the revenue growth observed during the period.

In the first years of the period this automatic revenue growth facilitated the reductions in personal and corporation income tax rates previously referred to. Subsequently, however, and especially in the Korean war years 1950–1952, tax rates on many revenue sources were increased. The substantial difference in total government spending increases during the latter half of the period following each great war provides a major part of the explanation of observed differences in tax structure policy, even though economic growth was robust in both periods.

The government's desire to finance the Korean war defence expenditures on a pay-as-you-go basis could account for the across-the-board tax rate increases, discussed above. This major increase was coupled with cautious forecasts of economic growth and the concomitant rise in tax revenues. The economy grew more rapidly than expected and actual tax revenues exceeded the predicted estimates. Finance Minister Abbott referred in his 1952 budget speech to the difficulties of forecasting tax revenues in such unsettled times, but was "gratified" to be able to devote the resultant surpluses to debt reduction.[58] Scott Gordon notes the extent to which actual revenues exceeded forecast revenues, and actual budgetary balance exceeded forecast budgetary balance in each year from fiscal 1945–46 through 1953–54.[59] Fiscal 1950–1952 are unique years in Canada's fiscal history, because the surpluses generated to pay down the debt occurred when the government was effecting substantial increases both in spending and in tax rates on almost all revenue sources.

Conclusions:
Tax and Reduce the Debt

This discussion leads to three conclusions on the evolution of the revenue structure during each of the periods following the great wars. First, post-war governments persistently pursued a budgetary policy that enabled them to reduce the twin wartime legacies of high debt and onerous tax burdens. Second, in addition to the substantial reduction in war-related defence spending, the sources of finance used to effect this policy of debt and tax rate reduction were sales tax rate increases and a buoyant revenue system responding to a growing economy. Third, the various revenue structure changes during the post-war periods can be explained by changes in relative political cost functions at a time when the level and mix of government expenditures was changing dramatically. Post-war Canadian federal governments chose revenue structures that minimized the political costs of financing their spending and redeeming some of the national debt.

These findings differ from the general interpretation of Canada's financing of expenditures during the two post-war periods. These two extended periods are the only ones in Canada's one hundred and twenty-three year fiscal history in which ministers of finance not only planned to generate surpluses and reduce the debt but did, in fact, achieve these objectives. This was an important national government policy accomplishment and is neglected in the literature. Surplus generation and debt reduction during the 1920s are ignored.[60]

Surplus generation and debt reduction during the 1946–1954 period are acknowledged by some writers, but are not discussed as components of a major post-war policy thrust.[61] What is discussed as the most important of the second post-war period policy thrust is the adoption of Keynesian stabilization policy as an integral component of budget making. Nevertheless, I argue in this study that fiscal stabilization policy played a minor role in shaping the revenue structure of the federal government after the second great war.[62]

One view expressed in the literature has been that stabilization objectives and fiscal policy seen from a normative perspective, became very important features of post-war government policy, and had a major impact, both stabilizing the economy and shaping the revenue structure.[63] The view that budgets ought to be stabilizing has even been extended back through time and used to criticize earlier governments for not pursuing such a goal.[64]

Another approach has resulted in a much more critical evaluation of budgetary policy from a normative perspective, and a characterization of policy in the second post-war period as ineffective or perverse, insofar as the goal of stabilization is concerned.[65] Such studies have tried to determine how well the federal government used its taxing and spending policies as part of a desirable fiscal policy aimed at stabilizing the economy. Each study has covered slightly different time periods, used somewhat different criteria for ranking or evaluating policy, and employed some common and some different primary sources or methods of analysis. Even so, their conclusions have been remarkably similar: the most charitable assessment found fiscal policy adequate no more than forty percent of the time, whereas the least favourable found it to be perverse (destabilizing) at least forty percent of the time.[66]

This poor performance of fiscal policy as an instrument of economic stability can be more readily understood within a comprehensive positive model of revenue structure, in which stabilization is just one of the many objectives that governments attempt to pursue, and moreover, in which the other objectives carry larger political weight. Politicians may feel constrained by voter reactions. Election year budgets may be expansionary no matter what the economic climate may be. The voters' belief that large surpluses are "overtaxation" and large deficits spell "fiscal irresponsibility or ruin" can prevent a finance minister from increasing tax rates during inflationary times and decreasing them in recessions.[67]

The present study provides an explanation for observed budgetary policy and revenue structure changes after the second great war. Keynesian fiscal stabilization policy had a minor influence on the revenue policy of federal governments;[68] the active pursuit and achievement of surpluses and debt reduction was much more important during the first nine years. This period of debt reduction, and the period of debt reduction after the first great war, stand in marked contrast with the remaining one hundred and five years of Canadian fiscal history.

This study accounts for revenue structure changes that have been observed but not explained by others. For example, some writers have noted the significant reduction in tariff rates after the first great war and in personal income tax rates after the second.[69] This study explains such reductions within a comprehensive model of revenue structure, with strong public opposition focused on these two heavily criticized wartime taxes. This approach is illuminating during the early years of the first post-war period, in which tariff cuts were combined with the introduction of a new sales tax and substantial increases in its rates.

Over 1924–1926 the manufacturers' sales tax rate, the personal income tax rate and the corporation income tax rate were reduced for the first time since the birth of these taxes. This study explains these reductions in terms of a political response to increasing opposition to such high taxes during a minority government period prior to an expected election, when a more rapidly growing economy was stimulating revenue buoyancy.

The sales tax rate was increased during the Korean war period, in contrast with its constancy during the second great war. The present study accounts for these differences by way of the strong policy thrust for debt reduction after the second great war and the absence of price controls during 1950–1952.

Finally, the contribution of the new sales tax in the early 1920s, and the post-war reduction in government expenditure in both periods have been noted by others as factors that helped reduce the high level of wartime taxes. However, a complete picture of the important role of the three major sources of financing the post-war debt reduction and tax rate reduction has not emerged. The present study focuses on these three major sources of funds: the dramatic reduction in defence-related spending, the critically important contribution of the sales tax, and the revenue buoyancy that accompanied the strong performance of the economy.

Of these three sources of funds for financing extensive debt reduction, only the large reduction in defence-related government expenditures is uniquely related to wartime spending. During peacetime a government determined to reduce the debt could still rely on the sales tax and, with luck, a growing economy. However, any planned reduction in government expenditures would face the opposition of voters whose benefits were being reduced. I, for one, would expect that peacetime debt reduction, as a political objective, would be much more difficult to achieve than immediate post-war debt reduction.

Chapter 8

Financing Depression

Introduction

The previous chapter analyzed the unique combination of circumstances that led to a substantial reduction in the national debt after each of the two great wars. This chapter continues the analysis of the evolution of government revenue structure in peacetime with an examination of the deficit financing and tax choices during the great depression of the 1930s.

The Canadian economy experienced a major disruption during the depression. National income dropped 50 percent between 1928 and 1933. Unemployment soared from a trivial 2 percent in 1929 to 20 percent in 1933. The value of imports plummeted by 69 percent over the same period. By 1939 national income was still short of the level it had been a decade earlier.[1]

Dominion spending grew modestly over the 1930s as a whole.[2] By historical standards the government spending increases were not unduly large.[3] Government expenditures, as a percentage of national income (presented in Chart 1-2), rose during the early years of the great depression because national income fell sharply.[4]

The interesting fiscal action during the great depression of the 1930s centred on the financing of this spending. Chart 8-1 provides a snapshot of the major revenue sources for selected years during the great depression. Customs and excise revenues plunged during the first few years.[5] The debt reduction of the 1920s gave way to new borrowing and deficit financing emerged as a very important financing source. The general sales tax, declining in importance in the late 1920s, got a new lease on life, to such an extent that it had become the pre-eminent revenue source by fiscal 1938. The corporation income tax declined in importance until the mid-1930s and then increased its share of total income significantly. The personal income tax share was approximately constant until the late 1930s, during which it rose slightly.[6]

It is these substantial revenue structure changes that merit analysis within the conceptual framework of this study. In the present chapter I first examine the borrowing choices and then review the tax choices of governments during the depression. The major findings are contrasted with the existing literature in a concluding section.

Back to Borrowing

Deficit financing quickly emerged as the major source of government financing during the early years of the depression. The surpluses of the 1920s vanished, to be replaced by very substantial borrowing to finance the spending of the government. In the fiscal period 1932–1936 deficit financing accounted for at least one-quarter of total financing.[7] Deficit financing tapered off somewhat after fiscal 1936, but in general it was a substantial source of funds during the depression years.

This response was not significantly different from that of governments during the earlier great depression of 1873–1896.[8] I have not examined this latter period in detail, but the reader will recall from Chapter 3 the budgetary policies of finance ministers which were aimed at keeping indirect tax rates low in order to encourage immigration. Deficit financing was used regularly to finance government spending throughout this period. Chart 1-2 in Chapter 1 illustrated the rise both in the spending indicator, reflecting in part declining national income, and in borrowing as a proportion of national income. This increase in borrowing resulted in the first of the five waves of debt creation illustrated in Charts 7-1 and 7-2 of the previous chapter.

During both great depressions national income fell; so did the value of imports and customs duties revenues automatically fell with them, causing governments to search out additional sources of finance. During both periods borrowing became a much more important source of financing government spending.

What distinguished the depression of the 1930s from that of 1873–1896 (or the entire period preceding the first great war, for that matter) was that finance ministers pursued a policy of active deficit financing but called for a move towards a balanced budget. The reader will recall from the discussion in Chapter 4 that after the first great war, finance ministers altered their views on deficit financing, and called for — and pursued — debt reduction policies. The severity of the depression rendered it impractical to plan for the budget surpluses that could be used to reduce the national debt. Finance Ministers relied heavily on borrowing, but in their policy views they attached considerable importance to the achievement of a balanced budget.

Finance ministers Rhodes of the Conservatives during the first half of the depression and Dunning of the Liberals during the second half expressed similar views on desired budgetary policy. They both called for a balanced budget, claiming that their policies were moving the government accounts in that direction, and they argued that such balance was necessary for the return of prosperity.[9] Dunning's strong views on balancing the budget had the support of Prime Minister MacKenzie King

Chart 8-1

**Major Revenue Sources During the Great Depression,
as a percentage of Total Financial Requirements (TFR),
Canada, Fiscal 1931, 1932, 1933, 1935, 1938 and 1939.**

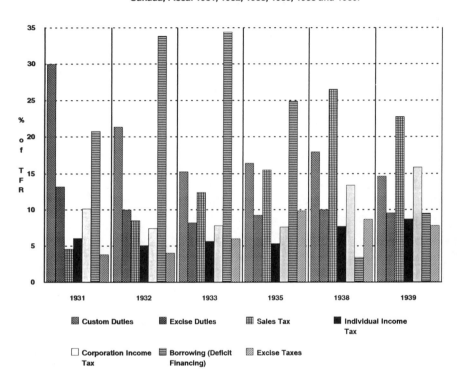

Source: Table B-3

throughout the preparations of the budgets of 1936, 1937 and 1938, although in the last of these three budgets King wanted a balanced budget in order that "tax reductions [could be] brought in before the election expected in 1939".[10]

This desire to balance the budget in a time of substantial deficits, was part of the context of depression borrowing and tax policies.

Tax Choices During the Depression

The economic environment of the 1930s set the scene in which governments eagerly sought for revenue. They tapped the bond market extensively as they quickly adapted to insufficient tax revenues by deficit financing. As indicated previously, they also drew on all of the major tax sources.

Acting as his own Minister of Finance Prime Minister Bennett, in June 1931, presented his first budget speech and set the tone of Conservative revenue-raising policy for the next four years. With regard to taxation policy he argued that

> Two principles have to be borne in mind; first . . . in a period of great depression departures from known practised methods of taxation should be as few as possible . . . The second is that taxes should be as light as possible, having regard to the conditions which prevail.
>
> (Bennett, 1931:54)

The use of the expression 'light taxes' implied that the government would be prepared to finance part of its spending by borrowing. Application of the maxim "an old tax is a good tax" meant that no major new revenue source would be tapped; instead, the existing revenue sources would be drawn upon more intensively.

The re-emergence of the sales tax as a major revenue-raiser during the 1930s laid to rest any wistful hope that the tax might wither away. The robust revenue-raising capacity of the sales tax during the early 1920s had clearly not been forgotten by the policy makers of the early 1930s; the same can be said, apparently, of the policy makers of the 1980s. With declining imports and incomes resulting in falling customs and income tax revenues, governments turned to the revenue source which was broadly based — even allowing for exemptions — had relatively low collection costs, and had been generating less opposition, mainly because of the declining rates of the late 1920s. Because of falling commodity prices, the substantial increase in the sales tax rate from one to four percent, announced in Bennett's 1931 budget speech, took some time to generate commensurate increases in revenues, even though the amount collected did rebound by the end of the fiscal year. Later increases in the sales tax rate, effected by both Conservatives and Liberals, brought the rate to 8 percent in 1936.

Prime Minister King's desire to use the 1938 budget to pave the way for a successful election, expected in 1939, led him to consider the sales tax, and he encouraged Dunning to lower the 8 percent rate to 6 percent just three days before the budget speech. Dunning responded two days later by suggesting the exemption of building materials. King praised this "admirable stroke" which would divert discussion away from tariff changes and would prove widely popular.[11]

The well-known volatility of the customs and excise duties, attributable to their dependence on incomes and prices, accounted for most of the automatic declines in tax revenues from these two sources. The strong revenue buoyancy of the tariff had, during the latter half of the 1920s, provided some of the scope for surpluses that were used to reduce the debt. As national income and prices fell during the early 1930s that same revenue buoyancy worked in reverse — revenues fell automatically.

The changes in the shares of these duties in total financial requirements reflected both revenue base elasticity and discretionary policy changes concerning rates.[12] The Conservatives returned to power in 1930 and tariff rates were raised towards the end of the year. The very substantial tariff increases introduced in the 1931 budget to protect domestic industry were the most significant since the 1879 National Policy Tariff.[13] In 1932 tariff rates were increased again. These very substantial tariff increases failed to halt the major decline in customs revenues during the early years of the depression. In the fiscal period 1934–1937 tariff rates were reduced.

The major excise duty change during the depression years was a reduction in the levy on spirits from $7 to $4 per gallon in 1935, representing an attempt to "protect our revenues . . . [by] eliminating illicit sales which would otherwise continue as a constant menace to our revenues".[14] The yield of such duties had fallen greatly since the boom days of the late 1920s, and lower spirit prices in the United States were encouraging smuggling and bootlegging as well.[15] Once again a Minister of Finance was acknowledging that costs of collection and compliance were shaping the actions he was taking in an attempt to increase revenues. Or, as Finance Minister Rhodes preferred to phrase it, "Our gain will be at the expense of the existing illicit trade".[16]

It has been pointed out that the personal income tax revenue share remained more or less constant, with a slight rise towards the end of the decade. Given that incomes fell during the early part of the 1930s, it is clear that effective tax rates had to be raised in order to generate this result. However, the first Conservative budget of the 1930s planned to reduce effective personal income tax rates. Bennett proposed (1) to apply a two percent income tax on investment income of non-residents; (2) to exempt "dividends from Canadian corporations, up to $10,000, . . . from taxation, to the extent of one half the income of the taxpayer"; and (3) to introduce a "somewhat increased" level of exemptions and a revised rate schedule that would start at "one percent with one percent added for each additional $1000 of income until the maximum . . . of 25 percent".[17] The last two proposals would have decreased effective tax rates for high-income taxpayers, with the highest marginal tax rate falling from 40 to 25 percent.

Dividends had been included in income for tax purposes in the 1926 Liberal budget. The Conservatives had immediately opposed such a move as "double taxation", and had expressed concerns that capital would seek out American investment opportunities where, even though the corporation income tax rate was higher, dividends received were free of tax. Bennett, then leader of the opposition, was one of the most persistent critics of this "double taxation" proposal:

> . . . if capital is to be twice taxed we shall find that people will refuse to invest in Canadian enterprises . . . and inevitably they will withdraw that money and invest it in the United States.
> (Bennett, *House of Commons Debates*, May 18, 1926:3517;
> see also 3516, and June 10, 1926:4306–4308)[18]

The business community had also opposed the inclusion of dividends in the definition of income and had continued their vocal opposition to such "double taxation" throughout the latter half of the 1920s.[19]

In these circumstances, it is hardly surprising that a Conservative Prime Minister would propose changing the tax treatment of dividends so that a dividend recipient

> . . . will not pay a second tax on his dividends, because it has already been paid through the tax paid by the company. That was the law at one time and is still the law in most countries.
> (R.B. Bennett, 1931:59)

The revenues foregone through this and the rate structure proposals were to be made up in part, as the reader will recall, by the stiff three-point increase in the sales tax rate announced in the same budget.

It is possible that the Conservative government of R.B. Bennett judged that the political benefits from effective income tax rate reductions for wealthy and business taxpayers would exceed, at the margin, the political costs of increasing sales tax revenues. If so, it made a serious political mistake. The opposition attack on this "rich man's budget" was relentless, and included criticisms that Mr. Bennett and his wealthy friends stood to benefit directly from the tax reductions.[20]

Bennett claimed during the budget debate that the proposed exemption levels and rate structure were prepared by the commissioner of taxation and "that bill was submitted to me on the night before the budget was presented". He added that he had no knowledge "at the moment what the effect of the proposed income tax legislation would have been upon my personal income tax".[21] This prompted one Mr. Euler to sympathize with the Prime Minister as a "very, very busy man" and to point out that

> . . . it is highly desirable . . . where legislation of such far-reaching importance, financial and otherwise, is to be introduced, that the finance minister should acquaint himself with the provisions of the proposed bill prior to its introduction.
>
> (*House of Commons Debates*, July 16, 1931:3857)

The Minister of Finance eventually withdrew the proposals and the government proved to have learned its lesson well. The personal income tax changes of the budgets of 1932, 1933 and 1935 all had the effect of increasing the effective tax rate on personal income. The budget of 1932 raised the highest marginal tax rate from 40 to 52.5 percent. The pre-election budget of 1935 announced a graduated surtax on investment income in excess of $5000 and on earned income in excess of $14,0000, and introduced a graduated gift tax to discourage gifts as an escape route from the higher tax rates.

Even with the reductions in personal exemptions contained in the 1932 and 1933 budgets, the personal income tax was still very much a tax on income recipients in the middle-upper and higher brackets. Given the narrow base of the tax the effective tax rate increases led to, at most, a very modest rise in the personal income tax share of the total financial requirements by the end of the decade. When this fact is considered together with the substantial rise in the sales tax share throughout the period and the significant increase in the corporation income tax share during the later years, it seems clear that the personal income tax was not utilized as a major revenue-raiser during the great depression.

These observations are consistent with the hypothesis that governments interpreted the political costs of additional personal income taxation as exceeding at the margin the political costs of additional sales taxation. A piece of indirect evidence can be found in the absence of further personal income tax rate increases when the Liberals returned to power after the 1935 election. The new government did, however, increase the sales tax rate from 6 to 8 percent in its budget of 1936.

Government utilization of the corporation income tax differed significantly from its handling of the personal income tax. As incomes and profits fell drastically during the first few years of the depression, revenues from the tax on corporation profits fell too. Governments responded by increasing the tax rate in 1931, 1932, 1933, 1935 and 1936. These tax structure changes, although accompanied by some improvement in the economy, did not result in an increase in corporation income tax revenues until fiscal 1935, but between then and the end of the decade the relative importance of the tax doubled, in terms of its contribution to total financial requirements. Bennett established in his 1931 budget the crucial significance of the corporation income tax as a revenue source when, under a strong opposition attack, he withdrew all his income tax proposals except the increase in the corporation income tax rate from 8 to 10 percent. Subsequent corporation income tax rate increases — not accompanied by much explanation or political opposition within the House — brought the rate to 15 percent by 1936.

The last revenue source of any significance consists of the excise taxes. These taxes had been declining in importance during the 1920s, and they reflected the commodity price decreases of the first three years of the depression.[22] The government responded by expanding the array of excises during the early part of the period, imposing a special excise tax of one percent on all imports in 1931, and raising it to three percent in 1932, and also imposing a special excise tax of 2 cents per pound of sugar in 1933.[23] These excises were gradually reduced or eliminated during the 1934–36 period.

Dominion governments did not make any sustained effort to seek out new revenue sources during the depression. However, several forays into new tax fields did take place, one of which is described below. It is consistent with the positive model of this study according to which, when the political cost curve of a previously untaxed revenue source falls, additional tax revenues became available to the goverment of the day at a very low cost.[24]

The President of the United States revalued gold from $20.67 to $35.00 an ounce in 1934, thereby generating a large windfall profit for the gold-mining industry. Finance Minister Rhodes drew attention, in his 1934 budget speech, to "the extraordinary increase in profits" for gold producers which were generated by "circumstances entirely external to this particular industry" and the "extraordinary gains which were the basis of this tax" in his 1935 budget. Rhodes also gave a detailed and reasoned explanation, based on costs of collection and compliance, of the reasons why it would be necessary to use an ad valorem tax on value rather than the theoretically preferable tax on excess profits from gold production.[25]

The Minister levied a tax of 10 percent on the value of gold "deposited at the Mint for sale" (all gold produced in Canada was so deposited). With great optimism, he stated that "it is believed that there can be no legitimate objection to [such] a tax".[26]

This optimism might have been based on the notion that any tax on "windfall" profits would have a neutral effect on the market, leaving allocative decisions unaltered. It is reasonable to suppose that a tax on unexpected extraordinary profits in the gold-producing industry, in addition to leaving investment and business decisions unaltered, would appear to the government as a low risk source of revenue, (politically speaking) extracted from a few taxpayers. In addition, voters could be informed that the gold tax would "replace the revenue lost by the reduction in the tax on sugar", an unpopular tax borne by most consumers.[27]

The Minister's confidence must have been short-lived. Opposition to the tax as a tax on production rather than a tax on excess profits, was manifested both inside the House and from the industry itself.[28] As a result the government was persuaded to change the structure of the tax. Three successive changes were made to the original proposal. First, the form of the tax was changed to a 25 percent levy on the difference between the old and the new price of gold. Second, it was restricted to those mines that paid dividends. Finally, a credit against the tax was allowed for income tax paid by gold mines on 1934 operations. The tax which Rhodes believed would meet no objections and would generate $10 million in additional revenues in actual fact generated considerable political pressure on the government and yielded $4 million;[29] it expired on May 31, 1935.

Consider, next, the package of tax policies contained in the pre-election budget of 1935. The budget announced reductions in the British preferential tariff, a very large decrease in the duty on spirits and the elimination of the special excise tax on imports entering under the British preferential tariff. In addition, Rhodes announced an increase in the corporation income tax rate, a new graduated surtax on investment income and a new graduated tax on gifts.[30] The tax reductions applied to a wide array of consumption and investment goods and one popular commodity, liquor. Many consumers would benefit, and western farmers would welcome the tariff reductions. The tax increases and new taxes would affect a small number of high-income taxpayers.[31]

This was a very political budget, intended to serve the same purpose as the 1917 introduction of the income tax: preservation of a Conservative government. Blair Neatby has argued that the aim of Bennett's New Deal broadcasts, made to the nation in January 1935, was to convince voters that the Conservative Party that he led was one of reform, devoted to measures that would spell "the end of *laissez-faire*" and produce active government intervention in many areas of policy.[32] Faced with a newly established socialist party and increasing Liberal strength in the provinces, the Conservatives sought to use the watchward "reform" as a means of retaining support.

The 1935 budget is consistent with an election strategy directed at reform-minded voters. The surtax on investment income and the graduated gift tax, were expected to dispel voters' fears, engendered by the embarrassing proposals contained in Bennett's first budget in 1931, that this government "favoured the wealthy", and also to appeal strongly to the same sectors of labour and agriculture that had pleaded for "conscription of wealth" prior to the summer of 1917 and supported the Conservative government when an income tax was introduced. This was most decidedly not a "rich man's budget", the charge levelled by the opposition during the 1931 budget debate. The reductions in commodity-based taxes noted above would benefit low- and middle-income voters, including the vitally important western farmers, and would alienate only smugglers and bootleggers.[33]

The New Deal "reform" strategy, and the 1935 political budget, were not sufficient to prevent the Conservatives from being defeated.[34] The tax policies of the 1935 budget survived, however, and were continued by the Liberal government of MacKenzie King. In 1936 the Liberals, who had often been vocal critics of the sales tax, increased the sales tax rate to 8 percent.

Conclusions:
Choosing the Revenue Mix
During the Depression

In conclusion, government revenue structure policy during the great depression exhibited several noteworthy features. First, building on the maxim that "an old tax is a good tax" or, in the terminology of this study, an old tax has a lower political cost at the margin than an untried new revenue source, the government fell back on two lifesavers to tide it through the stormy seas of the 1930s: deficit financing and the sales tax. As the sales tax revenue expanded and became the most important source of funds for the government, deficit financing was reduced.

Secondly, revenues from customs and excise duties fell; and while the protective tariff increases of the early 1930s did nothing to revive the former, a substantial reduction in liquor duties was partially successful in reviving excise revenues.

Third, governments of the 1930s, after a false start in 1931, increased effective tax rates on personal incomes just sufficiently to maintain the relative importance of the tax within the family of Dominion taxes, and raised corporation income tax rates high enough to strengthen the relative importance of the tax as a revenue raiser.

These major features of the revenue policy of the 1930s reflect a concerted set of policies, assembled with due regard to political costs aimed at generating additional revenues to meet a level of total government spending which was increasing only modetly in a period when revenues from the given tax structure were declining sharply. The government was in the fortunate position of having available to it a wide array of old taxes that could be drawn upon. When the government did attempt to to open up a new tax source — the gold tax — it did so because it expected that the political costs of introducing and collecting the tax would be low. Finally, the budget of 1935 was a pre-election political attempt to capture the support of those who were voicing a strong demand for vertical equity.

The search for additional revenues during the 1930s was neither haphazard nor indiscriminate. It reflected deliberate and cautious choice by governments from the available alternatives. The changing revenue mix resulting from their policies is reflected in Charts 4-4 and 4-5 of Chapter 4 and in Chart 8-1 in this chapter.

This interpretation of deficit financing and tax choices in the depression years, 1931–1939, differs from other interpretations in the literature. For the most part writers have interpreted the Dominion's search for revenues, and the parallel efforts of provincial and municipal governments, as a haphazard, chaotic, non-fiscal assault on the taxpayer, undertaken in order to minimize the deficit and balance the budget.

This interpretation is especially apparent in the very normative view of the Royal Commission on Dominion-Provincial Relations:[35]

> . . . the Dominion, faced successively with the emergencies of war, the financial débâcle of its developmental program, and the depression, turned to an *ad hoc* and somewhat indiscriminate imposition of taxes throughout nearly the whole field . . .

Ad hoc and indiscriminate tax policies do not need any explanation, and the Commission did not offer one. Tax policies which can be so characterized call for disapproval, and the Commission expressed disapproval:

> . . . when non-fiscal criteria become of dominant importance in shaping taxation policy, not only are new complexities and inequities introduced, but unexpected strains are thrown on other parts of the system . . .

As examples, the Commission referred to the protective customs tariff, "which ceases to be revenue-producing", tobacco and liquor taxes which are "frequently footballs of conflicting policies", and personal income taxes and succession duties, for which "the exemptions provided and the rate of progression are frequently determined by non-fiscal and non-economic influences and political pressures".[36] The Commission had, nevertheless, a strong preference for these last two taxes because they were the only "forms to which any scientific principles of progressivity can be applied".[37]

The Commission noted that

> . . . the present situation in Canadian public finance represents a wide departure from the conception of the Fathers of Confederation and from the spirit of the financial settlement which they devised.

With no analysis of how "political pressures" and "non-fiscal criteria" had played a role in bringing about such a state of affairs, it proceeded to call for "a better allocation of taxing powers and responsibilities". The failure of the Commission to understand the critically important role of these "political pressures" was a serious drawback; it reduced the probability that its recommendations on the distribution of taxing powers among the various levels of government would be accepted.[38] That, however, is the subejct for another time.

The Commission's report set the tone for the approaches of other analysts and later Finance Ministers to the tax policy of the 1930s. "Tax jungle" and "fiscal chaos" became the regular epithets to describe the supposed scramble for revenues by the provincial and Dominion governments.[39] Harvey Perry argues that the taxpayer

> . . . was attacked from all sides with violence that had no precedent . . . and the Canadian tax structure . . . was reduced to utter confusion . . . all jurisdictions turned on the taxpayer with an unprecedented ferocity . . . [in a] devastating attack.
>
> (Perry, 1955:255 and 303)[40]

The positive model of revenue structure in Chapter 2 does not assign to the taxpayer the role of a hapless, helpless victim of a rapacious government that taxes indiscriminately. It is based on the view that the government, in order to survive, chooses its revenue mix in such a way as to minimize the total political opposition it faces from taxpayers. Exogenous changes in the relative political costs of taxing the diverse revenue sources will cause the government to alter its revenue mix in a predictable fashion. It is the taxpayer's political opposition that shapes the government's revenue choices.

The discussion in this chapter demonstrates that taxpayer opposition shaped the government's revenue choices during the depression years. The drastic fall in national income and associated custom and excise revenues greatly increased the political costs per dollar's worth of these revenue sources relative to all other revenue sources. Governments expanded their use of old taxes, especially the productive sales tax, and of deficit financing. Strong political opposition forced Bennett to abandon plans to reduce taxes on upper-income Canadians; and the memory of this "rich man's budget" may have generated some voter scepticism when Bennett later tried to don the mantle of reform and substantially increase taxes on the rich. When windfall profits for gold producers occurred Finance Minister Rhodes moved quickly to tax this new low cost revenue source, and in response to strong opposition revised it three times.

Only John Due has acknowledged that government revenue policy during the depression reflected a response to differing political pressures, rather than an indiscriminate attack on the taxpayer. He argues that the

> . . . revenue needs of the depression forced abandonment of the plan of eliminating the [sales] tax, and firmly re-established it in the tax structure . . . [the government used the tax] to avoid either higher deficits or unpopular increases in other taxes.
>
> (Due, 1951:13 and 14)

By inference, the "unpopular increases in other taxes" would have exceeded the known unpopular increases in the sales tax.

Finally, Dominion governments during the 1930s were not committed to the goal of minimizing the deficit and balancing the budget, as against all other objectives of budget policy. I have noted those circumstances in which reductions in tax rates were proposed (1931 budget), or were actually reduced (budgets of 1934–1939), thus counteracting a thrust to balance the budget. And those strong believers in fiscal restraint and budget balance — Dunning and King — crafted a budget in 1938 that, with its sales tax exemption for building materials, would appeal to voters in the forthcoming election. And as Chart 8-1 demonstrates, the actual deficits during the 1930s were very large.

It can therefore be stated that revenue structure policy during the great depression reflected neither a single overriding objective nor an indiscriminate attack upon the taxpayer. It was rather a reflection of the difficult and sometimes unsuccessful attempt of governments to choose their additional revenues in such a way as to take into account the various political costs of alternative revenue sources.

Chapter 9

Financing Tax Reform Achievements 1963–1990

The nature of politics is to reconcile conflicting interests in order to bring about acceptable and workable solutions . . . there is inevitably a conflict of values and interests on the question [of tax reform] which can be resolved only through the political system . . . the political system thus fulfils with respect to the "buying" of tax reform the role of the market system with respect to the buying of apples.

(Richard Bird, "The Tax Kaleidoscope: Perspectives on Tax Reform in Canada," 1970a:452 and 453)

Introduction

This study builds upon the idea of an equilibrium revenue structure that minimizes total political costs of financing a given level of government spending. Through time, shifts in government spending levels and in the political costs of taxing the various revenue sources can lead to gradual modification in the equilibrium revenue structure, for a given number of revenue sources. Modifications of this kind are defined as revenue structure changes.

Major exogenous shocks of two kinds — a substantial increase in government spending and a significant change in the political costs of taxing one revenue source as compared with others — can lead to discrete changes in the equilibrium revenue structure. New revenue sources may be taxed for the first time and existing taxes repealed. These substantial alterations in the revenue structure are defined as tax reform.

Given that there are winners and there may be losers in all major tax reforms and revenue structure changes, it is in the government's interest to adopt a strategy or process of tax reform that allows it to assess the potential political costs and political benefits of any major tax proposals. I have discussed two such tax reform strategies in Chapter 2: a consultative process and a budget process. These different tax reform strategies are chosen by governments under different sets of circumstances in order to effect tax reform with minimal political damage.

During the past twenty-five years federal governments in Canada have achieved five major reforms of the tax structure. The tax reform of 1971 included capital gains for the first time in the definition of income for tax purposes and repealed federal estate taxes. The tax reform of 1974 indexed the personal income tax so that only increases in real income would be taxed. The tax reform of 1981–83 reversed the indexation reform of 1974 and eliminated and/or reduced many tax preferences for the personal and corporation income taxes. The tax reform of 1988 reduced tax preferences again and converted many exemptions and deductions into tax credits. The tax reform of January 1, 1991 transformed the manufacturers' sales tax into the Goods and Services Tax. This latter change gave rise to a fascinating exercise in tax reform polemics, of which I defer discussion until the next chapter.

After the second great war, and especially from the early 1950s onward, the three major taxes exhibited remarkably diverse behaviour, illustrated in Chart 9-1. The personal income tax share, as a percentage of total financial requirements, rises sharply until about 1975, declines, then rises again from 1985 onwards. The corporation income tax share declines from the early 1950s, though with considerable variation around this trend, until 1984, after which it evens off. The manufacturers' sales tax share declines during the 1950s, rises throughout the 1960s and declines until 1983, after which it rises again. The old age security fund taxes, which comprise equal numbers of percentage points of these three major taxes, are included in Chart 9-1 as well (see Appendix B for the treatment of these taxes). Chart 9-2 illustrates, by way of contrast, the behaviour of the other revenue sources for selected years from fiscal 1963 to 1990.

The expanding role of the personal income tax, the decreasing importance of the corporation income tax and the somewhat variable status of the manufacturers' sales tax — growing in importance in recent years — provide the subject of discussion in this chapter and the next.

In this chapter I employ the model of Chapter 2 to account for and to illuminate the first four tax reforms. The discussion that follows presents, for each major tax reform, the underlying causal forces that led to major changes in the tax structure, the choice of tax strategy that facilitated this reform and the results actually achieved. A concluding section summarizes the findings and contrasts them with the standard interpretation in the taxation literature.

Chart 9-1

**Major New Revenue Sources and OAS Taxes,
as a percentage of Total Financial Requirements (TFR),
Canada, Fiscal 1950-1990.**

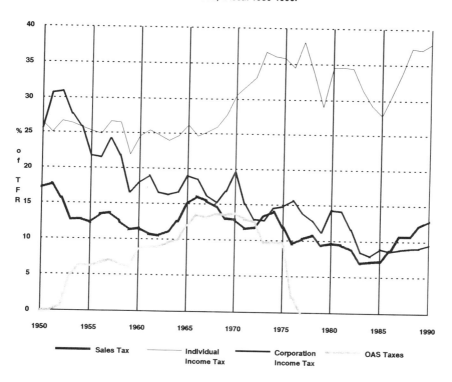

Source: Table B-3

Chart 9-2

Other Revenue Sources , as a percentage of Total Financial Requirements (TFR), Canada, Selected Fiscal Years, 1963 - 1990.

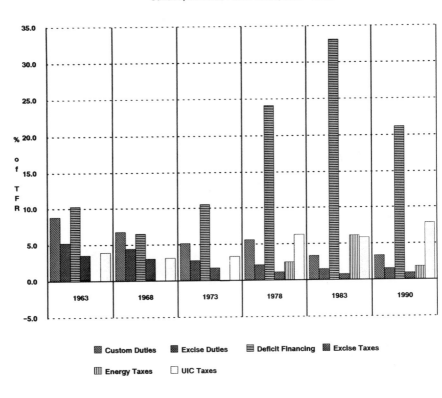

Source: Table B-3

Is a Buck a Buck? 1963–1971

A preference for fairness in the tax system was one of the strongest themes that influenced federal tax policy from 1917 through 1990. This preference for both vertical and horizontal equity in the tax structure strengthened during the two great wars, facilitating the birth of the graduated personal income tax in 1917 and its growth to full adulthood during 1940–43. After the war tax rates were reduced and exemptions increased, but the tax still applied to well over half the working population and the top marginal rates were very high.[1]

This provided a potential for taxpayer resistance to higher financial requirements. The exclusion of capital gains from income for tax purposes interfered with both horizontal equity and vertical equity, given the concentration of such income among high income taxpayers. These structural features of the tax system provided the context within which a stronger preference for fairness and equity developed during the late 1950s and the 1960s.

The thrust in favour of equity and social programs is perhaps more visible on the federal government's spending side of the budget. Beginning with unemployment insurance payments in 1942, followed by family allowance payments in 1944, the first universal old age security pensions in 1952, the Canada Assistance Plan, the Canada Pension Plan-Quebec Pension Plan in 1966, the guaranteed income supplement for the elderly in 1967, Medicare in 1969 and the revised unemployment insurance plan in 1971, the policy orientation has been directed to improving the economic welfare of low-income families in preference to that of high-income families.

The counterpart to this increased demand for social programs, aimed in part at reducing the inequality in the distribution of income, was an increased preference for equity and fairness in the tax system.[2] Income that escaped tax completely, such as capital gains income, became the focal point for taxpayer resistance to further increases in other tax rates. From this new situation originated a drive for reform of the personal income tax. Fairness in the tax system mattered to the public and policy makers.

A second impetus for change in the tax system was the sharpened federal-provincial conflict over shared and non-shared tax sources, following the second great war. Vertical tax competition was a modest theme that influenced federal tax policy. The provinces' increased spending during the 1950s and 1960s gave rise to growing and, at times, stridently voiced provincial demand for increased access to and a larger piece of the personal income, corporation income and succession duties pie. The post-war institutional experimentation with the tax collection and tax sharing arrangements was the most notable outcome of these federal-provincial battles over the financing instruments of the state and especially over the three occupied revenue sources.[3]

These forces making for change — a preference for fairness in the tax system and vertical tax competition between the federal government and provincial governments during the 1950s and early 1960s — provided the context for widespread criticism of the personal and corporation income taxes.[4] In 1962 the Conservative government of John Diefenbaker appointed the Royal Commission on Taxation under the chairmanship of Kenneth Le M. Carter to investigate and make recommendations on the federal tax system. In this way a strategy of wide-ranging consultation on tax reform was initiated.

The Commission invited briefs and held public hearings, thereby providing a forum for dispassionate — and some passionate — discussion of faults, defects and problems in the tax system. It also conducted a very comprehensive in-house program of research into the economic, administrative and legal aspects of the tax system.

The Carter Commission reported in February 1967, and the Liberal Minister of Finance, the Honourable Mitchell Sharp, called for submissions from interested groups and individuals which the government would receive before taking a position. Its first position appeared as a White Paper on Tax Reform in November 1969. Further debate was encouraged through hearings on the White Paper, conducted by the House of Commons Standing Committee on Finance, Trade and Economic Affairs and by the Senate Standing Committee on Banking, Trade and Commerce. The government's second position appeared as Bill C-259, the tax reform bill introduced in June 1971, which, in slightly amended form, emerged as the final tax reform legislation.

This extensive consultative process of tax reform allowed the government to gauge the intensity and scope of opposition to, and support for, the Commission's recommendations, its own White Paper proposals and its various legislative initiatives. At each stage in the process expected voter responses could be taken into account by deleting, modifying or pressing ahead with the various elements of the tax reform proposal.

The dominant thrust of the Royal Commission on Taxation, in its exhaustive *Report* and numerous complex recommendations, was equity or fairness in taxation. The principle of equity and its popularization in the phrase "a buck is a buck is a buck" are central to the ensuing public debate, and the Commission stated its views on equity forcefully:

> When faced with these hard choices we have consistently given the greatest weight to the equity objective . . . If equity were not of vital concern taxes would be unnecessary. The state could simply commandeer what it

needed. . . .

The first and most essential purpose of taxation is to share the burden of the state fairly among all individuals and families. Unless the allocation of the burden is generally accepted as fair, the social and political fabric of a country is weakened and can be destroyed. . . . We are convinced that scrupulous fairness in taxation must override all other objectives where there is a conflict among objectives.

We believe that horizontal equity is achieved when individuals and families with the same gains in discretionary economic power pay the same amount of tax.. . . . We believe that vertical equity is achieved when individuals and families pay taxes that are a constant proportion of their discretionary power.[5]

This equity principle led the Royal Commission to recommend the inclusion of all sources of income in a broadened income tax base. The inclusion of capital gains income for the tax purposes would have the most substantial effect on both horizontal and vertical equity.

The response of those most directly affected was critical, negative and sustained. Political pressure was brought to bear on the government to oppose the Royal Commission's recommendations and the overriding importance attached to equity.[6]

The 1969 White Paper on Tax Reform adopted "fairness in taxation", as defined by the Royal Commission, as the first objective of tax reform, although its specific reform proposals had a more limited potential to achieve the equity principle.[7] The 1971 tax reform legislation reflected an even more restricted approach to comprehensive tax reform than had the White Paper; nevertheless it still embodied an equity thrust, directed towards "a more balanced and fairer approach to taxation of incomes".[8]

The base-broadening proposal to include capital gains for taxation purposes, had not only become a more modest proposal by 1971, but was also generating much less opposition than initially. The proposal, having overcome "people's deep-seated reluctance to accept rapid changes in matters which they think concern them intimately", was now "an idea whose time had come".[9] It would appear that the lengthy process of debate and discussion served to reduce political opposition sufficiently to allow this reform measure to become legislation.

By the late 1960s the institutional tax-sharing arrangements between the federal government and the provinces with respect to estate revenues, a shared revenue source, were such that the federal government collected the tax and transferred 75 per cent to the provinces. In addition, Alberta and Saskatchewan were, by 1971, rebating their share of the estate tax to the taxpayer, in an attempt to attract persons with substantial capital.[10] The federal government was absorbing considerable opposition to a tax which it collected (see Chart 4-3), but most of which accrued to the provinces, and which, it seemed, the provinces were about to erode through competition.

The general tax collection agreements for the personal and corporation income taxes provide a high degree of tax harmonization in the Canadian federal system.[11] So long as the provinces define their tax bases similarly to the federal tax base, the federal government acts as the collection agency on behalf of the provinces. The tax collection agreements provide a positive benefit to Canada's fiscal system.[12] They can also be used as a bargaining instrument by those provinces that oppose certain tax reform proposals because of their possible effect on provincial tax revenues.

The provinces opposed some of the original Royal Commission recommendations and the White Paper proposals, such as those concerning removal of the special tax provision for the mineral and oil industries.[13] They also objected strongly to the recommendation on deemed realization of capital gains at death, and intervened actively to overturn it.

The provinces argued that adding deemed realization of capital gains at death was a form of severe and unfair double taxation on estates. Even though the revenue source defined as value of estate, is not the same base as the revenue source defined as net capital gains valued at the time of death, the strong opposition of the provinces that linked the two taxes led the federal government to repeal its estate tax. This repeal cost the federal government 25 percent of the revenues from the tax, in return for which they received grudging provincial acceptance of capital gains taxation, including the deemed realization at death feature and 76.6 percent of the revenues.[14]

The vertical tax competition between the provinces and the federal government accounted for the death of the federal estate and gift taxes as part of the tax reform adjustment. The federal government wanted to retain the tax collection agreement with the provinces on the personal and corporation income taxes after the passage of tax reform.[15] The tax reform proposals would affect the revenues of the provinces. It was therefore important for the government to gauge correctly the magnitude and depth of opposition of the provinces to the reform package, in order to ensure that it would finally go through without disrupting the tax collection agreements.

The consultative tax reform strategy allowed this information on provincial opposition to emerge. It made it possible for the government to mould its final tax reform legislation so as to achieve a major base-broadening through taxation of capital gains, while retaining the tax collection agreements. At the same time, it resulted in the death of the federal estate tax.

The forces for change in the federal tax system — an increasing preference for equity and a sharpened post-war vertical tax competition — were aided and encouraged by the Royal Commission on Taxation, and following the lengthy consultative process of tax reform, resulted in the 1971 tax reform legislation. The main features of the final package of legislated changes are described below.

Personal income tax marginal tax rates were reduced. Whereas they had previously ranged over nineteen tax brackets, from 12 percent on the first $900 of taxable income to 60 percent on taxable income exceeding $400,000, they now began at 6 percent on the first $500 of taxable income and rose to 47 percent on taxable income exceeding $60,000 over a range of thirteen tax brackets.[16] Personal exemptions, deductions, various allowances and limits for RRSPs were increased. These two sets of changes resulted in a revenue loss of about $685 million.

The tax base was broadened by including in taxable income one-half of net capital gains, unemployment insurance benefits, adult training allowances and several other items, for a revenue gain in excess of $290 million. The dual rate structure of the corporation income tax was altered and estate and gift taxes were eliminated.[17] The total package of changes would, it was predicted, generate a revenue loss of approximately $350 million. This initial increase in deficit financing would soon vanish through general revenue growth.

The broadening of the base, which is often discussed as the most significant outcome of a tax-reform debate which had lasted nearly ten years, was achieved by the inclusion of one-half of net capital gains in income for tax purposes.[18] This broadening of the tax base increased both horizontal and vertical equity. The short-term increase in deficit financing, the permanent extensive tax concessions (lowered marginal tax rates and increased exemptions, deductions and tax expenditures) and the death of federal estate and gift taxes were the prices paid by the government in order to achieve this move in the direction of greater equity.

Indexing the Personal Income Tax, 1972–74

If the government of Canada is sincere about fighting inflation, if it is sincere about justice, if it is sincere about honesty and fair dealing with the people it is serving . . . [it can] get rid of its vested interest in inflation. . . . What a government that I lead will do, is henceforth to calculate personal net income for federal tax purposes in constant dollars.

(Stanfield, 1972:2267)

Inflation had been increasing during the latter part of the 1960s, at the same time as the public debate on tax reform was influencing the way in which the federal government was restructuring the tax system. Because of the progressive income tax structure — even though reformed — inflation resulted in an increase in effective tax burdens even when real incomes remained constant. In addition, the substantial increases in federal government spending during the 1960s and the early 1970s gave rise to a demand that this growth should be decelerated, and possibly accompanied by a degree of fiscal restraint. Finally the long period of decline in the ratio of debt to gross national product had muted demand for debt reduction.

These three underlying forces led to the indexing of the personal income tax in 1974.

The average annual rate of price increase from the mid-1960s to 1973 was almost three times larger than it had been during the preceding thirteen years.[19] The early 1970s witnessed an acceleration in the inflation rate. A generalized inflation of all incomes and prices, proceeding at the same rate, results in constant real incomes. However, a graduated income tax system in which legislated exemptions and deductions do not increase at the same rate as inflation raises tax liabilities at a rate exceeding the rate of growth in incomes and government expenditures.[20] Consequently, effective tax rates rise, although real incomes and real government spending are unchanged.

This phenomenon has two very important characteristics: it is inequitable and it is automatic or "hidden". It is inequitable because inflation does not increase all effective tax rates equally. In practical terms it squashes tax brackets, as taxpayers are shoved into a higher bracket, and it reduces the value of exemptions and deductions. This "bracket creep" or "taxpayer shove" causes a larger increase in the effective tax rates for lower- and middle-income taxpayers (for whom the tax brackets are narrower to start with) and low-income taxpayers with taxable incomes just below the initial exemption and deduction levels. Higher-income taxpayers, and especially those in the open-ended tax bracket, experience smaller increases in effective tax rates. The consequence is that, through an extended period of inflation, an unindexed personal income tax structure results in less vertical equity than was initially provided for by the legislators. The tax system becomes less fair. Several researchers have documented this inequitable increase in effective tax rates up to 1973.[21]

The increase in effective tax rates is automatic and "hidden", in the sense that it does not require legislative approval.[22] A legislated tax increase provides the opportunity for political opposition to crystallize around the proposal, and therefore carries political costs of the sort we have been discussing in this study. Consequently, a hidden tax increase generated by inflation will be politically less costly than a legislated tax increase, if all other factors are held constant.[23] In the period under study, however, some other factors were not constant.

The hidden increase in effective tax rates offers the government a choice between three alternative uses of those funds: an increase in government spending, a decrease in deficit financing (and ultimately a reduction in the size of the debt) and a legislated reduction in statutory tax rates.

In the decade preceding 1974 federal spending increased substantially. In 1963–1973 the growth of federal total expenditures averaged approximately 12 percent annually, and federal spending as a percent of gross national product increased from 16 to 21 percent (see Chart 1-2).[24] It was known at the time that an unindexed personal income tax system facilitated this increase in government spending.[25] The Ministers in charge of spending departments eagerly sought after the "bonus" or "windfall" revenues which the system produced.[26]

It is plausible to hypothesize that, after such rapid growth in government spending, some degree of voter restraint on future increases in spending would emerge and influence government behaviour. This potential demand for some fiscal restraint would limit the use of funds for the first of the three options noted above: using the increased tax revenues to increase government spending. The attempt — admittedly unsuccessful — of the Department of Finance and Treasury Board "to contain the growth of federal expenditures during the first Trudeau mandate"[27] may have been an early indicator of this increasing preference for slower spending growth.

The national debt, relative to the size of the economy, declined from a peak of 101 percent in 1946 to a trough of 15 percent in 1974. The last previous year in which the ratio of debt to gross national product had been this low was 1915. The reader will recall this from Charts 7-1 and 7-2 in Chapter 7.[28] Even though federal governments used deficit financing regularly throughout the 1960s, the expansion of the economy was strong enough to shrink the relative significance of the debt. There was no active demand for debt reduction during the early 1970s. Consequently, there was no pressure on the Minister of Finance to resort to using the funds for the second policy option noted above — using the increased tax revenues to reduce the debt.

The strong preference for fairness in the tax system did not vanish after the 1971 tax reform legislation. Increasing inflation rates, especially during the early 1970s, led to an automatic increase in effective tax rates through bracket creep, and thus distorted the vertical equity dimension of the personal income tax. There existed a latent demand for tax rate reduction that would restore the fairness of the personal income tax.

These factors — some demand for fiscal restraint, absence of demand for deficit reduction and debt control and latent demand for tax rate reduction to restore the fairness of the tax system — resulted in political pressures to index the personal income tax. These pressures surfaced between the budget debate of 1972 and Finance Minister Turner's indexation proposal in the 1973 budget. The Leader of the Opposition, the Honourable Robert Stanfield, speaking in the debate on Mr. Turner's 1972 budget, advanced a specific proposal for complete indexation of the personal income tax. Mr. Stanfield's detailed proposal addressed the problems discussed above and contained provisions

> . . . for removing the government's vested interest in inflation, for controlling the government's percentage of the GNP, for increasing parliamentary control over taxation and spending. . . . Everybody concerned about government waste, *everybody concerned about the government taking more of the GNP without anybody's permission, should enthusiastically support the proposal.*
>
> (Stanfield, 1972:2268–2269, emphasis added)

This proposal became an important plank in the election platform of the Progressive Conservative Party during the October election of 1972. The Conservatives stressed the fairness of the indexation proposal, the return of parliamentary control over any required increase in tax rates and the fiscal restraint inherent in a policy of maintaining the government spending share in GNP.[29] The Conservatives increased their support substantially and the Liberals were reduced to a minority government. This electoral outcome is consistent with widespread support for the indexation proposal and with the concomitant strengthening of increased voter demand for the slower growth in government spending that Mr. Stanfield repeatedly stressed. The minority Liberal government certainly noted how popular the indexation proposal was with many voters.[30]

Finance Minister Turner's February 1973 budget had to gain support from one of the two opposition parties if it were to pass through the House. The budget must be of such a kind that, if it were defeated in the House, it would enable the Liberals to increase their electoral support in the election that would follow. It therefore included several attractive tax and transfer proposals designed to attract support[31] and one major reform of the tax system: indexation of the personal income tax system.

The Minister of Finance employed a budget strategy of tax reform to implement this significant reform of the personal income tax system: it was announced on February 19, 1973 and came into effect on January 1,

1974. The Minister knew it was a fundamental reform of the tax system, and said so, as he proposed

> . . . an income tax measure of fundamental importance. . . . What I want to do is eliminate [the automatic increase in personal income taxes even though real incomes have not changed, which is] an unfair and unintended result from our tax system . . . this proposal is a major innovation in tax philosophy and practice . . . [it] will be recognized everywhere as a bold and sensitive response to a rather fundamental tax problem . . . [it] puts Canada in the vanguard of countries with advanced tax systems.
>
> (Turner, 1973:17, 18, 19)

Moreover, the indexation proposal was generally interpreted in this sense, although only James Brown went so far as to suggest that the Canadian Tax Foundation consider erecting "a statue of John Turner . . . to commemorate this outstanding contribution to taxpayers' rights".[32]

The budget speech and accompanying debate focused on the elimination of the "unintended", "hidden", "unfair" increase in taxes which occurs when inflation pushes taxpayers into higher income brackets. With such automatic tax increases eliminated, any government attempt to increase future spending relative to GNP would necessitate legislated tax rate increases. These two features of indexation had been discussed publicly for a year. The widespread support for indexation reflected support for a future reduction of taxes in an inflationary setting and for a slower growth of government expenditures.

The budget strategy of tax reform was based on a correct prediction that, with many known winners and fewer unorganized losers, a speedy process of tax reform could be implemented. In one sense the public debate and election campaign of 1972 had provided the data and information on voter preferences for future tax and spending restraint that enabled the government to package a major tax reform, announce it on February 19, 1973 and implement it by January 1, 1974. The official opposition party enthusiastically supported the indexation proposal.

The new system was the product of underlying forces for change, detected by the official opposition and amplified throughout the public political debate during 1972, combined with a budget strategy of tax reform. The major exemptions — basic personal exemption, the marital exemption, the dependent exemptions and the exemptions for the aged, the blind and the disabled — were indexed for inflation, together with the bracket limits. The inflation factor was lagged somewhat and not all exemptions and deductions were indexed, but it was nevertheless a major reform.[33]

One aspect of the new structure had important implications for future levels of government spending and taxing. So long as government expenditures increased no more rapidly than the rate of inflation, and revenues from non-personal taxes automatically increased as rapidly as the rate of inflation, an indexed personal income tax would generate sufficient revenues to finance future spending: deficit financing need not grow.

Deficit financing did, however, increase considerably during the latter half of the 1970s. The reasons lie, not in the indexed personal income tax system, but in legislated changes in the other two variables, and these will be discussed in the next chapter.

Increasing Equity and Decreasing Indexation, 1981–1983

I dedicate myself in this and succeeding years to maintaining a fundamental sense of fairness in our society . . . [achieved via] a major overhaul of the personal tax system. [these tax changes ensure that the] tax burden is shared equitably by all Canadians . . . [the adjustment of all to a non-inflationary environment] will be much easier if everyone feels he is being treated fairly. That is why I have put so much emphasis on restraint with equity.

(MacEachen, 1981:2, 5 and 10)

Restraint with Equity: The Policy Context

The policy context preceding the tax reforms announced in the November 1981 budget comprises the causal forces that led to a change in tax structure and several known parameters of the political environment.

The preference for fairness in the tax system may have been weakened immediately after the exhausting tax reform debate of 1963–1971, but it continued to permeate budgetary policies.[34] Finance Ministers Turner, MacDonald and Chrétien during the 1970s, expressed a continuing concern that the tax, transfer and social spending actions of governments should maintain the real economic capacity of low-income Canadians during inflationary periods and, where possible, increase it.[35] Towards the end of the 1970s new information on the extent to which both horizontal and vertical equity were affected by tax expenditures — the revenues foregone as a result of exemptions, deductions and credits — became available as an input into proposed budgetary policy.[36]

From 1974 through 1980 federal spending increased at approximately the same rate as during the preceding decade, but given a more rapid increase in gross national product, the share of spending in national output remained constant at about 20–21 per cent for some years and then declined to 18 percent.[37] The demand for some fiscal restraint, noted above in connection with the indexation of the personal income tax, may have helped to determine these outcomes.

From approximately 1972 onwards deficit financing increased in importance, as compared with tax financing. In addition, deficit financing increased more rapidly than national income (see Chart 7-1 in Chapter 7), generating a rise in the ratio of debt to gross national product from 15 percent in 1974 to 25 percent in 1980. This was the first continuous rise in the proportion of the national debt to the size of the economy since the end of the second great war, and the first peacetime rise since the great depression of the 1930s. The change in the borrowing-taxing mix created the conditions conducive to the emergence of a demand for debt reduction (analyzed in Chapter 7) and, at the very least, a more widespread concern over the magnitude of borrowing undertaken to finance total federal expenditures.[38]

Given the more or less constant share of government spending in the economy and the rising share of borrowing during the middle and late 1970s, the total share of taxation in the economy declined. This latter change will be discussed in the next chapter, but, by way of preview, I would comment that horizontal tax competition led finance ministers to reduce the effective corporation income tax rate, thereby reducing considerably the revenues from this tax.

As previously stated the combination of stronger demand for equity in the tax system, continuing pressure for some fiscal restraint and an increased demand for deficit reduction and debt control provided the underlying political pressures for tax reform or at least a major revenue readjustment. These pressures for tax reform emerged in a political environment that contained three known characteristics.[39]

First, the debate leading up to the 1971 tax reform legislation, and the actual achievement of reform, leave no doubt that any tax reform proposal that intends to remove one or more tax preferences in order to achieve greater equity in the tax system will generate strong taxpayer opposition. The stimulating debate following publication of the Carter Report and Finance Minister Benson's White Paper on Tax Reform revealed to all, and especially to astute politicians, the depth of the antagonism which many businessmen harboured against the notion of equity, and the willingness of all sectors who perceived their financial interests to be threatened by "tax reform" to deploy resources through political lobbying at all levels in an attempt to alter or stop such reform.

Every finance minister after Benson would know this. The minister would be aware that strong, special interest group opposition, expressed through intense lobbying, would take shape in reaction to any tax reform proposed in the name of equity. A finance minister committed to such a tax reform package would prepare for this battle with the strongest possible armaments. At the strategic level this would mean informing those who stood to gain how much they would gain through the enhanced equity, and convincing them of the truth of such assertions. At the tactical level this successful battle plan would mean providing convincing quantitative evidence of: (1) the distortions in horizontal and vertical equity because of tax expenditures; and (2) behavioural responses of the suppliers of resources to the elimination or restriction of these tax expenditures. A final tactical component would consist of the introduction of transitional arrangements or "grandfather" clauses, spelling out precisely how activities launched when the pre-reform tax expenditures were in force would be handled after the reform.

The second known characteristic is the "price" to be paid for buying base-broadening. The 1971 tax reform legislation, which broadened the income tax base also included a reduction in marginal tax rates, especially those applying to middle and higher incomes. This "price", which increased between the White Paper proposals and the 1971 legislation, would take the form of an estimate of the reduction in marginal tax rates necessary to buy grudging acceptance of any future base-broadening which might be initiated for reasons of equity.

Finance Minister MacEachen, Prime Minister Trudeau and many members of the government in power in 1981 had participated in, and implemented the tax reform of ten years earlier. They knew, approximately, the price to be paid in tax rate reduction for the purpose of effecting a base-broadening reform. They knew that, if the initial tax rate reduction were too low, the predicted opposition to tax reform would oblige them to adopt an amended solution involving either larger tax rate cuts or less base-broadening (i.e., fewer tax expenditures would be eliminated).

The third known characteristic is the information that the government had acquired, prior to the 1980 fall budget, on the short-run political costs of de-indexing the personal income tax. In late May, 1980, the Prime Minister, the Minister of Finance and Deputy Minister of Finance, Ian Stewart, all stated publicly that the government was considering de-indexing the personal income tax as one of its alternative methods of increasing revenues in order to reduce deficit financing.[40] The press reaction was immediate and strongly critical.[41] The Progressive Conservatives promised to oppose the de-indexing proposal at every stage. On September 26, 1980, they launched a national advertising campaign to persuade voters to take the same attitude.[42] The fall 1980 budget did not, in fact, remove the indexation of the personal income tax.

The exercise provided the government with valuable information on the extent of political opposition to a separate proposal to de-index the personal income tax. The short-run political costs would have to be reduced if the government, in pursuit of the longer-run benefits which would accrue to it from automatic increases in effective tax rates due to inflation, should ever decide to remove the indexation feature. The government might also conclude that it would be helpful to have this potential short-run political opposition dispersed across several tax and transfer proposals on any future occasion in which it might again propose to de-index the personal income tax; in this way, it would have a greater chance of achieving its objective.

The Consultative Tax Reform Strategy

The underlying pressures for tax reform, operating in the environment described in the preceding section, led the Minister of Finance to choose a consultative strategy of tax reform that was initiated by his budget of November 18, 1981. The budget proposed to: (1) reduce personal income tax rates for middle and upper income taxpayers (for a revenue loss of $1,295 million), eliminate or reduce many tax expenditures (for a revenue gain of $2,145 million), eliminate or restrict many corporation income tax expenditures (for a revenue gain of $1,245 million); (2) use the net gain in tax revenues of $2,095 million to reduce borrowing, and (3) repeal the manufacturers' sales tax and introduce a new wholesale sales tax.

This package of major tax reforms is at least as substantial as Finance Minister Benson's White Paper tax reform proposals of twelve years earlier, and more comprehensive (encompassing reforms to the personal income tax, the corporation income tax and the manufacturers' sales tax). The Minister of Finance may have intended to shorten the consultative process that would accompany the strong business opposition to the content of his budget speech, but he knew that there would be such opposition and he knew that some such consultative process would occur.

It is a thesis of this study that a government will choose a consultative strategy of tax reform when it is uncertain about the magnitude of the changes in the underlying political costs of taxing various revenue sources. The consultative strategy is chosen in order to extract critically important information on those political costs (in other words, political opposition) and to guide the government as it amends, adjusts and alters its tax reform proposals into a politically acceptable package. Finance Minister MacEachen's 1981 budget launched such a process.

The objective of the budget proposals initiated by MacEachen on November 11, 1981 and legislated by Finance Minister Lalonde on March 30, 1983 was to achieve an increase in equity in the personal income tax, an increase in the proportion of tax financing to debt financing, and a partial de-indexation of the personal income tax.

The Finance Minister introduced his November 1981 budget with the clear commitment to equity and fairness in the tax system quoted earlier. That commitment to horizontal and vertical equity was still in place when he announced the first major set of revisions 39 days later:

> [this tax reform package] will improve the basic fairness of the tax system and ensure that tax preferences are more carefully targeted to economic objective. Those are the *fundamental principles* of the tax measures and *I have no intention of altering them*, not today nor at any time during the consideration of necessary legislation.
>
> (Office of the Honourable Allan J. MacEachen, 1981a:1, emphasis added)

The actual tax structure changes intended to eliminate or restrict tax expenditures as part of broadening the base would have had the combined effect of enhancing both vertical and horizontal equity.[43]

The package of proposed tax reforms was designed to produce a net increase in taxes in order to permit a planned reduction in the deficit. The Minister's awareness of the political costs of any further increase in the deficit was reflected in his firm commitment to reduce future deficit financing by increasing financing through taxes:

> I believe we must reduce our deficit and our borrowing requirements substantially — even more than I proposed a year ago . . . The corporate sector must also contribute to the reduction of the federal deficit. . . . I have set myself the task of cutting back the deficit in the next two fiscal years.
>
> (MacEachen, 1981:1, 4 and 8)

The significance attached to reducing the deficit by raising taxes was underlined by the Minister's later statement:

> . . . the question was not *whether* to raise additional tax revenue but *how* . . . Should I increase the load on those already carrying it, or should I spread the burden more evenly? I chose to spread the burden more evenly.[44]

The government knew that the business community and special interest groups would react negatively, but it did not know the full intensity with which various pressure groups would respond. Therefore, its initial tax reform proposals were aimed at stimulating opposition in order to allow it to gauge more accurately how much tax expenditure elimination it could achieve at minimum total political cost.

The Minister of Finance, and the government as a whole, seem to have been poorly prepared to fight the political battles and public opposition that they knew would arise in response to the initial tax reform proposals. They were in possession of documented evidence of vertical and horizontal inequity in the tax system. They failed, however, to target the potential winners from tax reform in such a manner as to secure their effective support after the budget speech. The Minister of Finance did not have the quantitative evidence on behavioural responses of the suppliers of resources to the elimination or restriction of tax expenditures. Some studies of this kind were launched after the budget, to counter the more strident critics' assertion that there would be emigration of skilled people and a capital "strike". The Minister of Finance did not have a complete, well-prepared set of transitional arrangements or "grandfather" clauses to accompany the tax reform proposals. The lack of these standard elements of any budget increased uncertainty and encouraged additional opposition to the proposals.

This apparent lack of preparation for the battle that would surely follow a tax reform package aimed at increasing fairness in the tax system is consistent with a consultative tax reform strategy aimed at flushing out information on the strength of opposition. The budget proposals did generate hostile, and in some cases vitriolic, opposition from affected parties and special interest groups, and even from more ordinary voters.[45] The government listened to these voices and sent the sales tax reform proposals to a committee of outside experts for examination and review (I return to this part of the reform process in the next chapter). In addition, the government substantially adjusted its other tax reform proposals on three occasions: December 18, 1981, June 28, 1982 and October 27, 1982.[46] The budget presented in November, 1981 finally became law as Bill C-139, on March 30, 1983.[47]

Throughout this evolving process of adjustment and amendment three features stand out. First, the adjustments all served to reduce the number and/or the extent of the base-broadening tax reforms. Second, the objective of increasing the proportion of tax financing to deficit financing was maintained. Finally, the institutional vehicle for achieving these two results was a permanent increase in "hidden" tax rates in an inflationary setting.

Each of the three adjustments limited the broadening of the personal and corporate income tax bases that would have occurred if the initial tax reform proposals had remained intact. These changes reduced the equity thrust of tax reform and also the planned gain in revenue. The changes embodied in revisions two and three were accomplished through government policy statements that de-emphasized equity. Finance Minister MacEachen's June 1982 budget speech made no reference to "tax preferences", "equity" or "fairness" of the tax system, thereby presenting a stark contrast with his eloquent plea for equity in the November budget.[48] Finance Minister Lalonde's October statement on the revisions to the tax reform proposals renamed tax preferences as "tax incentives", and set out six basic principles that would "guide" the Minister, not one of which mentioned equity or fairness.[49] By the time these revisions were introduced the recession was severely affecting national income and the government was more intent on stimulating private sector activity than on reminding the business sector of the equity thrust of tax reform.

Each of the three revisions of the tax reform proposals continued to emphasize the importance of shifting the financing mix away from deficit financing towards tax financing. The severe recession of 1982 increased the passive deficit substantially. This change in economic circumstances did not alter the policy thrust aimed at securing additional tax revenues that would replace some part of borrowing, even though borrowing requirements were rising.[50] This was also a period of very high interest rates, so that the cost of borrowing, per dollar's worth of revenue raised, was also rising, and thereby reinforcing the government's determination to shift the revenue structure in the direction of a larger taxing share.

This combination of a reduced equity objective, with its accompanying revenue loss, and the maintenance of a deficit financing objective made it necessary to recoup the revenue loss somewhere else in the tax system.[51] At the time of the June 1982 budget there was still strong, organized opposition from many special interest groups, and from the business community, to the tax reform proposals as revised on December 18, 1981. The Minister of Finance proposed to de-index partially the personal income tax. He also proposed, as part of a two-year restraint program, to partially de-index old age security pensions, family allowance payments and retired public service pensions.[52]

These proposals were unpopular and did generate opposition, but the opposition was diffused across several disparate interest groups and not targeted specifically at the effective tax increase achieved thorough partial de-indexation. The Progressive Conservative Party did not repeat its 1980 promise to win political support through a six-city advertising campaign that would attack the de-indexing proposal.[53] The diffusion of opposition across many proposals for tax reform and de-indexation, and the absence of a focal point around which unorganized voters might group to direct the attack on the partial de-indexation of the personal income tax, reduced the short-run political costs of deindexation.

As already noted one essential objective of the entire consultative tax reform process was to achieve some de-indexation of the personal income tax, thereby generating automatic increases in effective tax rates in an inflationary environment.

The 1982 budget was an important political blueprint for action in accordance with the consultative tax reform strategy. There is some evidence that the budget speech was drafted and written by Cabinet, with much less input than usual from officials of the Department of Finance.[54] The Cabinet devoted time and attention to the partial de-indexation of the personal income tax proposal, and specifically rejected a proposal from the Finance Department that a surtax on income be used to raise additional revenues. It preferred partial de-indexation to a surtax as a means of raising the tax revenues that would permit diminished recourse to borrowing.

The partial de-indexation proposal was stated to be for just two years. However, a departure from full indexation, even though temporary, would in principle mean that a further departure would encounter even less opposition. The benefit to a government of a partially indexed personal income tax in an inflationary setting is the automatic increase in revenues which are politically less costly than an increase in tax rates by means of legislation. By 1981 the Liberal government was responding to an increased demand for deficit reduction and debt control through an institutional change that would finance deficit reduction at low political cost. In 1985 the Conservative government responded to the continuing and rising demand for deficit reduction and debt control through a similar institutional change (a different version of partial de-indexation).[55]

Achieving Restraint with Equity

The forces for change in the federal tax system — an enhanced preference for equity, a continuing demand for some fiscal restraint and an increased demand for deficit reduction and debt control — were, as we have seen, effected through a somewhat messy consultative process of tax reform and aided by a reduction in opposition to de-indexation; they resulted in the 1983 tax reform legislation known as Bill C-139. This final tax reform package included the following provisions.

The tax rates on taxable incomes up to $24,464 remained unchanged, but tax rates for middle- and upper-income taxpayers, which had ranged from 28 percent on taxable income in the bracket $24,464–$31,136 to 43 percent on taxable income in excess of $133,440, were reduced to a range of 25 percent to 34 percent on incomes in excess of $53,376 (for a planned revenue loss of $1,295 million in fiscal 1983–84). The tax brackets were reduced in number from thirteen to ten.[56] The tax reform package also included the elimination and/or restriction of five major and many minor tax expenditures (for a revenue gain of $2,847 million) and the partial de-indexation of the personal income tax (for a revenue gain of $650 million).

The net increase in revenues would be devoted to reducing the amount of deficit financing. As noted above the sales tax reform proposal, in response to strong objections from business, was sent to a committee of outside experts for review.

Finance Minister MacEachen's initial proposals to eliminate and/or restrict tax expenditures were wide ranging but concentrated in six areas: the income averaging provisions, capital cost allowances during the year of purchase of an asset, the capital gains reserve provisions on property sales, the interest cost deduction for investment, the dividend tax credit and the tax treatment of employee benefits in three areas. These, along with the extension of the corporate surtax, would have provided $3,055 million of the $3,390 million planned revenue gain.[57] Finance Minister Lalonde's achieved tax reform excluded action in two areas — the interest cost deduction for investment and employee health and dental benefits — and delayed or modified a few proposals, for a reduction of $543 million in the initial planned revenue gain. However, most of the initial reform proposals became law, and the automatic increase in revenues from partial de-indexation of the personal income tax more than made up for the reduction in revenue gain from other sources.

In short, the 1981–1983 tax reform process achieved an increase in horizontal and vertical equity in the tax system through a major initiative that eliminated or reduced tax expenditures, an important shift in the financing mix away from deficit towards tax financing, and the partial de-indexation of the personal income tax system. The latter reform was of great importance since it would assure future governments of a politically less costly means of increasing tax revenues that could be used to reduce the deficit and control the growth in debt. The government chose a tax reform strategy that would increase the probability of success in achieving some de-indexation and the strategy worked.

International Tax Competition, 1987–1988

Statutory corporate tax rates in Canada are above those in United States and other countries, and without early implementation of significant reductions in Canada the gap would widen. If the gap between Canada and U.S. rates were not narrowed, considerable income-earning activities would shift to the United States. The gap would also encourage firms with operations in both countries to arrange their operations so as to allocate more of their taxable income outside Canada. *The result of such shifts would be less economic activity in Canada and a significant erosion of our corporate tax revenues.* The proposed reduction in Canadian statutory tax rates is designed to avoid these results.

(Wilson, 1987d:12, emphasis added)

The 1986 United States Tax Reform Act provided the major impetus for further reform of the Canadian federal tax structure. The U.S. tax reform reduced marginal tax rates for personal income tax, collapsed the number of income tax brackets to three, and broadened the tax base by removing or restricting personal tax expenditures. In addition, the U.S. tax reform reduced nominal corporation income tax rates, altered the foreign tax credit rules and broadened the tax base by removing and restricting some tax expenditures (for example, capital gains became taxable in full). The U.S. tax reforms were politically popular.

These tax reforms, in addition to reducing effective tax rates, made the U.S. tax system more neutral with regard to its effect on alternative sources of economic activity. These changes, in turn, increased the costs other countries would incur if they maintained tax structures that were significantly different from the reformed U.S. tax structure, in a world characterized by multinational corporations, considerable mobility of capital and some mobility of highly skilled labour. The exogenous shock of U.S. tax reform increased substantially the political costs of financing federal government spending in Canada with the existing tax system.

The pressure for tax reform in Canada was immediate and substantial. Finance Minister Wilson was acutely aware of the significance of the United States corporate and personal income tax reforms for revenue bases in Canada. He reiterated throughout the 1987–1988 tax reform debate in Canada, the need to make the Canadian tax system "competitive with other countries, particularly the United States".[58]

The three previous tax reforms discussed in this chapter were entirely the result of domestic forces for change. The 1987–1988 tax reform was primarily caused by an external force — the major United States tax reform — that increased the political costs of horizontal tax competition in relation to all other political costs of raising revenues.

There were two other kinds of political pressure for change that shaped the structure of the tax reform proposals: a continuing preference for fairness in the tax system and a continuing demand for deficit reduction and debt control. Finance Minister Wilson echoed the tone of his predecessors Benson, in 1971, and MacEachen, in 1981, in articulating "fairness" as an important, fundamental objective of the tax system. This preference for both horizontal and vertical equity found expression, not only through the various base-broadening proposals, but also through the conversion of exemptions into credits, a feature not found in the United states tax reforms. Finance Minister Wilson continued to reflect this preference for fairness and equity in the tax system throughout the tax reform debate.[59]

The demand for deficit reduction and debt control that had emerged towards the end of the 1970s and that influenced Finance Ministers MacEachen and Lalonde throughout the 1981–83 tax reform process, continued to shape revenue structure policy throughout Mr. Wilson's tenure of office as Minister of Finance. The tax reform proposals were crafted in such a way as to maintain revenue neutrality and so avoid additions to deficit financing and the size of the national debt. Mr. Wilson repeatedly stressed the point that tax reform would not add to the national debt.[60] Even though the gain from corporation income tax revenue would fall short of the personal income tax revenue loss, interim changes in the manufacturers' sales tax would make up the difference. This deliberate packaging of the tax reform components in order to maintain revenue neutrality is significant in light of the Minister's appraisal of the manufacturers' sales tax as a "silent killer of jobs" and his intention to replace it with a more efficient tax.

The three underlying forces — the increased cost of horizontal tax competition due to the 1986 United States tax reform, the continuing preference for equity in the tax system and the continuing demand for deficit reduction and debt control — led to pressure for tax reform in Canada. The government chose a consultative strategy of tax reform as its means of effecting change.

The government launched its formal consultative process in October 1986 with a Blue Paper, entitled *Guidelines for Tax Reform in Canada*, that set out the broad principles for comprehensive tax reform and encouraged voter feedback.[61] Fairness, neutrality, international competitiveness and simplicity were the goals to be sought after. Base-broadening, through elimination or reduction of special privileges, deductions and other provisions relating to the personal and corporate income taxes and the general sales tax, coupled with rate reductions, would be the instrumental changes employed to achieve these objectives. The revenue mix would shift away from personal income tax revenues towards a larger share of tax revenues "from the corporate and sales tax systems".[62]

Finance Minister Wilson's February 1987 budget outlined briefly the broad contours of the forthcoming tax reform package and reinforced the call for consultation and taxpayer response.[63] The Minister introduced the detailed White Paper, *Tax Reform 1987*, on June 18, 1987 and invited formal consultation, feedback and discussion on the tax reform proposals.[64] The comprehensive tax reform package was divided into a Stage 1 reform of the personal and corporation income taxes which would proceed immediately; and a Stage 2 reform of the manufacturers' sales tax that would entail further discussions of three possible replacement taxes, and would proceed after completion of the first set of reforms.

Debate on Stage 1 was encouraged through hearings on the White Paper, conducted by the House of Commons Committee on Finance and Economic Affairs and the Senate Committee on Banking, Trade and Commerce.[65] The Conservative government's second statement of position, which incorporated some recommended changes, appeared as a *Notice of Ways and Means Motion to Amend the Income Tax Act* in December, 1987, which, with some later technical refinements, became the tax reform legislation of 1988.[66]

The final package of legislated changes included the following provisions. The personal income tax marginal rates, which had ranged over ten tax brackets from 6 percent on the first $1,320 of taxable income to 34 percent on taxable incomes in excess of $63,347, were collapsed into three tax rates: 17 percent, 26 percent and 29 percent, on taxable incomes of up to $27,500, 27,500–55,000 and over 55,000 respectively.[67] The major exemptions and some deductions were converted to tax credits, thereby rendering them more beneficial to low income taxpayers.[68] These changes more than offset the increase in the first bracket tax rate from 6 to 17 percent. The base was broadened through an increase in the proportion of net capital gains that would be taxable, a decrease in the divided tax credit, the elimination of the $1000 investment income deduction and the restriction of several other tax expenditures.[69] These personal income tax reforms were expected to result in a revenue loss of $2.6 billion by fiscal 1991–92.[70]

The corporation income tax rates were reduced and the base was broadened through reductions in capital cost allowances, an increase in the proportion of capital gains to be included in income for tax purposes and the additional restrictions on the investment tax credits.[71] These corporate income tax reforms were expected to yield a revenue gain of $1.5 billion by fiscal 1991–92. The revenue shortfall of $1.1 billion was made up through interim changes in the manufacturers sales tax, pending the sales tax reform of Stage 2.[72] Stage 1 of tax reform was designed to be a revenue-neutral exercise in order to prevent an increase in the deficit.[73]

Conclusions:
Shaping Tax Reforms, 1963–1990

Canada's most recent fiscal history has revealed itself to be a quarter-century of federal tax reform. The present chapter has examined the underlying forces making for major changes in the determinants of the revenue structure, the tax reform strategies chosen by various governments and the actual results obtained through the ensuing tax reform processes. Federal governments, for the most part, employed a consultative tax reform strategy that served to generate data on the strength and magnitude of political opposition, and thereby aided those governments in shaping a package of politically acceptable tax reforms. This was true of the tax reforms of 1971, 1983 and 1988, each of which achieved a reduction in marginal tax rates and a broadening of the base of the personal income tax.

This conclusion differs from the judgment of the taxation literature, which is for the most part normative. The 1971 tax reform legislation differs from the 1967 tax reform recommendations of the Royal commission on Taxation. Most writers on taxation have noted those differences and the active influence exercised by lobbyists and special interest groups played in shaping them. They have interpreted this process of modification very pessimistically and have seen it as a government defeat. John Head refers to a "significant retreat . . . [and a] . . . watering down of the capital gains proposals."[74] Meyer Bucovetsky and Richard Bird, although sympathetic to the idea that tax reform is the outcome of a political and social process, still conclude that the 1971 tax reform "represents a major retreat from the government White Paper, and a *fortiori*, from the [Carter] Report".[75] Harvey Perry, one of the commissioners, and an astute observer of tax policy in Canada for almost fifty years, notes that "the grand designs crumbled under concerted taxpayer pressure".[76] David Wolfe concludes that "Inevitably, the Liberal government caved in under this sustained pressure from the business community".[77] Allan Maslove argues that the achieved tax reform "was only a pale reflection of the Carter Commission's recommendations. . . . The pressure brought to bear by the potential losers . . . forced the government to retreat from the Carter design".[78]

The death of the estate and gift taxes has also been described in negative terms. John Head argues that "the government chose to pay a disastrously heavy price for deemed realization at death . . . [the] . . . disastrous decision to abandon the federal estate and gift taxes . . . [was influenced by the provinces, resulting in] . . . the chaotic death tax situation".[79] John Bossons describes the decision as "retrograde . . . From a social point of view [it] . . . serves mainly to increase the concentration of wealth and to reduce social mobility".[80] Bucovetsky and Bird refer to the estate tax as being, "caught in the cross-fire over the tax treatment of capital gains at death", and the decision to repeal the tax as "surprising" and "startling".[81] Only Douglas Hartle, the Director of Research of the Royal Commission on Taxation, reflecting on the decision to abandon estate and gift taxes adopts an approach similar to that which underlies the positive model of this study:

> . . . the revenues were small and the aggravation enormous. The liquidity problems and/or the locked-in problems created by the conjunction of taxes imposed on large estates and of the deemed realization of capital gains at death jeopardized the inclusion of capital gains in income. Faced with the option of dropping either the estate tax or the taxation of capital gains the federal authorities chose the former rather than the latter. And who can blame them faced with that choice?
>
> (Hartle, 1987:55)[82]

The present study stresses that the federal government's consultative tax reform strategy generated important data that enabled the government to shape and mould the final tax reform package. The "screams of anguish" from potential losers, the threats of a "capital strike", and the intervention of some provinces on behalf of important industries were all valuable inputs into the shaping of the final tax reform package.[83] The government achieved a significant broadening of the personal income tax base by including in income — for the first time in Canadian fiscal history — one half of net capital gains, and it repealed the estate tax.

If we now review the reform of 1983, we find that legislation differs from the tax reform proposals of the 1981 budget speech. Most writers on taxation have noted these differences and the active, almost verbally abusive role that business groups, lobbyists, and other special interest groups played in determining those differences. They have interpreted the outcome of the process as a government defeat and the 1981 budget as a mistake, politically unwise, MacEachen's "greatest failure", a "disaster", a "fiasco" or a "debacle".[84] The government is seen as having buckled under the lobbyists' blows and having achieved, at best, a very modest reform. Allan Maslove argues that "almost every proposal, save the marginal rate reductions, was withdrawn or severely watered down."[85]

I have demonstrated in this chapter that the base-broadening reforms with significant effect on revenue survived intact and, with the exception of the restricted interest expense deduction and the employee health and dental benefits proposal (which were scrapped), most other changes amounted either to delay in the introduction of a proposal or to amendments that had a minor impact on revenues. The public debate, which may have been especially bruising for Finance Minister MacEachen, allowed the government to achieve not only a significant broadening of the personal income tax base but also a shift in the financing mix from borrowing to additional tax revenues and a partially de-indexed personal income tax.

Only Harvey Perry has noted that the Finance Minister "achieved 90 percent of his objective . . . it is a rare political accomplishment to have achieved most of one's objective and at the same time leave protesters convinced that they were the winners."[86] This interpretation is consistent with the general tenor of my conclusions. In addition, the explanation of the 1981–83 tax reform process in this book addresses an issue that has puzzled some writers: the apparent memory loss of the entire Liberal cabinet and government concerning their own tax structure changes of the preceding fifteen years.[87]

The 1988 tax reform legislation differs only marginally from the tax reform proposals of the 1987 White Paper with respect to the personal income tax and the corporation income tax. The tax reform package, the origins of which lay primarily in the 1986 United States tax reform, was effected through a consultative tax reform strategy, resulted in lower tax rates and modestly broadened tax bases for both the personal and corporate income taxes.

These conclusions are broadly similar to those of the literature. Most writers on taxation in Canada have taken note of the extensive consultations that laid the ground work for the White Paper and later, the legislation. The opposition was muted. The 1987–88 tax reform does seem to be "a model of a well-managed reform process."[88] In large part, this appearance of a tranquil consultative process is the result of an initial set of base-broadening tax reform proposals that were much more modest than the base-broadening amendments secured by Finance Ministers Benson and MacEachen in 1971 and 1983 respectively.

In addition, the major impact that the United States Tax Reform Act of 1986 had on the design of Finance Minister Wilson's White Paper proposals has been widely acknowledged.[89] The horizontal tax competition hypothesis H-10 is dressed up as "international tax competitiveness", and it is seen as fuelling the political pressures for Canadian tax reform.

The one major tax reform discussed in this chapter that was not achieved by means of a consultative tax reform strategy is the indexation of the personal income tax in 1974. This was a major change achieved through a budget reform strategy that responded in a minority government situation, to hidden inflation-induced increase in effective tax rates and an increased demand for slower growth in government spending unaccompanied by any demand for deficit and debt control. This conclusion differs in emphasis from the literature.

Most writers on taxation have praised the indexation of the personal income tax from a normative perspective, concerned with the maintenance of equity in personal taxes, and the elimination of "hidden" tax increases that are not legislated by Parliament.[90] This study focuses on the positive factors that explain and account for this tax reform, specifically, an increasing voter demand for slower growth in government spending and the absence of any expressed demand for deficit reduction and debt control.

Several writers have employed a more positive framework for analyzing tax indexation.[91] David Good accounts for the indexation decision as the outcome of a correct assessment, by the Minister of Finance and the Department of Finance, of the "political climate", and the absence of opposition from ministers in charge of spending departments, who had neither the time "nor the capability" to consider the implications of the indexation proposal.[92] I reject this model of government, according to which the Minister of Finance is more politically sensitive and more knowledgeable about the lifeblood of government — taxing and spending — than the other members of cabinet.[93] Besides, no Minister who was aware of the public debate during 1972 could fail to be aware of the implications of indexing for future spending plans.

Good is correct in arguing that political climate is important. But it is the changes in political climate — the phenomena I have defined as the political costs of taxation — that lead governments to change and reform their tax systems. It was external changes of this kind during the inflation of the late 1960s and early 1970s that brought pressure to bear upon the Minister of Finance and enabled him to gain agreement from, his cabinet colleagues to index the personal income tax system. Other factors were the political appeal of indexation during the election campaign of 1972 and the minority government situation in which Mr. Turner prepared his 1973 budget.

Chapter 10

The Deficit, the Debt and the GST

> . . . sales tax reform will provide a more stable foundation on which the
> government can maintain vital public services and effectively manage the
> problem of Canada's debt.
>
> (Wilson, 1989:14)

Introduction

The sales tax, like some heroic knight of romantic tales, has come to
the rescue of the damsels, deficit and debt, three times during the past
seventy years. Immediately after the first great war the government introduced a sales tax, in part to finance a reduction in the substantial
wartime debt. Sales tax revenues soared and the surpluses of the 1920s
were in fact used for debt reduction. At the beginning of the great
depression in the 1930s the government reversed five years of annual reductions in the rate of the tax and increased the rate sharply, in order
to reduce the deficit financing that accompanied a collapse of other revenue sources. Sales tax revenues grew substantially and deficit financing
became less important. Finally, several years after the second great war
the government increased the manufacturers' sales tax rate in order to
finance a continued reduction in the substantial wartime debt. Sales tax
revenues rose and the surpluses were used to reduce the debt.[1]

The sales tax knight is again being summoned to rescue the fair
damsels, deficit and debt. He arrived in the shiny new armour of the
Goods and Services Tax.

In the present chapter I return to the early 1970s in order to pick
up two themes that, along with the tax reforms discussed in Chapter
9, shaped the evolution of the revenue structure throughout the 1970s
and the 1980s. The first theme deals with the deficits that led to the
emergence of the fifth wave of debt creation noted in Chapter 7. The
second relates to the attempts of federal governments to reform the sales
tax, culminating in a lively public debate on the Goods and Services
Tax.

Riding the Fifth Wave of Debt Creation

The rapidly growing national debt puts Canada's future in jeopardy. . . .
Ottawa must stabilize and reduce the public sector debt as a share of
national income (reducing the annual *deficit* alone isn't enough). This is
the only moral, financially prudent, thing to do.
          (W.A. MacDonald, "Deficit: The No. 1 Threat to Canada's Future",
                    Globe and Mail April 6, 1989, A7, emphasis original)

There have been five surges or waves of debt creation in Canada, from
Confederation to the present. Chart 7-2 shows the crests and troughs of
the first four waves which, I argued earlier, were heavily influenced by
federal choices during the financing of wars and depressions.[2] The fifth
wave of debt creation began in the mid-1970s and is still rising — the
debt to gross national product ratio has increased from 15 percent in 1974
to 53 percent in 1989. The deep recession of 1981–82 contributed to this
wave of debt creation, but there were three additional factors, the origins
of which go back to the tax policy choices of the 1970s. These policy
choices included (1) the reduction in effective corporate income tax rates
(on manufacturing and processing profits, on small business and through
regional differentiation investment tax credits), (2) the proliferation of
tax expenditures in the personal income tax base and (3) the reductions
in the effective sales tax rate. The indexation of the personal income tax
in 1974 did not contribute to this wave of debt creation. The three tax
choices are discussed below.

Federal government spending, relative to the size of the economy, increased substantially from the mid-1960s through the mid-1970s, tapered
off for a few years, rose sharply during the early 1980s, and has been declining ever since 1984 (see Chart 1-2 in Chapter 1). The very high interest rates associated with the inflation of 1979–81 forced up government
outlays on interest payments, and continuing high interest rates during
the latter part of the 1980s have kept this form of spending high. The
deep recession of 1981–82 caused a fall in national income and a rise
in federal spending linked to automatic stabilizers, such as unemployment insurance payments, to rise. The sharp rise in unemployment to
13 percent, and its slow decline to a range which, by 1988, approximated
the "natural" rate of unemployment of 7.5 percent, kept unemployment
insurance benefit payments and government spending high.[3]

However, the growth in government spending was never more than
a minor contributor to increasing deficits and the fifth debt wave. The
major cause of the increase in deficit financing from the mid-1970s onwards was the decline in total tax revenues relative to the size of the
economy. The total tax indicator rose at about the same rate as the
total government spending indicator until the mid-1970s.[4] Then it fell

sharply between 1975 and 1979, after which it edged up. In other words, total tax revenues had fallen well before the recession of 1981–82 reduced them further.

The first tax choice that created conditions conducive to the gathering wave of debt creation was a package of reductions in the effective corporate income tax rate, which was intended, primarily to apply to manufacturing and processing firms, but was eventually extended to other sectors. Finance Minister Turner initiated this preferential treatment for manufacturing and processing profits in his budget of May, 1972 by proposing to reduce the statutory tax rate to 40 percent and to allow manufacturing and processing firms a two-year depreciation write-off of machinery and equipment.[5]

Turner continued this preferential treatment in his June, 1975 budget by proposing a 5 percent investment tax credit for new building, machinery and equipment purchased by firms in the manufacturing and processing sectors and in several other.[6] Finance Minister MacDonald, in his 1977 budget, extended the permissible time and increased the rates of the investment tax credit in regionally depressed areas.[7] Finance Minister Chrétien increased the basic and regionally differentiated rates of the investment tax credit in his budget of November, 1978 and made the credit permanent.

This package of reductions is interesting because all these Finance Ministers expressed concern about the need to maintain international competitiveness, especially with manufacturing and processing firms in the United States. The government's corporate tax choices were responses to horizontal tax competition with the latter country which had introduced a number of institutional changes in the early 1970s to enhance the worldwide competitiveness of its manufacturing and processing firms. The effect was to reduce substantially effective corporate income tax rates in the United States,[8] and Canada followed suit.

Finance Minister Turner underlined this policy thrust repeatedly:

> . . . tax treatment of companies engaged in manufacturing and processing will now compare very favourably with that in other nations, particularly the United States . . . *this radical revision of the corporate tax system as it affects manufacturing and processors will require us to forego revenue* . . . but these should not be regarded so much as a cost to the federal treasury as a major investment by the nation that over time will repay itself in terms of creating jobs for our workers and increasing prosperity for all Canadians.
>
> (Turner, 1972:9, emphasis added)

The reduction in the tax burden born by [manufacturing and processing] industries . . . will enable them to offset the serious competitive threat posed by the substantial tax subsidies for exports made available in the past year to U.S. corporations.

(Turner, 1973:2)

. . . the surtax will not apply to the profits from manufacturing and processing in Canada. I believe it is essential to maintain the reduction in the tax burden on that vitally important sector to enable it to strengthen its international competitive position. *Canadian manufacturers and processors continue to be vulnerable to foreign competition as a result of the extensive use being made of the U.S. DISC tax provisions*, the favourable tax treatment provided to manufacturers in other countries. . . .

(Turner, 1974a:18, emphasis added)

Finance Ministers MacDonald and Chrétien acted in a similar manner.[9]

This tax policy aimed at reducing the effective corporate income tax rate on manufacturing and processing firms in order to maintain their international competitiveness, is consistent with the horizontal tax competition hypothesis H-10. The impact on corporate income tax revenues is evident in the decreasing importance of such revenues, a trend which, with considerable variation, had continued since the early 1950s. Corporation income tax revenues, in proportion to the size of the economy, had also been declining since the early 1950s. This is illustrated in Chart 10-1.

The second package of tax choices was the proliferation of tax expenditures that followed and in part was a response to the tax reform legislation in 1971. This package of tax choices that narrowed the base of the personal income tax has been noted by others.[10] It helped to curb the growth in federal personal income tax revenues.

Finance Minister Benson, as part of the 1971 tax reform, increased the limits on deductions for contributions to pension plans and registered retirement savings plans and introduced an employment expense allowance. Finance Minister Turner increased the exemption for the elderly and the basic personal exemption; and he also introduced the post-secondary student deduction, the deduction for interest and dividend income, the registered home ownership savings plan deduction, the pension income deduction and the personal tax credit with a minimum and maximum limit (which he subsequently raised). Finance Minister MacDonald increased the limits on deductions for contributions to pension plans and registered retirement savings plans, the dividend tax credit, the personal tax credit, the employment expense deduction limit and the capital loss that could be offset against other income. Finance Minister Chrétien introduced registered retirement investment fund deductions and increased the maximum employment expense deduction.[11] The consequent narrowing of the personal income tax base contributed to the relative decline of the personal income tax as a financing source for the government's spending, especially after 1975. This pattern is illustrated in Chart 10-1.

The third package of tax choices consisted of two reductions in the effective rate for the manufacturers' sales tax. During the 1960s and 1970s many trading countries adopted a value-added tax on consumption, making their exports more competitive than Canadian exports, which carried the added input cost of the manufacturers' sales tax. In addition, Finance Ministers Turner in 1974 and Chrétien in 1978 interpreted the economy as requiring some fiscal stimulus and chose to provide it through the manufacturers' sales tax. Turner reduced the tax rate on building and construction materials from 12 to 5 percent, and Chrétien reduced the rate on all other manufactured goods except alcoholic beverages and tobacco products, from 12 to 9 percent.[12] These tax rate choices contributed to the declining relative importance of sales tax revenues from about 1974 through 1983, as illustrated in Chart 10-1.

By the mid-1970s the federal government's three major revenue sources — the personal income tax, the corporation income tax and the manufacturers' sales tax — were declining in relative importance as financing sources for the government's spending. In 1976 the government abandoned the fiction of a separate Old Age Security Fund and folded the OAS taxes (comprised of equal percentage points of these three major taxes) into the Consolidated Revenue Fund (see Charts 9-1 and 10-1). The three taxes combined represent the major component within the total tax indicator of Chart 1-3 in Chapter 1 that declines after 1974.

The tax policy initiative that increased revenues during the 1970s — the birth of energy taxes — while not substantial enough to offset the decline in the major revenue sources, was more than enough to aggravate the friction between oil-rich Alberta and the federal government; difficult relations continued well into the 1980s. This federal government attempt to share in the windfall gains to the petroleum sector occasioned by the worldwide increase in oil prices provoked substantial opposition, reflecting vertical tax competition, to the expanding family of energy taxes and the National Energy Program. By the late 1980s all that was left of these taxes was an excise tax on gasoline and on aviation gas and diesel fuel. The birth, growth and decline of the energy taxes are illustrated in Charts 4-3 and 4-6 of Chapter 4.[13]

With the exception of these energy taxes, decisions on revenue mix adopted by the federal government contributed to the increases in deficit financing during the latter half of the 1970s. The decisions were taken in

Chart 10-1

**Major New Revenue Sources and OAS Taxes,
as a percentage of GNP, Canada, 1950-1989.**

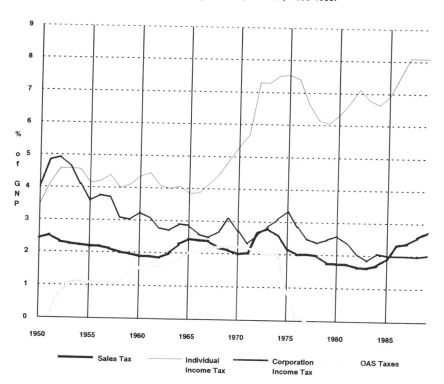

Source: Table C-3

response to foreign tax incentives and value-added taxes, the domestic demand for tax expenditures, and a perceived need to stimulate the economy and reduce unemployment. The deep recession of 1981–82 strengthened the trend towards deficit financing which, together with the national debt, rose in proportion to national income.

The magnitude of deficit financing and the national debt emerged as issues that have influenced every Minister of Finance since the Honourable John Crosbie declared, in his ill-fated budget of 1979, that the "fundamental objective of our fiscal plan is to bring about a steady reduction in our deficits."[14] The fiscal plans of the Liberals MacEachen and Lalonde and the Conservative Wilson have consistently and continually been devoted to reducing deficit financing and stabilizing the ratio of debt to gross national product.

I argued in Chapter 7 that voters with a demand for a public sector capable of responding to and managing instability in the economy and crises of a political or economic nature might, when the public debt reached some "order of magnitude", view deficit financing and the public debt as threats to such stability. After the two great wars this demand for debt reduction was strong enough, when coupled with several other factors, to result in surpluses which were used to reduce the absolute size of the national debt. In the peacetime 1980s the rising ratio of debt to gross national product, and the increasing portion of federal spending required to pay the interest on the national debt, could have triggered this demand for deficit reduction and debt control. The stimulus of such a demand is concern about the government's ability to manage instability or a crisis situation.

The fifth wave of debt creation is perceived as an issue of concern and political consideration. The quotation at the beginning of this section, taken from an article by a corporate tax lawyer in the firm of McMillan Binch, is representative of the strongly held views of many businessmen on the issue of the deficit and the debt.[15] Moreover, by April of 1989 several opinion polls reported that concern about the deficit among Canadians had deepened considerably.[16] It is not clear whether there exists a constituency or a winning coalition that would support the increased taxes or reduced government spending required to reduce deficit financing to zero, or to generate the surpluses necessary to effect a reduction in the absolute level of the debt.

What is of more immediate practical relevance is that federal governments — both Liberal and Conservative — have turned to that white knight of past rescues, the manufacturers' sales tax, in their search for increased tax revenues that will accommodate reduced deficit financing. The sales tax rate has been increased several times since 1983. Moreover, sales tax reform has been on the political agenda since 1975. The increasing importance of the sales tax is analyzed in the following section.

Reforming the Sales Tax

> The federal sales tax is unfair and inefficient. It is a silent killer of jobs. It levies a higher tax — on average, one-third higher — on domestic manufacturers than on competing imports. . . . The base is narrow and similar goods can have very different burdens of tax. The sales tax is coming under increasing pressure and reform is increasingly urgent.
>
> (Wilson, 1987:13)

The first major reform of the federal sales tax, in 1924, has been described in Chapter 7. It was converted from a two-stage turnover tax into a one-stage manufacturers' sales tax. Finance Minister Wilson's transformation of the manufacturers' sales tax into a value-added tax on consumption of most goods and services, effective as of January 1, 1991, is the second major reform of the sales tax.

In this section I examine the attempts to reform the sales tax using the conceptual framework of Chapter 2. First, I discuss the underlying forces that led to the sales tax reform proposals. Then I describe briefly the sales tax reform proposals that preceded, and laid the groundwork for, Finance Minister Wilson's sales tax reform. Third, I analyze the tax reform strategy chosen, and finally I consider what was accomplished by this tax reform.

The Causes of Sales Tax Reform

The manufacturers' sales tax, through its effects on relative prices, distorted production and consumption choices, thereby impairing the neutrality and equity of the tax system. These distortions stimulated imports at the expense of domestic production and reduced Canada's exports. Finding itself at a competitive disadvantage Canadian business demanded a more broadly based consumption tax that would exclude inputs from the tax base. Domestic producers of taxable goods in competition with imports, and exporters of all Canadian goods and services had together constituted one source of pressure for reform of the manufacturers' sales tax at least since the mid-1950s.[17]

Canada, as a trading country, was in an awkward, exposed position. Since 1960, a year in which no country had a value-added tax on consumption, some sixty countries had reformed their indirect tax systems to include such a tax; seventeen of these had done so since 1984.[18] A value-added tax is important for a trading country because it is the only form of sales tax that permits the tax component of the cost of producing a good to be eliminated for exports. It is a tax that does not reduce the international competitiveness of exports. In contrast, the Canadian manufacturers' sales tax discouraged exports because the tax component of input costs was built in. As a result, during the 1970s and especially the 1980s, many other exporting countries became more competitive than Canada.

These forces for change reflect the increased cost of horizontal tax competition, in accordance with hypothesis H-10, in a world of highly interdependent trading economies during a period of increased competition and reduced barriers to trade. The Canada-United States Free Trade Agreement, which will dismantle tariffs on most goods and many services by 1999, is one of several institutional changes that will increase the flow of goods and services among countries and increase the rewards to those firms and countries that maintain a high degree of international competitiveness.

The manufacturers' sales tax was a very non-neutral tax. In addition to its bias in favour of imports and against exports it had a narrowly defined consumption base which excluded all services and many goods such as food, clothing and footwear; it therefore created an incentive for producers to channel resources into efforts to convert taxable goods into non-taxable categories of goods, by means of departmental pressure and legal challenges. These actions increased costs and, when they were successful they narrowed the tax base still further. The definition of the base gave producers a powerful incentive to separate their marketing and distribution costs from their production costs in order to exclude the former two elements from the tax base. This legal tax avoidance device was used frequently during the 1980s and had the effect of restricting the base and reducing the revenues from the tax. In consequence the rate had to be increased, thereby creating political costs, merely for the purpose of raising the same level of tax revenues. In addition, the certainty and predictability of sales tax revenues were reduced.

A second underlying pressure for reform was the demand for deficit reduction and debt control that emerged during the latter part of the 1970s. This demand for deficit reduction had been stimulated, in part, by the higher interest rates and the concomitant increase in the political costs of borrowing during the 1980s, and reflects a desire to shift the total financing mix away from borrowing and towards taxation. Such a shift, viewed within a conceptual framework in which relative political costs of taxing different revenue sources are important, can be expected to lead to a broadening of the bases and to some reduction in the effective tax rates for the non-borrowing revenue sources. This demand for deficit reduction gave impetus to the thrust of the 1980s for a tax reform that would broaden the bases and lower the tax rates for the personal income tax and the corporation income tax. As we have seen, finance Ministers MacEachen and Wilson presided over the accomplishment of these reforms. They also launched major initiatives aimed at broadening the base and reforming the sales tax.

The increased demand for deficit reduction has been a source of political pressure in favour of increasing revenue from the sales tax, as well as the personal income tax and the corporation income tax. Finance Minister Lalonde increased the manufacturers' sales tax rate in 1984 and Finance Minister Wilson increased it still more in 1986 and 1989. A more broadly based, more comprehensive and more neutral sales tax allows the same amount of revenue to be raised with a lower tax rate. Consequently, such improvements will result, other things being equal, in a more efficient economy. Eventually, income growth in the economy will generate an automatic increase in tax revenues from the corporation and individual income taxes and other federal taxes. These revenues will be available for further reductions in deficit financing.

To sum up, the two major forces for reform of the manufacturers' sales tax have been increased costs of horizontal tax competition and the increased demand for deficit reduction and debt control.

Earlier Attempts to Reform the Sales Tax

In 1956 the Sales Tax Committee, a group of distinguished businessmen appointed by the Minister of Finance, recommended that the manufacturers' sales tax be shifted to the wholesale level.[19] In 1967 the Royal Commission on Taxation recommended that the tax be replaced by a federal retail sales tax on most goods and services, which would then be negotiated over to the provinces in lieu of further tax points on the personal income tax and the corporation income tax.[20] In 1975 Finance Minister MacDonald, in a discussion paper that accompanied his June budget, recommended shifting the tax to the wholesale level. He invited interested parties to make representations, with a view to introducing legislation "sometime after mid-1976".[21]

The government's response to the representations and briefs was the 1977 *Report of the Commodity Tax Review Group*.[22] This 1977 report firmly rejected a retail sales tax because of the difficulties of reaching an agreement with the provinces over the coverage of the base and concluded that the only feasible choice lay between an improved manufacturers' sales tax and a wholesale tax. The report favoured a wholesale sales tax, on grounds of its greater neutrality and the complexity of the administrative problems associated with eliminating the defects in the manufacturers' sales tax.

In the budget of November 1981 Finance Minister MacEachen proposed to reform this area of taxation by replacing the manufacturers' sales tax with a wholesale sales tax, effective July 1, 1982. The sales tax reform proposal, like many of the Minister's 1981 budget proposals, came in for considerable criticism, and the implementation date was delayed, eventually until mid-1984.[23]

Mr. MacEachen's successor, Marc Lalonde, appointed a committee of outside experts to examine the structural problems of the manufacturers' sales tax, consider alternative solutions and evaluate the wholesale tax proposal. The Federal Sales Tax Review Committee rejected the shift of the sales tax to the wholesale level and exhorted the government to consider instead a value-added tax on consumption that would be jointly administered with the provinces.[24] Finance Minister Lalonde's 1984 budget speech accepted the committee's recommendations not to shift the sales tax to the wholesale level.[25] This ended the Liberals' attempt to reform the sales tax, six months before an election that would install a Conservative government.

A Consultative Tax Reform Strategy

> My officials have been examining the value-added tax. . . . Our intention is to move to a new system that will encourage growth, improve equity, and yield revenues sufficient to replace the federal sales tax, to end the surtaxes I have announced today, and to provide adequate offsets for low-income Canadians.
>
> (Wilson, 1986:16)

The new government had to take account of the two forces for change — increased costs of horizontal tax competition and stronger demand for deficit reduction and debt control — and the strong business opposition encountered by previous attempts to shift the sales tax to the wholesale level. It chose a consultative tax reform strategy as its means effecting reform of the manufacturers' sales tax. This strategy, as the reader will recall, provides crucial data on the potential political opposition. The government expects strong political opposition. It also is fully prepared to "retreat" from its initial "bargaining position" in order to legislate a tax reform that minimizes the political costs of financing its spending.

Finance Minister Wilson had been preparing, since the beginning of his term of office, the way for a possible value-added tax on a broad consumption base. In a series of statements — his discussion of economic renewal in November, 1984, the 1986 budget speech, the 1986 Blue Paper on *Guidelines for Tax Reform in Canada* and the February 1987 budget speech — he referred to the need to eliminate the distortions of the manufacturers' sales tax, to consider seriously the imposition of a more broadly based sales tax on consumption, and to increase the share of total revenues raised by the sales tax.[26]

The Minister launched his sales tax reform proposals in his *White Paper on Tax Reform of June 18, 1987*, as part of his comprehensive tax reform. The initial sales tax reform proposal called for a value-added tax that would encompass most consumption goods and services, and would raise sufficient revenue to replace the existing manufacturers' sales tax, allow for a further reduction in the personal income tax rate for middle-income taxpayers, permit removal of the surtax on personal income, and fund a substantially enhanced refundable sales tax credit for lower-income taxpayers.[27] The Minister's proposals included three alternative structures for the tax: a national sales tax taking the form of a tax administered jointly by the federal and provincial governments, with a common base and the potential for different provincial tax rates, a federal goods and services tax that would allow virtually no exemptions from the tax base, and a federal value-added tax that would allow for more exemptions of goods, services and/or sectors from the tax base.[28]

The government initiated extensive discussions with the provinces, the business community and other interested parties, amidst some concern, on the part of anxious voters, about the effects of such a major tax change on individuals.[29] Finance Minister Wilson announced on December 16, 1987 that municipalities, hospitals, school boards, colleges and universities would not be subject to more tax than they were under the current manufacturers' sales tax system and that no tax would apply to basic groceries or to prescription drugs and certain medical services.[30] The federal government and the provinces discussed the feasibility of a combined national sales tax throughout 1987, 1988 and early 1989, but agreement on the definition of a common base seemed elusive.

The federal government decided to act alone and Finance Minister Wilson declared in his 1989 budget speech that

> *The present (sales) tax is widely recognized as being fundamentally flawed. It is hidden, unfair and damaging to our economy. . . .* The new (sales) tax will be called the Goods and Services Tax. It will replace the existing federal sales tax on January 1, 1991. It will be imposed at a rate of 9 percent on a very broad base, including the vast majority of goods and services consumed in Canada. Basic groceries, prescription drugs and medical devices will not be taxed. Residential rents, child care, legal aid and most health, dental and educational services will be tax-exempt. Special measures will be adopted to minimize the compliance burden for small business.
>
> *. . . sales tax reform will provide a more stable foundation on which the*

government can maintain vital public services and effectively manage the
problem of Canada's debt. It will bring an overall improvement in the
fairness of the tax system. It will make federal sales taxation more visible
to the consumer. And it will result in major gains in economic output in
the range of $9 billion a year.

(Wilson, 1989:13, 14, emphasis added)

The 9 percent GST would generate revenues of $24 billion in 1991. These
revenues would replace $18.5 billion that the federal manufacturers' sales
tax would have produced; *this latter figure included the extra $2 bil-*
lion for deficit reduction generated by the April 1989 budget tax rate
increases.[31] In addition, the revenues would finance the increased refundable sales tax credits for taxpayers of low and modest income by
$2.4 billion, replace the revenues foregone as a result of reducing the mid-
dle personal income tax rate from 26 to 25 percent ($700 million), and
finance the expected price effects on transfer payments ($2.2 billion).[32]

The GST Technical Paper set out the details of the sales tax reform proposal and invited feedback from affected businesses and interest groups.[33] In addition, the House of Commons Standing Committee
on Finance held public hearings across the country and examined the
Technical Paper and the draft GST legislation. The Committee was the
recipient of numerous expressions of opposition to the GST proposal and
served as a focal point for those who objected to it.

The objections were strong and can be grouped into two major categories. First, there were many businesses, trade associations and special
interest groups which opposed the GST and called for their service, economic activity and/or consumption to be "exempted" or "tax free".[34]
They provided living examples of the folk saying quoted on page 1 of this
book: "don't tax you, don't tax me, tax that fellow behind the tree".

Second, many objections were raised to a tax rate of 9 percent, as
compared with some lower rate, such as 7 percent. These concerns cen-
tered on the potential that a 9 percent rate had for affecting the general
price level in the short term, and ultimately influencing wage settlements
over a somewhat longer period. The possibility that the tax might significantly increase inflation led to pleas for a rate of 7 percent.[35]

The Blenkarn Committee presented its report to Parliament on November 27, 1989 and recommended the lower rate. The committee suggested
that the foregone revenues be recouped by the following means: by reducing the refundable sales tax credits and the fiscal offsets for the price
indexing effects, leaving the middle rate for the personal income tax at
26 percent, re-introducing excise taxes on the "sin" products (to maintain total revenue from alcoholic beverages and tobacco products when
the MST rate of 19 percent would be replaced with a GST rate of 7 per-

cent) and introducing a new trade-up tax on resale housing.[36] The latter proposal provoked strong critical reactions, especially from the housing industries.[37]

On December 19, 1989 the Minister of Finance unveiled his restructured GST proposal.[38] The government had responded to some concerns raised during the consultative process and to some of the strongest opposition to its initial proposals. Some business groups expressed grudging acceptance, and opposition to the GST became somewhat less intense.[39]

During 1990, the GST bill was passed in the House of Commons, and examined by the Senate Committee on Banking, Trade and Commerce, which held hearings during the summer and early fall. The hearings provided another opportunity for opposition to the tax reform proposal to crystallize, and for the lively, though unilluminating, debate which took place in the expanded Senate before the bill's approval on December 13, 1990.

Goodbye MST: Hello GST

The government's restructuring of the sales tax proposal on December 19, 1989 resulted in a 7 percent GST that will provide revenues of $19.5 billion. The two-point reduction in the rate of tax lowered planned revenues by $5.9 billion; it also lowered the offsetting refundable sales tax credits, the housing rebates and the indexing adjustments to personal income tax and to transfer payments to persons and provinces. The remaining foregone revenues will be recouped by leaving the middle rate of personal income tax at 26 percent, increasing the sin taxes, increasing the surtax on high income taxpayers, raising the tax rate on large corporations and reducing government expenditures.[40]

The sales tax reform package which substituted the goods and services tax for the manufacturers' sales tax can be illustrated with the aid of Table 10-1. The August 1989 estimate of GST revenues with a 9 per cent rate included the replacement of MST revenues and fiscal offsets of $5.4 billions, but it was net of the revenues that would be raised to finance housing rebates of $0.9 billions, the small business compensation fee of $0.6 billions and the rebates in respect of the public sector purchases, for which no estimate was provided. The revenue loss from reducing the GST rate from 9 to 7 percent was a reduction in gross revenues, and is recorded as such in Table 10-1 (except for the unknown amount generated in order to provide rebates for the public sector purchases).

This sales tax reform has resulted in a base-broadening and a rate reduction that increase horizontal equity, vertical equity and efficiency in the tax system. The improvement in horizontal equity is due to the breadth of the coverage of the tax base. Two families with identical incomes and identical total consumption levels who consume different proportions of goods, as compared with services, will no longer be taxed differently.

The improvement in vertical equity comes from two sources: the increase in the refundable sales tax credits for families of low and modest income, and the inclusion of many services in the tax base. The sales tax credit for a single parent with one child increases from $210 to $480, for a single person who maintains his or her own household from $140 to $290, and for a four-person family, comprising of two adults and two children from $420 to $580.[41] The income threshold above which the credits will be gradually phased out rises from $18,000 to $24,800. The credit amounts and threshold levels are indexed for inflation in excess of three percent.

The sales tax credits reduce effective GST tax burdens for families with incomes up to $35,000 to $45,000, as compared with the MST tax burdens. The declining sales tax credit for some middle-income families and the absence of any credit for families in the middle-upper and high brackets raise the GST tax burden, as compared with the MST tax burdens. The sales tax pattern is therefore less regressive and more progressive than the pattern of the manufacturers' sales tax.[42] The inclusion of services in the tax base, many of which, such as entertainment, travel and personal care services, absorb a higher proportion of income of middle-and upper-income families, will also improve the vertical equity of the tax system.[43]

The improvement in efficiency is the result of including most consumption in the tax base and taxing only value added at a uniform rate. Imports will be taxed in exactly the same way as domestic production; inputs used in production will not be taxed; and the tax as a percentage of final price will be the same, regardless of the number of stages in the production process.[44] The elimination of divergent effective tax rates on identical products will be a major gain in efficiency and will eventually lead to gains in national income.

In conclusion the substitution of GST for MST will make the federal tax system fairer and more neutral, and this too will increase efficiency. It will provide a more predictable and stable source of tax revenues to finance the federal government's expenditures. These benefits will greatly outweigh the costs of increased administration and compliance associated with a value-added tax.

Strong opposition to the sales tax reform persisted into the fall of 1990. Many ordinary Canadians found it hard to believe that they were paying a federal sales tax "hidden" in the price of every car, refrigerator, piece of furniture, toaster, rug and many other goods that they bought.

Table 10-1
The Goods and Services Tax Package

Item	Revenue Impact (billions of 1991 dollars)
Uses of Funds	
MST removal	18.5
Enhanced GST credit	1.2
Indexation offsets	0.9
Administration costs	0.2
Housing rebates	0.5
Total	21.3
Sources of Funds	
GST at 7 percent	19.5
Increased high income surtax	0.2
Increased excises on alcohol, tobacco and motive fuels	0.7
Increased large corporations tax	0.2
Reduced government expenditures	0.7
Adjustments in tax base	0.1
Total	21.4

Sources:
Hon. Michael H. Wilson, *Goods and Services Tax, An Overview*, and *Goods and Services Tax, Technical Paper*, (Ottawa: Canada, The Department of Finance, August, 1989) and *Goods and Services Tax*, (Ottawa: Canada, The Department of Finance, December 19, 1989). Individual items do not add up to totals, due to rounding.

The prices of these goods will fall during the first half of 1991 and the prices of clothing, entertainment, travel and other services will rise, as the more "visible" GST replaces the MST. This change from a hidden to a visible tax accounts for part of the continuing opposition of many citizens.[45]

Conclusions:
Sales Tax Reform For Debt Control

I have attempted in this chapter to illuminate the roles three major elements — sales tax, deficit and debt — played in the evolution of Canada's revenue structure during the past fifteen years.

The large federal deficits and increasing national debt of the 1980s were primarily the result of tax policy choices during the 1970s that reduced the effective tax rates of the three major federal taxes, and of the macro-policy decisions that, in part, engineered the deep recession of 1981–82 with its consequent automatic stabilization effects. The increase in the ratio of deficit to GNP until 1984, and the continuing rise in the ratio of debt to GNP ratio were not caused by indexation of the personal income tax in 1974 or by the increased rate of government spending during the 1980s (especially after 1984).

Some writers on taxation have acknowledged the role of the cuts made in the 1970s in the effective corporate income tax rate, or of the extension of the tax expenditures for the personal income tax in the same period, in reducing tax revenues and contributing to the deficits of the late 1970s.[46] There has been little discussion of the significant extent to which the tax policy choices concerning the three major taxes combined — the corporate income tax, the personal income tax and the manufacturers' sales tax — all served to reduce total tax revenues and to raise the requirement for borrowing. It is the sharp decline in total tax revenues, as a percentage of GNP, that increased deficit financing, in proportion to GNP during the same period. Federal government spending, relative to GNP, did not rise. Moreover, it was the exogenous shock of changes in U.S. corporate income tax rates, operating through horizontal tax competition, that impelled Canada's Ministers of Finance to reduce effective corporate income tax rates, thereby generating the decline in revenue from this important revenue source.[47]

In a generalized inflation, in which prices and incomes are rising at the same rate, the indexation of the tax system and transfer payments to persons will not increase the deficit. Tax revenues, transfer payments and national income will all increase at the same rate. Consequently taxes, transfers, and total spending, each considered as a percentage of GNP, will not change. The indexation of the personal income tax in 1974 (which was substantial but not complete) and the indexing of transfer payments to persons (which was also not complete) did not alter these important ratios. Some writers and the popular press have mistakenly inferred that the deficits of the late 1970s were caused by such indexation policies.[48]

Finally, the attempts to reform the sales tax, and the reform that substituted a new GST for the old MST, have been generated by international tax competition and a stronger demand for deficit reduction and debt control. Given the lack of success, in the case of Finance Ministers MacDonald and MacEachen, in transforming the MST into a wholesale sales tax, and uncertainties about potential opposition to a value-added tax on consumption, Finance Minister Wilson and the Conservative government chose a consultative strategy of tax reform. The government pursued that strategy assiduously, and modified its proposals in consequence, first by exempting basic foods, prescription drugs and medical services from the base well in advance of the 1988 election, then by choosing to move separately after agreement with the provinces proved difficult to achieve and finally, in response to the public debate of 1989 and the Blenkarn Committee report, by reducing the tax rate to 7 percent.

Many public commentators who have observed this process have interpreted it as a "bungled introduction of the sales tax", a political mistake, or a string of retreats on the part of Finance Minister Wilson.[49] It was no such thing. Tax reform has to be achieved by politicians in a political context. A component of that political context is the survival rule, and a consultative tax reform strategy is one effective way of achieving both reform and survival together. By adopting such a strategy, the Conservative government achieved the first major reform of the sales tax since 1924.[50]

Chapter 11

Conclusion:
Financing Federal Spending, Past, Present and Future

Nothing shows so clearly the character of a society and of a civilization as does the fiscal policy its political sector adopts . . .
(Schumpeter, *History of Economic Analysis*, New York: Oxford University Press, 1954:769)

The Contours of Revenue Structure Policy

In this final chapter the findings are summarized from the long-range perspective of the entire one hundred and twenty-three year period. The most important determinants of political costs are reviewed, together with their role in the evolution of the revenue structure. In addition, the various "political mistakes" that have occurred from time to time are drawn together and analyzed. The general conclusions draw attention to the evolution of the various components of the revenue structure throughout the entire period. The book concludes with a brief, speculative glimpse of the future.

The Determinants of Political Costs

The determinants of political costs have shaped the broad contours of revenue structure policy as it evolved from Confederation in 1867 through 1990. A preference for fairness or equity, based on ability to pay, grew from a minor influence during the first fifty years of revenue structure policy to an overwhelmingly important factor during the next seventy-three years. It was the major determinant of the introduction of income taxes during the first great war and the substantial expansion of the base and the increase in the rates of personal income tax, that occurred during the second great war. In addition, considerations of equity have highlighted the tax reform discussions and achievements of the past twenty-five years. In other words, hypothesis H-8b, which identified the tax preference for fairness or equity, is strongly supported by the qualitative data, especially during the two great war periods.

There are three determinants of political cost that have had a significant effect on the evolution of the revenue structure throughout the entire fiscal history of Canada, although their importance has declined: the good credit standing of the country, horizontal tax competition and vertical tax competition. In the early years the good credit standing of the national government and the associated low cost of government borrowing emerged as a major influence and retained that position until the end of the first great war. No Minister of Finance ignored the cost of borrowing in his budget speech.

Horizontal tax competition also emerged early as a major determinant of political costs. Considerations of "what tax levels are in neighbouring states" not only shaped indirect taxes — the tariff and excise duties — but also led all governments to avoid imposition of a direct tax on incomes for fifty years. Throughout the period a comparison of Canadian tax rates with rates in competing countries, especially the United States, was a regular feature of budget speeches. Horizontal tax competition has come to play a more modest, though still significant, role during the last seventy-three years. A comparison of Canadian personal income tax rates with rates in the United States has regularly been included in budget speeches of Ministers of Finance. Those Ministers have acknowledged, by their revenue choices, that they have been influenced by considerations of horizontal tax competition; examples are: Gordon, who had a nasty encounter with horizontal tax competition and was forced to withdraw his proposal for a non-resident takeover tax; Turner, MacDonald and Chrétien, who through a variety of tax changes, reduced the effective corporation income tax rate on manufacturing and processing firms in order to maintain the international competitiveness of those firms; and Wilson, who launched his 1987–1988 reform of personal and corporate income tax rates in response to and in order to remain competitive with, similar tax reforms in the United States.

Vertical tax competition was a major determinant of the evolution of the revenue structure during the first fifty years after Confederation. Considerations of this kind at a time when many municipal governments, and eventually two provinces were applying taxes on incomes influenced the decision to reject a direct tax on incomes, despite the acknowledged need for additional revenues. Vertical tax competition became a less important factor after 1917 although it continued to play a significant role. After the second great war innovative tax-sharing arrangements between the federal and provincial governments emerged from the conflict caused by joint occupancy of some tax bases. The conflict continued however, through the time of the provinces' strong opposition to some of the tax reform proposals of the late 1960s, through the disputes over the taxation of energy resources during the 1970s and through the provincial opposition to the federal government's plans to transform the manufacturers' sales tax into a goods and services tax.

The costs of compliance, collection and enforcement had a modest influence on revenue structure throughout the entire period. The possibility that high tax rates on some items of consumption would encourage smuggling served as a constraint on tariff rates and excise duty rates. The greater scope for fraud on ad valorem duties, as compared with excise duties, led to a switch from the former to the latter. Administrative experimentation with methods of income tax collection, and concern over tax avoidance, emerged as important elements in revenue policy choices.

Base elasticity was a major determinant of political costs during the first fifty years after Confederation, but had a more modest impact during the next seventy-three years. The elasticity of the revenue base against which the tariff was applied for a long time was an important determinant of the structure of revenues. As the revenue sources subject to tax increased in number, base elasticity of the tariff declined in importance, although minsters of finance counted on revenue elasticity of income and consumption bases to help them secure their total financial requirements.

A preference for taxes on sin had a modest influence on revenue structure during the first fifty years and a minor influence thereafter. Nondrinking finance ministers were willing to make use of taxpayers' guilt attached to the consumption of spirits (while showing some empathy for the beer-drinkers) and to smoking, in order to increase taxes on revenue sources that carried a negative connotation. The finance ministers of the 1880s and 1890s demonstrated creative ingenuity by constructing the notion of "voluntary" taxes on spirits and tobacco, that could be avoided by drinking tea, coffee and water! Finance Minister Foster, who joyously proclaimed his abstinence from tobacco and intoxicating liquor in 1889, firmly asserted that there would be voluntary taxes on liquors and tobacco "so long as Canada is a country." The fiction of "voluntary" taxes on some consumption preferences continues to be crafted by finance ministers of more recent vintage.

Finally, a preference for contracyclical fiscal policy had a very minor effect on the structure of revenues after the second great war. Several finance ministers voiced a fiscal policy appropriate to the pursuit of stabilization and then proceeded to implement a very different tax policy. Other determinants influenced revenue structure to a much greater extent and their influence was acknowledged.

In summary, the broad contours of revenue structure policy of the past one hundred and twenty-three years have been moulded by the following determinants, in declining order of importance — a desire for fairness, the good credit standing of the country, horizontal tax competition, vertical tax competition, the costs of administration, base elasticity, a preference for sin taxes and a minor preference for contracyclical fiscal policy (hypotheses H-8b, H-7, H-10, H-9, H-12, H-13, H-8a and H-8c respectively).[1] There is little or no evidence to show that the other potential determinants of political costs had any effect on the evolution of the revenue structure.

Since this study is focused on the national government, it is not particularly surprising that constitutional considerations and horizontal tax shifting seem to be insignificant; they would probably weigh more heavily with a provincial or a municipal government (see hypotheses H-4, H-5, H-6 and H-11). Moreover, given the findings on the extensive use of deficit financing, it was to be expected that volatility of a revenue base would not be a significant factor (hypothesis H-14). I initially hypothesized that a government would be politically embarrassed by the appearance of unplanned deficits attributable to a volatile revenue base, and would therefore avoid such volatile bases. The federal governments of Canada, far from being embarrassed by deficits, embraced borrowing as a friendly revenue source, along with an expanding family of taxes. Furthermore, the most volatile source of revenue, the tariff, although it was acknowledged by finance ministers, governments and observers alike to be a "fairweather friend", continued to provide a major share of total financing until the 1930s.

Political Mistakes

I argued in Chapter 2 that political mistakes in a government's revenue structure decisions could be interpreted in terms of the conceptual framework in such a way as to provide support for the positive model of that framework. Several political mistakes have been noted in the preceding eight chapters. It may now be useful to consider them altogether.

A political mistake regarding revenue structure is defined as a situation in which the government so misjudges or misreads the relative political costs of proposed tax changes, that it either suffers defeat, or, in response to observed opposition, amends its budget proposals; the amendments will be presented before the budget is approved in the House of Commons or in the budget speech of the following year. The initial budget speech defines the government's revenue structure proposals, based on a certain perception of political acceptability. As it is politically embarrassing to change a tax proposal after it is announced in a budget, it is reasonable to suppose that the government will agree to such change only if refusal to change would occasion still more serious political difficulties for the government. The initial perception of political acceptability is proven inaccurate by the very strength of the observed opposition. The government now attempts to correct its mistake, a move consistent with the positive model of this study, according to which the survival rule is not neglected by astute ministers of finance.

Since 1867 only two ministers of finance have submitted budgets that were defeated in the House and have thereby precipitated a general election. Liberal Finance Minister Turner's budget of May 1974 was defeated in a minority House, and it was then used as a successful election plank that helped the Liberals to return with a majority rule. Conservative Finance Minister Crosbie's budget of December 1979 was defeated in a minority House, and the election that followed returned the Liberals to power with a majority government. Politicians would be happy to make more mistakes of the first kind, but would prefer to be spared abiding failures!

Only five ministers of finance have experienced the embarrassment of amending their budget proposals perforce, in response to great opposition.[2] The budget proposals of Fielding in 1922, Bennett in 1931, Rhodes in 1934, Gordon in 1963, and Wilson in 1985 misread their political acceptability, and suffered substantial revision before passing. Fielding tried to increase taxes substantially on a variety of goods because he wished to avoid action that would "add enormously to the public debt". He was led, by strong opposition, to reduce the proposed tax increases on confectionary, soft drinks, beer and porter, cigarettes and raw beet sugar; and the increase in the public debt was greater than he had originally planned.

Bennett planned to exempt some dividend income from taxation and to change exemptions and the rate structure of the personal income tax in such a way as to lower effective tax rates for high-income taxpayers. The opposition attacked this "rich man's budget" relentlessly and the Minister of Finance eventually withdrew the proposals. It was a political miscalculation that dogged the Conservatives for the next four years.

Rhodes tried to capture some of the windfall profits of the gold-mining industry in 1934, after the United States had revaluated the price of gold. He proposed a 10 per cent tax on the value of gold produced in Canada, confidently concluding that "there can be no legitimate objection to [such] a tax". There were, in fact strong objections to the proposal, inside and outside Parliament; and the Finance Minister introduced several significant changes that lowered the revenues from the tax, before repealing it entirely in his 1935 budget.

Gordon, in his 1963 budget, proposed a tax on non-resident takeovers of Canadian companies and increased the rate of withholding tax on dividends paid to non-residents. He withdrew the proposed takeover tax almost immediately, in the face of furious opposition. Continuing opposition to the withholding tax differential led him to withdraw in it his 1964 budget.

Wilson attempted to de-index old age security pensions in his 1985 budget. This proposal gave rise to a flood of objections, and to biting assertions that the government was undermining the "sacred trust", so recently affirmed by the Prime Minister. The proposal was dropped.

The governments of Bennett, Rhodes and Wilson had comfortable majorities in Parliament and some time to go before the next election. Their behaviour is consistent with the prediction on the behaviour of the government contained in the model in Chapter 2.

In addition to these political mistakes, there were four occasions on which ministers of finance introduced tax changes in one budget that, in response to opposition or to reactions that the minister had failed to foresee, were repealed or altered in the following budget. Fielding in 1922–1923, Rhodes in 1934–1935 and Abbott in 1951–1952 misread the extent to which smugglers were able to syphon off a good part of the revenue expected from increased duties on cigarettes, spirits and cigarettes respectively.[3] Each minister placed the blame for lost revenues on smugglers but it is clear that in each case an error in judgment had been committed and, in response to these external actions, the Minister altered his tax policy accordingly.

It was not smugglers, but ordinary wage-earners who caused a change in Finance Minister Ilsley's refundable tax over 1943–1944. Finance Minister Ilsley defended the refundable tax passionately, in the face of strong opposition and a disbelief that the money would ever be refunded, arguing that "it would be political suicide for any government" not to refund the refundable tax in the post-war era. The Minister misread the extent of opposition and continued scepticism on the part of taxpayers, some of whom, with the introduction of the refundable tax, would face a top marginal rate of 98 per cent. In the final outcome the Minister withdrew the tax.[4]

Fielding in 1922, Gordon in 1963, Turner in 1974 and Crosbie in 1979 were in the unenviable position of being finance minister in a minority government situation, in which the cost of a political mistake would be felt directly.[5] It is also clear, however, that having a solid majority was no protection for finance ministers that misread the political costs of revenue extraction.

Steps taken by these ministers to alter their tax proposals demonstrate that they and their governments were politically sensitive to overt, demonstrated opposition by voters. It is reasonable to suppose that their sensitivity extended to the opposition they had tried to forestall in the original design of the proposals. In short, federal governments have behaved in a manner that is consistent with the central thesis of this study — that governments, in search of electoral support, will minimize the total political costs of raising a given level of financing.

The Content of Revenue Structure Policy

Two major conclusions emerge from the entire preceding analysis of government financing policies. First, governments have used deficit financing and borrowing as an active element of revenue structure policy, and not just as a "balancing" item. Second, governments have consistently adopted new tax sources, and abandoned old ones, in response to significant changes in political costs. This behaviour has been most pronounced at the birth of the three major federal taxes.

In addition, there are five observations, reflecting these conclusions, that emerge from the preceding discussion and apply to more time-specific patterns of taxing, borrowing and spending. These latter include: the similarities in borrowing and differences in taxing for the purpose of financing wartime spending, the unique phenomenon of postwar debt reduction, the revenue choices during the great depression, the tax reform strategies of the past quarter century and the link between debt creation and sales tax reform during the past fifteen years.

The Joys of Deficits and Borrowing

From the time of Confederation federal governments have regularly borrowed significant amounts to finance their total spending. The determinants affecting the political costs that led governments to choose an increase in borrowing, in preference to an increase in tax rates on existing tax bases or to the introduction of a new tax, altered through time. Initially governments pursued a policy of setting low customs and excise duty rates, and engaging in high public spending on "nation- building" activities, in order to attract and keep immigrants and to coax the remaining colonies into the Union.

Those governments expressed concern that high tax rates might encourage mobile labour to settle elsewhere, thus reflecting the political costs of horizontal tax competition. For the same reason they rejected proposals to introduce a new tax on incomes. In addition, government reluctance to tax a source that some municipalities and two provinces were already taxing, reflected the political costs of vertical tax competition enhanced by the effort to bring in the remaining colonies. These same considerations, that inhibited governments from utilizing tax sources more extensively, encouraged them to seek higher levels of spending. Thus, the demand for borrowing extensively followed directly from choice among potential revenue sources made in such a way as to finance a growing level of spending at a minimum political cost.

During each great war period, deficit financing accounted for the largest share of financing the rapid growth in federal spending. In each case the political costs of borrowing fell relatively to the costs of alternate revenue sources. The patriotic fervour aroused by war bond issues during the early years of each war led to oversubscriptions. Finance Ministers White and Ilsley responded rationally by making more extensive use of the borrowing revenue base, as compared with the existing tax bases. During the later years in each war period the respective finance ministers resorted to considerable moral persuasion to keep the cost of borrowing low and to shame bondholders into not redeeming their issues.

The great depressions following 1873 and 1930 were also periods when deficit financing accounted for a substantial share of total financial requirements. The use of borrowing in the 1880s reflected the policy thrusts noted earlier which were aimed at keeping the tax burden on a young, growing nation as light as possible. The use of borrowing in the 1930s reflected a government objective of keeping taxes as light as possible in a time of depression. The policy makers of the 1930s differed from their counterparts of earlier times in that they proclaimed their adherence to the principle of a balanced total budget, while at the same time borrowing in order to meet spending objectives without imposing onerously high tax rates.

Federal governments considered deficit financing to be an alternative revenue source. Policy decisions about the way in which total financial requirements would be met were based on a comprehensive evaluation of the various political factors affecting the position of the government of the day. Given such a framework for policy making, it was normal that deficit financing and borrowing should be regularly used for substantial contributions to total financial requirements.

The Search for New Revenue Sources: Healthy Tax Births

Between July 25, 1917 and January 1, 1924 the government created three major new taxes: the personal income tax, the corporation profits tax and the general manufacturers' sales tax. These three taxes have had a profound impact on the evolution of the revenue structure ever since.

After rejecting a direct tax on incomes for fifty years, the government altered course on July 25, 1917 and introduced an income tax on persons and corporations. In the midst of war, an increased preference for a graduated tax on incomes emerged — a "conscription of wealth" to match the conscription of men — especially as it was seen by western farmers and eastern workers as a substitute for further increases in tariff rates. Some opposition Liberal members were especially vocal supporters of a direct tax on incomes. The income tax was one element in a package of government actions used to entice such Liberals to join the Union team, which won the subsequent election. In addition, as the United States had increased its income tax rates during the preceding period, the potential loss of labour and capital to that country was reduced: horizontal tax competition became less costly to Canada. Finally, the fact that it was now possible to apply higher tax rates to personal income and corporate profits than had formely been contemplated (and rejected) meant that the administrative cost per dollar's worth of tax revenue had fallen. The change in these determinants of political costs provided the thrust in favour of introducing a direct tax on incomes when financial needs increased.

The income tax was not introduced as a temporary tax. The Minister of Finance, in the remarks with which he introduced the tax and during the parliamentary debate that followed, did not promise to repeal the tax when the war was over. Given the determinants enumerated above, the pressures for a direct tax on incomes were direct and permanent. The vocal advocacy of numerous members of the House of Commons reflected the expressed demand of farmers and workers. This demand was most forcefully expressed by Mr. Carvell (Liberal) when he claimed that the income tax "will never be abolished, because the good sense of the people of Canada will see it is kept in effect for all time."[6]

In 1920 the government introduced a general sales tax, in part to meet financial requirements and in part to reduce the debt, which had built up rapidly during the war. An equally important factor was the increasingly high political cost of the tariff, which led the government to seek out a (potentially) low-cost alternative source of revenue. The additional wartime customs duty, added to the normal tariff rates, stimulated considerable organized political opposition, especially from farm groups. The early post-war reduction and elimination of the wartime customs duty created a need for additional revenues, and a sales tax, levied at a low rate on many consumer items did not encounter organized opposition. The expected high costs of collection of a tax on sales at the retail level encouraged the government to adopt initially a two-stage turnover tax.

The personal income tax, corporation income tax and manufacturers' sales tax, once introduced, became permanent features of the structure of revenues utilized by the government of Canada. The forces that led to their introduction guaranteed that this would happen. There was one type of revenue source, however, that was drawn upon temporarily, had very low political costs associated with it, and subsequently vanished: excess profits. I include within this category the excess profits tax introduced during each of the two great wars and the gold tax introduced in 1934.

These revenue sources had a number of features in common. In each case they emerged as part of a unique set of circumstances that, for the most part, were not attributable to efforts of the firms or individuals involved. Extremely strong wartime demand for limited goods made it possible to obtain extraordinarily high profits, if only for a short time. The existence of such profits, received by some citizens when other citizens were being made to pay higher taxes on goods through the wartime customs duty, and some citizens were being called upon to fight and possibly to die, provided the context in which these "high", "extraordinary", "excessive", "exploitive" profits were seen as a potential revenue source involving very low political costs. The payers of such taxes did object to them. However, given the wartime context, there was more political support to be gathered by taxing such profits than by letting them escape.

With the passing of the emergency or the special set of circumstances (and the response of market forces to such circumstances) the "extraordinary" profits vanish, the revenue base vanishes, and, even in the absence of a legislated removal of the tax, the tax revenues from this source approach zero. The temporary nature of the revenue source leads to the introduction of a tax whose life will be short. The excess profits tax did, in fact, die after each great war.

A similar, although less dramatic, set of circumstances surrounded the birth and death of the gold tax during the 1930s. The revaluation of the price of gold in the United States allowed windfall profits to be received by Canadian gold mines on their current level of production. The government judged that the political costs of taxing this new, short-term source of revenue would be low, and introduced a tax on gold. Unfortunately the tax was not designed in such a way as to tax just the excess or windfall profits; opposition increased, the political costs turned out to be much higher than expected, and the tax was eliminated much sooner than the Minister had planned.

Evolution of the Revenue Structure

The active use of deficits and borrowing, and the constant search for new revenue sources are reflected in a number of more time-specific patterns of taxing, borrowing and spending.

First, Canada displayed creative flair in financing federal government spending during each of the two great war periods; it relied heavily on borrowing which became the most important single source of revenues, and its use of the major tax sources of revenue differed considerably in each war period.

War, with its attendant sacrifices on the battlefield, fostered a heightened sense of patriotism among many citizens, thereby increasing their willingness to lend money to the government at modest interest rates. Such patriotism, fuelled by the exhortations of ministers of finance during both war periods, led to a reduction in the political costs of borrowing as compared with those of taxing, and this accounted for the dramatic increase in deficit financing as a share of total financial requirements.

The birth of new taxes in the period 1917–1923, and a heightened sense of sharing sacrifices in wartime accounted for the great differences in the major sources of tax financing during the two war periods. Application of the principle that an "old tax is a good tax" accounts for part of this difference. The most important tax source of financing during the first great war was the tariff, and during the second great war it was the personal income tax. High tariff rates during the first war period antagonized western farmers and eastern workers sufficiently to call forth strong political support for the introduction of the direct tax on incomes and the general sales tax. By the time of the second great war the expanded family of taxes provided ample scope for relying on "old taxes" and great potential for financing the growth in expenditures.

In each war period concern with sharing sacrifices and establishing fairness in the tax system, based on ability to pay, led to an increased demand for equity. This demand stimulated the political support that contributed to the birth of the income tax in 1917. During the second great war the government's strongly expressed belief that income taxes would "distribute the financial and economic sacrifices of the war", according to a citizen's "means and responsibilities", whereas the sales tax would distribute "these burdens harshly and unfairly" made explicit the political support in the country for the vigorous expansion and utilization of the personal income tax and the neglect of the manufacturers' sales tax.

Second, significant debt reduction in Canada has been a post-war phenomenon. After each war governments steadily pursued a budgetary policy that enabled them to reduce the twin legacies of war: a greatly enlarged national debt and "enormous tax burdens". These surpluses available for debt reduction, viewed as a share of total financial requirements ranged from 4 to 23 percent for ten years after the first great war and from 2 to 36 percent for eight years after the second great war.

After each war the patriotic holders of war bonds redeemed them rapidly in order to finance consumption that had been restricted during war time and to obtain the higher market rates of interest. In addition, voters who, after the war, judged the rapid build-up of the debt during wartime as a potential threat to stability in the economy and to the government's ability to respond to and manage crises were demanding debt reduction (and displaying some willingness to incur the price of such a reduction). These two forces propelled the demand for a policy of debt reduction and led post-war governments to adopt such a policy.

Even so, major tariff reductions, especially favouring western farmers, were quickly enacted after the first great war, and after the second war substantial personal and corporate income tax rate reductions immediately passed into law. Such policies reduced the potential surpluses available for debt reduction, and it can theredore be said they did, in fact, constitute the most important objective of post-war fiscal policy. Early post-war governments demonstrated a fine understanding of the process of weighing the political benefits of tax rate reductions against the political benefits to be obtained from even further reductions in the size of the national debt.

The sources of finance used to implement this dual fiscal policy of debt and tax rate reduction were substantial reductions in war-related defence spending, sales tax rate increases and a buoyant revenue system responding to a growing economy. Widespread political agreement that wartime defence expenditures could be cut drastically allowed post-war governments to distribute a major portion of the burden of financing debt reduction in such a manner as to minimize the political cost of the operation. This may explain why Canada's federal governments succeeded in reducing the national debt substantially only during the two post-war periods. In peacetime it is much more difficult, politically, to distribute the cost of debt reduction through cuts in expenditures that have widespread political support at minimum political cost to the government.

The remaining sources of finance were not related to wartime activities. However, the demand for debt reduction after the first great war engendered Canada's first general sales tax and stimulated its robust growth during the 1920s. The demand for debt reduction after the second great war was strong enough to withstand the defence expenditure increases of the Korean war, and was effected by tax rate increases on most revenue sources during fiscal 1950–52, including the manufacturers' sales tax. Once again, the sales tax came to the aid of debt reduction.[7]

The buoyancy of the economy during each post-war period, and the automatic growth in revenues that reflected this buoyancy, contributed significantly to the surpluses. The same general observation applies to the economy in the early twentieth century and the surpluses that Finance Minister Fielding used to reduce the debt.

The third observation has to do with revenue structure choices during the depression. Federal financing policies of the 1930s reflected a coherent set of objectives, formulated with due political care and aimed at generating additional revenues to meet a modestly increasing level of total government spending. Governments accepted the fact that revenues from the given tax structure were declining sharply because of the depression. They were in the fortunate position of already having available a wide array of old revenue sources that could be drawn upon with less opposition than would have been the case for new revenue sources.

Two sources were drawn upon extensively: deficit financing and the sales tax. The sales tax revenue share expanded until it became the most important revenue source of the government, and deficit financing was reduced accordingly.

Federal government revenue policy did not, as had been alleged, contribute to a "tax jungle" in the 1930s, nor was it a haphazard, chaotic, assault committed on the taxpayer in order to balance the budget. It was rather the case that taxpayer opposition and expected voter responses shaped governments' revenue choices. Taxpayer opposition forced Bennett to withdraw his 1931 budget proposals to reduce income taxes for Canadians in the upper income brackets and forced Rhodes to revise his 1934 gold tax proposal. The Conservative reform budget of 1935, which preceded an election, was intended to tax the rich heavily but was not sufficient to erase memories of the earlier "rich man's budget". The Liberal pre-election budget, prepared by King and Dunning in 1938, exempted building materials from the sales tax, not as an implementation of Keynesian stabilization fiscal policy, but as a measure expected to be "widely popular" among the electorate in the forthcoming election.

The fourth observation concerns the strategies federal governments have followed in accomplishing major tax reforms. Governments during the past twenty-five years have, for the most part, employed a consultative strategy to generate information on the strength, magnitude and intensity of political opposition to initial reform proposals. This essential information guided ministers of finance as they worked to shape the proposals into a package of politically acceptable tax reforms. This was the procedure followed on the occasion of the tax reforms of Benson (1971), MacEachen (1981–83), and Wilson (1988), each of which achieved a reduction in tax rates and a broadening of the bases for the personal income tax and the corporation income tax.

These legislated reforms, especially the first two, differed from the initial proposals, but the process is not to be characterized as one of "defeat", "failure", or "disaster". The "screams of anguish", the threat of a "capital strike" and all such vigorous expressions of opposition were valuable inputs, that guided ministers of finance in shaping politically viable tax reforms in a world of considerable uncertainty. Benson in 1971, and MacEachen in 1981–83, achieved substantial base broadening and rate reduction for personal and corporation incomes taxes. Wilson in 1988 achieved a modest base broadening and rate reduction: these tax reforms, unlike the earlier ones, were initiated primarily in response to external forces: the 1986 Tax Reform Act in the United States and international tax competitiveness.

Finance Minister Turner employed a budget, instead of a consultative strategy for the purposes of his most important tax reform, the indexation of the personal income tax in 1973–74. Mr. Turner introduced this major change in response to the hidden inflation-induced increase in effective tax rates of the early 1970s, an emerging demand for some fiscal restraint, the political appeal of indexation during the 1972 election campaign and the minority government context within which the 1973 budget was designed.

Finally, we must recall the link between sales tax reform and debt control. The deficits of the late 1970s, and the large deficits and rising ratio of debt to national income in the 1980s were caused primarily by federal tax policy choices of the 1970s and the recession of 1981–82. Effective tax rates for the three major revenue sources were reduced — on corporate incomes in response to tax cuts in the United States, on personal incomes through the proliferation of tax expenditures and on manufacturers' sales for international tax competition and stabilization purposes. Total tax revenues as a percentage of national income fell, well before the 1981–82 recession.

The recession produced, through the operation of the automatic stabilizers of the fiscal system, a substantial rise in spending, a fall in revenues and a consequent increase in the deficit. During the five to six years that it took for unemployment to decline to its "natural" rate, unemployment insurance payments continued to reinforce higher spending levels and deficit financing.

This deficit financing, and the resulting expansion of the national debt have become issues of public concern. Finance Ministers Crosbie, MacEachen, Lalonde and Wilson all presented budgets that were devoted, in part, to the reduction of borrowing and the stabilization of the ratio of the debt to national income. The achievements to date have been modest. It is not clear whether there exists in Canada a winning coalition that would support the substantial increase in tax rates or the significant cuts in government programs that would encourage a minister of finance to decrease new borrowing to zero, not to mention the possibility of generating the surpluses needed to reduce the absolute size of the national debt.

And this is where the sales tax came to the rescue. The attempts to reform the manufacturers' sales tax since 1975, and the reform actually achieved which substituted a value-added GST for the MST on January 1, 1991, were the consequences of international tax competition and an emerging demand for deficit reduction and debt control. The Conservative government, keeping in mind the experience of two failed Liberal attempts to transform the manufacturers' sales tax into a wholesale sales tax, employed a consultative strategy to extract data on the strength, magnitude and intensity of political opposition to its initial proposal to convert the manufacturers' sales tax into a goods and services tax. This information on voter feedback and critical opposition guided Finance Minister Wilson as he reshaped the initial proposals into something politically more acceptable by explicitly exempting basic foods from the tax base well before the 1988 election, by consulting with, and then acting apart from, the provinces when agreement seemed difficult, and by reducing the tax rate from 9 to 7 percent.

The MST rate was increased several times during the 1980s, in order to increase consumption-based tax revenues and reduce deficit financing. The sales tax reform facilitates this continuing contribution to deficit reduction. In addition, the greater economic growth that will result from the sales tax reform will automatically increase revenues from the personal income tax, the corporation income tax and the new GST. These tax revenue increases will accommodate further reductions in the deficit and enhance control over the proportion of debt to the size of the economy.

Chart 11-1 illustrates these characteristics of the revenue structure — the vitally important role of borrowing, the search for new revenue sources and the dynamic evolution of that structure — that has financed federal spending since Canada has existed as a nation.[8]

Chart 11-2 provides a somewhat different perspective on the fiscal history of Canada. It describes the changing composition of consumption-based taxes, income-based taxes, deficit financing and a residual category of 'other' taxes throughout the entire period.[9] The most striking phenomenon is the continuing long-run decline in the importance of consumption-based taxes and the increasing importance of income-based taxes, especially after the second great war. The variability in the share of total revenue of these major kinds of taxes, and in the share represented by deficit financing, must also be noted.

Revenue Structure:
Back to the Future

In developing the model used in this study I alluded to several issues that might weaken the validity of the conceptual framework. Let us return to these topics before we attempt to speculate on the future.

The Model Revisited

The model depicts the politician as a passive player who attempts to minimize the political costs of raising a required level of revenue in a competitive political marketplace. I spoke of a survival rule, which ordains that a politician must offer the most "acceptable" tax package in order to gain and/or retain power. I did not mention personal agendas, integrity, or political platforms other than proposals regarding the level of government expenditures. The only element in the model that attributes to the victory-seeking politician the margin of manoeuvre within which he or she can offer a tax package distinct from those of competitors is the interpretation of the political costs. In support of the model I will examine three issues: simplifying assumptions, political leadership and hidden agenda.

First, it is certainly true that simplifying assumptions have been made, but they do not alter the predictive power of the model. This model of political behaviour, like all economic models, is a simplification of reality that attempts to represent the main dynamics of the real world. In particular, this study focuses on the revenue-raising aspects of our political system and a simplifying assumption is made to the effect that the required expenditure level is given. Similar models have been developed to show politicians maximizing political benefits from government spending for a given level of revenues. A general political equilibrium would be derived by simultaneously determining a level and a mix of both expenditures and financing that would maximize the net political benefits. In such a complete model, the politicians would interpret unclear signals of the political benefits of various levels and types of expenditures and at the same time interpret vague signals of the political costs of accompanying levels and types of taxation.

Given such an integration of the simultaneous determination and interpretation of both sides of the budget, there is obviously far greater scope for politicians to offer diverse budgetary platforms. Their subjective interpretations of political benefits and political costs may, of course,

Chart 11-1

**Major Revenue Sources, as a percentage of GNP,
Canada, Selected Calendar Years, 1870-1989.**

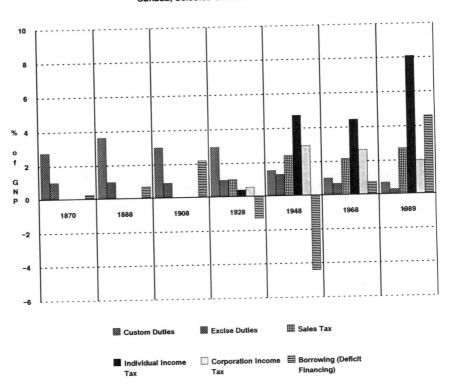

Source: Table C-3

Chart 11-2

The Financing of Total Government Expenditures (TGE), by Major Revenue Sources, Canada, Fiscal 1868-1990.

Values greater than 100% are Surpluses.

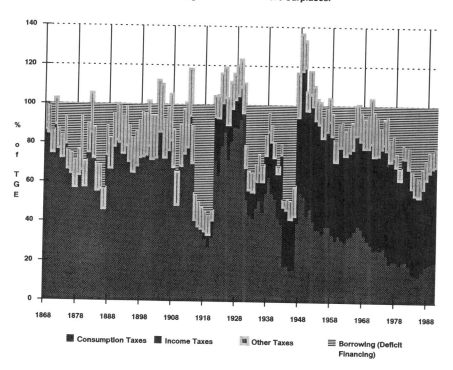

Source:Table B-4

be biased by their own preferences. Hence, the positive model of revenue structure allows for a far more varied mixture of political platforms than may initially appear to be the case. The simplifying assumptions made in the model do not prevent the politician from behaving in a manner different from what is observed in our political system.

Second, there is some scope for politicians to behave as leaders rather than as passive followers, but this issue does not create excessive difficulties. I have assumed that the politician faces a set of exogenously determined political cost curves. The political costs are not directly observable, but their potential determinants are. The politician must interpret, estimate, gauge or otherwise divine the magnitude of those political costs, for this is the only way to ensure political survival. The assumption that cost curves are fixed for a set of voter preferences and that the politician cannot change voter preferences is of critical importance. Because of it, the politician in this model is a passive responder.

The reader may be aware of the fact that a similar economic model exists for firms that maximize profits and consumers that maximize utility. Firms, in order to survive and thrive, respond passively to the exogenously determined tastes and preferences of consumers. The firm is not able to alter these preferences or to create a demand for a product that was previously not present in the consumer's preference ranking. Advertising is explained as an informational medium which allows the consumer to make clear distinctions between available products. Firms cannot sell products the consumers do not wish to buy, so that the market is limited by initial consumer preferences. Over time preferences change but these changes are not due to promotional activities of the firm.

The assumption of exogenously determined consumer tastes and preferences has not gone unchallenged. John Kenneth Galbraith claims that firms (specifically large multinationals) are able to "create their own demand" by changing the preferences of consumers and that, through promotional activities they shift the product demand curve outwards.[10] If Galbraith's hypothesis is an accurate description of the real world, it undermines almost all economic models. Microeconomic models would be incapable of determining a solution if preferences were not given. Most economists have rejected this critique; we continue to posit that promotional activities merely give information about the product to the consumer and that, if this is what the consumer is searching for, the product will be purchased.

The positive model of political equilibrium, containing passive politicians and active voters, is similar to the model of economic equilibrium containing passive firms and active consumers. The politicians in one firm (political party) face a set of voter preferences and offer for sale a product (a package of expenditure benefits coupled with a package of taxes and deficit financing) to the consumers (voters). The voter allocates his or her budget of one vote to the political party that offers the most preferable package, given his or her initial tastes and preferences. The politician participates in numerous promotional activities to sell his or her bundle of goods: advertising is carried on in newspapers, radio and television; live demonstrations are given, past performances are cited as evidence of guaranteed quality; and stress is placed on the faults of alternative packages offered for sale by competing political parties.

Do these promotional activities change the preferences of voters to a point where political cost curves are shifted? Or, alternatively, do they serve only as an informational medium which enables the voter to decide which package is most preferable? If the former question is answered affirmatively and the politicians within a political party are able to shift political cost curves, then the model loses its predictive power. Politicians, instead of playing a passive, responding role would be taking leadership action to change political preferences and thereby shift political cost curves.

It is difficult to determine with certainty which hypothesis most accurately describes the real world. At what point does the eloquent speech of the politician as philosopher-king cease to be merely an uncertainty-reducing informational tool and become an irresistible weapon of persuasion? At what point is the exhortation of the politician as war bond seller transferred from the efforts of a cheerleader to reaffirm voters' preferences for such bonds into a sermon, shaming bondholders into changing their behaviour? In my judgment the historical record is consistent with a model wherein, for the most part, politicians and political parties are responsive to voter preferences and exogenous shocks.

We have seen considerable variation in revenue structure and in total financial requirements relative to national income during the one hundred and twenty-three year period. I have described, explained and accounted for this evolution of the revenue system without once having had to rely on the particular political coloration of the party in power. The substitution of one firm called Liberal for another firm called Conservative, or vice versa, has had no appreciable impact on the evolution of the revenue structure.

More specifically, tax and deficit policies advocated in opposition have been blended into revenue structure decisions of the government that were indistinguishable from previous governments' decisions. The Conservative government that introduced the sales tax in 1920 became an opposition party that strongly opposed the increase in the tax rates legislated by the Liberal government a few years later. In the 1930s the Liberal opposition opposed the increases in the manufacturers' sales tax rate legislated by the Conservative government, but readily increased the rate of this tax as soon as they returned to power. The Liberal government that tried unsuccessfully, in the years 1975–1983, to transform the manufacturers' sales tax into a more efficient wholesale sales tax, became an opposition party that strongly opposed the Conservative government's transformation of the sales tax into an even more efficient and equitable value-added tax imposed on most goods and services.

The political mistakes that we noted earlier in this chapter were a painful jolt to the ministers of finance who so seriously misread the political acceptability of a particular tax proposal. They are also further evidence of the inability of politicians on the governing side of the house to alter political cost curves in their favour. Patriotic love of country during the second great war was not sufficient to enable Finance Minister Ilsley to persuade Canadian taxpayers to accept a refundable tax. Concern over energy supplies and deficit financing, in the late 1970s, was not sufficient to enable Finance Minister Crosbie to persuade Canadian taxpayer-voters to accept the "short term pain for long term gain" represented by major increase in taxes on gasoline and fuel oil, and his government went down to defeat.

Opinion polls have become an invaluable tool for the politician, most notably, when election time approaches; the frequency of polling then increases to a frenzied pace, and rarely a day passes without some 'startling' revelation of voter preference being exposed by a poll. Political parties often contract pollsters to determine the public's opinion on issues, appearances of a leader, and other activities designed to extract voter preferences. Political platforms are adjusted to cater to these preferences. The foregoing observations support the hypothesis that, with regard to financing, politicians face a set of political cost curves and respond in such a way as to offer a package most suitable for the perceived desires of the electorate.

The third issue is the possibility that there may be some limited role for a hidden agenda, but it is in no way detrimental to the model. In this context, a hidden agenda is a set of actions that are undertaken by the politician in a covert manner to satisfy goals that have not been publicly defined. It is not necessarily a pejorative term; a hidden agenda may be carried out for altruistic reasons, although more commonly we think of power-hungry politicians surreptitiously using political power for personal gain. Politicians, political parties and their policies are under intense scrutiny mediated through the political competition of one or more alternative governments in waiting, in-depth investigative reporting and the research of the occasional curious academic. Consequently, there is little scope for hidden agendas with respect to taxation and borrowing policies. Clandestine taxation is unlikely — most of us are intensely aware of the shrinkage of our real income as a result of taxation, even supposedly "hidden" sales taxation.

The Future Taxing and Borrowing Story, 1991–2000

Given this brief summary of the highlights of financing federal spending from 1867 to the present and the confirmation of the strength of the conceptual framework, let us set caution aside and speculate on the continuing evolution of the revenue structure — say, to the year 2000. Finance ministers of the present and future governments will respond in a predictable fashion to changes in the political environment, possibly with a long lag, possibly fumbling through painful political mistakes.

The personal income tax will continue to be the most prominent member of the federal revenue structure family, and continuing domestic demand for fairness in taxation and external changes emanating from the United States will influence the extent to which its share in total financial requirements rises or falls slightly. The mobility of some individuals will, as it has since at least 1874, cause federal governments to change Canadian tax rates in response to major changes in similar tax rates in the United States. The introduction of an individual income tax in 1913 and the rapid increase in its rates in the United States was a major cause of the introduction of the personal income tax in 1917. The 1986 tax reform in the United States, which lowered marginal rates and broadened the base, was the major cause of the 1988 tax reform legislation in Canada which contained similar changes. It can be predicted that future changes in United States personal income tax rates will have a similar impact on Canadian tax reform.

Canadian finance ministers are pinched not only by external pressures from the United States but also by domestic preferences for fairness in the tax system. The highest wartime marginal tax rate of 98 percent has been reduced to 29 percent, exclusive of the current surtaxes. The base has been correspondingly broadened. The internal domestic pressures for fairer taxes was largely responsible for the Benson reforms of 1971 and the MacEachen reforms of 1981–83. To the extent that these preferences of Canadian voters continue, we can expect to see future reductions in marginal rates coupled with further extensions of the base: the day of the flat rate tax is at hand!

The domestic preferences for fairness, except in time of war, have reflected primarily a thrust towards "equal treatment of equals". Only when great wartime crises have required some to make the ultimate sacrifice have the conditions made it relatively easy for governments to introduce strongly progressive tax rates. If no such crises arise in the future we need not expect that future ministers of finance will be so politically shortsighted as to finance spending through sharply progressive tax rates. The financing of a future "war on poverty" will not be accomplished through a steeply progressive income tax. It may not be undertaken at all, but that is a separate issue.

Unless there is a deep recession of the magnitude experienced in 1981–82, deficit financing will continue to decrease in importance as a financing source for total federal spending. The demand for deficit reduction and debt control has influenced every minister of finance since Crosbie in 1979. It has supported the decline, over 1984–1990, in deficit financing as a share of total financial requirements from 35 to 21 percent, and as a percentage of national income from 8.5 to 4.6. This demand will continue to pressure future ministers of finance into reducing new borrowing, if only gradually. Should interest rates continue to be high during the 1990s, their level will further encourage the shift away from deficit financing to greater use of taxation.

The new GST will continue the pattern established through the old MST since the early 1980s; it will increase in importance as a financing source for total federal spending, rising to at least the 16 and 19 percent at which the MST stood in 1966 and 1949 respectively, although not to the 27 and 30 percent attained, respectively, in 1938 and 1924. The domestic demand for deficit reduction and the external forces making for increasing international competitiveness caused the reform of the sales tax and will continue to operate throughout the 1990s. The new GST, purged of the biases against exports and in favour of imports that so afflicted the old MST, will be used actively by future finance ministers. The Conservatives have already absorbed the painful political costs of giving birth to the new tax. A future Liberal or N.D.P. government will find it in its political interests to continue drawing upon this revenue source (with possible minor alterations, such as full indexation of the refundable credits and the extension of tax-free or tax-exempt status to favoured items, such as books).

The increasing international integration of economies that has stimulated the GATT negotiations, the Canada-United States Free Trade Agreement and the GST will, when coupled with the increasing mobility of international capital, exercise its influence on the policy decisions of future finance ministers concerning the corporation income tax. Revenue from this tax will, barring a significant increase in rates of the corresponding tax in the United States, continue to account for a steady or very slightly increasing share of total financial requirements. In the

United States corporate income tax revenues declined in relative importance as a financing source from the early 1950s until the U.S. Tax Reform Act of 1986. We have observed the same pattern for Canadian corporate income tax revenues. And as Finance Ministers Turner, MacDonald and Chrétien lowered effective corporate tax rates during the 1970s in response to similar reductions in the United States, so too did Finance Minister Wilson, in his 1988 tax reforms, reduce the rates and broaden the base in response to American action. These tax reforms, for both countries, halted the declining importance of corporate income tax revenues and they may lead to an enhanced role for this tax throughout the 1990s. It can be predicted that future changes in United States corporate income tax rates will have an impact similar to that of the past on Canadian corporate tax changes.

The personal income tax, deficit financing, the GST and the corporation income tax are and will remain the high yield revenue sources, at least until the end of the century. Other predictions can be made. Now that the GST has been implemented and the federal government has sustained the substantial political costs of the initial tax substitution, provincial governments will find it financially rewarding to integrate their provincial sales taxes with the federal GST. The political costs of extending a transformed provincial goods and services tax to services will be largely offset by the reduced costs of collection, compliance and enforcement and the increased competitiveness of exports that no longer bear the sales tax cost on business inputs. With Quebec and Saskatchewan already planning to coordinate their sales taxes with the federal GST, there will be horizontal tax competition pressures on the other provinces to follow suit, so as not to lose their share of interprovincial trade.

If the trend to heightened voter concern for the environment continues, it will cause future finance ministers to tax environmentally destructive activities. A tax preference for sin taxes has motivated Finance Ministers to tax consumption of tobacco products and alcoholic beverages ever since Confederation. This tax preference could, in a similar fashion, be extended to encompass levies on consumption of environmentally negative products. Such initial tax forays as the federal differentiated excise tax rates on leaded and unleaded fuel may be harbingers of future revenue structure evolution.

I leave the reader with one last question. Will the continuing evolution of the Canadian revenue structure in an increasingly interdependent world lead to substantially increased tax harmonization between Canada and other countries, especially the United States; and will it lead to a significantly reduced scope for independent public policy actions on the part of the federal government? While I believe the answer is no, this story is for telling another time.

* * * * * *

What I hope I have achieved in the preceding pages is an increase in the reader's understanding of how federal governments have arrived at the taxing and borrowing choices that have financed their spending since the country came into being. An understanding of this kind may aid us as citizens to constrain, shape and mould future governments' spending and financing decisions as part of our search for the good society.

Appendix A

In Search of the Data
of Revenue Structure Variation

The Birth and Death of Taxes

This study focuses upon the historical evolution of revenue structure, which includes the birth, growth and death of taxes. Initially it is necessary to know when new taxes were introduced and when existing taxes were repealed. Tables A-1 and A-2 provide this information with respect to the major sources of revenue for the Dominion, provincial and municipal governments of Canada up to 1989.[1] Many taxes, especially those levied at the municipal level, precede the date of entry into Confederation. Municipal revenue sources were, in fact, not modified by Confederation, whereas provincial revenue sources were altered in a dramatic fashion. The reader will observe that over the entire period there have been more births than deaths! This is indeed a tax system which has been able to renew itself.

A detailed set of notes accompany Tables A-1 and A-2, but it may be helpful to elucidate the general structure. First, a date within brackets indicates the repeal or death of a tax; consequently Confederation began with a few births and a flurry of deaths. The Wartime Tax agreements are presented in the following format: a tax that was repealed by a province and not later re-introduced is treated as an ordinary death (for example, succession duties in Prince Edward Island); a tax that was repealed by a province and re-introduced at a later date has the initial year of repeal and the year just prior to rebirth included in brackets (for example, succession duties in British Columbia).

Second, the major revenue-raising taxes have been included at all levels of government. However, this procedure results in masking some births and deaths and excluding others. Excise and customs duties were imposed by the Dominion government for the first time in 1867 and are so recorded; this does not, however, take account of the fact that some additional duties and customs were added and some dropped several times throughout the years. Moreover, I have included only the major excise taxes selected: those on alcoholic beverages, autos, gasoline, tobacco products and amusements. This list is incomplete — especially during the two great war periods when many items were taxed by the Dominion government. Some limitation was necessary in order to render the table manageable.

Changes in the Revenue Structure

The growth of taxes and the variation in the structure of the tax systems of each government is the second important piece of information that is needed for the purposes of our analysis of revenue structure. This information can take the form of changes over time in (1) the structure of a particular tax and (2) the share of total revenues accounted for by each particular tax, through time. Tax structure changes — encompassing changes in statutory rates, base definition, exemptions, deductions and credits — are given in Perry's book, in his excellent Appendix A, and in some of the Tables in his Appendix C, for the major kinds of taxes levied by the Dominion and provinces up to 1954. Robin Boadway and Harry Kitchen have updated these sources.[2] The coverage for the municipalities is much less complete.

The data to calculate changes, for the three levels of government, in the share of total revenues occupied by each particular revenue source are, with two exceptions, not available before 1933. This paucity may reflect the virtual neglect of fiscal structure as a topic of analysis or, if we put the matter in more charitable terms, it may account for the fact that there exists no such analysis.

The first source of data which could be used to calculate the division of revenues among revenue sources is the work of the Rowell-Sirois Commission. The Commission compiled three kinds of evidence for the Dominion, provinces and municipalities. First, there are revenues and expenditures on current account for 1866, 1874 and 1896 derived from the various Public Accounts.[3] These data do not include capital expenditures. Second, the Commission generated, through a request to the provinces, "comparable" data, cross-checked against the various Public Accounts, for five years — 1913, 1921, 1926, 1930 and 1937: these data are comprehensive and detailed, providing expenditures and revenues on current and capital account and the total deficit or surplus for each level of government and for the entire federal system.

It can therefore be stated, for the three levels of government, adequate comparable data on the division of revenues among revenue sources are available for no more than a handful of years until 1937. This deficiency is especially serious, given the birth rate of new taxes before 1937, especially at provincial level.

The second source of data on the division of revenues among revenue sources is the invaluable collection of Appendices in Perry, noted earlier. The revenue information for the Dominion government is complete, except with respect to deficit financing, from 1867–1954: Table 6 of Appendix C, contains the revenues collected from each tax and total revenues as published in the Public Accounts for each year.

The readily available revenue information for the provinces is incomplete: Tables 12–20 of Appendix C, contain revenues collected from the principal revenue sources (but not *all* sources) as they appear in the Public Accounts for the various provinces, but no total estimate of revenues. Only the British Columbia data cover the entire period 1871–1954. Data for Alberta and Saskatchewan are virtually complete, starting in 1906 and 1907, respectively. However, data for Prince Edward Island, Nova Scotia, New Brunswick, Quebec, Ontario and Manitoba commence only in 1901, well after their entry to Confederation, and Newfoundland data are not included in the study at all. This lack of coverage for some years and lack of completeness for each year are serious deficiencies that limit the possibility of analyzing provincial tax policy in terms of the positive model of Chapter 2.

Very little revenue information is available for the municipalities: for thirteen municipalities across the country assessed valuations and taxes levied from 1901–1952 are provided. The tax coverage for these thirteen municipalities is less than complete; moreover, the tax data for Halifax, Toronto and Calgary begin in 1913, 1910, and 1914 respectively. These municipal tax data cannot be used to support any analysis at this time.

The Dominion-Provincial Conference on Reconstruction compiled data on a roughly comparable basis for 1933, 1937, 1941 and 1943, for the three levels of government.[4] The data are not consistent with the Rowell-Sirois data referred to above, and their level of detail is not as fine as that of the latter body of material. The revenue information on the Dominion government is complete for each revenue source in each of the four years, but the revenue information for the provinces and municipalities is not complete. Revenues for all provinces taken together, disaggregated by source of revenue, are available, and so are total net general revenues for each province. However, revenues, by source of revenue, for each individual province are not provided. The same deficiency exists for the municipal data. In addition, no deficit amounts are provided for any level of government.

The form of the data collected for the Dominion-Provincial Conference on Reconstruction became, with some adjustments, the framework for the revenue and expenditure data for 1945 and 1951 used by later Dominion-Provincial Conferences and by the Dominion Bureau of Statistics (D.B.S.) in fashioning its financial management statistics, which on a consistent basis continued beyond 1951. These latter data are available in finer detail, with revenues, by source of revenue, shown for each province.

These are the original three sources of published data on the revenues and expenditure of Canada's governments. For the period 1867 to 1951 there is a serious dearth of materials, especially for the provinces and the municipalities; data are available for fewer than fifteen years. This is a remarkable omission in the data base of a country that is one hundred and twenty-three years old.

All other published data sources on government revenues and expenditures that show any level of detail derive from these three sources. *Fiscal Facts*, compiled when Perry was at the Canadian Tax Foundation, draws upon all three of them, with special attention being given to the data of Perry's Appendices referred to above, updated to 1956.[5] In addition, data on Dominion expenditure from 1867 to 1956 are included.

The Historical Statistics of Canada uses the data of the Dominion-Provincial Conference on Reconstruction, later Conferences (and fills in for the years 1946 through 1950) with some adjustments, and the D.B.S. financial management statistics from 1951 onwards.[6] It presents some data from the Rowell-Sirois Commission material, but not in as fine detail. Finally, in a historical section supervised by Perry, *Historical Statistics of Canada* updates to 1960, with some revisions, Perry's work on revenues referred to above. At the municipal level it repeats the tabulation, originally calculated by Perry, of some taxes levied by 13 municipalities.

Richard Bird relies upon National Accounts statistics, which start in 1926 and have no detail for the municipalities and provinces, and the Reconstruction-Financial Management series, as his data base for the purpose of analyzing the growth in government spending from 1867 to the mid-1960s.[7] Some data for total government spending for seven years prior to 1926 are derived by Firestone, but the level of detail is inadequate for analysis.[8] Because of Bird's focus upon spending he makes virtually no use of revenue data, except in two cases. First, his proxy series for provincial spending from 1901 onwards is "net general revenue from own sources"; this is derived from *Historical Statistics*, which is in turn derived from the original Perry data referred to above.[9] Second, his partial proxy series for municipal spending from 1901 onwards is "taxes levied by selected municipalities", likewise derived from *Historical Statistics*, and ultimately from the original Perry data.[10]

A later study by Richard Bird relies mainly upon National Accounts statistics and some financial management statistics as the data base for the purpose of analyzing the *Financing of Canadian Government*.[11] The time period studied is limited to the years following the second great war.

It has been emphasized in this study that deficit financing, either through debt creation or through money creation, is an alternative source of revenue for a government, and it can be used to finance capital expenditures and current expenditures. At Confederation the Dominion government assumed the onerous debts of the colonies along with responsibility for transportation and other economic development expenditures.[12] During the nineteenth century, the artificial distinction between current and capital expenditure was deliberately manipulated by governments to show artificial surpluses on current expenditures that could ostensibly be used for meeting the debt obligations on capital account.[13]

Information on the value of the deficit is even more difficult to come by than tax structure data. The Rowell-Sirois Commission provided data on the deficits of the Dominion, provincial and municipal governments in the selected years they studied. Perry provides no data on the Dominion deficit; given his focus on revenues, there is no need for him to note expenditures and derive a balancing item. *The Historical Statistics of Canada* provides Dominion expenditures and revenues separately, without providing the balancing item. Data on provincial expenditures are partial and incomplete, as we have already found to be the case with revenues; consequently no accurate balancing item can be calculated. Municipal data are even less adequate.

It would seem, then, that, for a period dating back to 1867, only the deficit for the Dominion government can be calculated from readily available published sources, that is to say, either Perry's work or the original Public Accounts. However, even the Public Accounts data do not, in all cases, yield true figures for expenditures, revenues and the deficit. Several fictitious items distort the values of real expenditures and revenues, and consequently any calculated deficit or surplus. Georg Rich in his study, *The Cross of Gold*, adjusts the Public Accounts data to eliminate fictitious items and render the concept underlying the data closer to that of a national accounts basis for the years 1868–1914.[14]

The model developed in this study is applicable to all governments, Dominion, provincial and municipal, to the emergence of all taxes for each government, and to the changing revenue structure of each government. The available data impose severe limits on what can be accomplished.

The first stage of the research agenda is the revenue structure policy of the Dominion government. The Perry and Public Accounts data are available and the Rich adjustment has already converted the data for 1868–1914 into a usable form; this adjustment procedure is applied to the data for 1915–1990 in Appendix B. These sources allow us to use the positive model of this is study to analyze and to cast some light on the evolution of revenue structure policy at the federal level from 1867 to 1990.

Future Research Agenda

It is expected that this study will form one part of a long-range research investigation directed towards an analysis of the evolution of the revenue structure policies of all three levels of Canadian government. Examination of the tax structure policies of the provincial governments will constitute the next stage of the research agenda. Revenues and expenditures are available in the various provincial Public Accounts as far back as Confederation, even though they have not yet been extracted for research purposes. Data on expenditures and revenues by revenue source (including deficit financing) will be compiled from these sources.[15]

The final stage of the research agenda will be an analysis of the tax structure policies of some municipal governments. The municipal data, especially on revenues by revenue source, exist in scattered sources but have not yet been drawn together for research purposes. Ontario's data on municipal expenditures and revenues, appear in some detail in the Dominion Public Accounts for 1867 and several years following, after which they are found in the Ontario Sessional Papers. The Ontario Bureau of Industry Reports from the early 1880s until 1917, carried detailed municipal financial and spending data, which later appeared elsewhere in the sessional papers. The data for the municipalities of some of the other provinces are less detailed and less complete, but in almost all cases it seems that fairly comprehensive municipal series can be extracted.[16] Much of the municipal information has been compiled by Professor Urquhart at Queens, and this will facilitate the extraction of data in a suitable form.[17] In addition the *Statistical Yearbook of Canada 1894*, the *Quebec Statistical Yearbook 1914* and the *Royal Commission on Relations of Capital and Labour in Canada* of 1889, are useful sources for information on the financing of municipalities and cities.

One eventual by-product of this long-range research investigation will be the establishment, for the first time, of an adequate data base on the financing of Canadian government spending over long periods of time. Such a base will permit the testing of a host of hypotheses in addition to those of Chapter 2. It will be the indispensable instrument for the systematic study of such issues as the comparative growth rates of provincial or municipal governments, the variation, over time, in the centralization of revenues (as an indication of centralization or decentralization of government decision-making), and the role of transfer payments as revenues and expenditures change over long periods of time.

TABLE A-1

Births and Deaths of Taxes in Canada: Dominion and Provinces, 1793-1989

	Customs Revenue* (1)	Excise Duties* (2)	Real Property Tax (3)	Personal Property Taxes (4)	Personal Income Taxes[5] (5)	Poll Taxes (6)	Business Taxes[4] (7)	Natural Resource Revenues (8)	Succession Duties[5] (9)	Corporation Income Taxes[6] (10)	General Sales Taxes (11)	Alcoholic Beverages[7] (12)	Autos[8] (13)	Gasoline Products (14)	Tobacco Products (15)	Amuse- ment[9] (16)
Dominion	1867	1867	--	--	1917	--	--	1974	1941 (1971)	1918	1920	1920	1918	1942 (1947)	1922	1918 (1948)
Provinces																
PEI	(1873)	(1873)	1877	1920	1894 (1941-1961)	1877[10]	1894	1971	1894 (1947-1971) 1972 (1975)	1920 (1941-1961)	1960	1918	1914	1924	1941	1920
Nova Scotia	(1867)	(1867)	1917	--	1962	--	1903	1869	1892 (1947-1971) 1972 (1975)	1939 (1941-1961)	1959	1920	1912	1925	--	1920
New Brunswick	(1867)	(1867)	1917	--	1962	(1945)	1892	1901	1892 (1947-1971) 1972 (1975)	1938 (1941-1961)	1950	1920	1911	1926	1940	1918
Newfoundland	(1949)	(1949)	--	--	1917 (1949-1961)	--	--	1844[11]	1914 (1947-1971) 1972 (1975)	1917 (1949-1961)	1950	1925	1906	1949	1963	1953 (1968)
Quebec	(1867)	(1867)	--	--	1939 (1941-1953)	--	1882	1880	1892 (1985)	1932 (1941-1946)	1940	1921	1906	1924	1940	1932 (1965)
Ontario	(1867)	(1867)	1924	--	1936 (1941-1961)	--	1899	1826	1892 (1979)	1932 (1941-1946) 1947 (1952-1956)	1961	1918	1903	1925	1966	1916
Manitoba	(1870)	(1870)	1918 (1957)	--	1923 (1941-1961)	--	1900	1931	1893 (1947-1971) 1972 (1977)	1931 (1941-1961)	1967	1922	1908	1923	--	1915 (1918)
Saskatchewan	--	--	1906	--	1932 (1941-1961)	1919	1907	1931	1903 (1947-1971)	1931 (1941-1961)	1937	1915	1908	1928	1965	1933 (1967)
Alberta	--	--	1906	--	1932 (1941-1961)	--	1907	1931	1903 (1947-1971)	1932 (1941-1961)	1936 (1937)	1918	1912	1922	1969	1916 (1959)
British Columbia	(1871)	(1871)	1876 (1927)	1876 (1941-1961)	1876 (1941-1961)	1869[12] (1951)	1901	1871	1894 (1947-1971) 1963 (1977)	1901 (1941-1961)	1948	1917	1914	1923	1971	1917 (1963)

TABLE A-2

Births and Deaths of Taxes in Canada: Municipalities by Province, 1793-1989.

Municipalities by Province	Customs Revenue (1)	Excise Duties (2)	Real Property Tax (3)	Personal Property Taxes (4)	Personal Income Taxes (5)	Poll Taxes (6)	Business Taxes (7)	Natural Resource Revenues (8)	Succession Duties (9)	Corporation Income Taxes (10)	General Sales Taxes (11)	Selected Excise Taxes on: Alcoholic Beverage (12)	Autos (13)	Gasoline (14)	Tobacco Products (15)	Amusement (16)
PEI	--	--	1855[13]	1855 (1971)	1877 (1888)[14]	1870 (1972)	--	--	--	--	--	--	--	--	--	--
Nova Scotia	--	--	1831	1831 (1916)	1849 (1884)[16]	1866[15] (1971)	1916	--	--	--	--	--	--	--	--	--
New Brunswick	--	--	1822[17]	1822 (1967)	1831[18]	1822[19] (1965)	--	--	--	--	--	1822	--	--	--	--
Newfoundland	--	--	1852[20]	--	--	1942[21]	1951[22]	--	--	--	--	--	1942	1949[23]	--	1942
Quebec	--	--	1855	--	1855[24] (1939)	1870 (1980)	1870	--	--	--	1935[25]	1845	--	--	--	1965
Ontario	--	--	1793[26]	1850 (1904)	1850 (1936)[27]	1944 (1968)	1904	--	--	--	--	1868	--	--	--	--
Manitoba	--	--	1891	1891 (1906)	--	1965	1893	--	--	--	--	1922	--	--	--	--
Saskatchewan	--	--	1883	1883 (1908)	1883 (1932)	1885[28]	1893	--	--	--	--	--	--	--	--	1920
Alberta	--	--	1883	1883 (1904)	1883 (1932)	1885 (1958)	1893	--	--	--	--	--	--	--	--	--
British Columbia	--	--	1860[29]	1886 (1916)	1865[30] (1876)	1891 (1957)	1860	--	--	--	--	--	--	--	--	1920

Notes to Tables A-1 and A-2

* Dates in these two columns coincide with entry into Confederation. A date within brackets, ( ), indicates the repeal of a tax. Two dates within brackets indicate the period of repeal, after which the tax was reintroduced.

1. Includes land taxes at the provincial level: the B.C. land tax, introduced in 1869, eventually gave way to the real property tax of 1876; the P.E.I. land tax of 1877 was repealed in 1882 and reappeared as a real property tax in 1894.

   By 1988 those provinces still taxing real property (except New Brunswick and P.E.I.) were taxing unorganized areas where there was no municipal taxation. New Brunswick reversed the trend to a declining role for the provincial property tax in 1967 and instituted a new education tax and business tax based on the value of real property.

2. The personal property tax at the municipal level had become so haphazard in its administration that by the 1890s it was almost exclusively "a business tax on the inventory of merchants" (Perry, 1955:125). The personal property tax was first repealed by Winnipeg in 1893 and replaced by a business tax on floor space; in 1906 it was replaced in all Manitoba towns and villages by a business tax on rental value; the tax continued, in a very limited application in some cities. The tax in Ontario municipalities was repealed and replaced by a business tax on value of real estate in 1904. Edmonton and Calgary repealed it, replacing it by a business tax levied first of all on floor space (1904) and later on rental value (1916). Saskatchewan repealed the tax for all municipalities in 1908 and replaced it with the business tax on floor space. Halifax, which had first introduced the personal property tax in 1831, replaced it by a business tax on assessed value in 1916 (the tax continued, in a very limited fashion, in other municipalities through and beyond the time period of the table). In New Brunswick by 1875 the tax had been extended in a number of municipalities to tax corporations as well.

3. Personal income taxes were repealed in all provinces in 1941 in connection with the Wartime Tax Agreements. Various ensuing Tax Rental and Tax Sharing Agreements resulted in all provinces except Quebec re-entering the field in 1962; Quebec had already imposed a personal income tax in 1954.

4. All taxes on corporations by provinces and municipalities were repealed during the period of the Wartime Tax Agreements, 1941–1946 inclusive.

5. Succession duties were repealed in all provinces except Quebec and Ontario in 1947, in connection with the Tax Rental Agreements. British Columbia re-entered the field in 1963. Alberta and Saskatchewan, in 1967 and 1969 respectively, refunded to their citizens the revenues from death duties, and did not impose succession duties in 1972. The remaining provinces re-entered the field in 1972 and subsequently repealed such taxes.

6. Corporation income taxes were repealed in all provinces in 1941 in connection with the Wartime Tax Agreements. Various ensuing Tax Rental and Tax Sharing agreements resulted in all provinces except Quebec and Ontario re-entering the field in 1962; Quebec imposed a corporation income

tax from 1947 onwards, whereas Ontario imposed one from 1947–1951 and from 1957 onwards. All consenting provinces were required by the 1947 Agreement to impose a 5 percent income tax on corporations from 1947–1951 (this is not shown on the table), which was collected by the Federal government.

7. Includes excise taxes at the Dominion level, Liquor Control Board profits at the Provincial level and tavern licences, etc., at the Municipal level. Excise duties on alcoholic beverages and tobacco products have been applied by the Dominion government since 1867. In 1922 Manitoba returned to the municipalities one-half of liquor profits.

8. Includes excise taxes at the Dominion level and motor vehicle licences and fees at the Provincial and Municipal level.

9. Includes tax on amusements, pari-mutual bets and playing cards. Quebec vacated the amusement tax field in 1965 and left it entirely to the municipalities. Saskatchewan did the same later (cities in Saskatchewan had been allowed to levy amusement taxes since 1920), B.C. returned one-half of all amusement taxes to the municipalities from 1920 onwards; all provinces were still levying taxes on pari-mutual betting as of 1967.

10. Prince Edward Island introduced poll taxes first in 1877 and repealed them in 1882; it later re-introduced them in 1919 and 1920.

11. The collection of royalties or rent from land (for agriculture and timber uses) most likely began with the Act of 1844, but it was 1860 before royalties on mineral exploitation were provided for. These royalties and natural resources were repealed in 1872 and re-enacted in 1875. Mining taxes of a general nature were imposed only in 1949.

12. British Columbia repealed its first poll tax in 1913, reinstated it in 1917 and finally abolished it in 1951.

13. The first real property tax was imposed by Charlottetown in 1855; Summerside followed suit in 1877.

14. Summerside introduced a personal income tax in 1870 which was repealed in 1880; Charlottetown introduced such a tax in 1880 and it was repealed eight years later.

15. In Nova Scotia poll taxes were the principle source of revenues at Confederation; with the Act of 1888 not more than one-quarter of local revenues were to be raised by this means.

16. In Nova Scotia income was included in the personal tax base of the municipalities in 1835, but Halifax was the first municipality to introduce a clearly defined income tax in 1849.

17. The first real property tax was imposed in 1822 and repealed shortly after; by 1831 a few municipalities were using such a tax.

18. In New Brunswick a few municipalities had income taxes, but it was not until 1849 that such taxes were enforced aggressively. In 1908 the income tax was imposed on all municipalities by the provincial government.

19. In New Brunswick municipalities in 1822, one-half of local revenues were required to be raised by a poll tax; the ratio was reduced to one-eighth in 1831 and increased to one-sixth in 1875.

20. The first real property tax was an assessment based on rents or appraisal values of buildings, enacted by the Newfoundland Legislature for St. John's in 1852. In 1859 an additional water assessment charge was enacted. These two taxes were combined into a municipal property tax in 1888, at which time St. John's was incorporated as a Town with a municipal government. The real property tax is a local option except in St. John's, where it is mandatory.

21. St. John's had a poll tax prior to 1942, but the newer municipalities, created after 1942, relied much more extensively on this tax as a source of revenue. It is now used to a limited extent only.

22. St. John's converted its stock tax into a business tax (a property tax on rental value of businesses).

23. St. John's introduced a fuel and oil tax.

24. The first municipal income tax in Quebec was introduced in 1855 and repealed in 1870; however, Sherbrooke introduced an income tax in 1886 (repealed 1912), Sorel in 1889, Hull in 1893, Montreal in 1935 and Quebec City in 1939.

25. The first retail sales tax in Canada was imposed by the city of Montreal in 1935. It became the model for the Quebec retail sales tax in 1940 and between 1941 and 1943 five other municipalities followed suit (Valleyfield, Chicoutimi, St. Joseph d'Alma, Trois-Rivières and Sorel).

26. The real property tax was introduced early into the municipalities of Ontario (Upper Canada), but it was not until 1850 that extensive use was made of this revenue source.

27. The municipal income tax in Ontario, first introduced in 1850, was firmly entrenched by a strengthened law in 1866 and considerably broadened in definition in 1904.

28. The poll tax is authorized for use in Saskatchewan municipalities, but it is not currently in use.

29. The first real property tax was introduced by Vancouver Island in 1860; Vancouver followed suit in 1886.

30. Vancouver introduced a 1 percent tax on salaries in 1865; it was repealed when the provincial income tax was introduced in 1876.

Appendix B

Dominion Government Expenditure, Revenue and Budget Deficit, Canada 1868–1990

Dominion Expenditure, Revenue and Budget Deficit

The data on expenditure and revenue for 1868–1919 are derived from the comprehensive summary of expenditure, revenue, assets and liabilities found in Canada, *Public Accounts* for 1919 (Part I).[1] Georg Rich drew upon the same source for 1915 and adjusted the data to eliminate several fictitious items for the years 1868 through 1914.[2] I extended the adjustment procedure until 1919, when the format of presentation in the *Public Accounts* changed. The adjustment procedure is as follows. The data on expenditure represent total disbursements (24), excluding sinking fund allocations (25), the discount on loans (93), allowances to the provinces (93) and certain consolidated fund transfers (92). The data on revenue represent total receipts (25), excluding the premium on loans (95), and certain consolidated fund transfers (93). In addition, I deducted from both expenditure and revenue interest received by the government on investments (68), and receipts on account of the premium or discount on the exchange rate (69).

Government expenditure and revenue are therefore roughly equivalent to the modern national income version. Expenditure comprises net interest payments on the public debt, purchases of goods and services, and subsidies to the provinces and railway companies. Revenue includes receipts from all sources, except interest and the profit arising from the premium or discount on the exchange rate.

The data on expenditure and revenue for 1920–1942 are derived from the summary for the 1943 *Public Accounts* (pp. 44–50) and the *Public Accounts* for each individual year. The change in format in 1920 rendered redundant or unobtainable most of the adjustments referred to above — sinking fund allocations, the discount on loans, allowances to the provinces, certain consolidated fund transfers and the premium on loans.[3] A further change in the classification system of the accounts in

1936 created a new category of expenditures — government-owned enterprises — which included some items of account for the first time.[4] It also included others (occasional write-down of assets and non-active accounts) which were recorded on both the expenditure and revenue side of the budget. These latter are deducted from both expenditure and revenue in the data presented here. The revised disbursements and receipts classification of 1936 was extended back to 1930; consequently there is a slight discontinuity in the data between fiscal 1929 and 1930.

One further adjustment is made to the expenditure data for the years 1929 through 1933, in order to correct an error in expenditures for the year 1933 reported in official sources.[5] In fiscal 1933 a large item ($62.9 million), described as "accounts carried as active assets transferred to non-active", appeared for the only time in the account. This sum turns out upon closer examination to be comprised of two amounts that had been spent earlier.[6] The first component is loans to the Canadian National Railways during fiscal 1932, amounting to $41.1 million, that had initially been recorded as active loans (and thus repayable) but had been converted by the government into funds that could be used to meet the deficit on the Railways' accounts. Accordingly, the loan became a government expenditure and was recorded as such for fiscal 1933. It should have been recorded during the year in which it was spent, fiscal 1932, and I have made this correction.

The second component includes advances totalling $21.8 million, on loans to various Harbour Commissions over the years 1929–1932 for various projects; it was recognized in 1933 that these advances (all of which had been spent) could not be repaid. Consequently, the government converted the advances into expenditures and recorded them as such for fiscal 1933. These advances should have been recorded during the years in which they were spent, fiscal 1929–1932, and this correction has been made. The effect of these adjustments is to increase officially recorded expenditures slightly in fiscal 1929, 1930 and 1931, and substantially in fiscal 1932 and to reduce officially recorded expenditures by a significant amount in fiscal 1933. The corrected deficit for 1933 falls from $220 million to $158 million.[7]

It is possible that the corrected data for Dominion expenditures in the period fiscal 1929 through 1933 could affect the empirical work incorporated in any previous quantitative studies that tried to estimate the impact of government spending during a time period that included these critically important depression years.

The data for 1943–1951 are derived from the summary for the 1951 *Public Accounts* (pp. 102–106) and the *Public Accounts* for each individual year. In 1943 the *Public Accounts*, prepared by the Deputy Minister of Finance, and the report of the Auditor General were combined into one report, with much greater detail provided on expenditure.[8] Commencing with a $69,000 administrative expense in fiscal 1941, the Unemployment Insurance Commission began operations which entailed new taxes and generated new expenditures by the Dominion government. The *Public Accounts* record as expenditures on the budgetary accounts administrative expenses and the government's contribution to the Unemployment Insurance Commission (one fifth of total employer and employee tax contributions). The employer-employee tax contributions and the unemployment insurance benefits paid out are not recorded as revenues or as expenditures, but are treated instead as transactions of a separate account — the Unemployment Insurance Commission Account. A comprehensive picture of all government expenditure and all government revenue requires the inclusion of these transactions (net of the already recorded government contributions) and the treatment of any resulting deficit or surplus as a component of the total deficit or surplus of the government. Consequently, the following adjustment is made to the public accounts data, commencing in 1942. The employee-employer contribution tax is added to revenues, and unemployment insurance benefit payments, minus the government's contribution to the Unemployment Insurance Fund, are added to expenditures. This Unemployment Insurance Fund adjustment is made for the fiscal years 1942–1986.

The *Public Accounts* adopted this adjustment procedure in 1986 and revised their treatment of the unemployment insurance sector back to 1980.

The data for 1952–1967 are derived from Appendix No. 1 of the 1967 *Public Accounts* (pp. 9.4–9.5) and the *Public Accounts* for each individual year. Two additional adjustments are made to the *Public Accounts* data during this period. The first adjustment allows for the complete inclusion of the Old Age Security Fund transactions. The *Public Accounts* treat any deficit on the Fund's operations as an expenditure from the budget (this either appears as an authorized expenditure out of the consolidated fund or as a temporary loan from the Minister of Finance which is later forgiven and occasionally repaid out of a future fund surplus). Neither the old age security benefit payments nor the old age security taxes (on individual incomes, corporation incomes and manufacturers' sales) are recorded as part of budgetary transactions. A comprehensive picture of all government activity must include these transactions. Consequently, the following adjustment is made to the data for 1952–1976. The old age security taxes are added to revenues and old age security benefit payments, minus any deficit, is added to expenditures.[9]

The *Public Accounts* adopted this adjustment procedure in 1976; eventually the special old age security tax revenues were folded into the existing revenue sources.

The second adjustment involves the Defence Equipment and Replacement Account from fiscal 1951 through 1959.[10] Robert Will notes the distortions in expenditures that arise in the *Public Accounts* treatment of intragovernmental transactions and especially the magnitude of these large distortions for one of the largest special funds: the defence equipment replacement account.[11] The *Public Accounts* treat some part (but not all, except in 1950–51) of the voted allotments to the fund as ordinary expenditures of the budget. However, the real expenditures are the disbursements made out of the fund, and these disbursements bear no relationship to the allotments or the partial allotments for any given year. I have included as net expenditures, in connection with the Defence Equipment and Replacement Account, the difference between the ordinary expenditures credited to the account and the disbursements paid out it.

Stanley Winer and Walter Hettich used the methodology of this Appendix to derive the data for 1968–1985, for purposes of their own research.[12] I am extremely grateful to them for making their series available for use in my own study.

During this period, the social development tax appeared in 1969 and was folded into the reformed income tax in 1972 (it is included in column (8), Table B-2). In addition, a package of special energy taxes emerged (the Canadian ownership special charge, 1982–1986; oil export charges, 1974–1986; a special excise tax on gasoline, 1976–1990; the petroleum and gas revenue tax, 1981–1987; the natural gas tax, 1981–1984; special petroleum compensation charge in 1982 and the aviation and diesel fuel tax, 1986–1990). These revenue sources are grouped under 'energy taxes' and included in column (8), Table B-2. Federal estate taxes died in 1971 and any delayed revenues after 1975 are included in other miscellaneous taxes, which are included in column (12).

The separate Old Age Security Fund ceased to exist in 1976, and thereafter the old age security tax revenues were inseparable from the personal income tax revenues, corporation income tax revenues and sales tax revenues paid into the consolidated revenue fund. Benefit payments were made out of this fund. Consequently from 1976 onwards, the *Public Accounts* treated the 'fund' as it has been treated in this study. In 1986 the Unemployment Insurance Fund was integrated into the *Public Accounts* in a manner identical with its treatment in this study (*Public Accounts* data were adjusted back to 1980). As a result, there is a discontinuity in the data series over fiscal 1979–1980.

The data for 1986–1990 are derived from the *Public Accounts* for those years, and adjusted where necessary to conform with the methodology of this Appendix.

The budget deficit is calculated by subtracting total revenue, as derived above, from total expenditure, as derived above. A surplus appears with a minus sign. The deficit (surplus) for any year will encompass any separate deficits (surpluses) on the Unemployment Insurance Commission transactions, the Old Age Security Fund and the Defence Equipment and Replacement Account.

Dominion government expenditure, revenue and budget deficit (surplus), calculated in the manner described, are provided in Table B-1.

Comparison with Other Sources of Data

There exists only one other series for expenditure and revenue of the Dominion government which is continuous from 1868; it does, however, appear in three settings. Harvey Perry's *Taxes, Tariffs and Subsidies* contains a detailed compilation of total revenue and revenue sources for 1868–1954.[13] The Canadian Tax Foundation reproduces Perry's series on revenue, extends it to 1956, and adds expenditure of the Dominion government for 1868–1956.[14] Urquhart and Buckley, in an extensive section on government finances written by Perry, include Perry's series on expenditure and revenue with some revisions, and extend them to 1960.[15]

Perry's revenue series for 1868–1919 is identical with total receipts in Canada, *Public Accounts* for 1919 (p. 25). The series for 1921–1929 differs from total receipts of the summary tables in Canada, *Public Accounts* for 1943 (pp. 44–48), the source of the difference being the "special receipts and other credits" column (Perry's series records higher values than do the *Public Accounts*). There is no explanation in any of the three sources for the difference in this column. The series for 1930–1960 is identical with total receipts of the summary tables in Canada, *Public Accounts* for 1943, 1951 and 1967, which incorporate the revised format of 1936 (extended back to 1930), noted earlier in this Appendix. All three sources exclude the revenue from the employee-employer tax contributions for unemployment insurance from 1942 onwards. All three of them exclude the revenue generated by the old age security taxes from total budgetary revenue in 1952 and the following years, but Urquhart and Buckley provide the data in a separate set of columns (one for each of the three taxes).

Perry's expenditure series for 1868–1919 is identical with total disbursements exclusive of sinking funds in Canada, *Public Accounts* for

1919 (pp. 24–25). The series for 1921–1929 differs from total disbursements in the summary tables in Canada, *Public Accounts* for 1943, the source of the difference being the "Other Charges" column. There is no explanation for the derivation of this column. The series for 1930–1960 is identical with total disbursements in the summary tables referred to above, which incorporate the revised format of 1936 (extended back to 1930). The Canadian Tax Foundation, and Urquhart and Buckley, treat unemployment insurance expenditures and old age security benefit payments in the same way as does the *Public Accounts*, but the latter provide a separate column for old age security benefit payments.[16] Urquhart and Buckley have a separate column on expenditures from the Defence Equipment and Replacement Account for fiscal 1953–59; this is misleading, because if one were to add this column to total budgetary expenditures, the result would be a distortion of true expenditures on the account.[17]

In summary, Perry's series on expenditure and revenue include only one of the adjustments — the sinking fund allocation — which we made to the *Public Accounts* data in order to eliminate fictitious entries and render the data roughly comparable to figures prepared on a national accounts basis. These differences are most noticeable during the early years.[18] In addition, Perry's series include some adjustments for the years 1921–1929 for which we have not been able to find an explanation and which we do not include in the data presented here. Finally, they exclude a comprehensive treatment of three significant funds, two of which involve new taxes and therefore are important for our purposes.

Perry includes data on Dominion revenue only; consequently the question of a series for the deficit (surplus) does not arise. The Canadian Tax Foundation, and Urquhart and Buckley, include data on Dominion revenue and expenditure but no data on the deficit (surplus) implied by these series. Canada, *Public Accounts* for 1967 (pp. 9.2–9.3) provides a series on the deficit (surplus) which allows for only one of the adjustments — the sinking fund allocation — which we made to the data. This series on the deficit (surplus) derived from a comprehensive definition of Dominion expenditure and revenue is important, because the deficit has been one of the major sources of financing the Dominion government's expenditures.

Dominion Financial Requirements,
by Revenue Sources

The data on the separate revenue sources are drawn from the same sources and include the same adjustments as described above. I used Perry, Urquhart and Buckley and the *Public Accounts* to extract a breakdown of revenues, by source.[19] The "miscellaneous revenues" of Perry are adjusted in two respects. First, the Canada, *Public Accounts* for 1943, summary table is substituted for Perry's data for 1920–1929. Second, the four adjustments to revenue, noted above, are subtracted from the "miscellaneous revenues" of Perry.

The data include three revenue sources, not normally included as part of budgetary revenues, but discussed above in detail: unemployment insurance taxes from 1942 to 1990, old age security taxes from 1952 to 1976 and the value of the deficit (surplus).

Dominion government financial requirements, by revenue source, are shown in Table B-2. The percentage share of each source in total financial requirements is given in Table B-3.

Composition of Total Financial Requirements

The composition of total financial requirements, by four major categories of revenues — consumption, income, deficit financing and other — is derived in Table B-4 as follows. Consumption-based taxes include the following items from Table B-2: customs duties, excise duties, sales tax (including the old age security (OAS) portion), excise taxes and the excise-based energy taxes (special excise on gasoline, natural gas excise tax and aviation and diesel fuel excise tax).

Income-based taxes include the following items from the same source: individual income tax (including the OAS portion), corporate income taxes (including the OAS portion), non-resident income taxes, excess profits taxes and income-based energy taxes (petroleum and gas revenue tax). Deficit financing is borrowing and a surplus has a negative sign.

The residual 'other' category includes — again with reference to Table B-2: the remaining energy taxes (Canadian ownership special charge, oil export charges and the special petroleum compensation charge), estate taxes, post office revenues, miscellaneous revenues, special receipts and other credits and unemployment insurance (UIC) taxes.

The composition of total financial requirements, disaggregated for the four major categories, is shown in Table B-4 in millions of dollars and in percentages of total financial requirements.

TABLE B-1

Dominion Goverment Spending and Financing, Canada,
Fiscal & Calendar Years, 1868-1990. (Millions of Dollars)

Fiscal Year	Total Spending& Financing (1)	Revenue (2)	Deficit (3)	Calendar Year	Total Spending& Financing (4)	Revenue (5)	Deficit (6)	Debt (7)
1868	13.5	13.5	0.0	1868	13.3	13.3	0.0	0.0
1869	13.1	13.0	0.1	1869	15.3	14.1	1.3	1.3
1870	17.5	15.1	2.4	1870	17.9	17.0	1.0	2.3
1871	18.3	18.8	-0.5	1871	20.7	19.5	1.2	3.4
1872	23.0	20.2	2.8	1872	23.7	20.4	3.3	6.7
1873	24.3	20.5	3.8	1873	24.8	22.1	2.8	9.5
1874	25.3	23.6	1.7	1874	28.2	23.7	4.6	14.0
1875	31.1	23.7	7.4	1875	30.1	22.8	7.3	21.3
1876	29.0	21.8	7.2	1876	30.0	22.0	8.0	29.3
1877	30.9	22.2	8.7	1877	29.5	21.9	7.6	36.9
1878	28.1	21.6	6.5	1878	28.1	24.0	4.1	41.0
1879	28.1	26.4	1.7	1879	30.1	24.5	5.6	46.5
1880	32.0	22.6	9.4	1880	31.9	25.7	6.2	52.7
1881	31.8	28.8	3.0	1881	32.1	31.5	0.6	53.3
1882	32.4	34.2	-1.8	1882	36.5	35.0	1.5	54.8
1883	40.5	35.7	4.8	1883	43.2	33.8	9.4	64.2
1884	45.8	31.8	14.0	1884	45.5	31.5	14.0	78.2
1885	45.1	31.2	13.9	1885	49.8	31.1	18.7	96.8
1886	54.4	31.0	23.4	1886	46.7	32.9	13.8	110.6
1887	38.9	34.8	4.1	1887	40.5	34.9	5.7	116.2
1888	42.1	34.9	7.2	1888	40.6	36.2	4.5	120.7
1889	39.1	37.4	1.7	1889	38.9	38.1	0.9	121.5
1890	38.7	38.7	0.0	1890	38.2	38.1	0.1	121.6
1891	37.6	37.4	0.2	1891	37.8	36.6	1.2	122.8
1892	37.9	35.7	2.2	1892	37.6	36.3	1.3	124.1
1893	37.3	36.9	0.4	1893	38.2	36.0	2.3	126.4
1894	39.1	35.0	4.1	1894	39.1	33.8	5.3	131.7
1895	39.1	32.6	6.5	1895	39.9	33.9	6.0	137.6
1896	40.6	35.2	5.4	1896	40.0	35.8	4.3	141.9
1897	39.4	36.3	3.1	1897	39.9	37.6	2.3	144.1
1898	40.3	38.9	1.4	1898	43.7	41.9	1.8	145.9
1899	47.0	44.9	2.1	1899	47.8	47.1	0.7	146.6
1900	48.5	49.2	-0.7	1900	51.1	50.0	1.2	147.7
1901	53.7	50.7	3.0	1901	56.6	53.4	3.2	150.9
1902	59.4	56.1	3.3	1902	58.1	59.9	-1.8	149.1
1903	56.7	63.6	-6.9	1903	59.4	66.0	-6.6	142.5
1904	62.1	68.4	-6.3	1904	68.3	68.8	-0.5	142.0
1905	74.4	69.1	5.3	1905	76.5	73.5	3.1	145.0
1906	78.6	77.8	0.8	1906	81.4	83.3	-1.9	143.1
1907	63.1	66.5	-3.4	1907	101.8	92.7	9.1	152.2
1908	107.7	94.1	13.6	1908	122.5	85.9	36.6	188.8
1909	127.4	83.2	44.2	1909	114.0	94.9	19.1	207.8
1910	109.5	98.8	10.7	1910	116.3	111.8	4.6	212.4
1911	118.6	116.1	2.5	1911	129.8	130.1	-0.3	212.1
1912	133.5	134.7	-1.2	1912	139.4	158.9	-19.5	192.6
1913	141.3	166.9	-25.6	1913	170.6	162.6	8.1	200.7
1914	180.4	161.1	19.3	1914	223.7	137.5	86.2	286.9
1915	238.1	129.6	108.5	1915	307.9	158.8	149.1	436.0
1916	331.1	168.5	162.6	1916	441.2	213.7	227.6	663.5
1917	477.9	228.7	249.2	1917	537.8	248.8	289.0	952.5
1918	557.7	255.5	302.2	1918	660.6	292.5	368.1	1320.6
1919	694.9	304.8	390.1	1919	714.4	324.2	390.3	1710.8
1920	720.9	330.6	390.3	1920	475.5	391.2	84.3	1795.1
1921	393.7	411.4	-17.7	1921	356.1	373.0	-16.9	1778.3
1922	343.6	360.2	-16.6	1922	335.1	378.6	-43.5	1734.7
1923	332.2	384.7	-52.5	1923	330.4	390.5	-60.1	1674.7
1924	329.8	392.4	-62.6	1924	328.1	352.4	-24.4	1650.3
1925	327.5	339.1	-11.6	1925	332.6	364.8	-32.2	1618.2
1926	334.3	373.3	-39.0	1926	336.9	386.8	-49.9	1568.3
1927	337.8	391.3	-53.5	1927	345.9	411.4	-65.5	1502.8
1928	348.6	418.1	-69.5	1928	359.8	440.1	-80.3	1422.5
1929	363.5	447.4	-83.9	1929	387.3	441.1	-53.8	1368.7
1930	395.2	439.0	-43.8	1930	427.0	369.9	57.2	1425.8
1931	437.6	346.8	90.8	1931	474.9	328.4	146.5	1572.3
1932	487.3	322.3	165.0	1932	465.3	305.8	159.5	1731.8
1933	458.0	300.3	157.7	1933	449.7	310.1	139.6	1871.3

TABLE B-1

Dominion Goverment Spending and Financing, Canada,
Fiscal & Calendar Years, 1868-1990. (Millions of Dollars)

Fiscal Year	Total Spending& Financing	Revenue	Deficit	Calendar Year	Total Spending& Financing	Revenue	Deficit	Debt
	(1)	(2)	(3)		(4)	(5)	(6)	(7)
1934	446.9	313.4	133.5	1934	461.4	340.9	120.5	1991.8
1935	466.2	350.1	116.1	1935	508.0	359.0	149.0	2140.8
1936	521.9	361.9	160.0	1936	520.7	422.3	98.4	2239.2
1937	520.3	442.4	77.9	1937	520.4	487.6	32.8	2272.0
1938	520.4	502.7	17.7	1938	532.6	490.0	42.6	2314.6
1939	536.7	485.8	50.9	1939	613.7	512.0	101.8	2416.3
1940	639.4	520.7	118.7	1940	1057.8	745.0	312.7	2729.1
1941	1197.2	819.8	377.4	1941	1658.2	1299.3	359.0	3088.0
1942	1811.9	1459.1	352.8	1942	3654.7	2014.4	1640.3	4728.3
1943	4268.9	2199.5	2069.4	1943	4966.0	2585.0	2381.0	7109.2
1944	5198.3	2713.5	2484.8	1944	5134.5	2648.3	2486.2	9595.4
1945	5113.2	2626.6	2486.6	1945	5044.7	2863.5	2181.1	11776.5
1946	5021.8	2942.5	2079.3	1946	3175.5	2972.0	203.5	11980.0
1947	2560.0	2981.8	-421.8	1947	2184.9	2852.4	-667.6	11312.4
1948	2059.8	2809.3	-749.5	1948	2030.5	2715.9	-685.4	10627.0
1949	2020.7	2684.7	-664.0	1949	2271.5	2565.5	-294.0	10333.1
1950	2355.1	2525.7	-170.6	1950	2544.1	2927.3	-383.2	9949.9
1951	2607.1	3061.1	-454.0	1951	3395.8	3781.6	-385.8	9564.1
1952	3658.7	4021.8	-363.1	1952	4272.5	4471.8	-199.3	9364.8
1953	4477.1	4621.8	-144.7	1953	4577.5	4677.3	-99.8	9265.0
1954	4611.0	4695.8	-84.8	1954	4667.0	4499.8	167.3	9432.3
1955	4685.7	4434.4	251.3	1955	4750.9	4659.6	91.3	9523.5
1956	4772.6	4734.7	37.9	1956	5133.1	5276.3	-143.2	9380.4
1957	5253.3	5456.8	-203.5	1957	5557.4	5442.5	114.9	9495.3
1958	5658.7	5437.7	221.0	1958	6042.3	5179.2	863.1	10358.3
1959	6170.1	5093.0	1077.1	1959	6327.1	5642.3	684.8	11043.1
1960	6379.4	5825.4	554.0	1960	6646.5	6115.0	531.5	11574.6
1961	6735.5	6211.5	524.0	1961	7124.9	6309.6	815.3	12389.9
1962	7254.7	6342.3	912.4	1962	7278.3	6486.8	791.4	13181.3
1963	7286.1	6535.0	751.1	1963	7493.3	6833.8	659.5	13840.9
1964	7562.4	6933.4	629.0	1964	7912.0	7754.7	157.3	13998.2
1965	8028.5	8028.4	0.1	1965	8530.5	8573.4	-42.9	13955.3
1966	8697.8	8755.0	-57.2	1966	9526.0	9303.3	222.6	14177.9
1967	9802.0	9486.1	315.9	1967	10680.5	10064.8	615.7	14793.6
1968	10973.3	10257.7	715.6	1968	11796.1	11228.8	567.3	15360.9
1969	12070.4	11552.5	517.9	1969	13031.6	13299.1	-267.5	15093.4
1970	13352.0	13881.3	-529.3	1970	14404.3	14203.5	200.8	15294.3
1971	14755.1	14310.9	444.2	1971	16349.9	15483.5	866.5	16160.7
1972	16881.5	15874.3	1007.2	1972	21485.4	19429.5	2055.9	18216.6
1973	23020.0	20614.5	2405.5	1973	24948.6	23085.2	1863.4	20080.0
1974	25591.5	23908.8	1682.7	1974	30939.8	29244.8	1694.9	21775.0
1975	32722.5	31023.5	1699.0	1975	35790.7	30820.2	4970.5	26745.5
1976	36813.4	30752.4	6061.0	1976	38019.1	32252.1	5767.0	32512.5
1977	38421.0	32752.0	5669.0	1977	41724.0	32839.8	8884.3	41396.7
1978	42825.0	32869.0	9956.0	1978	48520.5	34409.5	14111.0	55507.7
1979	50419.0	34923.0	15496.0	1979	49081.0	38346.8	10734.3	66242.0
1980	48635.0	39488.0	9147.0	1980	55151.8	44582.0	10569.8	76811.7
1981	57324.0	46280.0	11044.0	1981	66687.8	53135.8	13552.0	90363.7
1982	69809.0	55421.0	14388.0	1982	80381.0	55922.0	24459.0	114822.7
1983	83905.0	56089.0	27816.0	1983	90154.8	58901.5	31253.3	146076.0
1984	92238.0	59839.0	32399.0	1984	101781.8	64939.0	36842.8	182918.7
1985	104963.0	66639.0	38324.0	1985	106868.8	71478.0	35390.8	218309.5
1986	107504.0	73091.0	34413.0	1986	110992.3	79435.3	31557.0	249866.5
1987	112155.0	81550.0	30605.0	1987	118779.0	90064.8	28714.3	278580.7
1988	120987.0	92903.0	28084.0	1988	127350.0	98615.8	28734.3	307314.9
1989	127471.0	98520.0	28951.0	1989	135007.5	106022.8	28984.8	336299.7
1990	136863.0	107867.0	28996.0					

Sources: Public Accounts of Canada, see Appendix B discussion for columns (1)-(4);
fiscal year ended on June 30 until 1906, on March 31 for 1907 and later years.
See Appendix C discussion for columns (5)-(9);
the debt is the cumulative total of all deficits minus surpluses (column 7). Surplus: -

TABLE B-2

Dominion Government: Total Financial Requirements, By Revenue Source, Fiscal 1868-1990 (Millions of Dollars)

Fiscal Year[1]	Custom Duties (1)	Excise Duties (2)	Sales Tax[2] (3)	Excise Taxes (4)	Individual Income Tax (5)	Corporate Income Tax (6)	Non Resident (7)	Excess Profits and as Noted[3] (8)	Estate Taxes (9)	Post Office Revenues (10)	Miscellaneous Revenues (11)	Special Receipts & other Credits[4] (12)	UIC Taxes (13)	Old Age Security Taxes[5] (14)	Deficit (Surplus) (15)	Total Financial Requirements (16)	Change in TFR (17)	Fiscal Year
1868	8.6	3.0		0.1						0.5	1.3				0.0	13.5	0.0	1868
1869	8.3	2.7		0.1						0.5	1.4				0.1	13.1	-0.4	1869
1870	9.4	3.6		0.1						0.6	1.4				2.4	17.5	4.4	1870
1871	11.8	4.3		0.2						0.6	1.8				-0.5	18.3	0.8	1871
1872	12.8	4.7		0.2						0.7	1.8	0.1			2.8	23.0	4.7	1872
1873	12.9	4.5		0.2						0.8	1.9				3.8	24.3	1.3	1873
1874	14.3	5.6		0.2						1.1	2.1	0.2			1.7	25.3	1.0	1874
1875	15.4	5.1		0.2						1.2	1.8	0.3			7.4	31.1	5.8	1875
1876	12.8	5.6		0.2						1.1	2.1				7.2	29.0	-2.1	1876
1877	12.6	4.9		0.2						1.1	2.5	0.9			8.7	30.9	1.9	1877
1878	12.8	4.8		0.2						1.2	2.6				6.5	28.1	-2.8	1878
1879	12.9	5.4		0.2						1.2	2.2	4.5			1.7	28.1	0.0	1879
1880	14.1	4.2		0.2						1.3	2.7	0.1			9.4	32.0	3.9	1880
1881	18.4	5.3		0.1						1.4	3.5				3.0	31.8	-0.2	1881
1882	21.6	5.9		0.0						1.6	3.2	1.8			-1.8	32.4	0.6	1882
1883	23.0	6.3		0.0						1.8	3.6	1.0			4.8	40.5	8.1	1883
1884	20.0	5.5		0.0						1.7	3.7	0.9			14.0	45.8	5.3	1884
1885	18.9	6.5		0.0						1.8	3.4	0.6			13.9	45.1	-0.7	1885
1886	19.4	5.8		0.0						1.9	3.6	0.3			23.4	54.4	9.3	1886
1887	22.4	6.3		0.0						2.0	4.1				4.1	38.9	-15.5	1887
1888	22.1	6.1		0.0						2.4	4.3				7.2	42.1	3.2	1888
1889	23.7	6.9		0.0						2.2	4.6				1.7	39.1	-3.0	1889
1890	23.9	7.6		0.0						2.4	4.8				0.0	38.7	-0.4	1890
1891	23.3	6.9		0.0						2.5	4.7				0.2	37.6	-1.1	1891
1892	20.4	7.9		0.0						2.7	4.7				2.2	37.9	0.3	1892
1893	20.9	8.4		0.0						2.8	4.8				0.4	37.3	-0.6	1893
1894	19.1	7.8		0.0						2.8	4.7				4.1	39.1	1.8	1894
1895	17.6	7.9		0.0						2.8	4.4				6.5	39.1	0.0	1895
1896	19.8	7.9								3.0	4.5				5.4	40.6	1.5	1896
1897	19.4	9.2								3.2	4.5				3.1	39.4	-1.2	1897
1898	21.6	7.9								3.5	5.9				1.4	40.3	0.9	1898
1899	25.2	9.6								3.2	6.9				2.1	47.0	6.7	1899
1900	28.2	9.9								3.2	7.9				-0.7	48.5	1.5	1900
1901	28.3	10.3								3.4	8.7				3.0	53.7	5.2	1901
1902	31.9	11.2								3.9	9.1	3.3			3.3	59.4	5.7	1902
1903	36.7	12.0								4.4	7.2				-6.9	56.7	-2.7	1903
1904	40.5	12.9								4.7	10.3				-6.3	62.1	5.4	1904
1905	41.4	12.6								5.1	10.0				5.3	74.4	12.3	1905
1906	46.1	14.0								5.9	11.8				0.8	78.6	4.2	1906
1907	39.7	11.8								5.1	9.9				-3.4	63.1	-15.5	1907
1908	57.2	15.8								7.1	14.0	0.4			13.6	107.7	44.6	1908
1909	47.1	14.9								7.4	13.4	0.1			44.2	127.4	19.7	1909
1910	59.8	15.2								8.0	15.7				10.7	109.5	-17.9	1910

TABLE B-2

Dominion Government: Total Financial Requirements, By Revenue Source, Fiscal 1868-1990 (Millions of Dollars)

Fiscal Year	Custom Duties (1)	Excise Duties (2)	Sales Tax (3)	Excise Taxes (4)	Individual Income Tax (5)	Corporate Income Tax (6)	Non Resident (7)	Excess Profits and as Noted (8)	Estate Taxes (9)	Post Office Revenues (10)	Miscellaneous Revenues (11)	Special Receipts & other Credits (12)	UIC Taxes (13)	Old Age Security Taxes (14)	Deficit (Surplus) (15)	Total Financial Requirements (16)	Change in TFR (17)	Fiscal Year
1911	71.8	16.9								9.1	18.2	0.1			2.5	118.6	9.1	1911
1912	85.0	19.3								10.5	19.9				-1.2	133.5	14.9	1912
1913	111.8	21.4								12.1	21.6				-25.6	141.3	7.8	1913
1914	104.7	21.4								13.0	22.0				19.3	180.4	39.1	1914
1915	75.9	21.5		0.1						13.1	19.0				108.5	238.1	57.7	1915
1916	98.6	22.4		3.7						18.9	24.9				162.6	331.1	93.0	1916
1917	134.0	24.4		3.9	7.9	1.4		12.5		20.9	33.0				249.2	477.9	146.8	1917
1918	144.2	27.2		4.0	13.2	7.1		21.3		21.3	37.5				302.2	557.7	79.8	1918
1919	147.2	30.3		13.9	32.5	13.9		33.0		21.6	49.5				390.1	694.9	137.2	1919
1920	168.8	42.7		17.7	39.8	38.9		44.1		24.5	12.5				390.3	720.9	26.0	1920
1921	163.3	37.1	37.6	25.0	31.7	28.0		40.8		26.7	14.0	1.9			-17.7	393.7	-327.2	1921
1922	142.4	36.8	61.3	25.1	25.7	28.5		22.8		26.4	13.6	0.3			-16.6	343.6	-50.1	1922
1923	118.1	35.8	89.8	27.9	25.1	31.1		13.0		29.0	11.8	8.5			-52.5	332.2	-11.4	1923
1924	121.5	38.2	98.0	27.2	23.9	31.7		4.8		28.9	12.1	9.7			-62.6	329.8	-2.4	1924
1925	108.1	38.6	63.2	22.6	18.1	29.3		2.7		28.8	11.7	4.7			-11.6	327.5	-2.3	1925
1926	127.4	42.9	72.9	22.9	23.2	33.3		1.2		30.3	12.9	2.2			-39.0	334.3	6.8	1926
1927	142.0	48.5	81.2	21.2	24.8	34.6		0.7		29.1	13.4	1.8			-53.5	337.8	3.5	1927
1928	157.0	57.4	70.6	16.7	27.2	41.8		1.0		31.6	14.5	6.9			-69.5	348.6	10.8	1928
1929	187.2	63.7	62.6	19.6	26.7	44.4		0.5		30.6	15.8	4.7			-83.9	363.5	14.9	1929
1930	179.4	65.0	44.1	27.7	24.8	36.5		0.2		33.3	15.2	11.6			-43.8	395.2	31.7	1930
1931	131.2	57.7	20.1	47.6	26.0	36.1				30.2	11.7	8.1			90.8	437.6	42.4	1931
1932	104.1	48.7	41.7	45.9	29.2	27.4				32.2	7.0	7.7			165.0	487.3	49.7	1932
1933	70.1	37.8	56.8	38.9	33.0	35.8				30.9	9.8	5.1			157.7	458.0	-29.3	1933
1934	66.3	35.5	61.4	42.5	35.5	27.4	4.8			30.9	9.7	0.6			133.5	446.9	-11.1	1934
1935	76.6	43.2	72.4	58.0	40.4	35.8	5.8			31.3	10.6	3.5			116.1	466.2	19.3	1935
1936	74.0	44.4	77.6	69.8	46.9	42.5	7.2			32.5	11.4	0.4			160.0	521.9	55.7	1936
1937	83.8	46.0	112.8	85.2	45.4	58.0	8.9			34.3	12.0	9.1			77.9	520.3	-1.6	1937
1938	93.5	52.0	138.1	131.6	103.5	69.8	10.1			35.5	11.7	6.4			17.7	520.4	0.1	1938
1939	78.8	51.3	122.1	185.5	296.1	85.2	9.9			35.3	10.0	4.2			50.9	536.7	16.3	1939
1940	104.3	61.0	137.4	348.0	484.1	77.9	11.1	24.0		36.7		15.6			118.7	639.4	102.7	1940
1941	130.8	88.6	179.7	311.4	698.4	131.6	13.0	135.0	7.0	40.4		1.2			377.4	1197.2	557.8	1941
1942	142.4	110.1	236.2	276.4	672.8	185.5	28.3	434.6	13.2	46.0		16.3	36.4		352.8	1811.9	614.7	1942
1943	119.0	138.7	232.9	341.3	686.6	348.0	28.1	428.7	15.0	48.9		26.5	57.4		2069.4	4268.9	2457.0	1943
1944	167.9	142.1	304.9	426.7	670.5	311.4	27.0	341.3	17.2	61.1		153.8	61.8		2486.8	5198.3	929.4	1944
1945	115.1	151.9	209.4	442.5	659.8	276.4	28.6	426.7	21.5	66.1		342.1	63.8		2486.5	5113.2	-85.1	1945
1946	128.9	186.7	212.2	227.0	762.5	217.7	28.3	442.5	23.6	68.6		608.9	62.7		2079.3	5021.8	-91.4	1946
1947	237.4	196.0	298.2	442.5	622.0	238.8	30.1	227.0	30.8	73.0		405.2	76.0		-421.8	2560.0	-2461.8	1947
1948	293	196.8	372.3	227.0	659.8	364.2	35.9	44.8	25.5	77.8		188.9	90.5		-749.5	2059.8	-500.2	1948
1949	223.0	204.7	377.3	262.8	762.5	492.0	43.4	-1.8	29.9	80.6		69.4	98.7		-664.0	2020.7	-39.1	1949
1950	225.9	220.6	403.4	172.4	622.0	603.2	47.5	10.2	33.6	84.5		13.8	104.3		-170.6	2355.1	334.4	1950
1951	295.7	241.0	460.1	231.7	652.3	799.2	61.6	2.4	38.2	90.4		54.6	130.7		-454.0	2607.1	252.0	1951
1952	346.4	217.9	573.5	318.1	975.7	1130.7	55.0		38.1	104.6	42.0	41.2	149.7	26.4	-363.1	3658.1	1051.6	1952
1953	389.4	241.4	566.2	288.7	1180.0	1240.1	53.7			111.9	49.8	83.1	155.7	223.7	-144.7	4477.1	818.4	1953

TABLE B-2

Dominion Government: Total Financial Requirements, By Revenue Source, Fiscal 1868-1990 (Millions of Dollars)

Fiscal Year (1)	Custom Duties (1)	Excise Duties (2)	Sales Tax (3)	Excise Taxes (4)	Individual Income Tax (5)	Corporate Income Tax (6)	Non Resident (7)	Excess Profits and as Noted (8)	Estate Taxes (9)	Post Office Revenues (10)	Miscellaneous Revenues (11)	Special Receipts & other Credits (12)	UIC Taxes (13)	Old Age Security Taxes (14)	Deficit (Surplus) (15)	Total Financial Requirements (16)	Change in TFR (17)	Fiscal Year
1954	407.3	226.7	587.3	310.5	1187.7	1191.2	53.8		39.1	111.0	54.5	74.5	159.1	293.1	-84.8	4611.0	133.9	1954
1955	397.2	226.5	572.2	267.5	1183.4	1020.6	61.3		44.8	131.3	52.6	28.8	158.3	289.9	251.3	4685.7	74.7	1955
1956	481.2	249.4	641.5	277.5	1185.6	1027.7	66.2		66.6	137.4	115.9		169.5	316.2	37.9	4772.6	86.9	1956
1957	549.1	271.4	717.1	285.4	1400.5	1268.3	76.4		79.7	145.8	104.7		186.8	371.6	-203.5	5253.3	480.7	1957
1958	498.1	300.1	703.2	250.0	1499.8	1234.8	64.3		71.6	152.9	102.4		189.1	371.4	221.0	5658.7	405.4	1958
1959	486.5	316.7	694.5	241.8	1353.5	1020.6	61.2		72.6	157.5	127.3		185.5	375.3	1077.1	6170.1	511.4	1959
1960	525.7	335.2	732.7	287.4	1566.6	1142.9	73.3		88.4	167.6	130.1		228.6	546.9	554.0	6379.4	209.3	1960
1961	498.7	344.9	720.6	290.7	1711.2	1276.6	88.2		84.9	173.6	143.7		275.3	603.1	524.0	6735.5	356.1	1961
1962	534.5	362.8	759.7	262.6	1792.7	1202.1	112.3		84.6	183.7	125.5		275.7	644.0	912.4	7254.7	519.2	1962
1963	645.0	381.9	806.0	260.4	1744.6	1182.8	129.1		87.1	192.8	127.8		286.4	691.1	751.1	7286.1	31.4	1963
1964	581.4	393.3	946.1	273.5	1865.1	1259.0	124.5		90.7	200.7	152.4		296.6	750.1	629.0	7562.4	276.3	1964
1965	622.1	411.4	1204.6	269.2	2103.3	1523.8	143.7		88.6	230.4	160.3		310.7	960.3	0.1	8028.5	466.1	1965
1966	685.5	445.9	1395.1	296.3	2142.5	1606.6	170.0		108.4	237.5	169.6		328.3	1169.3	-57.2	8697.8	669.3	1966
1967	777.6	461.0	1513.6	315.7	2473.8	1593.2	203.6		101.1	253.3	163.8		343.8	1285.6	315.9	9802.0	1104.2	1967
1968	746.5	488.6	1601.1	337.0	2849.6	1670.6	220.5	0.0	102.2	281.6	119.1		346.0	1494.6	715.6	10973.3	1171.3	1968
1969	761.7	509.3	1569.8	377.6	3356.4	2030.0	205.6	63.0	112.4	288.4	190.9	0.3	461.0	1626.1	517.9	12070.0	1097.1	1969
1970	818.3	518.8	1716.9	378.4	4085.1	2612.0	248.5	476.5	100.6	354.8	144.0	0.3	590.0	1837.1	-529.3	13352.0	1281.6	1970
1971	814.5	561.0	1707.5	403.2	4696.5	2218.5	258.2	566.2	119.9	337.6	119.3	0.3	594.0	1914.2	444.2	14755.1	1403.1	1971
1972	988.6	606.6	1984.7	388.4	5582.0	2183.1	287.7	408.4	132.0	403.8	127.6	0.3	663.0	2118.0	1007.2	16881.5	2126.4	1972
1973	1182.0	638.0	3052.0	400.0	8378.0	2920.0	292.0	15.6	60.9	470.0	163.0	0.4	763.0	2219.0	2405.5	23020.0	6138.5	1973
1974	1384.0	686.0	3590.0	408.0	9226.0	3710.0	324.0	287.0	14.3	480.0	265.0	61.0	1024.0	2496.5	1682.7	25591.5	2571.5	1974
1975	1809.0	748.0	3866.0	414.0	11710.0	4836.0	427.0	1669.0	7.0	486.0	264.0	14.0	1622.0	3158.5	1699.0	32722.5	7131.0	1975
1976	1887.0	815.0	3515.0	438.0	12709.0	5748.0	482.0	1488.0	10.0	444.0	322.0	7.0	2087.0	796.4	6061.0	36813.4	4090.9	1976
1977	2097.0	865.0	3929.0	485.0	14834.0	5363.0	451.0	1261.0		615.0	454.0	11.0	2528.0		5669.0	38421.0	1607.6	1977
1978	2312.0	882.0	4427.0	472.0	13988.0	5280.0	503.0	1030.0		773.0	541.0	70.0	2595.0		9956.0	42825.0	4404.0	1978
1979	2747.0	878.0	4729.0	499.0	14656.0	5654.0	568.0	844.0		903.0	503.0	66.0	2865.0		15496.0	50419.0	7594.0	1979
1980	3000.0	895.0	4698.0	502.0	16808.0	6951.0	787.0	1171.0		1118.0	684.0	77.0	2778.0		9147.0	48635.0	-1784.0	1980
1981	3788.0	1042.0	5429.0	573.0	19837.0	8106.0	867.0	1509.0		1109.0	618.0	96.0	3303.0		11044.0	57324.0	8689.0	1981
1982	3435.0	1175.0	6148.0	564.0	24046.0	8118.0	1018.0	4521.0		484.0	1039.0	99.0	4753.0		14388.0	69809.0	12485.0	1982
1983	2828.0	1274.0	5842.0	685.0	26330.0	7139.0	998.0	5147.0			814.0	120.0	4900.0		27816.0	83905.0	14096.0	1983
1984	3376.0	1356.0	6561.0	754.0	26967.0	7286.0	908.0	4168.0			1078.0	132.0	7259.0		32399.0	92238.0	8333.0	1984
1985	3794.0	1462.0	7592.0	850.0	29254.0	9379.0	1021.0	4479.0			1148.0	126.0	7553.0		38324.0	104963.0	12725.0	1985
1986	3971.0	1473.0	9345.0	1354.0	33008.0	9210.0	1053.0	3348.0			1484.0	107.0	8719.0		34413.0	107504.0	2541.0	1986
1987	4187.0	1470.0	11972.0	1455.0	37878.0	9885.0	1355.0	1965.0			1681.0	126.0	9558.0		30605.0	112155.0	4651.0	1987
1988	4385.0	1459.0	12927.0	1567.0	45125.0	10878.0	1162.0	2602.0			2166.0	144.0	10425.0		28084.0	120987.0	8332.0	1988
1989	4521.0	1453.0	15645.0	1506.0	48026.0	11730.0	1578.0	2646.0			1882.0	207.0	11268.0		28951.0	127471.0	6484.0	1989
1990	4587.0	2130.0	17672.0	1295.0	51895.0	13021.0	1361.0	2471.0			2461.0	226.0	10738.0		28996.0	136663.0	9392.0	1990

Source: Public Accounts of Canada See Appendix B for derivation

1. Fiscal year ended on June 30 until 1906 and on March 31 for 1907 and later years.
2. Gross Sales Tax Revenues less refunds of sales and other excises.
3. Business profits taxes (1917-1930) excess profits taxes (1941-1952) social development tax (1969-1973) and energy taxes (1974-1990).
4. Includes other miscellaneous taxes (and remnants of estate tax after 1975) from 1968 on.
5. Includes old age security individual income taxes corporation income taxes and sales taxes.

TABLE B-3

Dominion Government: Total Financial Requirements, By Revenue Source, Fiscal 1868-1990 (Percentages)

Fiscal Year	Custom Duties	Excise Duties	Sales Tax[2]	Excise Taxes	Individual Income Tax	Corporate Income Tax	Non Resident	Excess Profits and as Noted[3]	Estate Taxes	Post Office Revenues	Miscellaneous Revenues	Special Receipts & other Credits[4]	UIC Taxes	Old Age Security Taxes[5]	Deficit (Surplus)	Total Financial Requirements	Change in TFR	Fiscal Year
	(1)	(2)	(3)	(4)	(5)	(6)	(7)	(8)	(9)	(10)	(11)	(12)	(13)	(14)	(15)	(16)	(17)	
1868	63.7	22.2	0.0	0.7	0.0	0.0	0.0	0.0	0.0	3.7	9.6	0.0	0.0	0.0	0.1	100.0	0.0	1868
1869	63.4	20.6	0.0	0.8	0.0	0.0	0.0	0.0	0.0	3.8	10.7	0.0	0.0	0.0	0.8	100.0	-3.0	1869
1870	53.7	20.6	0.0	0.6	0.0	0.0	0.0	0.0	0.0	3.4	8.0	0.5	0.0	0.0	13.7	100.0	33.6	1870
1871	64.5	23.5	0.0	1.1	0.0	0.0	0.0	0.0	0.0	3.3	9.8	0.0	0.0	0.0	-2.7	100.0	4.6	1871
1872	55.7	20.4	0.0	0.9	0.0	0.0	0.0	0.0	0.0	3.0	7.8	0.8	0.0	0.0	12.2	100.0	25.7	1872
1873	53.1	18.5	0.0	0.8	0.0	0.0	0.0	0.0	0.0	3.3	7.8	0.0	0.0	0.0	15.6	100.0	5.7	1873
1874	56.5	22.1	0.0	0.8	0.0	0.0	0.0	0.0	0.0	4.3	8.3	1.2	0.0	0.0	6.7	100.0	4.1	1874
1875	49.5	16.4	0.0	0.6	0.0	0.0	0.0	0.0	0.0	3.9	5.8	0.8	0.0	0.0	23.8	100.0	22.9	1875
1876	44.1	19.3	0.0	0.7	0.0	0.0	0.0	0.0	0.0	3.8	7.2	0.0	0.0	0.0	24.8	100.0	-6.8	1876
1877	40.8	15.9	0.0	0.6	0.0	0.0	0.0	0.0	0.0	3.6	8.1	2.9	0.0	0.0	28.2	100.0	-6.6	1877
1878	45.6	17.1	0.0	0.6	0.0	0.0	0.0	0.0	0.0	4.3	9.3	0.0	0.0	0.0	23.1	100.0	-9.1	1878
1879	45.9	19.2	0.0	0.7	0.0	0.0	0.0	0.0	0.0	4.3	7.8	16.0	0.0	0.0	6.0	100.0	0.0	1879
1880	44.1	13.1	0.0	0.6	0.0	0.0	0.0	0.0	0.0	4.1	8.4	0.3	0.0	0.0	29.4	100.0	13.9	1880
1881	57.9	16.7	0.0	0.6	0.0	0.0	0.0	0.0	0.0	4.4	11.0	0.0	0.0	0.0	9.4	100.0	-0.6	1881
1882	66.7	18.2	0.0	0.3	0.0	0.0	0.0	0.0	0.0	4.9	9.9	5.6	0.0	0.0	-5.6	100.0	1.9	1882
1883	56.8	15.6	0.0	0.0	0.0	0.0	0.0	0.0	0.0	4.4	8.9	2.5	0.0	0.0	11.9	100.0	25.0	1883
1884	43.7	12.0	0.0	0.0	0.0	0.0	0.0	0.0	0.0	3.7	8.1	2.0	0.0	0.0	30.6	100.0	13.1	1884
1885	41.9	14.4	0.0	0.0	0.0	0.0	0.0	0.0	0.0	4.0	7.5	1.3	0.0	0.0	30.8	100.0	-1.5	1885
1886	35.7	10.7	0.0	0.0	0.0	0.0	0.0	0.0	0.0	3.5	6.6	0.6	0.0	0.0	43.0	100.0	20.6	1886
1887	57.6	16.2	0.0	0.0	0.0	0.0	0.0	0.0	0.0	5.1	10.5	0.0	0.0	0.0	10.5	100.0	-28.5	1887
1888	52.5	14.5	0.0	0.0	0.0	0.0	0.0	0.0	0.0	5.7	10.2	0.0	0.0	0.0	17.1	100.0	8.2	1888
1889	60.6	17.6	0.0	0.0	0.0	0.0	0.0	0.0	0.0	5.6	11.8	0.0	0.0	0.0	4.3	100.0	-7.1	1889
1890	61.8	19.6	0.0	0.0	0.0	0.0	0.0	0.0	0.0	6.2	12.4	0.0	0.0	0.0	0.0	100.0	-1.0	1890
1891	62.0	18.4	0.0	0.0	0.0	0.0	0.0	0.0	0.0	6.6	12.5	0.0	0.0	0.0	0.5	100.0	-2.8	1891
1892	53.8	20.8	0.0	0.0	0.0	0.0	0.0	0.0	0.0	7.1	12.4	0.0	0.0	0.0	5.8	100.0	0.8	1892
1893	56.0	22.5	0.0	0.0	0.0	0.0	0.0	0.0	0.0	7.5	12.9	0.0	0.0	0.0	1.1	100.0	-1.6	1893
1894	48.8	21.5	0.0	0.0	0.0	0.0	0.0	0.0	0.0	7.2	12.0	0.0	0.0	0.0	10.5	100.0	4.8	1894
1895	45.0	19.9	0.0	0.0	0.0	0.0	0.0	0.0	0.0	7.2	11.3	0.0	0.0	0.0	16.6	100.0	0.0	1895
1896	48.8	19.5	0.0	0.0	0.0	0.0	0.0	0.0	0.0	7.4	11.1	0.0	0.0	0.0	13.3	100.0	3.8	1896
1897	49.2	23.4	0.0	0.0	0.0	0.0	0.0	0.0	0.0	8.1	11.4	0.0	0.0	0.0	7.9	100.0	-3.0	1897
1898	53.6	19.6	0.0	0.0	0.0	0.0	0.0	0.0	0.0	8.7	14.6	0.0	0.0	0.0	3.5	100.0	2.3	1898
1899	53.6	20.4	0.0	0.0	0.0	0.0	0.0	0.0	0.0	6.8	14.7	0.0	0.0	0.0	4.5	100.0	16.6	1899
1900	58.1	20.4	0.0	0.0	0.0	0.0	0.0	0.0	0.0	6.6	16.3	0.0	0.0	0.0	-1.4	100.0	3.2	1900
1901	52.7	19.2	0.0	0.0	0.0	0.0	0.0	0.0	0.0	6.3	16.2	0.0	0.0	0.0	5.6	100.0	10.7	1901
1902	53.7	18.9	0.0	0.0	0.0	0.0	0.0	0.0	0.0	6.6	15.3	0.0	0.0	0.0	5.6	100.0	10.6	1902
1903	64.7	21.2	0.0	0.0	0.0	0.0	0.0	0.0	0.0	7.8	12.7	5.8	0.0	0.0	-12.2	100.0	-4.5	1903
1904	65.2	20.8	0.0	0.0	0.0	0.0	0.0	0.0	0.0	7.6	16.6	0.0	0.0	0.0	-10.1	100.0	9.5	1904
1905	55.6	16.9	0.0	0.0	0.0	0.0	0.0	0.0	0.0	6.9	13.4	0.0	0.0	0.0	7.1	100.0	19.8	1905
1906	58.7	17.8	0.0	0.0	0.0	0.0	0.0	0.0	0.0	7.5	15.0	0.0	0.0	0.0	1.0	100.0	5.6	1906
1907	62.9	18.7	0.0	0.0	0.0	0.0	0.0	0.0	0.0	8.1	15.7	0.0	0.0	0.0	-5.4	100.0	-19.7	1907
1908	53.1	17.7	0.0	0.0	0.0	0.0	0.0	0.0	0.0	6.6	13.0	0.0	0.0	0.0	12.6	100.0	70.7	1908
1909	37.0	11.7	0.0	0.0	0.0	0.0	0.0	0.0	0.0	5.8	10.5	0.3	0.0	0.0	34.7	100.0	18.3	1909
1910	54.6	13.9	0.0	0.0	0.0	0.0	0.0	0.0	0.0	7.3	14.3	0.1	0.0	0.0	9.8	100.0	-14.1	1910

TABLE B-3

Dominion Government: Total Financial Requirements, By Revenue Source, Fiscal 1868-1990 (Percentages)

Fiscal Year	Custom Duties (1)	Excise Duties (2)	Sales Tax (3)	Excise Taxes (4)	Individual Income Tax (5)	Corporate Income Tax (6)	Non Resident (7)	Excess Profits and as Noted (8)	Estate Taxes (9)	Post Office Revenues (10)	Miscellaneous Revenues (11)	Special Receipts & other Credits (12)	UIC Taxes (13)	Old Age Security Taxes (14)	Deficit (Surplus) (15)	Total Financial Requirements (16)	Change in TFR (17)	Fiscal Year
1911	60.5	14.2	0.0	0.0	0.0	0.0	0.0	0.0	0.0	7.7	15.3	0.1	0.0	0.0	2.1	100.0		1911
1912	63.7	14.5	0.0	0.0	0.0	0.0	0.0	0.0	0.0	7.9	14.9	0.0	0.0	0.0	-0.9	100.0	8.3	1912
1913	79.1	15.1	0.0	0.0	0.0	0.0	0.0	0.0	0.0	8.6	15.3	0.0	0.0	0.0	-18.1	100.0	12.6	1913
1914	58.0	11.9	0.0	0.0	0.0	0.0	0.0	0.0	0.0	7.2	12.2	0.0	0.0	0.0	10.7	100.0	5.8	1914
1915	31.9	9.0	0.0	0.0	0.0	0.0	0.0	0.0	0.0	5.5	8.0	0.0	0.0	0.0	45.6	100.0	27.7	1915
1916	29.8	6.8	0.0	1.1	0.0	0.0	0.0	0.0	0.0	5.7	6.9	0.0	0.0	0.0	49.1	100.0	32.0	1916
1917	28.0	5.1	0.0	0.8	0.0	0.0	0.0	2.6	0.0	4.4	6.7	0.0	0.0	0.0	52.1	100.0	39.1	1917
1918	25.9	4.9	0.0	0.7	0.0	0.0	0.0	3.8	0.0	3.8	7.1	0.0	0.0	0.0	54.2	100.0	44.3	1918
1919	21.2	4.4	0.0	2.0	1.1	0.0	0.0	4.7	0.0	3.1	1.7	0.0	0.0	0.0	56.1	100.0	16.7	1919
1920	23.4	5.9	0.0	2.5	1.8	0.0	0.0	6.1	0.0	3.4	3.6	0.0	0.0	0.0	54.1	100.0	24.6	1920
1921	41.5	9.4	9.6	11.1	8.3	0.2	0.0	10.4	0.0	6.8	4.0	0.5	0.0	0.0	-4.5	100.0	3.7	1921
1922	30.8	10.7	17.8	4.2	11.6	1.0	0.0	6.6	0.0	7.7	3.6	0.1	0.0	0.0	-4.8	100.0	-45.4	1922
1923	35.6	10.8	27.0	5.7	9.5	3.5	0.0	3.9	0.0	8.7	3.7	2.6	0.0	0.0	-15.8	100.0	-12.7	1923
1924	36.8	11.6	29.7	7.6	7.8	11.3	0.0	1.5	0.0	8.8	3.6	2.9	0.0	0.0	-19.0	100.0	-3.3	1924
1925	33.0	11.8	31.3	7.7	7.7	8.4	0.0	0.8	0.0	8.8	3.9	1.4	0.0	0.0	-3.5	100.0	-0.7	1925
1926	38.1	12.8	21.8	8.3	7.1	8.6	0.0	0.4	0.0	9.1	4.0	0.5	0.0	0.0	-11.7	100.0	-0.7	1926
1927	42.0	16.5	24.0	8.1	5.4	9.5	0.0	0.2	0.0	8.6	4.2	0.5	0.0	0.0	-15.8	100.0	2.1	1927
1928	45.0	16.5	20.3	6.5	6.7	8.7	0.0	0.3	0.0	9.1	4.3	2.0	0.0	0.0	-19.9	100.0	1.0	1928
1929	51.5	17.5	17.2	6.3	6.8	9.6	0.0	0.1	0.0	8.4	3.8	1.3	0.0	0.0	-23.1	100.0	3.2	1929
1930	45.4	16.4	11.2	5.4	6.9	9.5	0.0	0.1	0.0	8.4	2.7	2.9	0.0	0.0	-11.1	100.0	4.3	1930
1931	30.0	13.2	4.6	3.8	6.1	10.6	0.0	0.0	0.0	6.9	1.4	1.9	0.0	0.0	20.7	100.0	8.7	1931
1932	21.4	10.0	8.6	4.0	5.1	10.1	0.0	0.0	0.0	6.6	2.1	1.6	0.0	0.0	33.9	100.0	10.7	1932
1933	15.3	8.3	12.4	6.0	5.7	7.5	0.0	0.0	0.0	6.7	2.2	0.1	0.0	0.0	34.4	100.0	11.4	1933
1934	14.8	7.9	13.7	10.7	6.3	7.9	0.0	0.0	0.0	6.9	2.3	0.8	0.0	0.0	29.9	100.0	-6.0	1934
1935	16.4	9.3	15.5	9.8	6.8	6.1	1.1	0.0	0.0	6.7	2.2	0.1	0.0	0.0	24.9	100.0	-2.4	1935
1936	14.2	8.5	14.9	7.5	7.8	7.7	1.4	0.0	0.0	6.2	2.3	1.7	0.0	0.0	30.7	100.0	4.3	1936
1937	16.1	8.8	21.7	8.1	8.7	8.1	1.7	0.0	0.0	6.6	2.2	1.2	0.0	0.0	15.0	100.0	11.9	1937
1938	18.0	10.0	26.5	8.7	7.1	11.1	1.9	0.0	0.0	6.8	1.9	0.8	0.0	0.0	3.4	100.0	-0.3	1938
1939	14.7	9.6	22.8	7.8	8.6	13.4	1.8	0.0	0.0	6.6	0.0	2.4	0.0	0.0	9.5	100.0	0.0	1939
1940	16.3	9.5	21.5	4.9	16.3	15.9	1.7	2.0	0.0	5.7	0.0	0.1	0.0	0.0	18.6	100.0	3.1	1940
1941	10.9	7.4	15.0	8.9	11.3	12.2	1.1	7.5	0.0	3.4	0.0	0.9	0.0	0.0	31.5	100.0	19.1	1941
1942	7.9	6.1	13.0	12.1	13.4	11.0	1.6	10.2	0.4	2.5	0.0	0.6	0.0	0.0	19.5	100.0	87.2	1942
1943	2.8	3.2	5.5	6.3	13.2	10.2	0.7	8.2	0.3	1.1	0.0	3.0	0.0	0.0	48.5	100.0	51.3	1943
1944	3.2	2.7	5.9	6.6	13.7	8.2	0.5	6.7	0.3	1.2	0.0	6.7	2.0	0.0	47.8	100.0	135.6	1944
1945	2.6	3.0	4.1	6.7	9.3	6.0	0.6	8.5	0.3	1.3	0.0	12.1	1.3	0.0	48.6	100.0	21.8	1945
1946	9.3	3.7	4.2	5.8	26.2	5.4	0.6	17.3	0.4	1.4	0.0	15.8	1.2	0.0	41.4	100.0	-1.6	1946
1947	14.2	7.7	11.6	11.3	32.0	4.3	1.2	11.0	0.9	2.9	0.0	9.2	1.2	0.0	-16.5	100.0	-1.8	1947
1948	11.0	9.6	18.1	13.2	37.7	9.3	1.7	2.2	1.5	3.8	0.0	3.4	3.0	0.0	-36.4	100.0	-49.0	1948
1949	9.6	10.1	18.7	13.0	26.4	17.7	2.1	-0.1	1.3	4.0	0.0	0.6	4.4	0.0	-32.9	100.0	-19.5	1949
1950	11.3	9.4	17.1	7.3	25.6	24.3	2.0	0.4	1.3	3.6	0.0	2.1	4.9	0.0	-7.2	100.0	-1.9	1950
1951	9.5	9.2	17.6	8.9	25.0	25.6	2.4	0.1	1.3	3.5	0.0	1.1	5.0	0.0	-17.4	100.0	16.5	1951
1952	8.7	6.0	15.7	8.7	26.7	30.7	1.5	0.0	1.0	2.9	1.1	1.9	4.1	0.7	-9.9	100.0	40.3	1952
1953	8.7	5.4	12.6	6.4	26.4	27.7	1.2	0.0	0.9	2.5	1.1	1.9	3.5	5.0	-3.2	100.0	22.4	1953

TABLE 8-3

Dominion Government: Total Financial Requirements, By Revenue Source, Fiscal 1868-1990 (Percentages)

Fiscal Year[1]	Custom Duties (1)	Excise Duties (2)	Sales Tax[2] (3)	Excise Taxes (4)	Individual Income Tax (5)	Corporate Income Tax (6)	Non Resident (7)	Excess Profits and as Noted[3] (8)	Estate Taxes (9)	Post Office Revenues (10)	Miscellaneous Revenues[4] (11)	Special Receipts & other Credits (12)	UIC Taxes (13)	Old Age Security Taxes[5] (14)	Deficit (Surplus) (15)	Total Financial Requirements (16)	Change in TFR (17)	Fiscal Year
1954	8.8	4.9	12.7	6.7	25.8	25.8	1.2	0.0	0.8	2.4	1.2	1.6	3.5	6.4	-1.8	100.0	3.0	1954
1955	8.5	4.8	12.2	5.7	25.3	21.8	1.3	0.0	1.0	2.8	1.1	0.6	3.4	6.2	5.4	100.0	1.6	1955
1956	10.1	5.2	12.2	5.8	25.3	21.5	1.4	0.0	1.4	2.9	2.4	0.0	3.6	6.6	0.8	100.0	1.9	1956
1957	10.5	5.2	13.4	5.8	24.8	24.1	1.5	0.0	1.5	2.8	2.0	0.0	3.6	7.1	-3.9	100.0	10.1	1957
1958	8.8	5.3	13.7	5.4	26.7	21.8	1.1	0.0	1.3	2.7	1.8	0.0	3.3	6.6	3.9	100.0	7.7	1958
1959	7.9	5.1	12.4	4.4	26.5	21.8	1.1	0.0	1.2	2.6	2.1	0.0	3.0	6.1	17.5	100.0	9.0	1959
1960	8.8	5.1	11.3	3.9	21.9	16.5	1.0	0.0	1.4	2.6	2.0	0.0	3.6	8.6	8.7	100.0	3.4	1960
1961	8.2	5.3	11.5	4.5	24.6	17.9	1.1	0.0	1.3	2.6	2.1	0.0	4.1	9.0	7.8	100.0	5.6	1961
1962	7.4	5.1	10.7	4.3	25.4	19.0	1.3	0.0	1.3	2.5	1.7	0.0	3.8	8.9	12.6	100.0	7.7	1962
1963	7.4	5.0	10.5	3.6	24.7	16.6	1.3	0.0	1.2	2.5	1.8	0.0	3.9	8.9	10.3	100.0	0.4	1963
1964	8.9	5.2	11.1	3.6	23.9	16.2	1.5	0.0	1.2	2.7	2.0	0.0	3.9	9.5	8.3	100.0	3.8	1964
1965	7.7	5.2	12.5	3.6	24.7	16.6	1.8	0.0	1.2	2.7	1.9	0.0	3.9	9.9	0.0	100.0	6.2	1965
1966	7.7	5.1	15.0	3.4	26.2	19.0	1.8	0.0	1.1	2.9	1.7	0.0	3.8	9.9	-0.7	100.0	8.3	1966
1967	7.9	4.7	16.0	3.2	25.2	18.5	1.8	0.0	1.0	2.7	1.7	0.0	3.5	12.0	3.2	100.0	12.7	1967
1968	6.8	4.5	15.4	3.1	26.0	15.2	2.0	0.0	1.0	2.6	1.1	0.0	3.2	13.4	6.5	100.0	11.9	1968
1969	6.3	4.2	14.6	2.8	27.8	16.8	2.0	0.5	0.9	2.4	1.1	0.0	3.8	13.1	4.3	100.0	10.0	1969
1970	6.1	3.9	13.0	2.7	30.6	19.6	1.7	3.6	0.9	2.3	1.6	0.0	4.4	13.5	-4.0	100.0	10.6	1970
1971	5.5	3.6	12.9	2.3	31.8	15.0	1.9	3.8	0.8	2.3	0.8	0.0	4.0	13.8	10.5	100.0	10.5	1971
1972	5.9	3.6	11.6	1.7	33.1	12.9	1.7	2.4	0.8	2.0	0.8	0.0	3.9	13.0	6.0	100.0	14.4	1972
1973	5.1	2.8	11.8	1.6	36.4	12.7	1.7	0.1	0.3	1.9	0.7	0.3	3.3	12.5	10.4	100.0	36.4	1973
1974	5.4	2.7	13.3	1.3	36.1	14.5	1.3	1.1	0.1	1.5	1.0	0.1	4.0	9.6	6.6	100.0	27.9	1974
1975	5.5	2.3	14.0	1.2	35.8	14.8	1.3	5.1	0.0	1.6	0.8	0.0	5.0	9.8	5.2	100.0	12.5	1975
1976	5.1	2.2	11.8	1.3	34.5	15.6	1.3	4.0	0.0	1.8	0.9	0.2	5.7	9.7	16.5	100.0	4.4	1976
1977	5.5	2.3	9.5	1.1	38.1	14.0	1.2	3.3	0.0	1.8	1.2	0.2	6.6	0.0	14.8	100.0	11.5	1977
1978	5.4	2.1	10.2	1.0	32.7	12.3	1.1	2.4	0.0	2.3	1.3	0.2	6.1	0.0	23.2	100.0	17.7	1978
1979	5.4	1.7	10.3	1.0	29.1	11.2	1.1	1.7	0.0	1.9	1.0	0.2	5.7	0.0	30.7	100.0	17.7	1979
1980	6.2	1.8	9.4	1.0	34.6	14.3	1.6	2.4	0.0	0.7	1.8	0.2	5.7	0.0	18.8	100.0	-3.5	1980
1981	6.6	1.8	9.7	0.8	34.6	14.1	1.5	2.6	0.0	0.0	1.4	0.2	5.8	0.0	19.3	100.0	17.9	1981
1982	4.9	1.7	9.5	0.8	34.4	11.6	1.5	6.5	0.0	0.0	1.1	0.2	6.8	0.0	20.6	100.0	21.8	1982
1983	3.4	1.5	8.8	0.8	31.4	8.5	1.2	6.1	0.0	0.0	1.5	0.1	5.8	0.0	33.2	100.0	20.2	1983
1984	3.7	1.5	7.0	0.8	29.2	7.9	1.0	4.5	0.0	0.0	1.0	0.0	5.8	0.0	35.1	100.0	9.9	1984
1985	3.6	1.3	7.1	1.3	27.9	8.9	1.0	4.3	0.0	0.0	1.2	0.0	7.9	0.0	36.5	100.0	13.8	1985
1986	3.7	1.4	7.2	1.3	30.7	8.6	1.2	3.1	0.0	0.0	1.1	0.1	7.2	0.0	32.0	100.0	2.4	1986
1987	3.6	1.3	8.7	1.3	33.8	8.8	1.3	1.8	0.0	0.0	1.4	0.1	8.1	0.0	27.3	100.0	4.3	1987
1988	3.6	1.2	10.7	1.3	37.3	9.0	1.0	2.2	0.0	0.0	1.8	0.2	8.5	0.0	23.2	100.0	7.9	1988
1989	3.5	1.1	12.3	1.2	37.7	9.0	1.2	2.1	0.0	0.0	1.5	0.2	8.6	0.0	22.7	100.0	5.4	1989
1990	3.4	1.6	12.9	0.9	37.9	9.5	1.0	1.0	0.0	0.0	1.8	0.2	7.8	0.0	21.2	100.0	7.4	1990

Source: Public Accounts of Canada. See Appendix B for derivation.

1. Fiscal year ended on June 30 until 1906 and on March 31 for 1907 and later years.
2. Gross Sales Tax Revenues less refunds of sales and other excises.
3. Business profits taxes (1917-1930) excess profits tax (1941-1952) social development tax (1969-1973) and energy taxes (1974-1990).
4. Includes other miscellaneous taxes (and remnants of estate tax after 1975) from 1968 on.
5. Includes old age security individual income taxes corporation income taxes and sales taxes.

Table B-4

Composition of Total Financial Requirements (TFR), Canada,
Millions of Dollars and Percentages, Fiscal 1868-1990

Fiscal Year	Millions of Dollars				Percentage of TFR			
	Consumption Taxes (1)	Income Taxes (2)	Deficit (3)	Other Taxes (4)	Consumption Taxes (5)	Income Taxes (6)	Deficit (7)	Other Taxes (8)
1868	11.7	0.0		1.8	86.7	0.0	0.0	13.3
1869	11.1	0.0	0.1	1.9	84.7	0.0	0.8	14.5
1870	13.1	0.0	2.4	2.0	74.9	0.0	13.7	11.4
1871	16.3	0.0	-0.5	2.5	89.1	0.0	-2.7	13.7
1872	17.7	0.0	2.8	2.5	77.0	0.0	12.2	10.9
1873	17.6	0.0	3.8	2.9	72.4	0.0	15.6	11.9
1874	20.1	0.0	1.7	3.5	79.4	0.0	6.7	13.8
1875	20.7	0.0	7.4	3.0	66.6	0.0	23.8	9.6
1876	18.6	0.0	7.2	3.2	64.1	0.0	24.8	11.0
1877	17.7	0.0	8.7	4.5	57.3	0.0	28.2	14.6
1878	17.8	0.0	6.5	3.8	63.3	0.0	23.1	13.5
1879	18.5	0.0	1.7	7.9	65.8	0.0	6.0	28.1
1880	18.5	0.0	9.4	4.1	57.8	0.0	29.4	12.8
1881	23.9	0.0	3.0	4.9	75.2	0.0	9.4	15.4
1882	27.6	0.0	-1.8	6.6	85.2	0.0	-5.6	20.4
1883	29.3	0.0	4.8	6.4	72.3	0.0	11.9	15.8
1884	25.5	0.0	14.0	6.3	55.7	0.0	30.6	13.8
1885	25.4	0.0	13.9	5.8	56.3	0.0	30.8	12.9
1886	25.2	0.0	23.4	5.8	46.3	0.0	43.0	10.7
1887	28.7	0.0	4.1	6.1	73.8	0.0	10.5	15.7
1888	28.2	0.0	7.2	6.7	67.0	0.0	17.1	15.9
1889	30.6	0.0	1.7	6.8	78.3	0.0	4.3	17.4
1890	31.5	0.0	0.0	7.2	81.4	0.0	0.0	18.6
1891	30.2	0.0	0.2	7.2	80.3	0.0	0.5	19.1
1892	28.3	0.0	2.2	7.4	74.7	0.0	5.8	19.5
1893	29.3	0.0	0.4	7.6	78.6	0.0	1.1	20.4
1894	27.5	0.0	4.1	7.5	70.3	0.0	10.5	19.2
1895	25.4	0.0	6.5	7.2	65.0	0.0	16.6	18.4
1896	27.7	0.0	5.4	7.5	68.2	0.0	13.3	18.5
1897	28.6	0.0	3.1	7.7	72.6	0.0	7.9	19.5
1898	29.5	0.0	1.4	9.4	73.2	0.0	3.5	23.3
1899	34.8	0.0	2.1	10.1	74.0	0.0	4.5	21.5
1900	38.1	0.0	-0.7	11.1	78.6	0.0	-1.4	22.9
1901	38.6	0.0	3.0	12.1	71.9	0.0	5.6	22.5
1902	43.1	0.0	3.3	13.0	72.6	0.0	5.6	21.9
1903	48.7	0.0	-6.9	14.9	85.9	0.0	-12.2	26.3
1904	53.4	0.0	-6.3	15.0	86.0	0.0	-10.1	24.2
1905	54.0	0.0	5.3	15.1	72.6	0.0	7.1	20.3
1906	60.1	0.0	0.8	17.7	76.5	0.0	1.0	22.5
1907	51.5	0.0	-3.4	15.0	81.6	0.0	-5.4	23.8
1908	73.0	0.0	13.6	21.1	67.8	0.0	12.6	19.6
1909	62.0	0.0	44.2	21.2	48.7	0.0	34.7	16.6
1910	75.0	0.0	10.7	23.8	68.5	0.0	9.8	21.7
1911	88.7	0.0	2.5	27.4	74.8	0.0	2.1	23.1
1912	104.3	0.0	-1.2	30.4	78.1	0.0	-0.9	22.8
1913	133.2	0.0	-25.6	33.7	94.3	0.0	-18.1	23.8
1914	126.1	0.0	19.3	35.0	69.9	0.0	10.7	19.4
1915	97.5	0.0	108.5	32.1	40.9	0.0	45.6	13.5
1916	124.7	0.0	162.6	43.8	37.7	0.0	49.1	13.2
1917	162.3	12.5	249.2	53.9	34.0	2.6	52.1	11.3
1918	175.4	21.3	302.2	58.8	31.5	3.8	54.2	10.5
1919	191.4	42.3	390.1	71.1	27.5	6.1	56.1	10.2
1920	229.2	64.4	390.3	37.0	31.8	8.9	54.1	5.1
1921	281.6	87.2	-17.7	42.6	71.5	22.1	-4.5	10.8
1922	218.4	101.5	-16.6	40.3	63.6	29.5	-4.8	11.7
1923	262.7	72.7	-52.5	49.3	79.1	21.9	-15.8	14.8
1924	282.7	59.0	-62.6	50.7	85.7	17.9	-19.0	15.4
1925	235.0	58.9	-11.6	45.2	71.8	18.0	-3.5	13.8
1926	271.1	56.8	-39.0	45.4	81.1	17.0	-11.7	13.6
1927	298.9	48.1	-53.5	44.3	88.5	14.2	-15.8	13.1
1928	307.6	57.5	-69.5	53.0	88.2	16.5	-19.9	15.2
1929	336.4	59.9	-83.9	51.1	92.5	16.5	-23.1	14.1

Table B-4

Composition of Total Financial Requirements (TFR), Canada,
Millions of Dollars and Percentages, Fiscal 1868-1990

Fiscal Year	Millions of Dollars				Percentage of TFR			
	Consumption Taxes (1)	Income Taxes (2)	Deficit (3)	Other Taxes (4)	Consumption Taxes (5)	Income Taxes (6)	Deficit (7)	Other Taxes (8)
1930	309.7	69.2	-43.8	60.1	78.4	17.5	-11.1	15.2
1931	225.7	71.1	90.8	50.0	51.6	16.2	20.7	11.4
1932	214.1	61.3	165.0	46.9	43.9	12.6	33.9	9.6
1933	192.4	62.1	157.7	45.8	42.0	13.6	34.4	10.0
1934	210.8	61.4	133.5	41.2	47.2	13.7	29.9	9.2
1935	238.1	66.6	116.1	45.4	51.1	14.3	24.9	9.7
1936	234.9	82.7	160.0	44.3	45.0	15.8	30.7	8.5
1937	284.6	102.4	77.9	55.4	54.7	19.7	15.0	10.6
1938	328.8	120.3	17.7	53.6	63.2	23.1	3.4	10.3
1939	294.3	142.0	50.9	49.5	54.8	26.5	9.5	9.2
1940	334.0	134.4	118.7	52.3	52.2	21.0	18.6	8.2
1941	506.1	272.1	377.4	41.6	42.3	22.7	31.5	3.5
1942	708.5	644.9	352.8	105.7	39.1	35.6	19.5	5.8
1943	758.7	1294.8	2069.4	146.0	17.8	30.3	48.5	3.4
1944	956.3	1465.5	2484.8	291.7	18.4	28.2	47.8	5.6
1945	818.3	1319.1	2486.6	489.2	16.0	25.8	48.6	9.6
1946	821.5	1359.3	2079.3	761.7	16.4	27.1	41.4	15.2
1947	1022.1	1381.9	-421.8	577.8	39.9	54.0	-16.5	22.6
1948	1134.4	1286.9	-749.5	388.0	55.1	62.5	-36.4	18.8
1949	1067.8	1342.7	-664.0	274.2	52.8	66.4	-32.9	13.6
1950	1022.3	1270.9	-170.6	232.5	43.4	54.0	-7.2	9.9
1951	1228.5	1523.3	-454.0	309.3	47.1	58.4	-17.4	11.9
1952	1480.2	2165.8	-363.1	375.8	40.5	59.2	-9.9	10.3
1953	1627.3	2510.6	-144.7	483.9	36.3	56.1	-3.2	10.8
1954	1678.6	2488.3	-84.8	528.9	36.4	54.0	-1.8	11.5
1955	1606.5	2311.3	251.3	516.6	34.3	49.3	5.4	11.0
1956	1810.0	2332.8	37.9	591.9	37.9	48.9	0.8	12.4
1957	2002.3	2812.5	-203.5	642.0	38.1	53.5	-3.9	12.2
1958	1927.2	2859.6	221.0	650.9	34.1	50.5	3.9	11.5
1959	1913.1	2490.6	1077.1	689.3	31.0	40.4	17.5	11.2
1960	2151.0	2874.1	554.0	800.3	33.7	45.1	8.7	12.5
1961	2125.1	3179.5	524.0	906.9	31.6	47.2	7.8	13.5
1962	2204.5	3207.2	912.4	930.6	30.4	44.2	12.6	12.8
1963	2395.5	3171.8	751.1	967.7	32.9	43.5	10.3	13.3
1964	2526.1	3364.4	629.0	1042.9	33.4	44.5	8.3	13.8
1965	2890.5	3916.1	0.1	1221.8	36.0	48.8	0.0	15.2
1966	3344.9	4071.4	-57.2	1338.7	38.5	46.8	-0.7	15.4
1967	3627.4	4420.1	315.9	1438.6	37.0	45.1	3.2	14.7
1968	3717.7	4890.7	715.6	1649.3	33.9	44.6	6.5	15.0
1969	3746.5	5775.0	517.9	2094.0	30.9	47.6	4.3	17.3
1970	4009.8	7172.7	-529.3	3175.3	29.0	51.9	-3.8	23.0
1971	4060.0	7381.1	444.2	3516.0	26.4	47.9	2.9	22.8
1972	4636.8	8265.3	1007.2	3380.6	26.8	47.8	5.8	19.6
1973	6035.0	11856.0	2405.5	2555.0	26.4	51.9	10.5	11.2
1974	6965.5	13559.0	1682.7	3355.7	27.2	53.0	6.6	13.1
1975	7803.0	17523.5	1699.0	5683.0	23.9	53.6	5.2	17.4
1976	7229.6	19078.8	6061.0	4424.0	19.6	51.9	16.5	12.0
1977	7976.0	20448.0	5669.0	4328.0	20.8	53.2	14.8	11.3
1978	8691.0	19771.0	9956.0	2861.0	21.1	47.9	24.1	6.9
1979	9369.0	20878.0	15496.0	2870.0	19.3	42.9	31.9	5.9
1980	9516.0	24546.0	9147.0	3190.0	20.5	52.9	19.7	6.9
1981	11472.0	28837.0	11044.0	3753.0	20.8	52.3	20.0	6.8
1982	12756.0	34046.0	14388.0	7651.0	18.5	49.5	20.9	11.1
1983	12301.0	36427.0	27816.0	7361.0	14.7	43.4	33.2	8.8
1984	12957.0	37267.0	32399.0	9615.0	14.0	40.4	35.1	10.4
1985	14087.0	42217.0	38324.0	10335.0	13.4	40.2	36.5	9.8
1986	16898.0	45308.0	34413.0	10885.0	15.7	42.1	32.0	10.1
1987	20577.0	49591.0	30605.0	11382.0	18.3	44.2	27.3	10.1
1988	23009.0	57090.0	28084.0	12804.0	19.0	47.2	23.2	10.6
1989	25668.0	61439.0	28951.0	11413.0	20.1	48.2	22.7	9.0
1990	28098.0	66334.0	28996.0	13435.0	20.5	48.5	21.2	9.8

Source: See Appendix B for derivation.

Appendix C

Dominion Government Spending and Financing, Relative to National Income, Canada, 1870–1989

This appendix converts the data on Dominion government spending and financing by revenue source from a fiscal year basis to a calendar year basis and expresses the results as a percentage of national income. These measures indicate the relative importance of government spending and borrowing and of each of the major tax sources in the Canadian economy. They can be used to describe one aspect of the structure of the Canadian economy.

The structural estimates are derived in three steps. First, data on nominal gross national product (GNP), real GNP and the implicit price index for GNP are drawn from several sources. Professor Urquhart has provided, for the first time, estimates of GNP in current and constant dollars for the continuous period 1870–1926.[1] Leacy, Urquhart and Buckley, in the second edition of *Historical Statistics of Canada*, provide data on GNP in current and constant dollars from 1926 through 1976.[2] Statistics Canada supplies data on the revised gross domestic product basis from 1961 through 1986.[3] The data on GNP in current dollars for 1977 through 1986 are obtained from this source and GNP in real dollars is derived from it, on the basis of the available information. Similar data for years after 1986 are derived from later, annual, Statistics Canada publications.

This information on GNP in current and constant dollars, the implicit GNP price index and the year-over-year growth rate of real GNP, from 1870 continuously through 1989, is shown in Table C-1.

The second step involves the conversion of the budgetary data of Appendix B from a fiscal year basis to a calendar year basis. The government's *Public Accounts* are based on a fiscal year that ended on June 30th from 1868 through 1906, and for 1907 and all following years ended on March 31st. A simple conversion factor is applied, such that the proportion of each fiscal year that falls in a calendar year is allocated to that calendar year (for each item of Tables B-1 and B-2). Accordingly, half of fiscal 1868 and half of fiscal 1869 become calendar year 1868 (with a

similar treatment applying to all years through calendar 1905) and one-
quarter of fiscal 1908 and three-quarters of fiscal 1909 become calendar
1908 (with a similar treatment through calendar 1989). Calendar 1906
comprises one-half and two-thirds, respectively, of fiscal 1906 and 1907;
and calendar 1907 comprises one-third and three-quarters, respectively,
of fiscal 1907 and 1908.

These calendar year estimates of total financial requirements, by revenue source, and total government expenditures, are found in Table C-2
and summarized in Table B-1. The national debt in these tables is the
cumulative sum of deficit financing less surpluses, from Confederation
through 1989. This estimate of the national debt differs somewhat from
official published statistics on the debt, because the latter include any
debt in existence at the time of Confederation, and any additions to (or
subtractions from) the debt that are attributable to certain transactions
on the non-budgetary accounts which have not been integrated into the
quantitative measures of this study. Given these qualifications, the debt
estimates provided here — and especially the long-range pattern of these
estimates — conform closely to official data.

The third step involves expressing the total financial requirements, by
revenue source, and total government expenditures (the data of Table
C-2) as a percentage of current dollar GNP (the data of Table C-1) in
order to derive a measure of the proportion of the Dominion government
sector to national income in the Canadian economy. This information is
provided in Table C-3.

TABLE C-1

Gross National Product, Nominal and Real, Canada , 1870-1989 (Millions of Dollars)

Calendar Year	GNP Nominal	GNP Real	Price Index	Real Growth	Calendar Year	GNP Nominal	GNP Real	Price Index	Real Growth
1870	382.6	369.5	104		1930	5720.0	16174.0	35	-4.3%
1871	412.7	385.9	107	4.2%	1931	4693.0	14118.0	33	-12.7%
1872	447.3	382.8	117	-0.8%	1932	3814.0	12654.0	30	-10.4%
1873	487.8	419.3	116	9.5%	1933	3492.0	11811.0	30	-6.7%
1874	485.5	427.8	113	2.0%	1934	3969.0	13245.0	30	12.1%
1875	452.5	417.1	108	-2.5%	1935	4301.0	14279.0	30	7.8%
1876	421.7	391.1	108	-6.2%	1936	4634.0	14912.0	31	4.4%
1877	434.7	416.5	104	6.5%	1937	5241.0	16410.0	32	10.0%
1878	409.6	402.6	102	-3.3%	1938	5272.0	16545.0	32	0.8%
1879	445.1	441.8	101	9.7%	1939	5621.0	17774.0	32	7.4%
1880	482.0	462.1	104	4.6%	1940	6713.0	20277.0	33	14.1%
1881	568.7	527.9	108	14.0%	1941	8282.0	23194.0	36	14.4%
1882	618.9	547.2	113	3.8%	1942	10265.0	27497.0	37	18.6%
1883	611.5	545.7	112	-0.3%	1943	11053.0	28604.0	39	4.0%
1884	585.2	592.0	99	8.5%	1944	11848.0	29736.0	40	4.0%
1885	554.5	556.3	100	-6.0%	1945	11863.0	29071.0	41	-2.2%
1886	560.7	559.4	100	0.6%	1946	11885.0	28292.0	42	-2.7%
1887	611.1	579.0	106	3.5%	1947	13473.0	29498.0	46	4.3%
1888	630.3	616.1	102	6.4%	1948	15509.0	30231.0	51	2.5%
1889	655.8	620.9	106	0.8%	1949	16800.0	31388.0	54	3.8%
1890	685.4	657.4	104	5.9%	1950	18491.0	33762.0	55	7.6%
1891	703.5	679.9	103	3.4%	1951	21640.0	35450.0	61	5.0%
1892	700.3	676.2	104	-0.5%	1952	24588.0	38617.0	64	8.9%
1893	682.4	666.9	102	-1.4%	1953	25833.0	40605.0	64	5.1%
1894	651.4	700.6	93	5.1%	1954	25918.0	40106.0	65	-1.2%
1895	633.4	698.9	91	-0.2%	1955	28528.0	43891.0	65	9.4%
1896	640.8	680.7	94	-2.6%	1956	32058.0	47599.0	67	8.4%
1897	717.0	757.2	95	11.2%	1957	33513.0	48718.0	69	2.4%
1898	769.4	786.5	98	3.9%	1958	34777.0	49844.0	70	2.3%
1899	826.0	857.8	96	9.1%	1959	36846.0	51737.0	71	3.8%
1900	907.4	907.8	100	5.8%	1960	38359.0	53231.0	72	2.9%
1901	990.7	984.1	101	8.4%	1961	39646.0	54741.0	72	2.8%
1902	1119.6	1073.6	104	9.1%	1962	42927.0	58475.0	73	6.8%
1903	1178.2	1115.1	106	3.9%	1963	45978.0	61487.0	75	5.2%
1904	1205.8	1131.4	107	1.5%	1964	50280.0	65610.0	77	6.7%
1905	1361.5	1248.2	109	10.3%	1965	55364.0	69981.0	79	6.7%
1906	1525.9	1380.6	111	10.6%	1966	61828.0	74844.0	83	6.9%
1907	1728.4	1456.0	119	5.5%	1967	66409.0	77344.0	86	3.3%
1908	1653.8	1383.3	120	-5.0%	1968	72586.0	81864.0	89	5.8%
1909	1838.8	1520.4	121	9.9%	1969	79815.0	86225.0	93	5.3%
1910	2022.8	1655.4	122	8.9%	1970	85685.0	88390.0	97	2.5%
1911	2233.2	1770.7	126	7.0%	1971	94450.0	94450.0	100	6.9%
1912	2493.9	1905.4	131	7.6%	1972	105234.0	100248.0	105	6.1%
1913	2651.5	1979.8	134	3.9%	1973	123560.0	107812.0	115	7.5%
1914	2448.6	1835.6	133	-7.3%	1974	147528.0	111678.0	132	3.6%
1915	2688.6	1964.4	137	7.0%	1975	165343.0	113005.0	146	1.2%
1916	3242.7	2182.5	149	11.1%	1976	191031.0	119249.0	160	5.5%
1917	3991.9	2273.2	176	4.2%	1977	213308.0	304968.8	70	**
1918	4261.5	2141.4	199	-5.8%	1978	235654.0	317728.7	74	4.2%
1919	4367.4	1994.9	219	-6.8%	1979	268941.0	329593.4	82	3.7%
1920	5060.9	1992.0	254	-0.1%	1980	302064.0	334711.1	90	1.6%
1921	4073.8	1800.3	226	-9.6%	1981	344657.0	344657.0	100	3.0%
1922	4233.9	2060.9	205	14.5%	1982	361772.0	332884.7	109	-3.4%
1923	4555.3	2194.0	208	6.5%	1983	394114.0	345279.7	114	3.7%
1924	4501.5	2210.1	204	0.7%	1984	431249.0	366406.7	118	6.1%
1925	4995.7	2450.3	204	10.9%	1985	463656.0	384008.0	121	4.8%
1926	5345.3	2611.8	205	6.6%	1986	489264.0	395714.2	124	3.0%
1927	5561.0	15423.0	36	*	1987	535166.0	414658.5	129	4.8%
1928	6050.0	16831.0	36	9.1%	1988	584474.0	435098.4	134	4.9%
1929	6139.0	16894.0	36	0.4%	1989	629464.0	447049.2	141	2.7%

Source Notes: See Appendix C for discussion.
1. 1870-1926 Urquhart, 1900 Prices
2. 1927-1976 Historical Statistics, 1971 Prices
3. 1977-1989 National Income and Expenditure Accounts, 1981 Prices
* Index Changes to 1971 Dollars
** Index Changes to 1981 Dollars

TABLE C-2

Dominion Government, Total Financial Requirements, by Revenue Source, Calendar 1868-1989 (Millions of dollars)

Calendar Year	Custom Duties (1)	Excise Duties (2)	Sales Tax¹ (3)	Excise Taxes (4)	Individual Income Tax (5)	Corporate Income Tax (6)	Non Resident (7)	Excess Profits and as Noted² (8)	Estate Taxes (9)	Post Office Revenues (10)	Miscellaneous Revenues (11)	Special Receipts & other Credits³ (12)	UIC Taxes (13)	Old Age Security Taxes⁴ (14)	Deficit (Surplus) (15)	Total Financial Requirements (16)	Change in TFR (17)	Change Calendar Year
1868	8.5	2.9	0.0	0.1	0.0	0.0	0.0	0.0	0.0	0.5	1.4	0.0	0.0	0.0	0.1	13.3		1868
1869	8.9	3.2	0.0	0.1	0.0	0.0	0.0	0.0	0.0	0.6	1.4	0.0	0.0	0.0	1.3	15.3	2.0	1869
1870	10.6	4.0	0.0	0.2	0.0	0.0	0.0	0.0	0.0	0.6	1.6	0.1	0.0	0.0	1.0	17.9	2.6	1870
1871	12.3	4.5	0.0	0.2	0.0	0.0	0.0	0.0	0.0	0.7	1.8	0.1	0.0	0.0	1.0	20.7	2.8	1871
1872	12.9	4.6	0.0	0.2	0.0	0.0	0.0	0.0	0.0	0.8	1.9	0.1	0.0	0.0	3.3	23.7	3.0	1872
1873	13.6	5.1	0.0	0.2	0.0	0.0	0.0	0.0	0.0	1.0	2.0	0.3	0.0	0.0	2.8	24.8	1.1	1873
1874	14.9	5.4	0.0	0.2	0.0	0.0	0.0	0.0	0.0	1.2	2.0	0.2	0.0	0.0	4.6	28.2	3.4	1874
1875	14.1	5.4	0.0	0.2	0.0	0.0	0.0	0.0	0.0	1.1	2.3	0.5	0.0	0.0	7.3	30.1	1.8	1875
1876	12.7	5.3	0.0	0.2	0.0	0.0	0.0	0.0	0.0	1.2	2.6	0.5	0.0	0.0	8.0	30.0	-0.1	1876
1877	12.7	4.9	0.0	0.2	0.0	0.0	0.0	0.0	0.0	1.2	2.4	2.3	0.0	0.0	7.6	29.5	-0.5	1877
1878	12.9	4.8	0.0	0.2	0.0	0.0	0.0	0.0	0.0	1.2	2.5	2.3	0.0	0.0	4.1	28.1	-1.4	1878
1879	13.5	4.8	0.0	0.2	0.0	0.0	0.0	0.0	0.0	1.3	3.1	0.1	0.0	0.0	5.6	30.1	1.9	1879
1880	16.3	5.6	0.0	0.1	0.0	0.0	0.0	0.0	0.0	1.4	3.4	0.9	0.0	0.0	6.2	31.9	1.9	1880
1881	20.0	5.1	0.0	0.0	0.0	0.0	0.0	0.0	0.0	1.5	3.1	1.4	0.0	0.0	0.6	32.1	0.2	1881
1882	22.3	5.9	0.0	0.0	0.0	0.0	0.0	0.0	0.0	1.7	3.4	1.0	0.0	0.0	1.5	36.5	4.4	1882
1883	21.5	6.0	0.0	0.0	0.0	0.0	0.0	0.0	0.0	1.8	3.7	0.8	0.0	0.0	9.4	43.2	6.7	1883
1884	19.5	6.2	0.0	0.0	0.0	0.0	0.0	0.0	0.0	1.8	3.6	0.5	0.0	0.0	14.0	45.5	2.3	1884
1885	19.2	6.1	0.0	0.0	0.0	0.0	0.0	0.0	0.0	1.9	3.5	0.2	0.0	0.0	18.7	49.8	4.3	1885
1886	20.9	6.2	0.0	0.0	0.0	0.0	0.0	0.0	0.0	2.0	4.2	0.0	0.0	0.0	13.8	46.7	-3.1	1886
1887	22.9	6.5	0.0	0.0	0.0	0.0	0.0	0.0	0.0	2.2	4.5	0.0	0.0	0.0	5.7	40.5	-6.2	1887
1888	23.8	7.3	0.0	0.0	0.0	0.0	0.0	0.0	0.0	2.3	4.7	0.0	0.0	0.0	4.5	40.6	0.1	1888
1889	23.6	7.3	0.0	0.0	0.0	0.0	0.0	0.0	0.0	2.3	4.8	0.0	0.0	0.0	0.9	38.9	-1.7	1889
1890	23.6	7.4	0.0	0.0	0.0	0.0	0.0	0.0	0.0	2.5	4.7	0.0	0.0	0.0	0.1	38.2	-0.8	1890
1891	21.9	8.2	0.0	0.0	0.0	0.0	0.0	0.0	0.0	2.6	4.8	0.0	0.0	0.0	1.2	37.8	-0.4	1891
1892	20.7	8.4	0.0	0.0	0.0	0.0	0.0	0.0	0.0	2.8	4.8	0.0	0.0	0.0	1.3	37.6	-0.1	1892
1893	20.0	8.1	0.0	0.0	0.0	0.0	0.0	0.0	0.0	2.8	4.6	0.0	0.0	0.0	2.3	38.2	0.6	1893
1894	18.4	7.9	0.0	0.0	0.0	0.0	0.0	0.0	0.0	2.8	4.6	0.0	0.0	0.0	5.3	39.1	0.9	1894
1895	18.7	8.6	0.0	0.0	0.0	0.0	0.0	0.0	0.0	2.9	4.5	0.0	0.0	0.0	6.0	39.9	0.8	1895
1896	19.6	8.6	0.0	0.0	0.0	0.0	0.0	0.0	0.0	3.1	5.2	0.0	0.0	0.0	4.3	40.0	0.1	1896
1897	20.5	8.8	0.0	0.0	0.0	0.0	0.0	0.0	0.0	3.4	6.4	0.0	0.0	0.0	2.3	39.9	-0.1	1897
1898	23.4	9.8	0.0	0.0	0.0	0.0	0.0	0.0	0.0	3.2	7.4	0.0	0.0	0.0	1.8	43.7	3.8	1898
1899	26.7	10.1	0.0	0.0	0.0	0.0	0.0	0.0	0.0	3.3	8.3	0.0	0.0	0.0	0.7	47.8	4.1	1899
1900	28.3	10.8	0.0	0.0	0.0	0.0	0.0	0.0	0.0	3.7	8.9	0.0	0.0	0.0	1.2	51.1	3.4	1900
1901	30.1	11.6	0.0	0.0	0.0	0.0	0.0	0.0	0.0	4.2	8.2	1.7	0.0	0.0	3.2	56.6	5.5	1901
1902	34.3	12.5	0.0	0.0	0.0	0.0	0.0	0.0	0.0	4.6	8.8	1.7	0.0	0.0	-1.8	58.1	1.5	1902
1903	38.6	12.8	0.0	0.0	0.0	0.0	0.0	0.0	0.0	4.9	10.2	0.0	0.0	0.0	-6.6	59.4	1.4	1903
1904	41.0	13.3	0.0	0.0	0.0	0.0	0.0	0.0	0.0	5.5	10.9	0.0	0.0	0.0	-0.5	68.3	8.8	1904
1905	43.8	14.9	0.0	0.0	0.0	0.0	0.0	0.0	0.0	6.4	12.5	0.0	0.0	0.0	3.1	76.5	8.3	1905
1906	49.5	15.8	0.0	0.0	0.0	0.0	0.0	0.0	0.0	6.4	13.8	0.0	0.0	0.0	-1.9	81.4	4.9	1906
1907	56.1	15.1	0.0	0.0	0.0	0.0	0.0	0.0	0.0	7.3	15.1	0.3	0.0	0.0	9.1	101.8	20.4	1907
1908	49.6	15.1	0.0	0.0	0.0	0.0	0.0	0.0	0.0	7.9	17.6	0.2	0.0	0.0	36.6	122.5	20.7	1908
1909	56.6	16.5	0.0	0.0	0.0	0.0	0.0	0.0	0.0	7.9	15.1	0.2	0.0	0.0	19.1	114.0	-8.5	1909
1910	68.8	16.5	0.0	0.0	0.0	0.0	0.0	0.0	0.0	8.8	17.6	0.1	0.0	0.0	4.6	116.3	2.3	1910

TABLE C-2

Dominion Government, Total Financial Requirements, by Revenue Source, Calendar 1868-1989 (Millions of dollars)

Calendar Year	Custom Duties (1)	Excise Duties (2)	Sales Tax[1] (3)	Excise Taxes (4)	Individual Income (5)	Corporate Income Tax (6)	Non Resident (7)	Excess Profits and as Noted[2] (8)	Estate Taxes (9)	Post Office Revenues (10)	Miscellaneous Revenues (11)	Special Receipts & other Credits[3] (12)	UIC Taxes (13)	Old Age Security Taxes (14)	Deficit (Surplus) (15)	Total Financial Requirements (16)	Change in TFR (17)	Calendar Year
1911	81.7	18.7	0.0	0.0	0.0	0.0	0.0	0.0	0.0	10.2	19.5	0.0	0.0	0.0	-0.3	129.8	13.5	1911
1912	105.1	20.9	0.0	0.0	0.0	0.0	0.0	0.0	0.0	11.7	21.2	0.0	0.0	0.0	-19.5	139.4	9.6	1912
1913	106.5	21.4	0.0	0.0	0.0	0.0	0.0	0.0	0.0	12.8	21.9	0.0	0.0	0.0	8.1	170.6	31.3	1913
1914	83.1	21.5	0.0	0.1	0.0	0.0	0.0	0.0	0.0	13.1	19.8	0.0	0.0	0.0	86.2	223.7	53.1	1914
1915	92.9	22.2	0.0	2.8	0.0	0.0	0.0	0.0	0.0	17.5	23.4	0.0	0.0	0.0	149.1	307.9	84.2	1915
1916	125.2	23.9	0.0	3.9	0.0	0.0	0.0	9.4	0.0	20.4	31.0	0.0	0.0	0.0	227.6	441.2	133.4	1916
1917	141.7	26.5	0.0	4.0	0.0	0.0	0.0	19.1	0.0	21.2	36.4	0.0	0.0	0.0	289.0	537.8	96.6	1917
1918	146.5	29.5	0.0	11.4	5.9	1.1	0.0	30.1	0.0	21.5	46.5	0.0	0.0	0.0	368.1	660.6	122.9	1918
1919	163.4	39.6	0.2	16.8	11.9	5.7	0.0	41.3	0.0	23.8	21.8	0.0	0.0	0.0	390.3	714.4	53.8	1919
1920	164.7	38.5	28.2	37.1	27.7	12.2	0.0	41.6	0.0	26.2	13.6	1.4	0.0	0.0	84.3	475.5	-238.9	1920
1921	120.1	36.9	55.4	37.1	38.0	32.7	0.0	27.3	0.0	26.5	13.7	0.7	0.0	0.0	-16.9	356.1	-119.4	1921
1922	115.0	36.1	82.7	21.9	33.7	32.1	0.0	15.5	0.0	28.4	12.3	6.5	0.0	0.0	-43.5	335.1	-21.1	1922
1923	120.7	37.6	96.0	17.9	33.7	30.7	0.0	6.9	0.0	28.9	12.0	9.4	0.0	0.0	-60.1	330.4	-4.6	1923
1924	111.5	38.5	111.5	23.5	25.3	30.5	0.0	3.2	0.0	28.8	11.8	6.0	0.0	0.0	-24.4	328.1	-2.3	1924
1925	122.6	41.8	70.5	25.1	24.2	31.6	0.0	1.6	0.0	29.4	12.6	2.8	0.0	0.0	-32.2	332.6	4.5	1925
1926	138.4	47.1	79.1	27.2	19.6	29.9	0.0	0.8	0.0	31.0	13.3	1.9	0.0	0.0	-49.9	336.9	4.3	1926
1927	153.3	55.2	73.3	27.4	21.9	32.3	0.0	0.6	0.0	30.9	14.2	5.6	0.0	0.0	-65.5	345.9	9.0	1927
1928	179.7	62.1	64.6	23.8	24.4	34.3	0.0	0.3	0.0	32.6	15.5	5.3	0.0	0.0	-80.3	359.8	13.9	1928
1929	181.4	64.6	48.7	22.8	26.6	40.0	0.0	0.6	0.0	32.0	15.4	5.3	0.0	0.0	-53.8	387.3	27.5	1929
1930	143.3	59.5	26.1	21.6	26.8	43.8	0.0	0.3	0.0	31.0	12.6	9.9	0.0	0.0	57.2	427.0	39.7	1930
1931	110.9	51.0	36.3	17.8	25.3	38.5	0.0	0.1	0.0	31.7	12.4	9.0	0.0	0.0	146.5	474.9	47.9	1931
1932	78.6	40.5	53.0	18.9	25.7	36.2	3.6	0.0	0.0	31.2	8.2	7.8	0.0	0.0	159.5	465.3	-9.6	1932
1933	67.3	36.1	60.3	25.7	28.4	29.6	5.6	0.0	0.0	30.9	9.1	5.8	0.0	0.0	139.6	449.7	-15.6	1933
1934	74.0	41.3	69.7	42.6	26.1	33.7	6.9	0.0	0.0	31.2	9.7	1.7	0.0	0.0	120.5	461.4	11.7	1934
1935	74.7	44.1	76.3	40.7	31.0	40.8	8.5	0.0	0.0	32.2	10.4	2.8	0.0	0.0	149.0	508.0	46.6	1935
1936	81.4	45.6	104.0	41.2	34.9	54.1	9.8	0.0	0.0	33.9	11.2	1.2	0.0	0.0	98.4	520.7	12.7	1936
1937	91.1	50.5	131.8	44.4	39.2	66.9	10.0	0.0	0.0	35.2	11.9	6.9	0.0	0.0	32.8	520.4	-0.3	1937
1938	82.5	51.5	126.1	42.9	45.3	81.4	10.8	0.0	0.0	35.4	11.8	7.1	0.0	0.0	42.6	532.6	12.3	1938
1939	97.9	58.6	133.6	34.0	45.8	79.7	12.5	0.0	0.0	36.4	10.4	4.8	0.0	0.0	101.8	613.7	81.1	1939
1940	124.2	81.7	169.1	88.1	89.0	118.2	24.5	18.0	0.0	39.5	2.5	12.8	0.0	0.0	312.7	1057.8	444.0	1940
1941	139.5	104.7	222.1	191.6	248.0	172.0	28.2	107.3	5.3	44.6	0.0	4.8	27.3	0.0	359.0	1658.2	600.5	1941
1942	124.9	131.6	233.7	256.0	437.1	307.4	27.3	359.7	11.7	48.2	0.0	12.5	52.2	0.0	1640.3	3654.7	1996.4	1942
1943	155.7	141.3	286.9	323.7	644.8	320.6	28.2	430.2	14.6	58.1	0.0	24.0	60.7	0.0	2381.0	4966.0	1311.3	1943
1944	128.3	149.5	323.1	341.8	679.2	285.2	28.4	363.2	16.7	64.9	0.0	122.0	63.3	0.0	2486.2	5134.5	168.5	1944
1945	125.5	173.0	211.5	305.8	683.2	232.4	29.7	405.4	20.4	68.0	0.0	295.0	63.0	0.0	2181.1	5044.7	-89.8	1945
1946	210.3	178.0	276.7	291.5	674.5	233.5	34.5	438.6	23.1	71.9	0.0	542.2	72.7	0.0	203.5	3175.5	-1869.2	1946
1947	279.1	193.7	353.8	276.9	662.5	332.9	41.5	280.9	29.0	76.6	0.0	456.1	86.9	0.0	-667.6	2184.9	-990.6	1947
1948	240.5	196.6	376.1	265.2	736.8	460.1	46.5	90.4	26.8	79.9	0.0	243.0	96.7	0.0	-685.4	2030.5	-154.4	1948
1949	225.2	202.7	396.9	195.0	657.1	575.4	51.8	9.9	28.8	83.5	0.0	29.3	102.9	0.0	-294.0	2271.5	241.0	1949
1950	278.3	216.6	445.9	216.9	644.7	750.2	58.1	7.2	32.7	88.9	0.0	27.7	124.1	0.0	-383.2	2544.1	272.6	1950
1951	333.7	235.9	545.2	296.5	894.9	1047.8	56.7	4.4	37.1	101.1	31.5	44.4	124.1	19.8	-385.8	3395.8	851.7	1951
1952	378.7	223.7	568.0	296.1	1128.9	1212.8	54.0	0.6	38.1	101.1	47.9	72.6	154.2	174.4	-199.3	4272.5	876.7	1952
1953	402.8	230.4	582.0	305.1	1185.8	1203.4	53.8	0.0	38.9	111.2	53.3	76.7	158.3	275.8	-99.8	4577.5	305.0	1953

TABLE C-2

Dominion Government, Total Financial Requirements, by Revenue Source, Calendar 1868-1989 (Millions of dollars)

Calendar Year	Custom Duties (1)	Excise Duties (2)	Sales Tax[1] (3)	Excise Taxes (4)	Individual Income Tax (5)	Corporate Income Tax (6)	Non Resident (7)	Excess Profits and as Noted[2] (8)	Estate Taxes (9)	Post Office Revenues (10)	Miscellaneous Revenues (11)	Special Receipts & other Credits[3] (12)	UIC Taxes (13)	Old Age Security Taxes[4] (14)	Deficit (Surplus) (15)	Total Financial Requirements (16)	Change in TFR (17)	Calendar Year
1954	399.7	226.6	576.0	278.3	1184.5	1063.3	59.4	0.0	43.4	126.2	53.1	40.2	158.5	290.7	167.3	4667.0	89.5	1954
1955	460.2	243.7	624.2	275.0	1185.1	1025.9	65.0	0.0	61.2	135.9	100.1	7.2	166.7	309.6	91.3	4750.9	83.8	1955
1956	532.1	265.9	698.2	283.4	1346.8	1208.2	73.9	0.0	76.4	143.7	107.5	0.0	182.5	357.8	-143.2	5133.1	382.3	1956
1957	510.9	292.9	706.7	258.9	1475.0	1243.2	67.3	0.0	73.6	151.1	103.0	0.0	188.5	371.5	114.9	5557.4	424.2	1957
1958	489.4	312.6	723.2	243.9	1390.1	1074.2	62.0	0.0	72.4	156.4	121.1	0.0	186.4	374.3	863.1	6042.3	484.9	1958
1959	515.9	330.6	723.6	276.0	1513.3	1112.3	70.3	0.0	84.5	165.1	129.4	0.0	217.8	504.0	684.8	6327.1	284.8	1959
1960	505.5	342.5	749.9	289.9	1675.1	1243.2	84.5	0.0	85.8	172.1	140.3	0.0	263.6	589.1	531.5	6646.5	319.4	1960
1961	525.6	358.3	911.1	269.6	1772.3	1220.7	106.3	0.0	84.7	181.2	130.1	0.0	277.2	633.8	815.3	7124.9	478.4	1961
1962	617.4	377.1	794.4	261.0	1756.6	1187.6	124.9	0.0	86.5	190.5	127.2	0.0	284.3	679.3	791.4	7278.3	153.4	1962
1963	597.3	390.5	911.1	270.2	1835.0	1240.0	125.7	0.0	89.8	198.7	146.3	0.0	294.1	735.4	659.5	7493.3	215.1	1963
1964	611.9	406.9	1140.0	270.3	2043.8	1457.6	138.9	0.0	89.1	223.0	158.3	0.0	307.2	907.8	157.3	7912.0	418.7	1964
1965	669.7	437.3	1347.5	289.5	2132.7	1585.9	163.4	0.0	103.5	235.7	167.3	0.0	323.9	1117.1	-42.9	8530.5	618.5	1965
1966	754.6	457.2	1484.0	310.9	2391.0	1596.6	195.2	0.0	102.9	249.4	165.3	0.0	339.9	1256.5	222.6	9526.0	995.5	1966
1967	754.3	481.7	1579.2	331.7	2755.7	1651.3	216.3	0.0	101.9	274.5	130.3	0.2	345.5	1442.4	615.7	10680.5	1154.5	1967
1968	757.9	504.1	1577.6	367.5	3229.7	1940.2	209.3	47.3	109.9	286.7	173.0	0.3	432.3	1593.2	567.3	11796.1	1115.6	1968
1969	804.2	516.4	1680.1	378.2	3902.9	2466.5	237.8	373.1	103.6	338.2	155.7	0.3	557.8	1784.4	-267.5	13031.6	1235.5	1969
1970	815.5	550.5	1709.9	397.0	4543.7	2316.9	255.8	543.8	115.1	341.9	125.5	0.3	593.0	1894.9	200.8	14404.3	1372.7	1970
1971	945.1	595.2	1915.4	392.1	5360.6	2192.0	280.3	447.9	129.0	387.3	125.5	0.4	645.8	2067.1	866.5	16349.9	1945.6	1971
1972	1133.7	630.2	2785.2	397.1	7679.0	2735.8	290.9	113.8	78.7	453.5	154.2	45.9	738.0	2193.8	2055.9	21485.4	5135.5	1972
1973	1333.5	674.0	3455.5	406.0	9014.0	3512.5	316.0	219.2	26.0	477.5	239.5	25.8	958.8	2427.1	1863.4	24948.6	3463.3	1973
1974	1867.5	732.5	3797.0	412.5	11089.0	4554.5	401.3	1323.5	9.3	484.5	264.3	8.8	1472.5	2993.0	1694.9	30939.8	5991.1	1974
1975	2044.5	798.3	3602.8	432.0	12459.3	5520.0	468.3	1533.3	2.5	454.5	307.5	10.0	1970.8	1386.9	4970.5	35790.7	4850.9	1975
1976	2258.3	852.5	3825.5	473.3	14152.8	5459.3	458.8	1317.8	0.0	572.3	421.0	55.3	2417.8	199.1	5767.0	38019.1	2228.4	1976
1977	2638.3	877.8	4302.5	475.3	14149.5	5300.8	490.0	1087.8	0.0	733.5	519.3	67.0	2578.3	0.0	8884.3	41724.0	3704.9	1977
1978	2936.8	879.0	4653.5	492.3	14489.0	5560.5	551.8	890.5	0.0	870.5	512.5	74.3	2797.5	0.0	14111.0	48520.5	6796.5	1978
1979	3591.0	890.8	4705.8	501.3	16270.0	6626.8	732.3	1089.3	0.0	1064.3	638.8	91.3	2799.8	0.0	10734.3	49081.0	560.5	1979
1980	3523.3	1005.3	5246.3	555.3	19079.8	7817.3	847.0	1424.5	0.0	1111.3	634.5	98.3	3171.8	0.0	10569.8	55151.8	6070.8	1980
1981	2979.8	1141.8	5968.3	566.3	22993.8	8115.0	980.3	3768.0	0.0	640.3	933.8	114.8	4390.5	0.0	13552.0	66687.8	11536.0	1981
1982	3239.0	1249.3	5918.5	654.8	25759.0	7383.8	1003.0	2310.8	0.0	121.0	870.3	129.0	4863.3	0.0	24459.0	80381.0	13693.3	1982
1983	3689.5	1335.5	6381.5	736.8	26807.8	7249.3	930.5	4990.5	0.0	0.0	1012.0	127.5	6669.3	0.0	31253.3	90154.8	9773.8	1983
1984	3926.8	1435.5	7334.3	826.0	28682.3	8855.8	992.8	4412.8	0.0	0.0	1130.5	111.8	7479.5	0.0	36842.8	101781.8	11627.0	1984
1985	4133.0	1470.3	8906.8	1228.0	32069.5	9252.3	1045.0	4401.3	0.0	0.0	1400.0	121.3	8427.5	0.0	35390.8	106868.8	5087.0	1985
1986	4335.5	1470.8	11315.3	1429.8	36660.5	9716.3	1279.5	3630.8	0.0	0.0	1631.8	139.5	9348.3	0.0	31557.0	110992.3	4123.5	1986
1987	4487.0	1461.8	12688.3	1539.0	43313.3	10629.8	1210.3	2442.8	0.0	0.0	2044.8	191.3	10208.3	0.0	28714.3	118779.0	7786.4	1987
1988	4570.5	1454.5	14965.5	1521.5	45800.8	11517.0	1474.0	2635.0	0.0	0.0	1917.0	250.5	11057.2	0.0	28734.3	127350.0	7071.0	1988
1989		1960.8	17165.3	1347.8	50927.8	12698.3	1415.3	2514.8	0.0	0.0	2316.3	235.8	10870.5	0.0	28984.8	135007.5	8665.0	1989

Sources: See Appendix C for Discussion

1. Gross Sales Tax Revenues less refunds of sales and other excises.
2. Business profits taxes (1917-1930), excess profits tax (1941-1952), social development tax (1969-1973) and energy taxes (1974-1989).
3. Includes other miscellaneous taxes (and remnants of estate tax after 1975) from 1968 on.
4. Includes old age security individual income taxes, corporation income taxes and sales taxes.

TABLE C-3

Dominion Government, Total Financial Requirements, by Revenue Source, Calendar 1868-1989 (as a percentage of GNP)

Calendar Year	Custom Duties (1)	Excise Duties (2)	Sales Tax¹ (3)	Excise Taxes (4)	Individual Income Tax (5)	Corporate Income Tax (6)	Non Resident (7)	Excess Profits and as Noted² (8)	Estate Taxes (9)	Post Office Revenues (10)	Miscellaneous Revenues (11)	Special Receipts & other Credits³ (12)	UIC Taxes (13)	Old Age Security Taxes (14)	Deficit (Surplus) (15)	Total Financial Requirements (16)	Federal Debt (17)	Calendar Year
1870	2.8	1.1	0.0	0.0	0.0	0.0	0.0	0.0	0.0	0.2	0.4	0.0	0.0	0.0	0.2	4.7	0.6	1870
1871	3.0	1.1	0.0	0.0	0.0	0.0	0.0	0.0	0.0	0.2	0.4	0.0	0.0	0.0	0.3	5.0	0.8	1871
1872	2.9	1.1	0.0	0.0	0.0	0.0	0.0	0.0	0.0	0.2	0.4	0.1	0.0	0.0	0.7	5.3	1.5	1872
1873	2.8	1.0	0.0	0.0	0.0	0.0	0.0	0.0	0.0	0.2	0.4	0.0	0.0	0.0	0.6	5.1	1.9	1873
1874	3.1	1.1	0.0	0.0	0.0	0.0	0.0	0.0	0.0	0.2	0.4	0.1	0.0	0.0	0.9	5.8	2.9	1874
1875	3.1	1.2	0.0	0.0	0.0	0.0	0.0	0.0	0.0	0.3	0.4	0.1	0.0	0.0	1.6	5.8	4.7	1875
1876	3.0	1.1	0.0	0.0	0.0	0.0	0.0	0.0	0.0	0.3	0.6	0.5	0.0	0.0	1.9	6.6	6.9	1876
1877	2.9	1.2	0.0	0.0	0.0	0.0	0.0	0.0	0.0	0.3	0.6	0.5	0.0	0.0	1.7	7.1	7.1	1877
1878	3.1	1.1	0.0	0.0	0.0	0.0	0.0	0.0	0.0	0.3	0.6	0.0	0.0	0.0	1.0	6.8	8.5	1878
1879	3.0	1.3	0.0	0.0	0.0	0.0	0.0	0.0	0.0	0.3	0.8	0.0	0.0	0.0	1.2	6.9	10.0	1879
1880	3.4	1.0	0.0	0.0	0.0	0.0	0.0	0.0	0.0	0.4	0.8	0.2	0.0	0.0	1.3	6.8	10.4	1880
1881	3.5	1.0	0.0	0.0	0.0	0.0	0.0	0.0	0.0	0.3	0.7	0.3	0.0	0.0	0.1	6.6	10.9	1881
1882	3.6	1.1	0.0	0.0	0.0	0.0	0.0	0.0	0.0	0.3	0.6	0.2	0.0	0.0	0.2	5.7	9.4	1882
1883	3.5	1.1	0.0	0.0	0.0	0.0	0.0	0.0	0.0	0.3	0.6	0.1	0.0	0.0	1.5	5.9	8.9	1883
1884	3.3	1.1	0.0	0.0	0.0	0.0	0.0	0.0	0.0	0.4	0.6	0.1	0.0	0.0	2.4	7.1	10.5	1884
1885	3.5	1.1	0.0	0.0	0.0	0.0	0.0	0.0	0.0	0.4	0.6	0.0	0.0	0.0	3.4	7.8	13.4	1885
1886	3.7	1.1	0.0	0.0	0.0	0.0	0.0	0.0	0.0	0.4	0.7	0.0	0.0	0.0	2.5	9.0	17.5	1886
1887	3.6	1.2	0.0	0.0	0.0	0.0	0.0	0.0	0.0	0.4	0.7	0.0	0.0	0.0	0.9	8.3	19.7	1887
1888	3.6	1.1	0.0	0.0	0.0	0.0	0.0	0.0	0.0	0.4	0.7	0.0	0.0	0.0	0.7	6.6	19.0	1888
1889	3.6	1.1	0.0	0.0	0.0	0.0	0.0	0.0	0.0	0.4	0.7	0.0	0.0	0.0	0.1	6.4	19.1	1889
1890	3.4	1.1	0.0	0.0	0.0	0.0	0.0	0.0	0.0	0.4	0.7	0.0	0.0	0.0	0.0	5.9	18.5	1890
1891	3.1	1.1	0.0	0.0	0.0	0.0	0.0	0.0	0.0	0.4	0.7	0.0	0.0	0.0	0.2	5.6	17.7	1891
1892	2.9	1.2	0.0	0.0	0.0	0.0	0.0	0.0	0.0	0.4	0.7	0.0	0.0	0.0	0.2	5.4	17.5	1892
1893	2.9	1.2	0.0	0.0	0.0	0.0	0.0	0.0	0.0	0.4	0.7	0.0	0.0	0.0	0.3	5.4	17.7	1893
1894	2.8	1.2	0.0	0.0	0.0	0.0	0.0	0.0	0.0	0.4	0.7	0.0	0.0	0.0	0.8	5.6	18.5	1894
1895	3.0	1.3	0.0	0.0	0.0	0.0	0.0	0.0	0.0	0.5	0.7	0.0	0.0	0.0	0.9	6.0	20.2	1895
1896	3.1	1.3	0.0	0.0	0.0	0.0	0.0	0.0	0.0	0.5	0.8	0.0	0.0	0.0	0.3	6.3	21.7	1896
1897	2.9	1.2	0.0	0.0	0.0	0.0	0.0	0.0	0.0	0.4	0.9	0.0	0.0	0.0	0.2	6.2	22.1	1897
1898	3.0	1.3	0.0	0.0	0.0	0.0	0.0	0.0	0.0	0.4	1.0	0.0	0.0	0.0	0.3	5.7	20.1	1898
1899	3.2	1.2	0.0	0.0	0.0	0.0	0.0	0.0	0.0	0.4	1.0	0.0	0.0	0.0	0.1	5.6	19.0	1899
1900	3.1	1.2	0.0	0.0	0.0	0.0	0.0	0.0	0.0	0.4	1.0	0.0	0.0	0.0	0.3	5.8	17.7	1900
1901	3.0	1.1	0.0	0.0	0.0	0.0	0.0	0.0	0.0	0.4	0.8	0.2	0.0	0.0	-0.2	5.6	16.3	1901
1902	3.1	1.1	0.0	0.0	0.0	0.0	0.0	0.0	0.0	0.4	0.8	0.1	0.0	0.0	-0.6	5.7	15.2	1902
1903	3.3	1.0	0.0	0.0	0.0	0.0	0.0	0.0	0.0	0.4	0.9	0.0	0.0	0.0	0.0	5.2	13.3	1903
1904	3.4	0.9	0.0	0.0	0.0	0.0	0.0	0.0	0.0	0.4	0.8	0.0	0.0	0.0	0.0	5.0	12.1	1904
1905	3.2	1.0	0.0	0.0	0.0	0.0	0.0	0.0	0.0	0.5	0.9	0.0	0.0	0.0	0.2	5.7	11.8	1905
1906	3.2	0.9	0.0	0.0	0.0	0.0	0.0	0.0	0.0	0.4	0.8	0.0	0.0	0.0	-0.1	5.6	10.7	1906
1907	3.2	0.9	0.0	0.0	0.0	0.0	0.0	0.0	0.0	0.4	0.8	0.0	0.0	0.0	0.5	5.3	9.4	1907
1908	3.0	0.9	0.0	0.0	0.0	0.0	0.0	0.0	0.0	0.4	0.8	0.0	0.0	0.0	2.2	5.9	8.8	1908
1909	3.1	0.8	0.0	0.0	0.0	0.0	0.0	0.0	0.0	0.4	0.8	0.0	0.0	0.0	1.0	7.4	11.4	1909
1910	3.4	0.8	0.0	0.0	0.0	0.0	0.0	0.0	0.0	0.4	0.9	0.0	0.0	0.0	0.2	5.8	11.3	1910

TABLE C-3

Dominion Government, Total Financial Requirements, by Revenue Source, Calendar 1868-1989 (as a percentage of GNP)

Calendar Year	Custom Duties (1)	Excise Duties (2)	Sales Tax (3)	Excise Taxes (4)	Individual Income Tax (5)	Corporate Income Tax (6)	Non Resident (7)	Excess Profits and as Noted (8)	Estate Taxes (9)	Post Office Revenues (10)	Miscellaneous Revenues (11)	Special Receipts & other Credits (12)	UIC Taxes (13)	Old Age Security Taxes (14)	Deficit (Surplus) (15)	Total Financial Requirements (16)	Federal Debt (17)	Calendar Year
1911	3.7	0.8	0.0	0.0	0.0	0.0	0.0	0.0	0.0	0.5	0.9	0.0	0.0	0.0	0.0	5.8	9.5	1911
1912	4.2	0.8	0.0	0.0	0.0	0.0	0.0	0.0	0.0	0.5	0.8	0.0	0.0	0.0	-0.8	5.6	7.7	1912
1913	4.0	0.8	0.0	0.0	0.0	0.0	0.0	0.0	0.0	0.5	0.8	0.0	0.0	0.0	0.3	6.4	7.6	1913
1914	3.4	0.9	0.0	0.0	0.0	0.0	0.0	0.0	0.0	0.6	0.8	0.0	0.0	0.0	3.5	9.1	11.7	1914
1915	3.5	0.8	0.0	0.1	0.0	0.0	0.0	0.0	0.0	0.6	0.9	0.0	0.0	0.0	5.5	11.5	16.2	1915
1916	3.9	0.7	0.0	0.1	0.0	0.0	0.0	0.3	0.0	0.5	1.0	0.0	0.0	0.0	7.0	13.6	20.5	1916
1917	3.5	0.7	0.0	0.1	0.0	0.0	0.0	0.5	0.0	0.5	0.9	0.0	0.0	0.0	7.2	13.5	23.9	1917
1918	3.4	0.7	0.0	0.3	0.1	0.1	0.0	0.9	0.0	0.5	1.1	0.1	0.0	0.0	8.6	15.5	31.0	1918
1919	3.7	0.9	0.0	0.4	0.3	0.2	0.0	0.9	0.0	0.5	0.5	0.1	0.0	0.0	8.9	16.4	39.2	1919
1920	3.3	0.9	0.0	0.7	0.5	0.8	0.0	0.8	0.0	0.5	0.5	0.1	0.0	0.0	1.7	9.4	35.5	1920
1921	3.3	0.8	0.6	0.5	0.9	0.8	0.0	0.7	0.0	0.6	0.3	0.0	0.0	0.0	-0.4	8.7	43.7	1921
1922	2.9	0.9	1.4	0.5	0.8	0.7	0.0	0.4	0.0	0.7	0.3	0.2	0.0	0.0	-1.0	7.3	41.0	1922
1923	2.7	0.9	2.0	0.4	0.6	0.7	0.0	0.2	0.0	0.6	0.3	0.2	0.0	0.0	-1.3	7.3	36.8	1923
1924	2.6	0.8	2.1	0.5	0.6	0.6	0.0	0.1	0.0	0.6	0.3	0.1	0.0	0.0	-0.5	6.7	36.7	1924
1925	2.5	0.9	1.6	0.5	0.4	0.6	0.0	0.1	0.0	0.6	0.3	0.1	0.0	0.0	-0.6	6.3	32.4	1925
1926	2.5	0.9	1.4	0.5	0.4	0.6	0.0	0.0	0.0	0.6	0.2	0.1	0.0	0.0	-0.9	6.2	29.3	1926
1927	2.6	1.0	1.5	0.4	0.4	0.6	0.0	0.0	0.0	0.5	0.3	0.1	0.0	0.0	-1.2	5.9	27.0	1927
1928	2.8	1.0	1.3	0.4	0.4	0.7	0.0	0.0	0.0	0.5	0.3	0.2	0.0	0.0	-1.3	6.3	23.5	1928
1929	3.0	1.1	1.1	0.4	0.4	0.7	0.0	0.0	0.0	0.5	0.3	0.1	0.0	0.0	-0.9	6.3	22.3	1929
1930	3.0	1.0	0.8	0.4	0.5	0.8	0.0	0.0	0.0	0.5	0.3	0.2	0.0	0.0	1.0	7.5	24.9	1930
1931	2.5	1.1	0.8	0.3	0.5	0.8	0.0	0.0	0.0	0.7	0.2	0.2	0.0	0.0	3.1	10.1	33.5	1931
1932	2.4	1.1	1.4	0.4	0.7	0.9	0.1	0.0	0.0	0.8	0.2	0.2	0.0	0.0	4.2	12.2	45.4	1932
1933	2.1	1.1	1.7	0.7	0.7	0.8	0.1	0.0	0.0	0.9	0.3	0.2	0.0	0.0	4.0	12.9	53.6	1933
1934	1.9	1.0	1.8	1.2	0.8	0.8	0.1	0.0	0.0	0.8	0.3	0.1	0.0	0.0	3.0	11.6	50.2	1934
1935	1.9	1.0	1.8	1.2	0.7	0.9	0.2	0.0	0.0	0.7	0.3	0.1	0.0	0.0	3.5	11.8	49.8	1935
1936	1.7	1.0	2.2	0.9	0.8	1.2	0.2	0.0	0.0	0.7	0.3	0.1	0.0	0.0	2.1	11.2	48.3	1936
1937	1.8	1.0	2.5	0.9	0.9	1.3	0.2	0.0	0.0	0.7	0.2	0.1	0.0	0.0	0.6	9.9	43.4	1937
1938	1.7	1.0	2.4	0.8	0.8	1.5	0.2	0.0	0.0	0.7	0.2	0.1	0.0	0.0	0.8	10.1	43.9	1938
1939	1.7	1.0	2.4	0.8	0.8	1.4	0.2	0.3	0.0	0.6	0.2	0.1	0.0	0.0	1.8	10.9	43.0	1939
1940	1.8	1.2	2.5	0.6	1.3	1.8	0.2	1.3	0.0	0.6	0.0	0.1	0.1	0.0	4.7	15.8	40.7	1940
1941	1.7	1.3	2.7	1.1	3.0	2.1	0.3	3.5	0.0	0.5	0.0	0.2	0.3	0.0	4.3	20.0	37.3	1941
1942	1.2	1.3	2.3	2.3	4.3	3.0	0.2	3.9	0.1	0.5	0.0	1.1	0.5	0.0	16.0	35.6	46.1	1942
1943	1.4	1.3	2.9	2.9	5.8	2.9	0.2	3.1	0.1	0.5	0.0	2.5	0.5	0.0	21.5	44.9	64.3	1943
1944	1.1	1.3	2.6	2.6	5.7	2.4	0.2	3.7	0.2	0.5	0.0	4.6	0.5	0.0	21.0	43.3	81.0	1944
1945	1.1	1.5	2.0	2.5	5.8	2.0	0.2	3.4	0.2	0.6	0.0	3.8	0.6	0.0	18.4	42.5	99.3	1945
1946	1.8	1.6	1.8	2.1	5.7	2.0	0.2	2.1	0.2	0.6	0.0	1.8	0.6	0.0	1.7	26.7	100.8	1946
1947	2.1	1.5	2.3	1.7	4.9	2.5	0.3	0.6	0.2	0.6	0.0	0.6	0.6	0.0	-5.0	16.2	84.0	1947
1948	1.6	1.3	2.6	1.2	4.8	3.0	0.3	0.1	0.2	0.6	0.0	0.2	0.6	0.0	-4.4	13.1	68.5	1948
1949	1.3	1.3	2.4	1.2	3.9	3.4	0.3	0.0	0.1	0.5	0.0	0.2	0.6	0.0	-1.7	13.5	61.5	1949
1950	1.5	1.0	2.4	1.4	3.5	4.1	0.3	0.0	0.2	0.5	0.1	0.2	0.7	0.1	-2.1	13.8	53.8	1950
1951	1.5	1.0	2.5	1.4	4.1	4.8	0.3	0.0	0.2	0.5	0.1	0.2	0.7	0.7	-1.8	15.7	44.2	1951
1952	1.5	1.0	2.3	1.2	4.6	4.9	0.2	0.0	0.2	0.4	0.2	0.3	0.6	0.7	-0.8	17.4	38.1	1952
1953	1.6	0.9	2.3	1.2	4.6	4.7	0.2	0.0	0.2	0.4	0.2	0.3	0.6	1.1	-0.4	17.7	35.9	1953

TABLE C-3

Dominion Government, Total Financial Requirements, by Revenue Source, Calendar 1868-1989 (as a percentage of GNP)

Calendar Year	Custom Duties (1)	Excise Duties (2)	Sales Tax[1] (3)	Excise Taxes (4)	Individual Income Tax (5)	Corporate Income Tax (6)	Non Resident (7)	Excess Profits and as Noted[2] (8)	Estate Taxes (9)	Post Office Revenues (10)	Miscellaneous Revenues (11)	Special Receipts & other Credits[3] (12)	UIC Taxes (13)	Old Age Security Taxes[4] (14)	Deficit (Surplus) (15)	Total Financial Requirements (16)	Federal Debt (17)	Calendar Year
1954	1.5	0.9	2.2	1.1	4.6	4.1	0.2	0.0	0.2	0.5	0.2	0.2	0.6	1.1	0.6	18.0	36.4	1954
1955	1.6	0.9	2.2	1.0	4.2	3.6	0.2	0.0	0.2	0.5	0.4	0.0	0.6	1.1	0.3	16.7	33.4	1955
1956	1.7	0.8	2.2	0.9	4.2	3.7	0.2	0.0	0.2	0.4	0.3	0.0	0.6	1.1	-0.4	16.0	29.3	1956
1957	1.5	0.9	2.1	0.8	4.4	3.1	0.2	0.0	0.2	0.5	0.3	0.0	0.6	1.1	0.3	16.6	28.3	1957
1958	1.4	0.9	2.0	0.7	4.0	3.0	0.2	0.0	0.2	0.4	0.3	0.0	0.5	1.1	2.5	17.4	29.8	1958
1959	1.3	0.9	2.0	0.7	4.1	3.2	0.3	0.0	0.2	0.4	0.4	0.0	0.6	1.1	1.9	17.2	30.0	1959
1960	1.3	0.9	1.9	0.8	4.4	3.1	0.3	0.0	0.2	0.5	0.4	0.0	0.7	1.5	1.4	17.3	30.2	1960
1961	1.4	0.9	1.9	0.7	4.5	3.1	0.3	0.0	0.2	0.5	0.3	0.0	0.7	1.4	2.1	18.0	31.3	1961
1962	1.4	0.9	2.0	0.6	4.1	2.8	0.3	0.0	0.2	0.4	0.3	0.0	0.7	1.6	1.8	17.3	30.2	1962
1963	1.3	0.8	2.0	0.6	4.0	2.7	0.3	0.0	0.2	0.4	0.3	0.0	0.7	1.6	1.4	17.0	30.7	1963
1964	1.2	0.8	2.3	0.5	4.1	2.9	0.3	0.0	0.2	0.4	0.3	0.0	0.6	1.8	0.3	16.3	30.1	1964
1965	1.2	0.8	2.4	0.5	3.9	2.9	0.3	0.0	0.2	0.4	0.3	0.0	0.6	1.8	-0.1	15.7	27.8	1965
1966	1.1	0.7	2.4	0.5	3.9	2.6	0.3	0.0	0.2	0.4	0.3	0.0	0.5	2.0	-0.4	15.4	25.2	1966
1967	1.0	0.7	2.4	0.5	4.1	2.5	0.3	0.0	0.2	0.4	0.3	0.0	0.6	2.0	0.9	15.4	22.9	1967
1968	1.0	0.6	2.2	0.5	4.4	2.7	0.3	0.1	0.2	0.4	0.3	0.0	0.6	2.2	0.8	16.1	22.3	1968
1969	1.0	0.6	2.1	0.5	4.9	3.1	0.3	0.5	0.2	0.4	0.2	0.0	0.7	2.2	-0.8	16.3	21.2	1969
1970	1.0	0.6	2.0	0.5	5.3	2.7	0.3	0.6	0.2	0.4	0.2	0.0	0.7	2.2	-0.3	16.3	18.9	1970
1971	1.0	0.6	2.0	0.4	5.7	2.3	0.3	0.5	0.1	0.4	0.1	0.0	0.7	2.2	0.2	16.9	17.8	1971
1972	1.1	0.6	2.6	0.4	7.3	2.7	0.3	0.1	0.1	0.4	0.1	0.0	0.7	2.2	0.9	17.3	17.1	1972
1973	1.1	0.5	2.8	0.3	7.3	2.6	0.3	0.2	0.1	0.4	0.1	0.0	0.7	2.1	2.0	20.4	17.3	1973
1974	1.2	0.5	2.6	0.3	7.5	2.8	0.3	0.9	0.0	0.4	0.2	0.0	0.8	2.0	1.5	20.2	16.3	1974
1975	1.1	0.5	2.2	0.3	7.5	3.3	0.3	0.7	0.0	0.3	0.2	0.0	1.0	1.1	1.1	21.0	14.8	1975
1976	1.1	0.4	2.0	0.2	7.4	2.9	0.2	0.7	0.0	0.3	0.2	0.0	1.2	0.8	3.0	21.6	16.2	1976
1977	1.1	0.4	2.0	0.2	6.6	2.5	0.2	0.5	0.0	0.3	0.2	0.0	1.2	0.1	3.0	19.9	17.0	1977
1978	1.1	0.3	2.0	0.2	6.1	2.4	0.2	0.4	0.0	0.4	0.2	0.0	1.2	0.0	4.2	19.6	19.4	1978
1979	1.1	0.3	1.7	0.2	6.0	2.5	0.3	0.4	0.0	0.4	0.2	0.0	1.0	0.0	6.0	20.6	23.6	1979
1980	1.2	0.3	1.7	0.2	6.3	2.6	0.3	0.5	0.0	0.4	0.2	0.0	1.0	0.0	4.0	18.2	24.6	1980
1981	1.0	0.3	1.7	0.2	6.7	2.4	0.3	1.1	0.0	0.2	0.2	0.0	1.1	0.0	3.5	18.3	25.4	1981
1982	0.8	0.3	1.6	0.2	7.1	2.0	0.3	1.1	0.0	0.0	0.3	0.0	1.3	0.0	3.9	19.3	26.2	1982
1983	0.8	0.3	1.6	0.2	6.8	1.8	0.2	1.4	0.0	0.0	0.3	0.0	1.3	0.0	6.8	22.2	31.7	1983
1984	0.9	0.3	1.7	0.2	6.7	2.1	0.2	1.1	0.0	0.0	0.3	0.0	1.7	0.0	7.9	22.9	37.1	1984
1985	0.8	0.3	1.9	0.3	6.9	2.0	0.2	0.8	0.0	0.0	0.3	0.0	1.8	0.0	8.5	23.6	42.4	1985
1986	0.8	0.3	2.3	0.3	7.5	2.0	0.2	0.5	0.0	0.0	0.3	0.0	1.9	0.0	7.6	23.0	47.1	1986
1987	0.8	0.2	2.4	0.3	8.1	2.0	0.2	0.5	0.0	0.0	0.4	0.0	1.9	0.0	6.4	22.7	51.1	1987
1988	0.8	0.2	2.6	0.3	8.1	2.0	0.2	0.5	0.0	0.0	0.3	0.0	1.9	0.0	5.4	22.2	52.1	1988
1989	0.7	0.3	2.7	0.2	8.1	2.0	0.2	0.4	0.0	0.0	0.4	0.0	1.7	0.0	4.6	21.4	53.4	1989

Sources: See Appendix C for Discussion

1. Gross Sales Tax Revenues less refunds of sales and other excises.
2. Business profits taxes (1917-1930), excess profits tax (1941-1952), social development tax (1969-1973) and energy taxes (1974-1989).
3. Includes other miscellaneous taxes (and remnants of estate tax after 1975) from 1968 on.
4. Includes old age security individual income taxes, corporation income taxes and sales taxes.

Appendix D

Dates of Dominion/Federal General Elections, 1867–1990

Parliament	Date	Parliament	Date
1	Sept. 1867	18	Oct. 14, 1935
2	Sept. 1872	19	March 26, 1940
3	Jan. 22, 1874	20	June 11, 1945
4	Sept. 17, 1878	21	June 27, 1949
5	June 20, 1882	22	Aug. 10, 1953
6	Feb. 22, 1887	23	June 10, 1957
7	March 5, 1891	24	March 31, 1958
8	June 23, 1896	25	June 18, 1962
9	Nov. 7, 1900	26	April 18, 1963
10	Nov. 3, 1904	27	Nov. 8, 1965
11	Oct. 26, 1908	28	June 25, 1968
12	Sept. 21, 1911	29	Oct. 30, 1972
13	Dec. 17, 1917	30	July 8, 1974
14	Dec. 6, 1921	31	May 22, 1979
15	Oct. 29, 1925	32	Feb. 18, 1980
16	Sept. 14, 1926	33	Sept. 4, 1984
17	July 28, 1930	34	Nov. 21, 1988

Sources: *The Canada Year Book*, (1926:73–74; 1946:54; 1959:65) and *Canadian News Facts* (Vols. 2, 6, 13, 14, 18 and 22), Toronto: Marpep Publishing.

Appendix E

Budget Speeches

1867–1990

Year	Minister of Finance	Budget Date	Governing Party
1867	Rose, Hon. John,	Dec. 7.	Conservative
1868	Rose, Hon. John,	April 28.	"
1869	Rose, Hon. John,	May 7.	"
1870	Hincks, Sir Francis,	May 7.	"
1871	Hincks, Sir Francis,	March 10.	"
1872	Hincks, Sir Francis,	April 30.	"
1873	Tilley, Hon. S.L.,	April 1.	"
1874	Cartwright, Hon. R.J.,	April 14.	Liberal
1875	Cartwright, Hon. R.J.,	Feb. 16.	"
1876	Cartwright, Hon. R.J.,	Feb. 25.	"
1877	Cartwright, Hon. R.J.,	Feb. 20.	"
1878	Cartwright, Hon. R.J.,	Feb. 22.	"
1879	Tilley, Hon. S.L.,	March 14.	Conservative
1880	Tilley, Hon. S.L.,	March 9.	"
1881	Tilley, Sir Leonard,	Feb. 18.	"
1882	Tilley, Sir Leonard,	Feb. 24.	"
1883	Tilley, Sir Leonard,	March 30.	"
1884	Tilley, Sir Leonard,	Feb. 29.	"
1885	Tilley, Sir Leonard,	March 3.	"
1886	McLean, Hon. A.W.,	March 30.	"
1887	Tupper, Sir Charles,	May 12.	"
1888	Tupper, Sir Charles,	April 27.	"
1889	Foster, Hon. George,	March 5.	"
1890	Foster, Hon. George,	March 27.	"
1891	Foster, Hon. George,	June 23.	"
1892	Foster, Hon. George,	March 22.	"
1893	Foster, Hon. George,	Feb. 14.	"
1894	Foster, Hon. George,	March 27.	"
1895	Foster, Hon. George,	May 3.	"
1896	Foster, Hon. George,	Jan. 3.	"

Year	Minister of Finance	Budget Date	Governing Party
1897	Fielding, Hon. William S.,	April 22.	Liberal
1898	Fielding, Hon. William S.,	April 5.	"
1899	Fielding, Hon. William S.,	May 2.	"
1900	Fielding, Hon. William S.,	March 23.	"
1901	Fielding, Hon. William S.,	March 14.	"
1902	Fielding, Hon. William S.,	March 17.	"
1903	Fielding, Hon. William S.,	April 16.	"
1904	Fielding, Hon. William S.,	June 7.	"
1905	Fielding, Hon. William S.,	May 6.	"
1906a	Fielding, Hon. William S.,	May 22.	"
1906b	Fielding, Hon. William S.,	Nov. 29.	"
1908	Fielding, Hon. William S.,	March 17.	"
1909a	Fielding, Hon. William S.,	April 20.	"
1909b	Fielding, Hon. William S.,	Dec. 14.	"
1911	Fielding, Hon. William S.,	April 4.	"
1912	White, Hon. W.Thomas.,	March 13.	Conservative
1913	White, Hon. W.Thomas.,	May 1.	"
1914a	White, Hon. W.Thomas.,	April 6.	"
1914b	White, Hon. W.Thomas.,	Aug. 20.	"
1915	White, Hon. W.Thomas.,	Feb. 11.	"
1916	White, Sir Thomas,	Feb. 15.	Conservative
1917a	White, Sir Thomas,	April 14.	"
1917b	White, Sir Thomas,	July 25*.	"
1918	MacLean, Hon. A.K.,	April 30.	Unionist
	(acting for Sir Thomas White)		
1919	White, Sir Thomas,	June 5.	"
1920	Drayton, Sir Henry L.,	May 18.	"
1921	Drayton, Sir Henry L.,	May 9.	"
1922	Fielding, Hon. William S.,	June 12.	Liberal**
1923	Fielding, Hon. William S.,	May 11.	" **
1924	Robb, Hon. James A.,	March 24.	" **
	(acting for William S. Fielding)		
1925	Robb, Hon. James A.,	April 10.	" **
	(acting for William S. Fielding)		
1926	Robb, Hon. James A.,	April 5.	" **
1927	Robb, Hon. James A.,	Feb. 17.	"
1928	Robb, Hon. James A.,	Feb. 16.	"
1929	Robb, Hon. James A.,	March 1.	"
1930	Dunning, Hon. Charles. A.,	May 1.	"
1931	Bennett, Rt. Hon. R.B.,	June 1.	Conservative
1932	Rhodes, Hon. Edgar N.,	April 6.	"

Year	Minister of Finance	Budget Date	Governing Party
1933	Rhodes, Hon. Edgar N.,	March 21.	"
1934	Rhodes, Hon. Edgar N.,	April 18.	"
1935	Rhodes, Hon. Edgar N.,	March 22.	"
1936	Dunning, Hon. Charles. A.,	May 1.	Liberal
1937	Dunning, Hon. Charles. A.,	Feb. 25.	"
1938	Dunning, Hon. Charles. A.,	June 16.	"
1939a	Dunning, Hon. Charles. A.,	April 25.	"
1939b	Ilsley, Hon. J.L.,	Sept. 12.	"
	(acting for Charles. A. Dunning)		
1940	Ralston, Hon. J.L.,	June 24.	"
1941	Ilsley, Hon. J.L.,	April 29.	"
1942	Ilsley, Hon. J.L.,	June 23.	"
1943	Ilsley, Hon. J.L.,	March 2.	"
1944	Ilsley, Hon. J.L.,	June 26.	"
1945	Ilsley, Hon. J.L.,	Oct. 12.	"
1946	Ilsley, Hon. J.L.,	June 27.	"
1947	Abbott, Hon. D.C.,	April 29.	"
1948	Abbott, Hon. D.C.,	May 18.	"
1949a	Abbott, Hon. D.C.,	March 22.	"
1949b	Abbott, Hon. D.C.,	Oct. 20.	"
1950	Abbott, Hon. D.C.,	Sept. 7.	"
1951	Abbott, Hon. D.C.,	April 10.	"
1952	Abbott, Hon. D.C.,	April 8.	"
1953	Abbott, Hon. D.C.,	Feb. 19.	"
1954	Abbott, Hon. D.C.,	April 6.	"
1955	Harris, Hon. Walter,	April 5.	Liberal
1956	Harris, Hon. Walter,	March 20.	"
1957a	Harris, Hon. Walter,	March 14.	"
1957b	Fleming, Hon. Donald M.,	Dec. 6.	Progressive Conservative**
1958	Fleming, Hon. Donald M.,	June 17.	"
1959	Fleming, Hon. Donald M.,	April 9.	"
1960a	Fleming, Hon. Donald M.,	March 31.	"
1960b	Fleming, Hon. Donald M.,	Dec. 20.	"
1961	Fleming, Hon. Donald M.,	June 20.	Progressive Conservative
1962a	Fleming, Hon. Donald M.,	April 10.	"
1962b	Fleming, Hon. Donald M.,	Oct. 22.	" **
1963	Gordon, Hon. Walter,	June 13.	Liberal**
1964	Gordon, Hon. Walter,	March 16.	" **
1965	Gordon, Hon. Walter,	April 26.	" **

Year	Minister of Finance	Budget Date	Governing Party
1966a	Sharp, Hon. Mitchell,	March 29.	" **
1966b	Sharp, Hon. Mitchell,	Dec. 19.	" **
1967a	Sharp, Hon. Mitchell,	June 1.	" **
1967b	Sharp, Hon. Mitchell,	Nov. 30.	" **
1968	Benson, Hon. Edgar.J.,	Oct. 22.	Liberal
1969	Benson, Hon. Edgar.J.,	June 3.	"
1970a	Benson, Hon. Edgar.J.,	March 12.	"
1970b	Benson, Hon. Edgar.J.,	Dec. 3.	"
1971a	Benson, Hon. Edgar.J.,	June 18.	"
1971b	Benson, Hon. Edgar.J.,	Oct. 14.	"
1972	Turner, Hon. John N.,	May 8.	" **
1973	Turner, Hon. John N.,	Feb. 19.	" **
1974a	Turner, Hon. John N.,	May 6.	" **
1974b	Turner, Hon. John N.,	Nov. 18.	"
1975	Turner, Hon. John N.,	June 23.	"
1976	Macdonald, Hon. Donald S.,	May 25.	"
1977	Macdonald, Hon. Donald S.,	Mar. 31.	"
1978a	Chrétien, Hon. Jean,	April 10.	"
1978b	Chrétien, Hon. Jean,	Nov. 16.	"
1979	Crosbie, Hon. John,	Dec. 11.	Progressive Conservative**
1980	MacEachen, Hon. Allan J.,	Oct. 28.	Liberal
1981	MacEachen, Hon. Allan J.,	Nov. 12.	"
1982	MacEachen, Hon. Allan J.,	June 28.	"
1983	Lalonde, Hon. Marc,	April 19.	"
1984	Lalonde, Hon. Marc,	Feb. 15.	"
1985	Wilson, Hon. Michael,	May 23.	Progressive Conservative
1986	Wilson, Hon. Michael,	Feb. 26.	"
1987a	Wilson, Hon. Michael,	Feb. 18.	"
1987b	Wilson, Hon. Michael,	June 18.***	"
1988	Wilson, Hon. Michael,	Feb. 10.	"
1989	Wilson, Hon. Michael,	April 27.	"
1990	Wilson, Hon. Michael,	February 20.	"

* This is not a formal budget speech, but it marks the introduction of the income tax on persons and corporations.

** Designates a minority government.

*** This White Paper on Tax Reform has the significance of a budget speech, and has been treated as one.

Notes

Chapter 1: Introduction

1. Peacock and Wiseman (1967) and Bird (1970b).
2. Musgrave (1959:v–vi).

Chapter 2: A Positive Model of Revenue Structure

1. For an excellent survey of the development of taxation theory from writers preceding Adam Smith to the present see Musgrave (1985).
2. From an extensive literature see, for example: Hobbes (1651:386), Kaldor (1955), Bradford (1980), and Mieszkowski (1980), calling for a tax on consumption or expenditure; and Smith (1776, Vol. I:350; Vol. II:310, 333 and 337), Haig (1921), Simons (1938 and 1950), Goode (1980), and Graetz (1984), calling for a broad-based tax on income. For three recent volumes of tax reform proposals see: Roskamp and Forte (1981), Thirsk and Whalley (1982) and McLure (1983).
3. Rowell-Sirois (1940) and Royal Commission on Taxation (1967).
4. For a succinct summary of the major writings in this "sociology of fiscal politics" see Musgrave (1980). See also Schumpeter (1918) and Hinrichs (1966).
5. See Musgrave (1969:125–136 and 159–167).
6. Perry (1955). See also Perry (1953), Petrie (1952) and Due (1951, 1953 and 1964).
7. For attempts to explain structural features of particular taxes as an outcome of the political process see Gordon (1972), Lindsay (1972), O'Connor (1973) and Buchanan (1976). For several attempts to develop political models of taxation see Alt (1983), Hansen (1983) and Rose and Karran (1987).
8. Hettich and Winer (1984).
9. See, for example, Chiancone and Messere (1989), which includes twenty-seven papers from a recent conference on *Changes In Revenue Structures*. Two papers only — Wiseman (1989) and Brosio and Pola (1989) — discussed some aspects of an analytical model that could explain observed changes in revenue structures.
10. The public choice literature is the most likely source for a comprehensive theory of tax structure, tax reform and revenue structure change (to complement its theory of public expenditure growth). Yet three classic works are silent on these broader issues and others addressed in this study; see, for example, Buchanan and Tullock (1962), Downs (1957) and Brennan and Buchanan (1980). For several attempts to analyze tax reform within a context that is consistent with the general thrust of this book see Bird (1970a), Bird and Bucovetsky (1972) and Peacock (1981).
11. See, for example, Borcherding and Deacon (1972) and Bergstrom and Goodman (1973).
12. Buchanan (1976:23) succinctly summarizes the key differences between the small-number, unanimous-consent, revealed-preference model and the large-number model with complex political processes, less-than-unanimity voting

rules and incentives for masking preferences. In the latter case the

> ... bridge between taxes paid and benefits received, which seems direct in the small-number illustration, may all but disappear in the calculus of the citizen ... the absence of a unanimity rule implies that, for members of some groups, there need be no connection at all between taxes paid and benefits received.

See Winer (1983) for some evidence on the separation of spending and taxing decisions.

13. Even those few situations where there seems to be, on the surface, a direct link between taxes applied and benefits received, turn out, upon closer analysis, to be capable of generating — via a perceived separation of benefits received and taxes paid — political opposition. The social security funds with earmarked taxes are a case in point. The unemployment insurance fund in Canada was originally financed partly by earmarked taxes (on employers and employees), partly by a government contribution (equivalent to one fifth of the earmarked funds) out of the consolidated revenue fund and, when these sources were inadequate to cover benefit payments, the deficit was covered by funds out of the consolidated revenue fund. Thus, from the very outset the link between total benefits and total financing was *not* legislated. Second, an employee could know with some certainty, his or her taxes, but not the share of shifted employer taxes, nor employee contributions through the consolidated revenue account. The expected benefits would be even more vague. The point is *not* that the employee could not make reasonable estimates of all such taxes; it is rather that there was no direct link between expected benefits and expected tax payments.

14. It may be helpful to think of hypotheses H-2 and H-3 in terms of the marginal political cost function of Figure 2-1, below. A revenue source with few taxpayers, compared with a revenue source with many taxpayers, results in a marginal political cost function that has a higher intercept and lower slope.

15. I use the term advisedly. No less a philosopher than Hobbes argued that due to the sinful nature of consumption, because of its sinful nature, it ought to be taxed (see Hobbes, 1651).

16. A similar point is made in Pommerehne and Schneider (1982). For an opposing view, see Hettich and Winer (1984:68).

17. The argument can be extended to allow a provincial government to take into consideration the actions of American state governments and other similar jurisdictions.

18. This is one case where the policy prescriptions of the normative approach of the optimal theory of taxation are similar to the predictions of a positive theory of taxation. In general the optimal theory of taxation concludes that where factors are immobile and substitution away from taxed actively is very limited, efficiency losses are smallest: the normative prescription calls for high tax rates on immobile factors and low tax rates on mobile factors. Hypothesis H-10 predicts that, in order to minimize the total political costs of financing a given level of spending, governments will tax relatively

immobile revenue sources more extensively than relatively mobile revenue sources. In this case it is the potential economic cost of the reduced revenue source base that directly affects the perceived political cost function.

19. See, for example, McLure (1962), Hogan and Skelton (1973) and Sjoquist (1981).

20. Peacock (1981) notes that "innovations in tax collection" can cause tax reform and more extensive use of revenue sources for which the innovations have taken place. Musgrave (1969) stresses the costs of compliance, collection and enforcement as an element in the "tax handles" approach, noted above.

21. I refer specifically to "unplanned" deficits here, because elsewhere in this model deficits are planned (with consequent financing arrangements) as part of the system of financing total requirements. In the latter circumstances deficit is used without any qualifications.

22. This may be especially true for governments which can only borrow up to legislated debt limits and/or cannot create money.

23. See, for example, Niskanen (1971, Hettich (1975), Bush and Denzau (1977) and Orzechowski (1977). Wagner (1976) and Pommerehne (1978) examine the extent of 'fiscal illusion' created by an appropriate choice of tax structure. It is argued that more complex tax systems (those with more revenue sources for a given budget size) obscure the true effective tax rate, reduce the political costs of raising tax revenues and thus lead to larger public sectors. However, the choice of tax structure is effected by politicians and bureau officials play no special role in these models.

24. For a fascinating discussion of an insider's perceptive analysis of such creativity on the part of officials of the Department of Finance, see Bryce (1986).

25. Gaudet (1987) formally derives these three propositions of the model.

26. There may even be differences of opinion among the politicians on the government's side of the House as to the relative rankings of benefits and costs of proposed tax changes; the model implicitly assumes that any internal differences over the ranking of political costs of various revenue sources are resolved before the government responds.

27. To round out the picture one might add that the source of the initial menu of tax reform dishes could be, in the words of Peacock, "a Royal Commission of *éminences grisés* who are given wide scope in interpreting their terms of reference, and full opportunity to examine the comments and complaints of interest groups. This gives a government ample opportunity for gearing acceptance or rejection of the final recommendation of such bodies to its current view of its objective function" (Peacock, 1981:15–16).

28. Galbraith (1967).

29. See, Hettich and Winer (1984 and 1988) and Winer and Hettich (1988 and 1991).

30. Hettich and Winer (1984:71). Hettich and Winer note the importance of extending their analysis to allow for a more formal treatment of major changes in taxes, including the introduction of new taxes, but judge that their

cross-sectional empirical estimation is more appropriate for small marginal changes.

31. Hettich and Winer (1988) formally integrate administration costs into the theoretical model.

32. Given that a consumer wishes to maximize utility, he or she will choose a mix of goods and services such that relative prices are equated with the marginal rate of substitution among goods. A change in the price of one good, all other factors held constant, will lead the consumer to choose a different mix of goods and services in a predictable fashion.

Chapter 3: Attracting People and Building the Union: Dominion Revenue Policy, 1867–1917

1. The term, federal, gradually replaced Dominion in the years following the second great war. I have adopted the practice of designating the central government as federal in chapters 1 and 11; throughout the rest of the study Dominion is used to describe the government up to the end of the second great war. For a more detailed account of the economic and political problems facing the colonies before Confederation and the terms of the financial settlement at Confederation, see Rowell-Sirois (1940:29–46) and Perry (1955:20–48).

2. See Fielding (1904:15; 1905:8–11; 1906:17; 1909:16–19, and 1911:9–10).

3. See also Rose (1869:7), Cartwright (1877:2; 1878:19) and Tilley (1879:22).

4. I do not explore here the many avenues that Finance Ministers chose for the purpose of augmenting the revenues and diminishing the expenditures of the ordinary account in order to generate an apparent surplus while borrowing extensively to cover the expenditures on the extraordinary or capital account. After 1920 the arbitrary distinction between ordinary and capital expenditure was maintained for a while, but Finance Ministers "gave up the old custom of claiming credit for a surplus on ordinary account . . . they have compared total expenditure with total receipts" (Maxwell, 1934:147). Maxwell argues that, at least until 1920, the bulk of expenditures on extraordinary account were ordinary recurrent expenditures (railway subsidies, military equipment, iron and steel bounties, and maintenance and replacement expenditures for railways and canals and other public works long after the capital expenditure had been made). See also Villard and Willoughby (1918:60–62), Courtney (1914:498–499), and Buck (1949:69).

5. See Rose (1968:16).

6. See, for example, Rose (1868:28–29), Hincks (1870:5), Cartwright (1874:39; and 1878:16), Tilley (1881:36; and 1885:47–50) and Foster (1893:25 and 29). Such international tax comparisons are still being made; see Department of Finance (1978).

7. See Tilley (1873:20–23).

8. See Fielding (1910:1460–1462).

9. Tilley (1881:29). The desire to keep the rate of indirect taxation low in order to attract immigrants can also be found in Tilley (1882:6 and 19), Foster (1892:8 and 13) and White (1913:14).

10. Between 1867 and 1917 there are forty-six references to the "good credit standing" of the Dominion and the continuing search for the lowest interest rate at which the debt could be lodged.
11. Cartwright (1875:13, emphasis added).
12. Cartwright (1878:20).
13. Foster (1895:10).
14. White (1913:11).
15. Tilley (1881:27). The previous Liberal Minister of Finance, Sir Richard Cartwright, had expressed similar concerns in his budgets of 1876 (p. 27) and 1878 (p. 24) in which he argued against a high protective tariff.
16. The conceptual framework of this study treats all determinants that impinge upon political equilibrium as political costs. I see no analytical advantage in categorizing some effects of voters' expected behaviour on governments as economic (such as the emigration of people and their resources, which entails the economic cost of loss of revenue base), and some as political (such as the formation of lobby groups to pressure governments into altering behaviour). Any voter response that impinges upon political equilibrium carries a political cost.
17. White (1916:13).
18. The Minister's other reasons for rejecting the tax included the small expected revenue, the high cost of levying and collecting the tax, and the fact that incomes earned through joint stock companies were already subject to the business profits war tax (White, 1917:8).
19. Tupper (1888:31).
20. The reciprocity theme and direct taxation can also be found in Foster (1893:16).
21. Foster (1891:27).
22. Foster (1893:40).
23. The Minister's other reasons included the small expected revenue, the high costs of levying and collecting the tax and the "length of time which must elapse before it becomes productive" (White, 1915:16, 17).
24. White (1917:8).
25. See, for example, Cartwright (1876:27; 1877:31; and 1878:19 and 24), Tilley (1885:62), Foster (1893:32) and Fielding (1897:32).
26. See, for example, Cartwright (1874:35), Tilley (1882:20), MacLean (1886:44), Foster (1894:26) and White (1913:45).
    An exception to this general observation is found in Sir John Rose's second budget when he converted a specific duty on sugar into an ad valorem rate of duty because of the administrative difficulty of enforcing the diverse duties on different grades of sugar (Rose, 1868:18).
27. McLean (1886:44).
28. The counterpart of this argument is that during periods of rising prices, ad valorem duties are less costly politically than specific duties, because the latter require continuing revisions upward to maintain revenue levels. The switch from specific to ad valorem duties during the late 1970s provides an example of this type of political behaviour.

29. See Lower (1936:212, n. 68).
30. Tilley (1882:5).
31. The focus on luxuries as a source of taxation and the link between luxuries, including tobacco and spirits, and voluntary taxation, can be found in Cartwright (1874:34, and 1877:33), McLean (1886:9) and Fielding (1897:23–24, and 1906:304 and 310).
32. See, for example, Hincks (1870:18), Cartwright (1877:32), Tupper (1888:4), Foster (1891:11, and 1896:6), Fielding (1897:32) and White (1915:14).
33. See Musgrave (1959:60).
34. Higher taxes on luxuries and favourable treatment of farmers were called for in Foster (1894:13 and 21–22), decisions *not* to increase the tax on such broadly consumed necessities as sugar, oil and tea are referred to in Fielding (1902:15, 1904:38; and 1906:288) and the decision to reduce the tax on an article used extensively by the "working classes" is found in Foster (1904:40).
35. See Tilley (1882:41–42; and 1883:11).
36. See Cartwright (1876:27; and 1878:24).
37. See Foster (1893:21).
38. A tax on beer would not meet a horizontal equity criterion today, and it is hard to believe it would have done much better in 1891.
39. The data for government spending and financing on a fiscal year basis (derived in Appendix B) are used in this study for discussions of (i) changes in absolute levels, and (ii) changes in the share of one revenue source in total financial requirements. The data for government spending and financing on a calendar year basis (derived in Appendix C) are used, along with gross national product data (also in Appendix C), for discussion of changes in spending, financing and the various revenue sources relative to the size of the economy. 1870 is the first year for which Canadian data on national income exists.
40. Dominion spending rose, fell and underwent virtually no change in 33, 12 and 4 years respectively, in the fiscal period 1868–1917 (see Appendix Tables B-2 and B-3).
41. I am designating these sources as the Confederation revenue sources, because they are the most important sources of revenue initially used by Dominion governments under terms of the Confederation agreements. The other revenue sources during this period include post office revenues, miscellaneous revenues, miscellaneous indirect taxes (later referred to as excise taxes), and special receipts and other credits (see Appendix Table B-3).
42. On the whole, when customs duties revenues were increasing the relative importance of this revenue source was much more significant (generally: 1868–1875; 1880–1883, 1886–1891 and 1896–1913). When customs duties were falling the relative importance of this revenue source was near the low end of its share in total financial requirements (generally: 1876–1879, 1884–1885 and 1892–1895). See Appendix Tables B-2 and B-3.
43. Neither is the revenue buoyancy effect of the tariff an adequate explanation of the changing levels of government spending. See Table B-2, where years

of decreases in customs duties revenues are almost always years in which total government spending increased.

44. See Rich (1988:206). Domestic borrowing accounted for at least 45 percent of total Dominion borrowing until the mid-1880s; thereafter domestic borrowing declined rapidly to less than 10 percent of the total (until 1913).

45. In 1907 the fiscal year change resulted in a 9-month year for 1907 and a 15-month year for 1908; the uneven timing of revenues and expenditures most likely accounts for the modest surplus in 1907 and part of the substantial deficit in 1908.

46. See, for example, Caves (1976), Helleiner (1977), Dales (1966) and Innis (1972).

47. Perry (1955:52). See also: Bates (1939:35–38, 45), Bonomo and Tanner (1972), Bryce (1939), Chambers (1964), Hay (1966), Rich (1988), Rowell-Sirois (1940:61 and 81) and Taylor (1931).

48. Rich (1988:208). In addition, Rich concludes that the stabilizing role of foreign borrowing (to finance the deficit) was "largely automatic and derived from the fact that *the government did not attempt to balance the budget* when cyclical swings in customs revenues generated surpluses or deficits" (1988:211, emphasis added).

49. Rich (1988:207 and Tables 2-2 and 7-4). Rich notes that the Province of Canada (Ontario and Quebec) had acquired a poor credit rating and consequently had to pay a high interest rate on its bonds in London; "the new Dominion government inherited the Province's poor credit rating" (212; see also 188, 192 and 211 on minimizing the interest burden of the debt).

50. See Dales (1966), Innis (1972), Perry (1955) and Rowell-Sirois (1940).

51. Perry (1955:54–55).

52. Perry (1955:286–289).

Chapter 4: An Overview of Dominion Revenue Policy: 1918–1990

1. Sir Thomas White introduced the income tax on July 25, 1917 (Hansard: 3760–3779). Given the major significance of such a move for the Dominion's tax structure, I decided to treat Sir Thomas's speech as equivalent to a budget speech (White, 1917b).

2. See also Mr. A.K. Maclean (the new tax will "equalize taxation in this country") and Mr. Carroll ("I know of nothing as fair and just upon everybody as an income tax") in White (1917b:3766 and 3770).

3. Ilsley (1939b:6).

4. See Ilsley (1941:10, 12; 1942:3, 8; 1943:2, 5; 1944:10, 13; 1945:1, 7; and 1946:18).

5. See Drayton (1920:29), Robb (1927:14), Rhodes (1932:31; 1933:22; and 1935:26), Dunning (1936:27), Ralston (1940:13), Ilsley (1941:16), Abbott (1949a:11), Harris (1955:12), Fleming (1959:14), Gordon (1966a:9), (1966b: 11336), Benson (1968:8, 11, and 12; and 1971a:4, 5, 10, 12, 14, 22 and 33), Turner (1972:11 and 13; 1973:15, 16, 18, 19; 1974a:17 and 20; and 1974b:23, 24), Chrétien (1978b:11), Crosbie (1979:5), and Wilson (1985:12, 14 and 15; 1986:12 and 17; 1987a:12 and 13; and 1989:10, 11 and 14).

6. See Fielding (1922:46–50).
7. *Ibid*, 50.
8. See Ilsley (1943:17; and 1944:9–10).
9. See also White (1919:20), Rhodes (1933:24), Ralston (1940:10, 19–20), Ilsley (1945:5–7; and 1946:10–12), Abbott (1950b:419, 420; and 1953:11, 12 and 16), Fleming (1958:16; and 1959:14), Gordon (1964:10), Benson (1970b:1743), MacDonald (1976:16; and 1977:4), and Chrétien (1978b:10).
10. Fielding perfected the art of creative circumlocution in his 1923 budget speech, where, after noting that there would be a surplus on consolidated fund account and ordinary expenditures, added that capital expenditures and railway expenditures "will consume all of the surplus that I have mentioned and leave a *balance on the other side of the account*" (Fielding, 1923:6, emphasis added). Presumably, parliamentarians of the day were quick to detect that the Minister of Finance was actually acknowledging that, owing to a deficit on the total budgetary expenditures, the national debt would increase. As it turned out, a more buoyant economy than expected did generate a surplus on total account, allowing the Minister of Finance to reduce the debt.
11. See, for example, Robb (1924:6; 1925:1; 1926:1 and 9; 1927:1; 1928:1; 1929:1 and 18), Dunning (1930:11).
12. See also:Rhodes (1933:24: and 1935:30), and Dunning (1936:24; 1937:27; 1938:16; and 1939:11).
13. See also:Abbott (1949a:9; 1950a:7; 1952:6; and 1953:8, 10).
14. See also: Crosbie (1979:8, 16 and 20).
15. See MacEachen (1980:4 and 14; 1981:1, 2 and 5, and 1982:1).
16. See Lalonde (1983:20 and 21; and 1984:5), and Wilson (1985:5, 15, 19 and 20; 1986:1, 5 and 23; 1987:2, 6 and 13; 1988:2 and 5; and 1989:1, 3, 4, 10 and 15).
17. See also MacLean (1918:11), White (1919:20), Drayton (1920:11), Fielding (1922:10), Robb (1925:2; and 1927:9), Rhodes (1932:4, 12; and 1933:6), Dunning (1936:4; 1937:21; and 1939:8), Abbott (1949b:5, 6; 1950a:7, 11; and 1950b:424), Fleming (1959:10; and 1962:9), Benson (1970:1743), MacDonald (1977:7, 11), Crosbie (1979:3), and Wilson (1985:16; and 1989:2).
18. See Fielding (1923:5).
19. Sir Henry Drayton, in his 1920 budget speech, acknowledged provincial occupancy of the motor taxation field and responded by increasing the excise tax on all cars; in addition, he acknowledged the burden — especially on small theatres — of triple taxation of theatres and repealed the Dominion duty he had introduced one year previously (Drayton, 1920:22 and 23).
20. See Dunning (1937:4).
21. See Isley (1941:11; and 1943:22). The concern over high combined tax rates, first emphasized in Ralston (1940:14) continued into the post-war period: Abbott (1950b:423; and 1953:18), Gordon (1964:7), Benson (1971a:38), and Turner (1972:5 and 1974a:9 and 10).
22. Abbott (1948:15); see also Abbott (1947:18; 1948:15; and 1953:19), and Turner (1973:20).

23. Gordon (1965:17).
24. Abbott (1947:6).
25. Harris (1956:13, 14).
26. Benson (1971a:3). See also, Harris (1956:6, 7; and 1957:7, 8), Fleming (1959:9-10), and Wilson (1987b:2 and 9; 1988:4; and 1989:13).
27. See Fleming (1961:19-20; and 1962a:13, 36). For a more extensive discussion of the changes in fiscal revenue-sharing arrangements during the entire post-war period, see Perry (1955:547-566), Moore, Perry and Beach (1966:25-95), Lynn (1967:65-83), Strick (1978:107-121) and Auld and Miller (1982:352-372).
28. See Gordon (1964:7; 1965:18; and 1966a:9), Turner (1974b:12, 13; and 1975:33), MacDonald (1976:20) and MacEachen (1980:8 and 9).
29. See White (1917b:3765, 3767 and 3772).
30. *Ibid*, 3761, 3768 and 3769.
31. See White (1919:2526) and Drayton (1920:23).
32. See Robb (1928:18).
33. See Bennett (1931:59, 60).
34. See Abbott (1947:12).
35. Abbott (1947:16); he repeated the same procedure the following year (Abbott 1948:11-13); see also Ilsley (1944:6).
36. See Gordon (1963:13).
37. See Gordon (1964:12).
38. *Ibid*, 12.
39. See Gordon (1965:19-20).
40. See Benson (1971a:10).
41. See also Benson (1971a:11, 15,18,19 and 21).
42. See also Turner (1972:6, 7, and 8; 1973:2 and 3; 1974a:13; 1974b:20; and 1975:21), MacDonald (1977:12; and Chrétien (1978b:7).
43. See also Benson (1968:11 and 13; and 1971b:5), Turner (1972:18 and 19; 1974a:24 and 25), MacDonald (1976:28), Chrétien (1978a:9), Crosbie (1979: 11 and 17), MacEachen (1980:15; 1981:4; and 1982:7), and Lalonde (1983:16).
44. See Wilson (1987b:2, 7, 8 and 11; and 1988:2, 3 and 10).
45. Abbott's joust with smugglers was a strange affair. The Minister had already rejected an increase in cigarette taxes in his 1950 budget, precisely because of the threat of smuggling from the United States (Abbott 1950:423). After his retreat in 1952, noted in the text, cigarette sales increased, "a very encouraging (sign) from the point of view of the revenue collector", but continued smuggling led him to reduce the excise duty and customs duty still further in the following year (Abbott, 1953:20).
46. There were some concerns also expressed over administrative cost aspects of the sales tax (and its early competitor, the turnover tax); see, for example Drayton (1921:15), Fielding (1923:7-8) and Dunning (1936:27). By 1941 the sales tax's virtues, ease of administration and collection, were being extolled by Ilsley (1941:19).
47. See Ralston (1940:15).
48. See Ralston (1940:15) and Ilsley (1941:14).

49. See Ilsley (1942:9, 14–15).
50. See Robb (1926:14; 1927:14), Rhodes (1932:29), Abbott (1948:16), Harris (1957a:13), Turner (1974a:14) and Chrétien (1978b:12). See also:Abbott (1954:12), Harris (1957a:13) Fleming (1961:20), Benson (1969:6 and 7; and 1971a:3 and 20), Turner (1972:16 and 17; and 1973:13), MacDonald (1976:31), and Lalonde (1984:10, 11 and 12).
51. See Dunning (1938:32).
52. See Ilsley (1941:17–18).
53. Unforeseen administrative problems may have played a role in facilitating this change. Finance Minister MacEachen's initial proposal was to have the specific taxes on alcoholic beverages and tobacco adjusted quarterly, on the basis of indexes of the selling prices of the two products. Difficulties in utilizing such indexes and discussions with industry personnel eventually led to the CPI being used as the relevant price index. The de-indexation and discretionary tax increases in 1985 led to a *net increase* in tax revenues from the two excises of $135 millions and $245 millions for 1985 and 1986 respectively (Department of Finance, 1985:77 and 92–93).
54. See Robb (1926:13; 1927:13; 1928:13; and 1929:19) and Dunning (1930:19), for much the same enthusiasm.
55. See Rhodes (1932:1, 6 and 25; and 1933:6).
56. See Rhodes (1935:10 and 26), Dunning (1936:1; 1937:13, and 1938:17) and Ilsley (1941:3, 7).
57. See Abbott (1948:4, 6; 1949a:7; 1950a:6, 8; and 1951:7), Harris (1956:5; and 1957a:7), Fleming (1960a:16, 17), Gordon (1965:9), Benson (1969:1; and 1971a:9), and Wilson (1985:16).
58. See Mackintosh (1966) and Gordon (1966).
59. See Abbott (1947:11, 12; and 1949a:9, 10), Harris (1957a:11) and Gordon (1965:16; Gordon, in the face of an expanding economy and falling unemployment, defined the appropriate fiscal policy as an expansionary one).
60. Abbott (1949a), Harris (1957a) and Gordon (1965). See Appendix D for dates of all Dominion elections.
61. Abbott (1950b:419, 420, 423; and 1951:5, 11) and Fleming (1961:7, 28–29; and 1962a:6, 17–18).
62. For the most part then, hypothesis H-8c is rejected by a reference to observed tax structure policy.
63. See White (1918:16) for a similar argument.
64. See Fielding (1923:9).
65. See, for example, Ilsley (1941:20–21; 1942:18–20; 1943:20–22), Abbott (1950b: 423; and 1951:16) and Fleming (1959:21).
66. For the most part then, in contrast to the first fifty years of revenue structure policy, hypothesis H-8a is rejected by a reference to the qualitative data.
67. The reader is reminded of the broad classification scheme for ranking political costs, discussed as part of the research strategy in Chapter 1.

Chapter 5: Expansion of the Revenue Family: The Fecund Years, 1915–1923

1. A fourth new revenue source, excise taxes, was not trivial as a contribution to total tax revenues, but its future role in the revenue structure was not as important as the personal income tax, the corporation income tax and the general sales tax. See Charts 4-3 and 4-6 in the previous chapter. For details of the statutory and effective rate changes throughout the fecund years and beyond (1914 through 1939) see Perry (1955) and Appendix F (*not included in this book but available from the author upon request*).
2. See Charts 1-1 and 1-2, Chapter 1 and Appendix Table C-3.
3. Dominion expenditures increased to $238 millions in fiscal 1915, $331 millions in 1916, $478 millions in 1917, $558 millions in 1918, $694 millions in 1919 and $921 millions in 1920. See Table B-2.
4. For that matter, even the Progressives agreed with the general thrust of tax policy; they did have different answers for the question, "where can those taxes be best raised, without hurting too much?" (R. Forke, Leader of the Progressives, *House of Commons Debates*, 1923:921).
5. See White (1915:14 and 17).
6. *Ibid*, 14.
7. See the discussion in Chapter 2.
8. See White (1916:14).
9. See Sir Thomas's fascinating account in *The Story of Canada's War Finance*, where he reveals that the Income War Tax Act had been drafted and ready to introduce for almost a year prior to July 25, 1917 (White, 1921:52–53).
10. See White (1917b:3762 and 3769), where he argues that vertical equity considerations of fairness require some sacrifice from those whose incomes have grown substantially because of the war.
11. See Sharp (1971:68 and 112) and *The Grain Growers' Guide*, various issues.
12. Krever (1981:183); see also, Rowell-Sirois (1940:99–100) and Perry (1955:155).
13. Robin (1966:65–69).
14. Krever (1981:186); Sharp (1971:116, 124). *The Grain Growers' Guide* (June 20, 1917) argued that such a tax would reduce the opposition to conscription, and the Canadian Council of Agriculture modified its proposal to tax incomes directly by deleting the exemption level of $4000 (this would effectively bring all farmers into the tax base).
15. See M. Clark, *House of Commons Debates*, August 20, 1914:41; and *House of Commons Debates*, March 10, 1915:872.
16. For similar Liberal opposition pressure, see, *House of Commons Debates*, February 16, 1916:902, February 22, 1916:1025 and February 24, 1916:1086; and *House of Commons Debates*, April 24, 1917:738, May 15, 1917:1424–1425 and May 23, 1917:1688.
17. See also the comments of Hon. A.K. MacLean, Mr. Graham, Mr. Lemieux, and Mr. Macdonald in White, 1917b:3760–3793, 5475–5481, and 5883–5887.
18. This point kept resurfacing in the Minister's comments and the debate in the House (see White 1917b:3761, 3765 and 3772).

19. The earlier birth occurred during the Civil War in 1861, and the income tax expired in 1871.
20. See Baack and Rae (1985:611).
21. The 1913 income tax had a large exemption, with graduated rates of 1, 4, 5, 6 and 7 percent on incomes of $50,000–$75,000, $75,000–$100,000, $100,000–$250,000, $250,000–$500,000 and $500,000 and over, respectively. (*Congressional Record*, Washington, D.C., 1913: 1st session.)
22. See Witte (1985:87).
23. There was strong opposition in the United States to a graduated income tax. In the Congressional debate leading up to the 1894 income tax amendment, four hundred wealthy businessmen declared they were prepared to leave the country if the income tax was passed (McQuaig, 1987:24). It is not known whether they threatened to migrate to Canada.
24. By the end of fiscal 1921 income taxes on individuals and corporations accounted for 11.8 percent of total financial requirements. Since there was a surplus of 4.5 percent of total financial requirements that year, the income tax share can be interpreted as a share of total tax revenues (see Table B-3).
25. Horizontal tax competition is still guiding Canadian Finance Ministers; see Chapters 9 and 10.
26. The Minister argued that his earlier revenue estimates of $3–$4 million, based on the existing U.S. income tax rates, were superseded by current revenue estimates of $15–$20 million, based on the proposed new U.S. income tax rates. (White, 1917b:3768–3769 and 3760–3761).
27. See Sir Herbert Ames' comments during the debate on the 1918 budget speech (*House of Commons Debates*, 1918:1291), where he argued that not more than one hundred thousand taxpayers would be subject to the 1917 legislation. One year later, during the debate on the 1919 budget speech (*House of Commons Debates*, 1919:3545), Mr. F.F. Pardee, a long-time champion of the income tax, expressed fears that there "has not been a wholly sympathetic administration of the Income Tax Act". During the year that had just ended there were just 31,000 taxpayers and revenues of $6.5 millions.
28. See MacLean (1918:16 and 22) and note 1 above.
29. An interesting trade-off was negotiated with the railways in order to lower the cost of agricultural implements shipped to western farmers, a group who were flexing their political muscles. In exchange for the abolition of the 7.5 percent war customs duty on bituminous coal, the railways agreed to lower their shipping rates on agricultural implements being shipped from eastern Canada to western markets. The rates were equalized with the Chicago rates to similar Canadian destinations (White, 1919:21–23).
0. See also *House of Commons Debates*, 1918:1266, 1270 and 1294.
31. See also *House of Commons Debates*, 1919:3247–48, 3264–65, 3272, and 3280).
32. The Minister commented that
The income tax rate was substantially increased last year *so as to bring it up to the increased United States rates*. The increase was material . . .

The corporation tax was in like manner increased from 6 to 10 percent.
(Drayton, 1920:23, emphasis added)

33. The government expected that customs revenues would fall by $25 million of which $17 million would be due to the announced tariff rate reductions, and the remainder to declining import prices (White, 1919:25). It anticipated that the income tax rate increases would generate an extra $15 million (White, 1919:25; and Drayton, 1920:924).

34. See Drayton (1920:26–27).

35. *Ibid*, 25–26.

36. See Drayton (1921:14).

37. See Drayton (1920:24).

38. *Ibid*, 20–22.

39. *House of Commons Debates*, 1923:919, emphasis added; see also Drayton, 1920:22; *House of Commons Debates*, 1920:3609; Drayton, 1921:11; Fielding, 1922:25 and *House of Commons Debates*, 1923:924.

40. See Drayton (1920:3–4).

41. The estimate of foregone customs duty revenue is for fiscal 1919 (Drayton, 1920:27) whereas the sales tax revenue is for fiscal 1921 (Appendix Table B-2).

42. Perry (1955:222–223) argues that the "new-found power of the agrarian free trade group, now organized in the Progressive party, was largely responsible for the removal of the wartime increases in the tariff, and forced substantial reductions on farm implements at a time when all other taxes were being raised".

43. See, for example, *House of Commons Debates* (1921:3170 and 3396 where the sales tax is referred to as "high protection in disguise"); and Fielding, 1922:31. See note 1 of Appendix F for the rate changes.

44. Sir Henry emphasized the same point in the budget debate (see *House of Commons Debates*, 1921:3253).

45. See the discussion in Chapter 10.

46. For the derivation of the displacement hypothesis, see Peacock and Wiseman (1967).

47. See Bird (1970b:107–117), for an extensive critique of the model and empirical evidence for the displacement hypothesis.

48. Bird (1970a:454).

49. Gillis (1985:98).

50. I return to the demand for debt reduction in Chapter 7 below.

51. Boadway and Kitchen (1984:37). See also, Buck (1949:152), Bernier (1967:3–4), LaForest (1967:21), Rowell-Sirois (1940:98–100), Petrie (1952:32), Auld and Miller (1984:94 and 142), Krever (1981:187, 189) and Morton and Granatstein (1989:85).

52. See, for example, Toulin (1989), Coyle (1989), Simpson (1989 and 1991), Nichols (1990) and Corcoran (1991).

53. Perry (1955:144–149, 155 and 157).

54. Krever (1981:171; see also 173, 174–175, 179, 183 and 187).

55. See Krever (1981:188). These partisan bills included the Military Voters

Act, which facilitated the "voting of soldiers who, it was expected, would solidly support the Conservatives", and the Wartime Elections Act, which "extended the franchise to female relatives of soldiers and disenfranchised 'alien' voters who had come from ... countries where the mother tongue had been German" (and whose sympathies were often pro-Liberal). Ten days before the election the coalition Union team announced that all farmers would be exempted from compulsory enlistment.

56. MacLean, Guthrie and Carvell all made it into the cabinet, and MacLean became acting Minister of Finance in 1918.

57. See Sir James Lougheed, *Debates of the Senate of Canada*, August 29, 1917:721.

58. See, for example, Perry (1955:196–202), Due (1951:5–7; and 1957:147), Rowell-Sirois (1940:104), Auld and Miller (1984:189), Gillis (1985:68 and 98), and Bird (1970a:454, n. 33).

Chapter 6: Financing War

1. For the purpose of focusing the discussion in this chapter I define the two great war periods as fiscal 1914 through 1920 and fiscal 1940 through 1946. Total financial requirements increased by 411 percent and 835 percent during the two great wars, respectively (see Table B-3).

2. See Chart 1-2, Chapter 1 and Appendix Table C-3.

3. See Charts 4-4 through 4-6, Chapter 4 for the variation in the major revenue sources during the two war periods.

4. National Defence spending and war-related government spending are the classic examples of public or social goods that require collective provision and financing. In times of emergencies or wars the citizen demand for such public goods can be expected to increase substantially. See Musgrave (1959: Chapters 1 and 3) and Peacock and Wiseman (1967).

5. Ilsley (1943:1), as quoted at the beginning of this chapter.

6. Ilsley (1944:4), as quoted below.

7. The distinction between voluntary and compulsory is not as clear-cut as might be imagined. To the extent that a citizen is persuaded or coerced into believing that it is his or her duty to lend funds to the state, then this behaviour is not totally voluntary. Likewise, compulsory taxation, applied to all taxpayers, is a necessary condition (to minimize the free rider problem) for a collectivity of individuals to arrive voluntarily at decisions in their own best interests, with respect to the provision and financing of public goods. Nevertheless, the individual voter most likely perceives the two acts as "different".

8. See also White (1916:10 and 20; and 1917:10–11).

9. (White, 1916:7).

10. These war bond issues were oversubscribed as well: MacLean (1918:10–12) and Brown (1941:17).

11. See, for example, Deutsch (1940:528, 530 and 532), McIvor (1948:87) and Perry (1955:149).

12. See Ilsley (1939b:5; 1941:2; 1942:8, 9, 11, 22–23; 1943:6, 24; 1944:3, 10,

18–19; and 1945:13–14) and Ralston (1940:3).

13. This phrase is only partially descriptive of the available loanable funds during the first great war. In large part inflation of money and credit generated a redistribution of income away from fixed income earners and some wage earners towards business profits and individuals with higher incomes. It was the large incomes that were the source of most of the funds loaned to the government. For a more detailed analysis of this factor in the successful war financing, see Rowell-Sirois (1940:99–100, and 103) Deutsch (1940:531, 532 and 536–37) and McIvor (1948:87).

14. The analysis here is a positive theory of government financing throughout the war and post-war period. The normative case for loan financing of temporary wartime government spending in order to reduce extreme fluctuations in effective tax rates (which would result in increasing "tax friction" and inefficiencies) is developed in Musgrave (1959:567–568), where he concludes that "reliance on borrowing is a proper instrument of war finance".

15. See especially White (1916:13 and 1917:7).

16. Rowell-Sirois (1940:103).

17. See, for example, Deutsch (1940:527), Brown (1941:22), Gibson (1941:52), McIvor (1948:63, 86) and Perry (1955:149). Even O.D. Skelton, who was one of the government's sharpest critics on the subject of borrowing to finance the war, acknowledged that 100 percent tax financing of the war would be

> hardly practicable. It would mean too drastic a revolution in industry. It would discourage production. It would lead to concealment and evasion. *Borrowing is an indispensable policy in great wars.*
>
>   (Skelton, 1918:18, emphasis added)

18. See, for example, Ralston (1940:20–21), and Ilsley (1941:9; 1943:17; 1944:6, 9, 10–11; and 1945:6–7 and 10).

19. See Charts 4-4 and 4-6 and Table B-3. These observations are based on the level and trend of tax shares throughout the period.

20. The personal income tax of the second great war pales in significance when compared with deficit financing and it fell far short of the relative importance of the biggest tax raiser of the first great war: customs duties.

21. Other commentators have stressed the "abnormality" of profits in war time as *justifying* an excess profits tax. See, for example, Deutsch (1940:529), Skelton (1918:32) and Perry (1955:155). My point here is that the "abnormality" of such profits lowered the political cost of taxing them and accounted for the governments' extensive utilization of the excess profits revenue source during wartime.

22. White (1921:18).

23. Ralston (1940:10–11, and 19).

24. See Appendix Table B-3 for the modest changes in the share of these taxes as a percentage of total financial requirements during the second great war.

25. Perry (1955:360) estimates that before the war the personal income tax applied to no more than 250,000 persons.

26. The personal exemptions for singles and married persons were lowered from

$1000 to $750 and $2000 to $1500 respectively; and the tax rate structure was raised to 6 percent on the first $250 of taxable income, with the rate increasing in graduated steps, to 78 percent on taxable incomes over $500,000. The national defence tax was a flat rate tax: for singles it was 2 percent on incomes over $600 and less than $1200, and 3 percent on incomes over $1200; for married persons it was set at 2 percent on incomes over $1200 (Ralston, 1940:14–15).

27. In the 1941 budget the exemption level under the national defence tax was raised from $600 to $660 and the tax rates were raised from 2 and 3 percent to 5 and 7 percent; the rate structure under the personal income tax was adjusted upward, raising the lowest rate to 15 percent on the first $1000 of taxable income, with a maximum rate of 85 percent on incomes over $500,000 (Ilsley, 1941:13–14).

28. In the 1942 budget the two taxes were combined into one personal income tax, collected at source (or on a voluntary instalment plan) on a current basis. The flat rate tax, corresponding to the national defence tax with given exemptions, was 7 percent for married and single persons with incomes of $660–$1800, 8 percent for singles with incomes of $1800–$2999 and 9 percent for those with higher incomes; the exemptions under the graduated rate structure fell to $660, with a credit of $150 for married persons; rates were raised substantially — 30 percent on the first $500 of taxable income, with a maximum of 85 percent on incomes over $100,000, and an investment surtax of 4 percent was added.

29. The marginal tax rates are estimated by Perry (1955:368). In 1938 the highest marginal tax rate was 69.3 percent on taxable incomes in excess of $500,000; by 1943 all those with incomes in excess of $100,000 incurred the highest marginal tax rate of 98 percent.

30. Perry (1955:360).

31. Lord Keynes' initial proposal for compulsory savings to defer wage payment until after the war appeared in two articles in *The Times* on the 14 and 15 November, 1939. The expanded and more detailed proposal appeared as a pamphlet on 27 February, 1940, *How to Pay for the War: A Radical Plan for the Chancellor of the Exchequer*. See Moggridge (1978:40–155).

32. Ilsley (1942:10–11).

33. The six-month tax liability for 1942, amounting to $59 million (including interest at 2 percent), was refunded in March 1948; and the tax liability for 1943 and six months of 1944, totalling $237 million (including interest at 2 percent) was refunded a year later (Perry, 1955:364).

34. See, for example, Ilsley (1939:6; 1941:1, 10 and 13; and 1942:9 and 18).

35. See Ilsley (1942:18; and 1943:7).

36. See Plumptre (1941a:113–114) and Perry (1955:369).

37. It is also likely that the government was aware of the reduction in the effectiveness of inflation financing since the first great war, owing to the changed wage-setting rules that reduced the time-lag between price increases and wage increases. Keynes developed this argument in *How to Pay for the War*. See Moggridge (1978:43–44).

38. See Ilsley (1939b:5).

39. Ilsley (1945:9–10).

40. Ilsley (1945:2). I have not attempted to measure separately an inflation tax and the possible role that it may have played in the evolution of the tax system. It is a task that, given the magnitude of the current investigation, is best left to another time.

41. White (1916:10 and 14; and 1917:8).

42. See the discussion in Ralston (1940:12–13). For a discussion of the more significant aspects of the excess profits tax and difficulties of implementing it, see Perry (1955: Ch. 22).

43. Ilsley (1945:8).

44. Ilsley (1941:16); see Charts 4-3 and 4-6 in Chapter 4 for the contribution of both estate taxes and UIC taxes to total financial requirements. The treatment of UIC taxes in this study is discussed in Appendix B.

45. In the debate leading up to the introduction of the income tax in the summer of 1917 it was the Liberal opposition and not the government that most eloquently argued for a graduated tax on incomes in order to ensure that those most able to pay taxes to finance the war would actually be called upon to make such a sacrifice. Sir Thomas White first took up the "fairness" theme on the day he introduced the income tax, and if the ensuing Union government sounded very Liberal on the issue of progressive income taxation the reason was probably that three former Liberal champions of a graduated income tax were in the cabinet.

46. White (1915:14).

47. See Perry (1955:369–373). The excise tax rate on automobiles increased and ranged from 25 percent on cars valued at less than $9600 to 80 percent on cars valued over $1200.

48. See, for example, Skelton (1915 and 1918), Gibson (1941), Deutsch (1940), McIvor (1948 and 1958:105–108; 194–197), Brown (1941) Stikeman (1943), Parkinson (1940), Musgrave (1943), Perry (1953:18 and 30), and MacDonald (1985:64).

49. Perry (1955:142–149; 163–164 and 328–334).

50. MacDonald (1985:64).

51. McIvor (1948), Perry (1955).

52. McIvor (1948:86–87; and 1958:104, 114 and 197), Skelton (1915:86; and 1917:828–831), Musgrave (1943:309 and 314), and Perry (1955:*loc. cit.*).

53. McIvor (1948:65, 75 and 89), Gibson (1941:43), Plumptre (1940:123, 131), Parkinson (1940:420), and Perry (1955:*loc. cit.*).

54. See, for example, White (1921:32–33), Deutsch (1940:529, Skelton (1918:32; and 1917:823, 826 and 828), Perry (1955:155, 341–342) and MacDonald (1985:48).

55. Morton and Granatstein (1989:85–87).

56. See, for example, Deutsch (1940:527, 536), Stikeman (1943:358–359), McIvor (1948:63, 76–77, 81, 83 and 86–89; 1958:114 and 195–196), Brown (1941:22), Parkinson (1940:403 and 414–415) and Perry (1955:149, 155, 331–334, 363–364 and 367).

57. Parkinson (1940:403).
58. Stikeman (1943:358–359).
59. McIvor is emphatic on the role of educating the public: "If fiscal measures hitherto considered drastic are to be successfully introduced, *the public must first be taught to recognize their necessity*" (McIvor, 1948:63 and 87; and 1958:165, emphasis added). This is excellent advice to any Minister of Finance contemplating any major change in revenue structure at any time, and wishing to retain his or her job!

Chapter 7: Financing Post-War Debt Reduction

1. Fiscal 1903 and 1904 each had surpluses; the remaining seven surpluses occurred in fiscal 1871, 1882, 1900, 1907, 1913, 1957 and 1970 (see Table B-2).
2. During the five years, fiscal 1921 through 1925, Dominion spending fell by 54.5 percent, with most of it occurring during the first two years. The five years of reductions in spending after the second great war actually began in fiscal 1945, with most of the 61.3 per cent reduction occurring during fiscal 1947–1948. See Appendix Tables B-2 and B-3.
3. Dominion total tax revenues increased by 24 percent over fiscal 1920–1921, and then declined, with some fluctuation — 17 percent by fiscal 1925. Dominion total tax revenues increased by a trivial 2 percent over fiscal 1946–1947, and then declined 16 percent up to fiscal 1950. See Appendix Tables B-2 and B-3.
4. For growth rates in real national income, see Appendix Table C-1.
5. This observation combines the corporation income tax plus the excess profits tax as one overall tax on corporate profits. When the two taxes are observed separately, as in Chart 7-3, the share of the excess profits tax drops from 17 to 2 per cent of total financial requirements during 1947–1949, as the tax is phased out; whereas the corporation income tax share rises dramatically to a high of 31 per cent in 1951–1952, after which it declines slightly.
6. For the derivation of the theory of optimal provision and financing of a collective consumption good, see Musgrave (1958: Chapters 1 and 4), Samuelson (1954) and such recent references as Musgrave, Musgrave and Bird (1987: Chapters 3 and 4) and Boadway and Wildasin (1984: Chapter 4).
7. See Appendix C for several measures of the "magnitude" of the national debt: the current dollar value of the debt, the current dollar annual increase in the value of the debt, and the value of the debt relative to gross national product, annually, from 1870 through 1989.
8. It also provides no support for the displacement hypothesis, in any of its three variants. See Peacock and Wiseman (1967) and Bird (1970b:107–117).
9. Drayton (1920:3–4).
10. Fielding (1922:7).
11. See, for example, Robb (1924:6; 1925:1; 1926:1 and 9; 1927:1; 1928:1; 1929:1 and 18) and Dunning (1930:11).
12. Ilsley (1945:5), Abbott (1947:11; and 1948:10).

13. See also Abbott (1949a:9; 1950a:7; 1952:6, and 1953:8, 10).

14. See also Appendix Tables C-1 and C-3.

15. See note 1, Chapter 5. In addition, most of the special luxury excises of early 1920 were repealed by the end of the year, with a few left to die in the 1921 budget. The excess profits tax also withered away.

16. Bryce (1986:24–26) emphasizes the extent to which fiscal policy at the time reflected the

> need of [Prime Minister] Mackenzie King and his ministers of finance to woo the West and farmers in other parts of the country with concessions on the tariff.. . . [The selective tariff reductions] of 1922, 1923 and 1924 occurred when the minority Liberal government was seeking the support of the Progressives.

17. See Perry (1955:193) and Rowell-Sirois (1940:113–114). Fiscal 1922 covers the period April 1, 1921 through March 31, 1922; thus it includes much of 1921, when the recession was still in full swing (national income declined by 9.6 percent; see Appendix Table C-1).

18. Deficit financing accounted for 49 and 41 per cent of total revenue requirements in fiscal 1945 and 1946 respectively.

19. Ilsley (1946:7, 8).

20. Abbott (1948:6, 10).

21. There were several other tax rate increases. Excise duties on liquor were increased from $2.40 to $4.40 per imperial proof gallon in 1920 and to $9.00 in 1921. The increase in excise duties on cigarettes in 1922 was rescinded in the 1923 budget.

22. See, *House of Commons Debates*, 1921:2515–2650, 3016–3017, and 3608–3617.

23. See also, *House of Commons Debates, 1921*:3221, 3314–3315, 3396 and 3576.

24. See Mr. Reid's comments, *House of Commons Debates, 1921*:3396.

25. Fielding (1922:31).

26. *House of Commons Debates*, May 29, 1922:2242 and June 8, 1922:2661 respectively. See also Mr. Gardiner's comments, June 7, 1922:2627.

27. See, for example, *House of Commons Debates, 1922*:2293, 2601, 2626, 2662, 2666 and especially 2676 and 2883.

28. *House of Commons Debates*, March 7, 1923:915–928.

29. *Ibid*, 919, quoted at the beginning of Chapter 5; see also, for the government:924; for the Conservatives:920, and for the Progressives:921.

30. Sir Henry Drayton, *ibid*:919.

31. Lest it be thought that the proponents of "fiscal illusion" went unchallenged, it could be noted that Liberal supporters of the introduction of the income taxes argued their superiority on grounds of the *absence* of fiscal illusion (A.K. MacLean, in White 1917b:3767 and 3771).

32. It is hard to believe that this proposal stemmed solely from Mr. Steven's eloquent plea made two months earlier. Would that all backbenchers could have such an impact on the cabinet! A more likely stimulus for change was the strength of the Progressive Party in a minority government situation.

33. Mr. T.W. Bird, in his comments criticizing the regressivity of the tax, raised the possibility that the luxury taxes of Sir Henry Drayton's 1920 budget were introduced to make it "easier for the people to swallow the sales tax"; when these luxury taxes were repealed within seven months the Liberal opposition (now the government) "were silent; . . . they consented to its death". He continued,

Taxes are born and taxes die, both parties consenting thereto. We have this silent, invisible pact whereby the masses of the people always get the heavy end of the burden, and the well-to-do people get things easy.
(Bird, *House of Commons Debates*, May 15, 1923:2789)

34. Total expenditures increased by 15.2 percent, 12 percent, 40.3 percent, and 22.4 percent in fiscal 1950, 1951, 1952 and 1953 respectively.

35. Abbott (1950b).

36. Abbott (1951).

37. Abbott (1952). See Appendix B for a discussion of the OAS fund and its treatment in the consistent data base of this study. In 1976 the government abandoned the separate OAS taxes and folded them directly into the Consolidated Revenue Fund.

38. The building materials exemption was introduced in 1938 (Dunning, 1938:33), removed in 1941 (Ilsley, 1941:21) and re-introduced in 1945 (Ilsley, 1945:7). The exemption for machinery used in manufacturing processes was introduced in 1945 (Ilsley, 1945:7) and the heating fuel oil exemption in 1949 (Abbott, 1949b:8).

39. See the discussion in Chapter 6.

40. Drayton (1921:1–6) and Fielding (1922:6 and 11).

41. Fielding (1923:5 and 7).

42. Robb (1926:13; 1927:13; and 1929:19) and Dunning (1930:19).

43. See, for example, Perry (1955:194–195 and 220), Rowell-Sirois (1940:112–117), Safarian (1970:32–57) and Appendix Table C-1.

44. See note 1, Chapter 5.

45. See Perry (1955:223–226), and Bryce (1986:24–25).

46. See Bryce (1986:68–70) for a fascinating discussion of the political importance attached to Dunning's May 1930 budget, especially the proposed selective tariff rate reductions, designed to appeal to farmers. The Prime Minister confided to his diary that "This budget will be far reaching in its consequences. It will, I believe, win us the election." Unfortunately for Dunning and King, the Liberals lost.

47. Robb (1927:14; and 1929:18).

48. See Perry (1955) and Bryce (1986:25).

49. See Bryce (1986:26) and Neatby (1963:124).

50. See Table B-3.

51. Robb (1924:14).

52. See Bryce (1986:24 and 242, n. 5).

53. Robb (1927:13; 1928:13; and 1929:18). The sales tax rate reduction from two to one percent in the May 1930 budget would not have affected the revenues of fiscal 1930 (given the definition of the fiscal period) but would

have influenced the revenues of fiscal 1931.

54. The Minister of Finance, the Honourable William Fielding, was disappointed to find that after he had increased the duty on cigarettes from $6.00 to $7.50 per 1000 cigarettes in 1922, revenues from the duty fell, and he subsequently reduced the levy to $6.00 in 1923 (not without some stern warnings to smugglers!).

55. See Chart 4-5 in Chapter 4.

56. Real GNP grew, in successive years, from 1947 through 1953 at the following rates:4.3, 2.5, 3.8, 7.6, 5.0, 8.9, and 5.1 percent (see Appendix Table C-1).

57. See Ilsley (1946:4), Abbott (1947:1, 7, 10; 1948:4, 6; 1949a:7; 1949b:1; 1950a:6, 8; 1951:7; 1952:6 and 1953:5).

58. Abbot (1952:5–7); see also Abbott (1951:11).

59. Gordon (1966:43–44).

60. Perry (1955:297) refers to Finance Minister Drayton's intention to reduce the debt by introducing the sales tax in 1920, but does not make any further reference to planned or achieved debt reduction during the 1920s. Rowell-Sirois (1940:127) notes the prosperity and growth of the 1920s and the declining per capita Dominion debt (within the context of a rising per capita total government debt), without discussing the importance of the debt reduction. McIvor (1958:120) notes the boom period of the 1920s, but does not discuss the effect of this on Dominion revenues or the ability of the government to reduce the debt.

61. Perry (1955:387–88, and 443–448) and McIvor (1958:211).

62. See also the discussion in Chapter 4.

63. See, for example, Perry (1955:381–394; and 1989:151–156), Samuelson and Scott (1971:440), Strick (1978:147–153) and Stager (1988:227).

64. See Strick (1978:104, 140), and Lipsey, Purvis and Steiner (1985:577).

65. See, for example, Gordon (1966), Will (1967), Royal Commission on Taxation (1967), Auld (1969), Curtis and Kitchen (1975), Gillespie (1973 and 1978), and Auld and Miller (1982:297–320).

66. See Gillespie (1979) for a critical analysis of this literature, and a comparison of the findings in terms of adequate, inadequate and perverse policy actions. Federal fiscal policy scored adequate (correct direction and magnitude) only 11 to 37 percent of the time, inadequate (correct direction, insufficient magnitude) 21 to 56 percent of the time, and perverse (destabilizing:wrong direction), 30 to 42 percent of the time.

67. See, for example, Perry (1955:393), McIvor (1958:240), Will (1966:14, 20, 35 and 91), and Gordon (1966:30, 35, 42–43). Such beliefs help us to explain the budgetary policies of Finance Ministers during the early period following the second great war (when passive surpluses emerged and the public cried "overtaxation") and the late 1950s through early 1960s (when passive deficits occurred and the business community charged the government with "fiscal irresponsibility").

68. I anticipated such an outcome in Gillespie (1979). See also Campbell (1987). For an insider's view of Ministers' fiscal stabilization commitments during the 1950s, see former Assistant Deputy Minister Kenneth Eaton's sugges-

tion that

> Nowadays if [the Minister of Finance] should be fortunate enough to have an overflowing treasury he is liable to deliver a discourse on inflation and talk of surplus purchasing power in the hands of the public as a reason for not cutting taxes at a time when people are scrambling to make ends meet. Surplus purchasing power indeed! Or upon finding his budget badly out of balance he may blandly extol the virtue of *planned* deficits for stimulating the economy.
>
> (Eaton, 1966:3–4, emphasis original)

69. See, for example, Perry (1955:196–205, 222–225, and 396–400), Due (1951:6–10), Kemp (1923:216–217) and Bernier (1967:25–30).

Chapter 8: Financing Depression

1. For a more extensive discussion of the severity of the depression, see Bryce (1986:39–52), Perry (1955:253–284), Rowell-Sirois (1940:140–177) and Safarian (1970:1–17 and 88–98). See also the GNP data in Appendix Table C-1.

2. See Appendix Table B-3. Spending rose by 11 percent in fiscal 1931 and 1932, fell by 6 and 2 percent in the next two years respectively, rose by 3 and 12 percent during fiscal 1935 and 1936, remained constant over the next two years and rose by just 3 percent in fiscal 1939.

3. The expenditure data for the years fiscal 1929 through 1933 correct an error in the official figures. See Appendix B for a discussion of the error and the correction. One consequence is that the deficit for fiscal 1933 declines from the officially recorded $220 million (Perry 1955:254) to $158 million.

4. See Appendix Table C-3 for the years 1929–1939.

5. The collapse in imports accounted for the drastic decline (65 percent) in customs revenues between fiscal 1929 and 1934. See Perry (1955:253–284) and Safarian (1970:88–98).

6. See Appendix Table B-3.

7. See Appendix Table B-3.

8. The depression lasted from about 1873 to 1896 with three prosperous years, 1880–1882 (Perry, 1955:58–68 and 93; Rowell-Sirois, 1940:49 and 53). Deficit financing was a major source of revenues (over 20 percent) during fiscal 1875–1880 and 1883–1889. See Appendix Table B-3.

9. See the discussion of these themes in Chapter 4 and Rhodes (1932:32; 1933:24; and 1935:30) and Dunning (1936:24; 1937:27; 1938:16; and 1939:11).

10. Bryce (1986:60 and 113–119) discusses the orthodox commitment of Dunning to expenditure restraint and tax increases in order to achieve balanced budgets during these years. King's commitment to restraint was more political. In any case, total government spending did not change through fiscal 1937 and 1938 and increased by just 3 percent in fiscal 1939 (see Appendix Table B-3).

11. See the discussion of this budget-making process in Bryce (1986:119), where he quotes from King's Diaries for June 15 and 16, 1938.

12. See note 1, Chapter 5.

13. Perry (1955:279).
14. Rhodes (1935:28).
15. There were other changes in excise duties rates during the period, but they were minor. The rate for spirits had been set at $9.00 per gallon in 1921 and reduced to $7.00 in 1932.
16. Rhodes (1935:28).
17. Bennett (1931:59–60).
18. For the full tenor of the "double taxation" debate, see the critical comments of Mr. T.H. Stinson (*House of Commons Debates*, April 30, 1926:2983), Mr. J.D. Chaplin (3301), Mr. Euler (3449–3450) and Mr. Cahan (May 27, 1926:3778–3779).
19. Perry (1955:220–221).
20. See especially the critical attacks of Mr. Ralston (*House of Commons Debates*, June 4, 1931:2293–2306), Mr. Heaps (2315–2321), Mr. Lacroix (2321–2325), Mr. Spence (June 11, 1931:2533–2537), Mr. W.L. MacKenzie King (June 16, 1931:2664–2683 and 2691–2711), and Mr. Rinfret (June 18, 1931: 2777–2783).
21. Bennett, *House of Commons Debates*, July 16, 1931:3855.
22. See Appendix Tables B-2 and B-3.
23. The 2-cent-per-pound excise tax on sugar was a large revenue raiser; it accounted for excise tax revenues of $14.1 million during its first fiscal year (1934). This revenue accounted for the bulk of the $19.9 million increase in excise tax revenues from fiscal 1933 to 1934, and hence the bulk of the increase in relative importance of excise tax revenues during the depression (Appendix Tables B-2 and B-3, and Perry, 1955:Appendix Table A-10, pp. 636–637).
24. The other "new" tax was an export tax on liquor leaving Canada. The export tax, one of only a few up to that time, was a validation fee of 20 cents per gallon, and it lasted from 1934 until 1953 (Perry, 1955:271, 603 and 632).
25. Rhodes (1934:25–26; and 1935:27–28).
26. Rhodes (1934:26).
27. Rhodes (1934:25).
28. See Perry, (1955:277), and also *House of Commons Debates*, 1934: comments by Mr. Ralston (2439–2440), Mr. Bradette (2687–2688) and Mr. Hurtubise (2875).
29. Rhodes (1935:10) and Perry (1955:277).
30. See note 1, Chapter 5.
31. See Perry (1955:263).
32. Neatby (1972:64–69).
33. While the duty on spirits was reduced greatly, the effect expected by Rhodes was to divert consumption from the "illicit trade"; revenues did increase (Perry, 1955:269–270).
34. The Conservatives were reduced to 39 members in a House of 245 members. See Neatby (1972:61–69) for a discussion of the failure of the "reform" strategy based on Bennett's "psychological New Deal".

35. Rowell-Sirois (1940:213 and 217).
36. The Commission erred in stating that "excise duties on liquors and to-bacco (among other taxes) were sharply raised" (Rowell-Sirois, 1940:176 and 213). In fact, as I have demonstrated, excise duties on liquors were sharply lowered in an attempt to increase revenues.
37. *Ibid*, 214, 245 and 246.
38. The Commission recommended that the provinces (and municipalities) should permanently vacate the personal income tax, corporation income tax and the succession duty fields, and leave them entirely to the Dominion government. (Royal Commission on Dominion-Provincial Relations, 1940:Book II, Chapter 3).
39. See, for example, Lynn (1964:54–60), Moore, Perry and Beach (1966:10) and Strick (1978:104). In addition to Ilsley (1946:9, 12) and Abbott (1947:6), quoted in Chapter 6, see other examples of the continuing view of the depression years as a period of chaos in Dominion financing in Abbott (1949a:6), Harris (1956:13, 14; and 1957:7, 8) and Fleming (1959:9–10).
40. The analysis in this study is, of course, limited to the Dominion government. However, I do not expect that, when the Provinces have been studied within a similar conceptual framework, these conclusions will be significantly altered.

Chapter 9: Financing Tax Reform Achievements, 1963–1990

1. In 1948 the marginal tax rates ranged over nineteen tax brackets, from a low of 10 percent on taxable income up to $100 to a high of 80 percent on taxable income exceeding $250,000. A surtax of 4 percent applied to investment income.
2. For some evidence on the extent to which Canadian governments were suc-cessful in reducing income inequality over 1951–1969, see Gillespie (1980) and Normand, Hawley and Gillespie (1983).
3. See, for example, Moore, Perry and Beach (1966) and Lynn (1964).
4. Perry (1982:75–76) and MacDonald (1985).
5. Royal Commission on Taxation (1966:45).
6. For the tone of the critical reaction to the Carter *Report* and the later White Paper on Tax Reform, see Asper (1970). See also Bucovetsky and Bird (1972:17–18), Head (1972:56), Gardner (1981:246–248) and Wolfe (1988:357). For the scope of the critical responses, see the references cited in MacDonald (1985: Chapter VI).
7. See Benson (1969:6).
8. See Benson (1971:8). The reader will recall from Chapter 4 Finance Min-ister Benson's strong affirmation of the equity principle at the time of in-troducing the legislation.
9. Bird (1970a:453) and Brown (1977:41).
10. This is an example of horizontal tax competition at the provincial level.
11. Under the tax collection agreements all provinces except Quebec were and are party to the personal income tax arrangements. The agreeing provinces accept the deductions, exemptions and rate structure adopted by the fed-

eral government, and the federal government will accept tax credits, such as sales and property tax credits, that do not seriously impair the harmonization of the personal income tax system. All provinces except Ontario and Quebec in 1971 were party to the corporation income tax arrangements (Alberta now has a separate corporation income tax).

12. See Hartle (1987:37 and 55).

13. See Bucovetsky (1975) for an examination and evaluation of the active role the resource-rich provinces played in intervening on behalf of the oil and mineral industries.

14. The federal government, as part of the tax reform legislation, withdrew from 23.4 percent of the personal income tax revenue, allowing the provinces to apply their own income taxes. Given the very different bases of the estate tax and the deemed realization of death feature of capital gains taxation, the revenues gained did not make up for the revenues lost (see Canada, Department of Finance, 1980b:18).

15. See Bucovetsky (1975:103), Hartle (1987:52) and Maslove (1989:10).

16. Benson (1971:16–17). These are the federal tax rates; the combined federal-provincial tax rates prior to reform ranged from 11 to 61 percent respectively. After tax reform the first bracket rate declined from 17 percent in 1972 to 6 percent in 1976.

17. For further details of the legislation and expected revenue changes see Benson (1969 and 1971) and Gillespie (1978:28–29).

18. See, for example, Bossons (1972:45–67), Brown (1977) and Bucovetsky and Bird (1972).

19. See Bossons and Wilson (1973:185–186), Leacy, Urquhart and Buckley (1983:K8–18) and Appendix Table C-1 (for the implicit GNE price index).

20. See Vukelich (1972), Bossons and Wilson (1973) and Allan, Dodge and Poddar (1974, especially 355–357), for an analysis of the effects in terms of the federal personal income tax structure.

21. See Vukelich (1972) and Bossons and Wilson (1973).

22. See Vukelich (1972:342), Bossons and Wilson (1973:185–199), Auld and Miller (1982:112), and Musgrave, Musgrave and Bird (1987:345).

23. See Good (1980:30 and 67) and Hartle (1988:80).

24. See Appendix Tables B-3 and C-3.

25. Bossons and Wilson (1973:189–190) estimate that from 1964–1971 the revenues from direct personal taxes grew at an annual rate of 18.6 percent, whereas a completely indexed personal income tax system would have produced an annual rate of 13 percent. These revenue increases were available to finance spending increases. See also Vukelich (1972:342).

26. See Good (1980:30) and Hartle (1988:79).

27. See the discussion in Hartle (1988:79–80).

28. See also Appendix Table C-3.

29. Mr. Stanfield's initial proposal, for an indexed tax system put forward during the 1972 budget debate, still stands as a model of clear exposition, cogency and persuasiveness (Stanfield, 1972:2263–2269).

30. Hartle (1988:80).

31. The budget also included the controversial corporation profits tax reduction and two-year depreciation write-off of machinery and equipment, both for manufacturing and processing firms (initially proposed in the 1972 budget, but not passed at the time of the October election). See Turner (1973) and Gillespie (1978:21 and 31–34) for details.
32. Brown (1978:47). See also Bossons and Wilson (1973:185), Allan, Dodge and Poddar (1974), Perry (1982:102) and Maslove (1989:10, n. 10).
33. The inflation factor for year 4 is the percentage increase in the average CPI for the twelve months ending in September of year 3 over the average CPI for the twelve months ending in September of year 2.
34. See the discussion in Chapter 4 for the continuing policy thrust for equity in the tax system.
35. For an analysis and evaluation of the equity and income distribution policies of federal governments during the 1970s, see Gillespie (1978:5–15) and Doman (1980).
36. See, for example, Smith (1979), Canada, Department of Finance (1979, 1980 and 1981c) and Canada, Department of Finance (1985) for a more recent analysis.
37. See Appendix Tables B-3 and C-3.
38. This concern, reflected in the fiscal stance of Ministers of Finance, is documented more fully in the next chapter.
39. I first raised these issues in a more tentative discussion in Gillespie (1983b). Here they are integrated into an explanation of observed tax reform achievements from 1963 through 1990.
40. Finance Minister MacEachen first suggested that "the end of income indexation looms as a probability" in an interview with *Le Devoir* on May 24 (Vastel, 1980). Deputy Minister of Finance Ian Stewart acknowledged that "the total removal of indexing in the tax system is one thing that is being looked at" in his appearance before the Senate Standing Committee on National Finance on May 27 (Senate of Canada, 1980:2.31). Prime Minister Trudeau confirmed in parliamentary debate on June 2 that "the government is considering various possibilities and [removing indexation] is one of them" (*House of Commons Debates*, 1980:1626).
41. See, for example, Cheveldayoff (1980), Anderson (1980), Globe and Mail (1980 and 1980a), Young (1980), Cohen (1980), Montreal Gazette (1980), Bossons (1980) and Auld (1982:114).
42. The Progressive Conservative party targeted six cities and ran half-page messages that emphasized the party's claim to the indexing idea, provided examples of additional tax payments under de-indexing and called upon Canadians to speak up against de-indexing. Canadians did.
43. See Canada, Department of Finance (1981a:33; 1981b:15; and 1981c:18).
44. Office of the Honourable Allan J. MacEachen (1981a:1, emphasis original).
45. See, for example, Gillespie (1983b:975–976), McQuaig (1987:223–238) and Doern, Maslove and Prince (1988:65–66).
46. See Office of the Honourable Allan J. MacEachen (1981b), MacEachen (1982), Office of the Honourable Allan J. MacEachen (1982), Canada, De-

partment of Finance (1982b), and Lalonde (1982). These three major revisions in the initial tax reform proposals are described in detail in Gillespie (1983b: Table 1).

47. Bill C-139, *An Act to amend the statute law relating to income tax* (No. 2), SC 1980-81-82-83, C. 140. A fourth set of revisions (26 draft amendments of a technical nature) was proposed five days after Bill C-139 passed the House of Commons (Canada, Department of Finance, 1983).

48. See MacEachen (1982).

49. See Lalonde (1982, especially 3–4).

50. MacEachen forecast the deficit for fiscal 1982–1983 in his November 1981 budget at $10.5 billion. The June 1982 budget forecast the deficit at $19.6 billion; Mr. Lalonde's October 27 statement forecast it at $23.6 billion, and his 1983 budget forecast it at $25.3 billion.

51. Gillespie (1983b: Table 2) estimates the revenue loss for fiscal 1983–1984 at between $440 million and $543 million (accounting for between 21 and 26 percent of the planned tax revenue increase).

52. Partial de-indexation of the personal income tax was expected to generate an additional $1300 million in tax revenues during 1983 and 1984. The partial de-indexation of the other three programs would save $300 million in expenditures. Planned cuts in public service wages and other non-specified expenditures would save $1380 billion. The two-year total planned financing pool would be $3 million.

53. The Conservatives, in anticipation of their return to power, may have been dreaming fondly of using this "hidden" source of revenues, in stark contrast with Mr. Stanfield's plea ten years earlier for greater parliamentary control over tax rate increases and spending increases.

54. See Gwyn (1982), Janigan (1982) and Maslove (1989:19, n. 25).

55. Mr. MacEachen's de-indexation scheme fixed the inflation factor at 6 and 5 percent in 1983 and 1984 respectively, while expecting it to be 11.2 percent in 1983 and somewhat less in 1984 (Canada, Department of Finance, 1982a:28). Mr. Wilson's de-indexation scheme adjusts only for increases in the inflation factor in excess of three percent.

56. Canada, Department of Finance (1981b:13). These are the federal tax rates; the combined federal-provincial tax rates for the highest incomes prior to reform ranged from 60–65 percent and after tax reform ranged from 47–54 percent, depending on the province.

57. The elimination of the income averaging provisions and the restriction of capital cost allowances during the year of purchase of an asset to one-half the value of the allowance accounted for $1145 millions and $940 millions respectively within these totals for fiscal 1983–1984.

58. See, for example, Wilson (1987b:6; and 2, 7, 11; 1987c:1, 4, 21–22, 42 and 71; and 1987d:12 and 24), and Canada, Department of Finance (1986 and 1987a:56).

59. See the discussion in Chapter 4. See also Wilson (1987b; 1987c:1, 3, 7, 10, 28, 29–30, 39; and 1987d:1, 6, 19, 33, 38).

60. See Wilson (1987b:3, 9; and 1987c:2, 5, 58, 73–75; 1987d:3, 31), and

Canada, Department of Finance (1987a:2–3, and 119–128).

61. Wilson (1986b). Finance Minister Wilson's 1985 budget had rejected the notion of comprehensive tax reform (Wilson, 1985:15), while his February, 1986 budget had begun the process of corporation income tax reform by eliminating the general investment tax credit and the inventory allowance and announcing the gradual reduction in the corporate income tax rate (Wilson, 1986:12–13).

62. Wilson (1986b:6).

63. Wilson (1987a:11–13).

64. Wilson (1987b, 1987c, 1987d and 1987e).

65. House of Commons Committee on Finance and Economic Affairs (1987) and Senate Committee on Banking, Trade and Commerce (1987).

66. Canada, Department of Finance (1987a, 1987b and 1987c).

67. Wilson (1987c:27; and 1987d:69–70). These are the federal tax rates; the combined federal-provincial tax rates prior to tax reform averaged 53 percent for the highest tax rate bracket and after tax reform it averaged 45 percent.

68. This conversion involved the personal exemptions (basic, spousal, dependent children, age and disability) and such deductions as medical expenses, charitable contributions, the education deductions and deductions for unemployment insurance premiums and Canada/Quebec pension plan contributions.

69. The lifetime capital gains exemption of $500,000 (introduced by Finance Minister Wilson in his 1985 budget) was reduced to $100,000, the $500 standard employment expense deduction was eliminated, the gradual phase-in period for the enriched RRSP contribution limits was delayed, write-offs on MURBs, films, and earned depletion were restricted and allowable expenses for autos, home offices and business meals were tightened up. See Canada, Department of Finance (1987a, 1987b and 1987c) for details.

70. Canada, Department of Finance (1987a:126–128).

71. The general corporate income tax rate was reduced from 36 percent to 28 percent, the rate for manufacturing and processing was reduced from 30 to 26 percent (and eventually to 23 percent in 1991) and the small business rate was lowered from 15 to 12 percent. For the details of the base-broadening elements, see Wilson (1987d:98–128) and Canada, Department of Finance (1987a:51–98).

72. These changes included: shifting the sales tax to the wholesale level for a limited range of goods, applying the sales tax to sales by marketing companies linked to the manufacturer and levying the sales tax on telecommunication services at a rate of 10 percent.

73. The tax reform fiscal plan was designed to achieve revenue neutrality by year four, fiscal 1991–1992, and over the entire four-year period. This produces, given the immediate introduction of the personal income tax changes and the more gradual phasing in of the amendments to the corporation income tax, a sizeable net revenue loss during fiscal 1988–1989 and a net revenue gain, also sizeable, during fiscal 1989–1990. See:Wilson

(1987b:3; and 1987c:5, 23 and 73–77), and Canada, Department of Finance (1987a:119–128).

74. Head (1972:65).
75. Bucovetsky and Bird (1972:38 and 23).
76. Perry (1982:80).
77. Wolfe (1988:358).
78. Maslove (1989:10). See also Gardner (1981), which discusses six stages of retreat, MacDonald (1985), McQuaig (1987:156) and Farrow (1988:2).
79. Head (1972:57 and 66).
80. Bossons (1972:55).
81. Bucovetsky and Bird (1972:23 and 37).
82. Hartle (1987:37) is more explicit in arguing that the Commission implicitly assumed that the provinces would "meekly acquiesce" in the proposed changes in the federal personal and corporation income tax structure, even though such changes would affect the provincial tax bases. This failure to allow for legitimate provincial concerns at a time of increasing federal-provincial disagreements over tax revenue sources was a major omission in the Commission's grand design for tax reform.
83. Hartle (1987:43), Bucovetsky and Bird (1972:17–18), Gardner (1981:249 and 254) and Maslove (1989:9).
84. See, for example, Gwyn (1982), Doern (1982:9 and 10), McQuaig (1987:223–238), Doern, Maslove and Prince (1988:65–66), Farrow (1988:2), Maslove (1989:11–12, 23 and 27), Kennedy (1990) and Simpson (1990).
85. Maslove (1989:11).
86. Perry (1989:314).
87. See Doern, Maslove and Prince (1988:65), McQuaig (1987:223 and 238) and Maslove (1989:11). The interpretation is mine, but these writers express surprise or incomprehension at the government's lack of preparedness for the response of business groups, lobbyists and special interest groups, given previous experience of a reaction of exactly the same kind.
88. Carmichael, MacMillan and York (1989:57); see also Farrow (1988:2), Doern, Maslove and Prince (1988:70) and Maslove (1989:27–28).
89. See Bossons (1987), Hartle (1987:15–16), Doern, Maslove and Prince (1988:67), Courchene (1988:25), Timbrell (1988), Dodge and Sargent (1988:51–52), Carmichael, MacMillan and York (1989:99) and Maslove (1989:23).
90. See, for example, Bossons and Wilson (1973:185, 189 and 199), Allan, Dodge and Poddar (1974:360–362 and 369), Auld and Miller (1982:113–114) and Musgrave, Musgrave and Bird (1987:345).
91. See Good (1980) and Hartle (1988).
92. Good (1980:30).
93. Hartle (1988:79–81) adopts a similar model and concludes, in an almost normative vein, that it was a "gross error" to eliminate a "politically costless" increase in revenues as a result of inflation.

Chapter 10: The Deficit, the Debt and the GST

1. The sales tax revenue share measure illustrates these policy choices clearly

for the first post-war period, the 1930s and the second post-war period, in each period it peaked, respectively, at 29 percent (in 1924), 26 percent (in 1938) and 18 percent (in 1950) of total financial requirements:see Chart 9-1 and Table B-3.

2. See also, Chart 7-1 and the discussion in Chapters 7 and 8.

3. For the growth in government expenditures and total spending relative to gross national product, see Tables B-3, C-1 and C-3.

4. See Chart 1-3 in Chapter 1.

5. The proposal was not passed before the October election which resulted in a minority Liberal government, and it was repackaged in Mr. Turner's 1973 budget. When finally passed, the proposal was effective from May 8, 1972 for the fast write-off decision and January 1, 1973 for the tax rate reduction. In November 1974, with a majority government, Mr. Turner made the fast write-off permanent and exempted manufacturing and processing firms from his 10 percent corporate surtax.

6. The investment tax credit also covered petroleum, minerals, logging, farming and fishing, and was extended to research and development expenditures by Finance Minister MacDonald in his 1977 budget.

7. Mr. MacDonald's proposal to allow 3 percent of inventories to be deductible before calculation of corporation income tax reduced the effective tax rate further in 1977. Specifically, there were changes in the petroleum sector that defined the federal government's attempts to share in the windfall gains, attributable to the world-wide rise in oil prices and aggravated the friction between Alberta and Ottawa (vertical tax competition, again).

8. The share of corporation income tax revenues in total tax revenues in the United States demonstrates a similar pattern to Charts 9-1 and 10-1 for Canada. See J. Pechman's posthumous Presidential Address to the American Economic Association on December 29, 1989, "The Future of the Income Tax", *American Economic Review*, Vol. 80, No. 1 (March 1990:1–20).

9. MacDonald (1977:12) and Chrétien (1978a:9, and 1978b:7 and 11); see also Turner (1975:21).

10. See Winer and Hettich (1988:413–14) and Maslove (1989:10–11 and 16–19).

11. See Gillespie (1978:28–39) and Doman (1980) for a summary of the details of these tax choices of the 1970s.

12. Turner (1974b:19) and Chrétien (1978b:19). Turner also exempted clothing and footwear from the tax in 1974a:17.

13. The oil export charges were born in 1974 and died in 1986; the excise tax on gasoline was born in 1976 and is the most substantial existing energy tax today; the petroleum and gas revenue tax and the natural gas tax were born in 1981 and died in 1987 and 1985 respectively (although some revenues are still collected on previous sales); the Canadian Ownership special charge was borne in 1982 and died in 1986; and the excise tax on aviation gas and diesel fuel, born in 1986, still exists today.

14. Crosbie (1979:3); see also MacEachen (1980:4; 1981:1, 2 and 5; and 1982:1), Lalonde (1983:20 and 21; and 1984:5) and Wilson (1985:5 and 15; 1986:1, 5 and 23; 1987:2, 6 and 13; 1988:2 and 5; and 1989:1, 3, 4, 10 and 15).

In addition, see the separate studies of the deficit and the debt in Lalonde (1983b) and Wilson (1989c).

15. MacDonald (1989:A.7). See also Toulin (1988), Simpson (1989b) and the *Globe and Mail* (1990:A16, which refers in alarmist tones to "the crushing burden of the federal debt", the slow progress in "taming the unruly federal debt" and the "stock pile of debt".

16. Angus Reid Associates Inc. found that the deficit was number 2 on the list of the public's concerns, and Environics Research Group found that the percentage of Canadians who saw the deficit as an important problem had risen over four months from 50 to 60 percent (Kohut, 1989).

17. For a discussion of the inefficiencies of the positive import bias and the negative export bias, and the other reasons why the federal manufacturers' sales tax was non-neutral see any one of the various reports and white papers of the last thirty years: Sales Tax Committee (1956), Royal Commission on Taxation (1967), Canada, Department of Finance (1975 and 1977), MacEachen (1981 and 1982b), Federal Sales Tax Review Committee (1983) and Wilson (1987c and 1987e).

18. See Jenkins (1989:18–20) and Tait (1988:10–14). For a succinct but perceptive discussion of the intellectual foundations of the value-added tax, see Thirsk (1991) in the volume paying tribute to the "intellectual father" of the VAT, Carl Sumner Shoup (Eden, 1991).

19. Sales Tax Committee (1956).

20. Royal Commission on Taxation (1967). The Commission's first preference was a value-added tax on most goods and services, but it judged that such a tax would be administratively difficult to implement.

21. Canada, Department of Finance (1975:7). The Discussion Paper argued that a VAT type mechanism was best suited to a tax at the retail level with few exemptions. A sales tax at the wholesale level with some goods and most services exempt was not seen as justifying the added administrative costs of a VAT type mechanism.

22. Canada, Department of Finance (1977).

23. The first extension was proposed by MacEachen (1982b) and the second by Lalonde (1982). The strong business opposition centred on the added complexity and administrative costs of extending the tax to the wholesale level for what were perceived to be very small gains in efficiency. See Beauchesne (1983:35).

24. Federal Sales Tax Review Committee (1983:58).

25. Lalonde (1984:13).

26. See Canada, Department of Finance (1984:67) and Wilson (1986:16; 1986b:6 and 8; and 1987:13).

27. With the structure of the tax not yet determined it was not possible to choose a rate for the tax. However, the Department of Finance for illustrative purposes used a tax rate of 8 percent. See Wilson (1987b; 1987c:60; and 1987e:29).

28. For details of these proposals, see Wilson (1987c:65–70; and 1987e:47–58).

29. For a brief discussion of the debate in the early stages, and especially the

strongly critical reaction to any tax on food, see McQuaig (1987:331–333) and McSheffrey (1988:50–57 and 80–83).

30. See McSheffrey (1988:80–83).

31. See Wilson (1989a:12). The sales tax rates on alcoholic beverages and tobacco products, on telecommunication services, and on construction materials were increased by one percentage point; the rate on all other taxable goods was increased by one and a half percentage points.

32. See Wilson (1989b; and 1989d:33; and 1989e:43–45).

33. Wilson (1989e:9, 81, 97, 142, and 151).

34. To get some of the flavour of these special requests, reflected in 770 briefs, which ranged from book lovers (who requested exemption for this "food for the soul") through funeral service directors (who argued for their "essential service") to veterinarians (who estimate that the 7 percent GST will increase the demand for their euthanasia services by 7 percent), see Bagnall (1989) and Corcoran (1990).

35. See, for example, Freeman (1989a) and Riley (1989). Other objections surfaced, ranging from a call for inclusion of basic foods in the tax base (which would require higher refundable sales tax credits to low income-taxpayers) to a reduction in the "overly generous" refundable sales tax credits.

6. House of Commons (1989). The proposed trade-up tax on resale housing was expected to raise $1.6 billion of the total $5 billion in recouped revenues.

37. See Hazledine (1989) and Simpson (1989a).

38. Wilson (1989g).

39. See Freeman (1989b).

40. See Wilson (1989g:14–18) for details.

41. See Wilson (1989g:29–35) for the details of the refundable sales tax credits. The comparisons in the text are for 1990 with the MST and, for 1991 with the GST, and in both cases assume full eligibility for the credit.

42. See Wilson (1989g:19 and 31–35), where the sales tax pattern for families with children is progressive over low and modest incomes.

43. See, for example, Maslove (1990:33–34) and Brooks (1990:26, 28 and 37). Brooks is critical of the MST-GST tax reform proposal, and presents an alternative reform package that abolishes the MST and replaces the revenues with higher personal income tax revenues and several other additional taxes. However, he does acknowledge — and his empirical findings (Table 17) demonstrate the point — that the GST tax reform package results in a tax incidence pattern (tax payments as a percent of family income) that is progressive up to an income of $35,000–$45,000, and is less regressive than the existing MST tax incidence pattern for incomes over $45,000. Fifty-eight percent of family units have incomes of $45,000 or less, according to his study.

44. For the diversity of effective tax rates when expressed as a percent of product price, see Wilson (1987e:13 and 17; and 1989b:5 and 9).

45. See especially the discussion in Maslove (1990:40–42).

46. See, for example, Doern, Maslove and Prince (1988:24, 146–148), Maslove

(1989:21 and 23), McQuaig (1987:198 and 314) and Wolfe (1985:120–121; and 1988:360–365).

47. Boadway and Kitchen (1984:128–129) note that these tax rate cuts were in response to tax changes in the United States, but do not develop the implications for the increasing deficits of the late 1970s.

48. See, for example, Doern, Maslove and Prince (1988:24 and 206), Hartle (1988:69, 80, 82 and 87), and the *Globe and Mail* (1990).

49. See, for example, the *Globe and Mail* (1989), Cook (1989), Janigan (1989) and Winsor (1989).

50. The decision of the provinces of Quebec (on August 30, 1990) and Saskatchewan (on February 20, 1991) to merge their retail sales tax with the GST, and thus establish a broader provincial tax base and a lower tax rate by January 1, 1992, will increase the political pressures on other provinces to merge their sales taxes with the federal levy.

Chapter 11: Conclusion: Financing Federal Spending, Past, Present and Future

1. See Table 2-1 in Chapter 2.

2. I am not interested in minor technical changes, whether effected voluntarily or in response to opposition from some small select group of taxpayers. I am only interested in big political mistakes.

3. Fielding increased the excise duty on cigarettes by $1.50 per thousand in his 1922 budget and, in response to the effect of smuggling on decreasing consumption, rescinded it in his 1923 budget (p. 9). Rhodes reduced the duties on spirits in his 1935 budget (p. 28), as part of his plan to "stamp out the smuggling trade". Abbott increased the excise duty on cigarettes in his 1951 budget, but in response to excessive smuggling and decreased revenues, rescinded the increase in his 1952 budget (p. 15), and lowered the duty still further in his 1953 budget (p. 20) because of smuggling.

4. See Ilsley (1943:17; and 1944:9–10).

5. While these four budgets contained political mistakes, eighteen budgets were presented in minority government situations with no such political mistakes (see Appendix E).

6. As quoted in White (1917b:3770).

7. Fiscal 1950–1952 was a unique period of Canadian fiscal history. The pressures of war-related expenditures and a buoyant economy allowed the Finance Minister to increase tax rates on many revenue sources, finance the Korean war entirely on a pay-as-you-go basis, and generate surpluses that were used to reduce the debt. The key difference between this period of surpluses and other periods is that the surpluses were the outcome of increased tax rates, imposed across the board, that generated revenues in excess of spending.

8. See also Charts 1-1 and 1-2 of Chapter 1.

9. See Appendix B, Table B-4 for a detailed description of the revenue sources included in each of the four groups of taxes.

10. Galbraith (1967).

Appendix A: In Search of the Data of Revenue Structure Variation

1. The table is an extensively expanded version of Perry (1955:707), and draws upon Due (1964) and Canadian Tax Foundation (1967 and 1971).
2. Boadway and Kitchen (1984).
3. Rowell-Sirois Commission (1940:Book I, Table 4, p. 40 for 1866, and Table 12, p. 64 for 1874 and 1896).
4. Dominion-Provincial Conference on Reconstruction (1945).
5. Canadian Tax Foundation (1957).
6. Urquhart and Buckley (1965) and Leacy, Urquhart and Buckley (1983).
7. Bird (1970b).
8. Firestone (1958).
9. Bird (1970b: Table 26, pp. 268–271). There is one conceptual and one empirical problem in this proxy approach. Conceptually, revenue from own sources understates provincial spending by the amount of the deficit (and there were large deficits on capital account during the early years after Confederation) and the amount of the Dominion statutory subsidies (although, for spending by all three levels of government, there must necessarily be some netting out of intergovernmental transfers). Empirically, Bird's allocation of $1 million of "spending" in 1901 falls well short of the $4.9 million of revenues from "selected" revenue sources, given in *Historical Statistics* (1965).
10. Bird (1970b: Table 26, 268–271). There is a conceptual problem similar to the one discussed in the preceding note; in addition, not all municipalities and not all municipal taxes are included.
11. Bird (1979).
12. Prior to Confederation, the colonies were extensively involved in transportation and public works. Forty percent of direct government spending and seventy-five percent of colonial debt outstanding was on this account, with interest payments on the debt amounting to 29 percent of government spending. The collapse of the Grand Trunk railway during the 1850s led to a drying up of long term funds and a short term "exorbitant" rate of 8 percent (Perry, 1955:37–39). How times have changed!
13. See Villard and Willoughby (1918:60–62) and Maxwell (1934:147).
14. See Rich (1988: Chapter 7). For details of the adjustment procedure during the period covered by Rich and from 1914–1988, see Appendix B of this study.
15. As of writing, data has been extracted and arranged in an appropriate format for analysis for British Columbia (see Gillespie, 1988). Work is progressing on arranging the public accounts data for the provinces of Ontario, Nova Scotia and Manitoba.
16. For the early years, information may exist for major cities only (from the Treasurers' Reports for Montreal, Halifax and Winnipeg, one can extract expenditures, revenues by revenue source and deficit financing, although it is not a straightforward matter, given the changing format of such Reports). This may not pose a serious problem in provinces where, for many years,

only one or two such cities might account for major municipal spending and taxing.

17. Professor Urquhart has very kindly made available to me this very extensive body of information.

Appendix B: Dominion Government Expenditure, Revenue and Budget Deficit, Canada, 1868–1990

1. In the following, numbers in parentheses identify the pages in Canada, *Public Accounts* for 1919 (Part I).

2. Sinking fund allocations represented revenue earmarked for the retirement of outstanding bonds — not a real expenditure item. Allowances to the provinces are also fictitious:each province was awarded a debt allowance at Confederation, such that if the debt actually taken over by the Dominion government exceeded the debt allowance the province had to pay interest on the difference (and vice versa if the debt allowance exceeded the actual debt taken over); subsequently, the debt allowance was raised several times and on these occasions was treated as an expenditure item. See Rich (1988: Chapter 7) for a discussion of the other fictitious items.

3. The change in format, commencing fiscal 1920, is a mixed blessing. While sinking fund allocations are no longer included in disbursements (necessitating a deletion), much of the detail from which the precise calculations for 1868–1919 were derived was omitted. Apparently the Finance Department was in the midst of an economy drive and saw many of the tables as not "serving any useful purposes" (Canada, *Public Accounts* for 1920, Sessional Paper No. 2, 1921, p. vii).

4. Canada, *Public Accounts* for 1936, Part I, p. ix.

5. Urquhart and Buckley (1965:202; given their method of recording fiscal years, the error occurs in fiscal 1932).

6. See the detailed discussion in Rhodes (1933:12–14; and 1934:13–17).

7. See Perry (1955:254).

8. Canada, *Public Accounts* for 1943, Part I, Introduction of the Deputy Minister of Finance, pp. XII–XVI.

9. Given the treatment of these items in the public accounts, the value of old age security taxes equals the value of old age security benefit payments minus any deficit:thus the same amount gets added to both sides of the government's budget.

10. The account, established under section 3 of the *Defence Appropriation Act* of 1950, was an instrument for handling defence materials and supplies which the government transferred to member countries of NATO. The disbursements from the account include expenditure for actual equipment replacement for the Canadian armed forces plus direct cash outlays to purchase equipment for NATO or to train pilots: Will (1964).

11. *Ibid*, 47–50.

12. See Winer and Hettich (1991).

13. See Perry (1955:624–627).

14. See the Canadian Tax Foundation (1957:42–45, and 58–62).

15. One revision designed to keep the reader on his or her toes is the one-year shift of each fiscal year recorded in Perry's earlier work:fiscal 1868 for Perry (1955) and the Canadian Tax Foundation (1957) becomes fiscal 1867 in Urquhart and Buckley (1965:197–203).

16. The administrative expenses of the Unemployment Insurance Commission, and the government's contribution to them, are included in budgetary expenditure; unemployment insurance benefit payments are excluded from expenditure. Any deficit on the old age security fund is covered by the government and included as a budgetary expenditure; old age security benefit payments are excluded from expenditure.

17. Urquhart and Buckley (1965:202). We noted above that some part of the vote allotment in the Public Accounts is recorded as ordinary expenditure in the budgetary total. However, only the disbursement out of the account is a real expenditure. Therefore, to derive the value of net real expenditures to be added to the budgetary total, it is necessary to subtract ordinary expenditures credited to the account from disbursements out of the account. This procedure accords with the derivation of total disbursements found in Will (1964).

18. This fictitious effect is especially noticeable in 1873 (although it is not much less pronounced for 1874, 1884 and 1886). If the debt allowance to the provinces, amounting to $13.9 million, is *not* excluded — this is the procedure in the public accounts and other sources — the figure for recorded expenditure becomes unusually high. In *Canadian Fiscal Facts* "capital expenditures" for 1873 amount to $19.9 million, as compared with $7.9 million in the preceding year (Canadian Tax Foundation 1957:58). In Urquhart and Buckley (1965:202–203) "unclassified" expenditures total $14.8 million in 1873, as compared with $2.8 million in 1872.

19. See Perry (1955, Appendix Table 6), Urquhart and Buckley (1965:197–198) and Leacy, Urquhart and Buckley (1983).

Appendix C: Dominion Government Spending and Financing, Relative to National Income, Canada, 1870–1989

1. Urquhart (1986: Tables 2.1 and 2.9).
2. Leacy, Urquhart and Buckley (1983: Series F1–F55).
3. Statistics Canada (1988 and 1990: Tables II, 1, 3 and 4).

References

Allan, J.R., D.A. Dodge and S.N. Poddar, 1974. "Indexing the Personal Income Tax: A Federal Perspective." *Canadian Tax Journal*, Vol. 22, No. 4:355–369.

Alt, James E., 1983. "The Evolution of Tax Structures." *Public Choice*, Vol. 41:181–222.

Anderson, Ronald, 1980. "Politicians' Lives Easier with Inflationary Gains." *Globe and Mail*, June 3:B2.

Asper, I.H., 1970. *The Benson Iceberg: A Critical Analysis of the White Paper on Tax Reform in Canada*. Toronto: Clarke, Irwin and Co.

Auld, D.A.L., and F.C. Miller, 1982. *Principles of Public Finance, A Canadian Text*. Toronto: Methuen.

Baak, Bennett D., and Edward John Ray, 1985. "Special Interests and the Adoption of the Income Tax in the United States." *Journal of Economic History*, Vol. XLV, No. 3 (September):607–625.

Bagnall, James, 1989. "Death, Taxes and Bowling: a Shot at the GST." *Financial Post*, October 14:1.

Bates, Stewart, 1939. *Financial History of Canadian Governments*. A Study Prepared for the Royal Commission on Dominion-Provincial Relations. Ottawa.

Beauchesne, Eric, 1983. "Business's Budget-Bashing Campaign Paid Off." *Ottawa Citizen*, January 6:35.

Benson, Honourable E.J., 1969. *Proposals for Tax Reform*. Ottawa: Queen's Printer.

Benson, Honourable E.J., 1971. *Summary of 1971 Tax Reform Legislation*. Ottawa: Department of Finance.

Bergstrom, Theodore C., and Robert P. Goodman, 1973. "Private Demands for Public Goods." *American Economic Review*, Vol. 63 (June):280–296.

Bernier, Pierre C.D., 1967. *The Federal Sales Tax and Federal Fiscal Policies, 1920–1967*. Ottawa: Carleton University, M.A. Thesis.

Bird, Richard M., 1970a. "The Tax Kaleidoscope: Perspectives on Tax Reform in Canada." *Canadian Tax Journal*, Vol. 18, No. 5 (September–October):444–473.

Bird, Richard M., 1970b. *The Growth of Government Spending In Canada*. Canadian Tax Paper No. 51. Toronto: Canadian Tax Foundation.

Bird, Richard M., 1979. *Financing Canadian Government: A Quantitative Overview*. Toronto: Canadian Tax Foundation.

Boadway, Robin W. and David E. Wildasin, 1984. *Public Sector Economics*, 2nd ed. Toronto: Little, Brown and Co.

Boadway, Robin W. and Harry M. Kitchen, 1984. *Canadian Tax Policy*. Canadian Tax Paper No. 63. Toronto: Canadian Tax Foundation.

Boadway, Robin W., Neil Bruce and Jack M. Mintz, 1982. "Corporate Taxation in Canada: Toward an Efficient System." In Wayne R. Thirsk and John Whalley (eds.), *Tax Policy Options in the 1980s*. Toronto: Canadian Tax Foundation.

Bonomo, V. and J.E. Tanner, 1972. "Canadian Sensitivity to Economic Cycles in the United States." *Review of Economics and Statistics*, 54 (February):1–8.

Borcherding, Thomas and Robert T. Deacon, 1972. "The Demand for Services of Non-Federal Governments." *American Economic Review*, Vol. 62 (December):891–901.

Bossons, John, 1972. "Economic Overview of the Tax Reform Legislation." *Report of the Proceedings of the Twenty-Third Tax Conference, 1971*. Toronto: Canadian Tax Foundation, 45–67.

Bossons, John, 1980. "Ending Tax Indexing: Sneaking in Hidden Future Increases." *Globe and Mail*, June 6:7.

Bossons, John, 1988. "Sales Tax Reform: The Postponed Part of the Package." In Edward A. Carmichael (ed.), *Tax Reform: Perspectives on the White Paper*. Policy Study No. 4. Toronto: C.D. Howe Institute, 87–102.

Bossons, John and Thomas A. Wilson, 1973. "Adjusting Tax Rates for Inflation." *Canadian Tax Journal*. Vol. XXI, No. 3 (May–June):185–199.

Bradford, David F., 1980. "The Case for a Personal Consumption Tax." In Joseph A. Pechman (ed.), *What Should be Taxed: Income or Expenditure?* Studies of Government Finance. Washington, D.C.: The Brookings Institution, 75–113 and 113–125.

Brennan, Geoffrey and James M. Buchanan, 1980. *The Power to Tax, Analytical Foundations of a Fiscal Constitution*. London: Cambridge University Press.

Brooks, Neil, 1990. *Searching For An Alternative to the GST*. Discussion Paper 90.C.1, Studies in Social Policy. Ottawa: Institute for Research on Public Policy (February).

Brosio, Giorgio and Giancarlo Pola, 1989. "A Survey of Various Attempts to Explain the Distribution of Tax Revenues among Levels of Government." In Aldo Chiancone and Ken Messere (eds.), *Changes in Revenue Structure*, Proceedings of the 42nd Congress of the International Institute of Public Finance. Detroit: Wayne State University Press, 403–419.

Brown, F., 1941. "The History of Canadian War Finance, 1914–1920." In F. Brown, J. Gibson, and A.F. Plumptre (eds.), *War Finance in Canada*. Toronto: Ryerson Press.

Brown, James R., 1978. "Tax Reform — Six Years Later." *Report of the Proceedings of the Twenty-Ninth Tax Conference, 1977*. Toronto: Canadian Tax Foundation, 41–48.

Brown, Robert D., 1986. "Canadian Tax Reform: Can We Do Better the Second Time Around?" In *Report of Proceedings of the Thirty-Eighth Tax Conference*. Toronto, Canadian Tax Foundation, 3:1–3:31

Bryce, R.B., 1939. "The Effects on Canada of Industrial Fluctuations in the United States." *Canadian Journal of Economics and Political Science*, 5 (August):373–386.

Bryce, R.B., 1986. *Maturing in Hard Times, Canada's Department of Finance through the Great Depression.* Kingston: McGill-Queens University Press.

Buchanan, James M., 1976. "Taxation in Fiscal Exchange." *Journal of Public Economics*, Vol. 6:17–29.

Buchanan, James M. and Gordon Tullock, 1962. *The Calculus of Consent, Logical Foundations of Constitutional Democracy.* Ann Arbor: University of Michigan Press.

Buck, A.E., 1949. *Financing Canadian Government.* Chicago: Public Administration Service.

Bucovetsky, M.W., 1975. "The Mining Industry and the Great Tax Reform Debate." In A. Paul Pross (ed.), *Pressure Group Behaviour in Canadian Politics.* Toronto: McGraw-Hill, 87–114.

Bucovetsky, Meyer and Richard M. Bird, 1972. "Tax Reform in Canada: A Progress Report." *National Tax Journal*, Vol. 35, No. 1 (March):15–42.

Bush, Winston C. and Arthur T. Denzau, 1977. "Voting Behaviour of Bureaucrats and Public Sector Growth." In Thomas E. Borcherding (ed.), *Budgets and Bureaucrats, op. cit.*, 90–99.

Byatt, I.C.R., 1986. "U.K. Public Debt: Trends, Composition and Performance." In Bernard P. Herber (ed.), *Public Finance and Public Debt*, Proceedings of the 40th Congress of the International Institute of Public Finance. Detroit: Wayne State University Press, 97–110.

Campbell, Robert M., 1987. *Grand Illusions: The Politics of the Keynesian Experience in Canada, 1945–1975.* Peterborough: Broadview Press Ltd.

Canada, Department of Finance, 1975. *Federal Sales and Excise Taxation: Discussion Paper.* Ottawa: The Department.

Canada, Department of Finance, 1977. *Report of the Commodity Tax Review Group.* Ottawa: The Department.

Canada, Department of Finance, 1978. *The Tax Systems of Canada and the United States, A Study Comparing the Levels of Taxation on Individuals and Businesses in the Two Countries.* Ottawa: The Department (November).

Canada, Department of Finance, 1979. *Government of Canada Tax Expenditure Account; A Conceptual Analysis and Account of Tax Preferences in the Federal Income and Commodity Tax Systems.* Ottawa: The Department (December).

Canada, Department of Finance, 1980a. *Government of Canada Tax Expenditure Account; The Account of Tax Preferences in the Federal Income and Commodity Tax Systems 1976–1980.* Ottawa: The Department (December).

Canada, Department of Finance, 1980b. *A Review of the Taxation of Capital Gains in Canada.* Ottawa: The Department (November).

Canada, Department of Finance, 1981a. *The Budget in More Detail*. Ottawa: The Department (November 12).

Canada, Department of Finance, 1981b. *Budget Papers*, Supplementary Information and Notice of Ways and Means Motion on the Budget. Ottawa: The Department (November 12).

Canada, Department of Finance, 1981c. *Analysis of Federal Tax Expenditures for Individuals*. Ottawa: The Department (November).

Canada, Department of Finance, 1982a. *Budget Papers*, Supplementary Information and Notice of Ways and Means Motion on the Budget. Ottawa: The Department (June 28).

Canada, Department of Finance, 1982b. *Notice of Ways and Means Motions to Amend the Income Tax Act and the Income Tax Application Rules, 1971*. Ottawa: The Department (June 28).

Canada, Department of Finance, 1983. *Draft Amendments to the Income Tax Act*. Ottawa: The Department (April 5).

Canada, Department of Finance, 1984. "A New Direction for Economic Renewal", *Budget Papers*. Ottawa: The Department (November 8).

Canada, Department of Finance, 1985. *Account of the Cost of Selective Tax Measures*. Ottawa: Minister of Supply and Services Canada (August).

Canada, Department of Finance, 1986. "Opening Remarks by the Honourable Michael Wilson, Minister of Finance, at a News Conference", *Release*, No. 86–129. Ottawa: The Department (July 18).

Canada, Department of Finance, 1987a. *Supplementary Information Relating to Tax Reform Measures*. Ottawa: The Department (December 16).

Canada, Department of Finance, 1987b. *Tax Reform 1987, Notice of Ways and Means Motion to Amend the Income Tax Act*. Ottawa: The Department (December).

Canada, Department of Finance, 1987c. *Draft Income Tax Regulations, Legislation and Explanatory Notes*. Ottawa: The Department (December).

Canada, *Public Accounts*, 1919, (part 1). Ottawa: King's Printer.

Canada, *Public Accounts*, 1920, (part 1). Ottawa: King's Printer.

Canada, *Public Accounts*, 1936, (part 1). Ottawa: King's Printer.

Canada, *Public Accounts*, 1943, (part 1). Ottawa: King's Printer.

Canada, *Public Accounts*, 1951, (part 1). Ottawa: King's Printer.

Canada, *Public Accounts*, 1967, (part 1). Ottawa: Queen's Printer.

Canadian Tax Foundation, 1957. *Canadian Fiscal Facts*. Toronto: Canadian Tax Foundation.

Canadian Tax Foundation, 1967. *Provincial Finances 1967*. Toronto: Canadian Tax Foundation.

Carmichael, Edward A., Katie MacMillan and Robert C. York, 1989. *Ottawa's Next Agenda: Policy Review and Outlook, 1989*. Toronto: C.D. Howe Institute.

REFERENCES 335

Caves, Richard E., 1976. "Economic Models of Political Choice: Canada's Tariff Structure." *Canadian Journal of Economics*, 9, No. 2 (April):278–300.

Chambers, E.J., 1964. "Late Nineteenth Century Business Cycles in Canada." *Canadian Journal of Economics and Political Science*, 30 (August):391–412.

Cheveldayoff, Wayne, 1980. "Taxpayers May Lose Inflation Adjustment." *Globe and Mail*, June 2:1 and 2.

Chiancone, Aldo and Ken Messere (eds.), 1989. *Changes in Revenue Structure*, Proceedings of the 42nd Congress of the International Institute of Public Finance. Detroit: Wayne State University Press.

Cohen, Dian, 1980. "Grits Will Only Bleed Economy." *Ottawa Citizen*. June 9:7.

Cook, Peter, 1989. "The Minister Must Clear Up A Little Misunderstanding On Taxes." *Globe and Mail*, October 4:B2.

Corcoran, Terence, 1990. "Vets, Pets and Maoist Guerrillas Form Fatuous Lineup Againt GST." *Globe and Mail*, February 2:B2.

Corcoran, Terence, 1991. "Foundation Laid For Low-Inflation Era." *Globe and Mail*, February 28:B10.

Courchene, Thomas J., 1988. "Tax Reform: The Impact on Individuals." In Edward A. Carmichael (ed.), *Tax Reform: Perspectives on the White Paper*. Policy Study No. 4. Toronto: C.D. Howe Institute, 11–48.

Courtney, J.M., 1914. "Dominion Finance, 1867–1912." In Adam Shortt and A.G. Doughty (eds.), *Canada and Its Provinces*, Toronto: Publishers Association of Canada, volume 7:469–517.

Curtis, D.A. and H.M. Kitchen, 1975. "Some Quantitative Aspects of Canadian Budgetary Policy 1953–1971." *Public Finance*, Vol. XXX, No. 1:108–128.

Dales, J.H., 1966. *The Protective Tariff in Canada's Development*. Toronto: University of Toronto Press.

Deputy Minister of Finance, 1980. "Remarks before the Senate Committee on National Finance." In *Proceedings of the Senate Standing Committee on National Finance*. Ottawa: May 27.

Deutsch, J.J., 1940. "War Finance and the Canadian Economy, 1914–1920." *Canadian Journal of Economics and Political Science*, Vol. 6:525–542.

Dodge, David A. and John H. Sargent, 1988. "Tax Reform in Canada." In Joseph A. Pechman (ed.), *World Tax Reform, A Progress Report*, Washington, D.C.: Brookings Institution.

Doern, G.B., 1982. "Liberal Priorities 1982: The Limits of Scheming Virtuously." In G.B. Doern (ed.), *How Ottawa Spends Your Tax Dollars 1982*. Toronto: Lorimer, 1–36.

Doern, G. Bruce, Allan M. Maslove and Michael J. Prince, 1988. *Public Budgeting in Canada, Politics, Economics and Management*. Ottawa: Carleton University Press.

Doman, Andrew, 1980. "The Effects of Federal Budgetary Policies 1978–80 on the Distribution of Income in Canada." *Canadian Taxation*, Vol. 2:112–118.

Downs, Anthony, 1957. *An Economic Theory of Democracy.* New York: Harper and Row Publishers.

Due, John F., 1951. *The General Manufacturers Sales Tax in Canada,* Canadian Tax Paper No. 3. Toronto: Canadian Tax Foundation.

Due, John F., 1957. *Sales Taxation.* London: Routledge and Kegan Paul.

Due John F., 1964. *Provincial Sales Taxes.* Canadian Tax Paper No. 37. Toronto: Canadian Tax Foundation.

Eaton, A. Kenneth, 1966. *Essays In Taxation.* Canadian Tax Papers No. 44. Toronto: Canadian Tax Foundation.

Eden, Lorraine (ed.), 1991. *Retrospectives on Public Finance.* Fiscal Reform in the Developing World Series. Durham, N.C.: Duke University Press.

Farrow, Maureen, 1988. "Perspectives on the White Paper: An Overview." In Edward A. Carmichael (ed.), *Tax Reform: Perspectives on the White Paper.* Policy Study No. 4. Toronto: C.D. Howe Institute, 1–10.

Federal Sales Tax Review Committee, 1983. *Report of the Committee,* submitted to the Honourable Marc Lalonde, Minister of Finance (Wolfe D. Goodman, Chair). Ottawa, May.

Feldstein, Martin, 1976. "On the Theory of Tax Reform." *Journal of Public Economics,* Vol. 6:77–104.

Firestone, O.J., 1958. *Canada's Economic Development 1867–1953.* London: Bowes and Bowes.

Freeman, Alan, 1989a. "Taxing Food and Raising Rebates Would Help Poor, Economist Says." *Globe and Mail,* October 26:5.

Freeman, Alan, 1989b. "Tax Proposal Has Won Over Big Business, Labor Fuming." *Globe and Mail,* December 20:A1.

French, William, 1989. *Review* of D. Morton and J.L. Granatstein, *Marching To Armageddon, Canadians and the Great War." Globe and Mail,* March 25:C6.

Galbraith, John Kenneth, 1967. *The New Industrial State.* Boston: Houghton Mifflin Co.

Gandenberger, Otto, 1986. "On Government Borrowing and False Political Feedback." In Bernard P. Herber (ed.), *Public Finance and Public Debt,* Proceedings of the 40th Congress of the International Institute of Public Finance. Detroit: Wyane State University Press, 205–216.

Gardner, Robert, 1981. "Tax Reform and Class Interests: The Fate of Progressive Reform, 1967–72." *Canadian Taxation,* Vol. 3, No. 4 (Winter):245–257.

Gaudet, Ceo, 1987. "Modelling Discrete Changes in Tax Structure." Ottawa: Mimeo.

Gibson, J. Douglas, 1941. "Principles of War Finance." In F. Brown, J.D. Gibson and A.F. Plumptre (eds.), *War Finance in Canada.* Toronto: Ryerson Press.

Gillespie, W. Irwin, 1973. "The Federal Budget as Plan, 1968–1972." *Canadian Tax Journal*, Vol. 21, No. 1 (January–February):64–84.

Gillespie, W. Irwin, 1978a. *In Search of Robin Hood, the Effect of Federal Budgetary Policies During the 1970s on the Distribution of Income in Canada.* Montreal: C.D. Howe Research Institute, Canada Economic Policy Committee.

Gillespie, W. Irwin, 1978b. "Postwar Canadian Fiscal Policy Revisited, 1945–1975." *Carleton Economic Papers*, 78–23. Ottawa.

Gillespie, W. Irwin, 1979. "Postwar Canadian Fiscal Policy Revisited, 1945–1975." *Canadian Tax Journal*, Vol. 27, No. 3 (May–June):265–276.

Gillespie, W. Irwin, 1980. *The Redistribution of Income in Canada.* Carleton Library No. 124. Toronto: Gage Publishing Ltd.

Gillespie, W. Irwin, 1983a. "Tax Reform: The Battlefield, The Strategies, The Spoils." *Canadian Public Administration*, Vol. 26, No. 2 (Summer):182–202.

Gillespie, W. Irwin, 1983b. "The 1981 Federal Budget: Muddling Through or Purposeful Tax Reform?" *Canadian Tax Journal*, Vol. 31, No. 3 (November–December):975–1002.

Gillespie, W. Irwin, 1988. "British Columbia: Government Expenditure, Revenue and Budget Deficit, 1871–1968." *Canadian Tax Journal*, Vol. 36, No. 4 (July–August):924–953.

Gillis, Malcolm, 1985. "Federal Sales Taxation: A Survey of Six Decades of Experience, Critiques, and Reform Proposals." *Canadian Tax Journal*, Vol. 33, No. 1:68–98.

Globe and Mail, 1980. "To Gain From Inflation." Lead editorial, June 3:A6.

Globe and Mail, 1980a. "Without Representation." Lead editorial, October 1:6.

Globe and Mail, 1989. "To Replace a Sales Tax (3)." Lead editorial, August 7:A6.

Globe and Mail, 1990. "The Crushing Burden of the Federal Debt." Lead editorial, October 2:A16.

Good, David A., 1980. *The Politics of Anticipation: Making Canadian Federal Tax Policy.* Ottawa: School of Public Administration, Carleton University.

Goode, Richard, 1980. "The Superiority of the Income Tax." In Joseph A. Pechman (ed.), *What Should Be Taxed: Income or Expenditure?* Studies of Government Finance. Washington, D.C.: The Brookings Institution, 49–73.

Gordon, David M., 1972. "Taxation of the Poor and the Normative Theory of Tax Incidence." *American Economic Review, Papers and Proceedings.* Vol. LXII, No. 2 (May):319–328.

Gordon, H. Scott, 1966. "A Twenty Year Perspective: Some Reflections on the Keynesian Revolution in Canada." In S.F. Kaliski (ed.), *Canadian Economic Policy Since the War.* Montreal: Canadian Trade Committee, 23–46.

Government of Canada, 1945. *Proposals of the Government of Canada.* Dominion-Provincial Conference on Reconstruction. Ottawa: Government of Canada.

Government of Canada, 1946. *Dominion and Provincial Submissions and Plenary Conference Discussions.* Dominion-Provincial Conference (1945). Ottawa: Government of Canada.

Graetz, Michael J., 1984. "Can the Income Tax Continue to be the Major Revenue Source?" In Joseph A. Pechman (ed.), *Options for Tax Reform.* Washington, D.C.: The Brookings Institution, 39–73.

The Grain Growers' Guide, 1914. Winnipeg: The Grain Growers' Guide, June 24.

Gwyn, Richard, 1982. "Finance Department Loses Power and Prestige." *Ottawa Citizen,* July 6:6.

Haig, R.M., 1921. "The Concept of Income: Economic and Legal Aspects." In R.M. Haig (ed.), *The Federal Income Tax,* New York: Columbia University Press.

Hansen, Susan B., 1983. *The Politics of Taxation, Revenue Without Representation.* New York: Praeger Publishers.

Harberger, Arnold C., 1962. "The Incidence of the Corporation Income Tax." *Journal of Political Economy,* Vol. 70, June:457–483.

Hartle, Douglas G., 1987. "Some Analytical, Political and Normative Lessons From Carter." Paper delivered to a Conference on the Royal Commission on Taxation: Twenty Years Later. Toronto: Osgoode Hall Law School (March 26–27, mimeo).

Hartle, Douglas G., 1988. *The Expenditure Budget Process of the Government of Canada: A Public Choice-Rent-Seeking Perspective.* Canadian Tax Paper No. 81. Toronto: Canadian Tax Foundation.

Hay, K.A.J., 1966. "Early Twentieth Century Business Cycles in Canada." *Canadian Journal of Economics and Political Science,* 32 (August):354–364.

Hazledine, Tim, 1989. "Sales Tax Move Like Baronial Blackmail." *Globe and Mail,* December 7:A7.

Head, John G., 1972. "Canadian Tax Reform and Participatory Democracy." *Finanzarchiv,* Band 31, Heft 1:48–68.

Helleiner, G.K., 1977. "The Political Economy of Canada's Tariff Structure: An Alternative Model." *Canadian Journal of Economics,* Vol. 10, No. 2:318–325.

Hettich, Walter, 1975. "Bureaucrats and Public Goods." *Public Choice,* XXI (Spring):15–25.

Hettich, Walter and Stanley Winer, 1984. "A Positive Model of Tax Structure." *Journal of Public Economics,* Vol. 24, No. 4:67–87.

Hettich, Walter and Stanley L. Winer, 1988. "Economic and Political Foundations of Tax Structure." *The American Economic Review,* Vol. 78, No. 4:701–712.

Hinrichs, Harley, 1966. *A General Theory of Tax Structure Change During Economic Development*. Cambridge: Law School of Harvard University.

Hobbes, J., 1651. *Leviathan, or the Matter, Forme, and Power of a Commonwealth Ecclesiastical and Civil*, edited with an introduction by Michael Oakeshott. Oxford: Basil Blackwell, 1947.

Hogan, T. and R. Skelton, 1973. "Interstate Tax Exportation and States' Fiscal Structure." *National Tax Journal*, Vol. 26 (December):553–564.

House of Commons, 1989. *Report of the Standing Committee on Finance on the Goods and Services Tax*. Ottawa: November 27.

Innis, H.A., 1972. "A Defence of the Tariff." In R. Neill, *A New Theory of Value: The Canadian Economics of H.A. Innis*. Toronto: University of Toronto Press.

Janigan, Mary, 1982. "MacEachen Buys Time But Maybe Not for Himself." *MacLeans*. July 12:20–21.

Janigan, Mary, 1989. "Oops! They Goofed." *Globe and Mail, Report on Business*, Vol. 6, No. 6 (December):75–81.

Jenkins, Glenn P., 1989. "Tax Reform: Lessons Learned." Harvard Institute for International Development (mimeo).

Kaldor, N., 1955. *An Expenditure Tax*. London: Allen and Unwin.

Kemp, H.R., 1923. "Dominion and Provincial Taxation in Canada." *Annals of the American Academy of Political and Social Science*. Vol. 107 (May 1923):216–230.

Kennedy, Mark, 1990. "The Battle is on." *Ottawa Citizen*, September 29:B2.

Kohut, John, 1989. "Tories Will Face Selling Job After The Budget, Too." *Globe and Mail*, April 17:B1.

Krever, Richard, 1981. "The Origin of Federal Income Taxation in Canada." *Canadian Taxation, A Journal of Tax Policy*, Vol. 3, No. 4:170–188.

LaForest, Gerard V., 1967. *The Allocation of Taxing Power Under the Canadian Constitution*. Canadian Tax Papers No. 46. Toronto: Canadian Tax Foundation.

Lalonde, Honourable Marc, 1982. *Statement on the Economic Outlook and the Financial Position of the Government of Canada*. Ottawa: Minister of Supply and Services Canada, October 27.

Lalonde, Honourable Marc, 1983b. *The Federal Deficit In Perspective*. Ottawa: Canada, The Department of Finance (April).

Leacy, F.H., M.C. Urquhart and K.A.H. Buckley (eds.), 1983. *Historical Statistics of Canada, Second Edition*. Ottawa: Statistics Canada.

Lindsay, C.M., 1972. "Two Theories of Tax Deductibility." *National Tax Journal*, Vol. 25, No. 1:43–52.

Lipsey, R.G., D.D. Purvis and P.O. Steiner, 1985. *Economics*, 5th Edition. New York: Harper and Row.

Lower, A.R.M., 1936. *The Settlement and the Forest Frontier in Eastern Canada*. Vol. IX, *Settlement and the Mining Frontier*, By Harold A. Innis, Macmillan Co. of Canada (Toronto).

Lynn, James H., 1964. *Federal-Provincial Fiscal Relations*. Study No. 23, The Royal Commission on Taxation. Ottawa: Queen's Printer.

MacDonald, Leslie J., 1985. *Taxing Comprehensive Income: Power and Participation in Canadian Politics, 1962-1972*. Ph.D. thesis, unpublished. Ottawa: Carleton University.

MacDonald, W.A., 1989. "Deficit: The Number 1 Threat to Canada's Future." *Globe and Mail*, April 6:A7.

MacEachen, Honourable Allan J., 1980a. "Interview." *Le Devoir*, May 24.

MacEachen, Honourable Allan J., 1980b. *House of Commons Debates*, June 2:1626.

MacEachen, Honourable Allan J., 1982. *Proposal to Shift the Federal Sales Tax to the Wholesale Trade Level*. Ottawa: Department of Finance (April).

MacKintosh, W.A., 1966. "The White Paper on Employment and Income in its 1945 Setting." In S.F. Kaliski (ed.), *Canadian Economic Policy Since the War*. Montreal: Canadian Trade Committee, 9-21.

Maslove, Allan M., 1989. *Tax Reform in Canada: The Process and Impact*. Halifax: Institute for Research on Public Policy.

Maslove, Allan M., 1990. "The Goods and Services Tax: Lessons from Tax Reform." In Katherine A. Graham (ed.), *How Ottawa Spends, 1990-91, Tracking the Second Agenda*. Ottawa: Carleton University Press.

Maxwell, J.A., 1934. "The Distinction Between Ordinary and Capital Expenditure in Canada." *Bulletin of the National Tax Association*, Vol. XIX, No. 5 (February):146-148.

McCready, Douglas J., 1984. *The Canadian Public Sector*. Toronto: Butterworths.

McIvor, R. Craig, 1948. "Canadian War Time Fiscal Policy, 1939-45." *Canadian Journal of Economics and Political Science*, Vol. XIV:62-93.

McIvor, R. Craig, 1958. *Canadian Monetary, Banking and Fiscal Development*. Toronto: Macmillan Co. of Canada.

McLure, Charles E., Jr., 1967. "The Interstate Exporting of State and Local Taxes: Estimates for 1962." *National Tax Journal*, Vol. 20, No. 1:49-77.

McLure, Charles E. (ed.), 1983. *Tax Assignment in Federal Countries*. Centre for Research on Federal Financial Relations, Australian National University. Canberra: Australian National University Press.

McQuaig, Linda, 1987. *Behind Closed Doors, How the Rich Won Control of Canada's Tax System*. Markham: Viking Books.

McSheffrey, Kerry, 1988. *The Process of Tax Reform: Analyzed According to the Economic Model and to the Political Model*. Honours Thesis, School of Public Administration, Carleton University, Mimeo (April 1).

Mieszkowski, Peter, 1980. "The Advisability and Feasibility of an Expenditure Tax System." In H.J. Aaron and M.J. Boskin (eds.), *The Economics of Taxation*. Studies of Government Finance. Washington, D.C.: The Brookings Institution, 179–201.

Moggridge, Donald (ed.), 1978. *The Collected Writings of John Maynard Keynes*, Vol. XXII, *Activities 1939–1945, Internal War Finance*. London: Macmillan, Cambridge University Press.

Montreal Gazette, 1980. Editorial, "Sneaking in a Tax Hike." June 4.

Moore, A. Milton, J. Harvey Perry and Donald I. Beach, 1966. *The Financing of Canadian Federation, The First Hundred Years*. Canadian Tax Paper No. 43. Toronto: Canadian Tax Foundation.

Morton, Desmond and J.L. Granatstein, 1989. *Marching to Armageddon, Canadians and the Great War, 1914–1919*. Toronto: Lester and Orpen Dennys.

Musgrave, Richard A., 1943. "The Wartime Tax Effort in the United States, the United Kingdom and Canada." In *Proceedings of the 36th Annual Conference of the National Tax Association*, 300–322.

Musgrave, Richard A., 1959. *The Theory of Public Finance, A Study in Public Economy*. New York: McGraw-Hill.

Musgrave, Richard A., 1969. *Fiscal Systems*. New Haven and London: Yale University Press.

Musgrave, Richard A., 1980. "Theories of Fiscal Crises: An Essay in Fiscal Sociology." In Aaron and Boskin (see above, under Mieszkowski), 361–390.

Musgrave, Richard A., 1985. "A Brief History of Fiscal Doctrine." In Alan J. Auerbach and Martin Feldstein (eds.), *Handbook of Public Economics*, Vol. I. New York: North Holland, 1–59.

Musgrave, Richard A., Peggy B. Musgrave and Richard M. Bird, 1987. *Public Finance in Theory and Practice*. Toronto: McGraw-Hill.

Neatby, H. Blair, 1963. *William Lyon Mackenzie King*, Vol. 2. *The Lonely Heights, 1924–1932*. Toronto: University of Toronto Press.

Neatby, H. Blair, 1972. *The Politics of Chaos, Canada in the Thirties*. Toronto: Macmillan of Canada.

Nichols, Marjorie, 1990. "Tories Know GST Wound Won't Heal With Time." *Ottawa Citizen*, April 14:3.

Nielsen, Erik, 1989. *The House Is Not a Home*. Toronto: MacMillan.

Niskanen, William A., 1971. *Bureaucracy and Representative Government*. Chicago and New York: Aldine-Atherton.

Normand, Denis, Gilbert Hawley and W. Irwin Gillespie, 1983. "In Search of the Changing Distribution of Income During the Post-War Period in Canada and the United States." *Public Finance, Finances Publiques*, Vol. 38, No. 2 (December):267–281.

O'Connor, James, 1973. *The Fiscal Crisis of the State*. New York: St. Martin's Press.

Office of the Honourable Allan J. MacEachen, 1981a. "Notes for Remarks by the Honourable Allan J. MacEachen." *Release*, No. 81–127. Ottawa: December 18.

Office of the Honourable Allan J. MacEachen, 1981b. "Notes on Transitional Arrangements and Adjustments Relating to Tax Measures Announced November 12, 1981." *Release*, No. 81–126. Ottawa: December 18.

Office of the Honourable Allan J. MacEachen, 1982. "Notes on Draft Income Tax Legislation to Implement Budget Proposals." *Release*, No. 82–72. Ottawa: June 28.

Orzechowski, William, 1977. "Economic Models of Bureaucracy: Survey, Extensions, and Evidence." In Thomas E. Borcherding (ed.), *Budgets and Bureaucrats, The Sources of Government Growth*. Durham, North Carolina: Duke University Press, 229–259.

Parkinson, J.F., 1940. "Some Problems of War Finance in Canada." *Canadian Journal of Economics and Political Science*, Vol. 7:1–12.

Peacock, Alan, 1981. "Fiscal Theory and the "Market" for Tax Reform." In Roskamp and Forte (eds.), *Reforms of Tax Systems*. Proceedings of the 35th Congress of the International Institute of Public Finance. Detroit: Wayne State University Press.

Pechman, Joseph A., 1990. "The Future of the Income Tax." *American Economic Review*, Vol. 80, No. 1 (March):1–20.

Perry, J. Harvey, 1953. *Taxation in Canada*. Toronto: Canadian Tax Foundation and University of Toronto Press.

Perry, J. Harvey, 1955. *Taxes, Tariffs and Subsidies, A History of Canadian Fiscal Development*. 2 vols. Toronto: Canadian Tax Foundation and University of Toronto Press.

Perry, J. Harvey, 1982. *Background of Current Fiscal Problems*. Canadian Tax Paper No. 68. Toronto: Canadian Tax Foundation.

Perry, J. Harvey, 1989. *A Fiscal History of Canada — The Postwar Years*. Canadian Tax Paper No. 85. Toronto: Canadian Tax Foundation.

Petrie, J. Richards, 1952. *The Taxation of Corporate Income In Canada*. Toronto: University of Toronto Press.

Plumptre, A.F.W., 1941. *Canadian War Finance: A Study of Wartime Economic, Financial and Price Policies and Developments in Canada, September 1939 to December 1940*. Washington, D.C.: Office of Price Administration and Civilian Supply.

Plumptre, A.F.W., 1941a. *Canadian War Finance*. Washington, D.C.: U.S. Office for Emergency Management.

Pommerehne, Werner W., 1978. "Institutional Approaches to Public Expenditures: Empirical Evidence from Swiss Municipalities." *Journal of Public Economics*, Vol. 9, No. 2 (April):255–280.

Pommerehne, Werner W. and Friedrich Schneider, 1982. "Does Government in a Representative Democracy Follow a Majority of Voters' Preferences?: An Empirical Examination." In M. Hanusch (ed.), *Anatomy of Government Deficiencies*. Detroit: Wayne State University Press.

Rich, Georg, 1988. *The Cross of Gold: Money and the Canadian Business Cycle 1867–1913*. Ottawa: Carleton University Press.

Riley, Susan, 1989. "The GST: Rare Displays, Tender Concern." *Ottawa Citizen*, October 1:A10.

Robin, Martin, 1966. "Registration, Conscription and Independent Labour Polities, 1916–1917." In R. Cook., C. Brown and C. Berger (eds.), *Conscription 1917*. Toronto: University of Toronto Press, reprinted from *Canadian Historical Review*, Vol. XLVII, No. 2 (June):60–77.

Rose, Richard and Terence Karran, 1987. *Taxation by Political Inertia, Financing the Growth of Government in Britain*. London: Allen and Unwin.

Roskamp, Karl W. and Francesco Forte, 1981. *Reforms of Tax Systems*. Proceedings of the 35th Congress of the International Institute of Public Finance. Detroit: Wayne State University Press.

Rowell-Sirois Commission, 1940. *Report of the Royal Commission On Dominion-Provincial Relations*. Book I Canada: 1867–1939. Book II Recommendations. Book III Documentation. Ottawa: Government of Canada.

Royal Commission on Taxation, 1966. *Report*, 6 vols. Ottawa: Queen's Printer.

Safarian, A.E., 1970. *The Canadian Economy in the Great Depression*. The Carleton Library No. 54. Toronto: McClelland and Stewart Ltd.

Sales Tax Committee, 1956. *Report to the Minister of Finance*. Ottawa: Queen's Printer.

Samuelson, Paul A., 1954. "The Pure Theory of Public Expenditure." *Review of Economics and Statistics*, Vol. XXXVI (November):387–389.

Samuelson, Paul A. and Anthony Scott, 1971. *Economics*, 3rd Canadian Edition. Toronto: McGraw Hill.

Sandmo, Agnar, 1976. "Optimal Taxation: An Introduction to the Literature." *Journal of Public Economics*, Vol. 6:37–54.

Schumpeter, Joseph, 1918. "The Crisis of the Tax State", translated by W.F. Stolper and R.A. Musgrave, in A. Peacock, *et al.* (eds.), *International Economic Papers*, Vol. 4. London: Macmillan & Co., 1954, 5–38.

Schumpeter, Joseph, 1954. *History of Economic Analysis*. New York: Oxford University Press.

Senate of Canada, 1980. *Proceedings of the Standing Senate Committee on National Finance*. First Session, Thirty-Second Parliament, May 27:2A, 1–31 and 2, 30–39.

Sharp, Paul F., 1971. *The Agrarian Revolt In Western Canada, A Survey Showing American Parallels*. New York: Octagon Books.

Simons, Henry, 1938. *Personal Income Taxation. The Definition of Income as a Problem of Fiscal Policy.* Chicago: University of Chicago Press.

Simons, Henry, 1950. *Federal Tax Reform.* Chicago: University of Chicago Press.

Simpson, Jeffrey, 1989. "A Milch Cow Called The GST." *Globe and Mail,* September 8:6.

Simpson, Jeffrey, 1989a. "The Rate's Progress." *Globe and Mail,* November 28:A6.

Simpson, Jeffrey, 1989b. "To Recover from a Bad Decade." *Globe and Mail,* December 20:A6.

Simpson, Jeffrey, 1990. "He Who Haunts Us Still." *Globe and Mail,* October 27:C12.

Simpson, Jeffrey, 1991. "The Ominous Thin Edge of an Ill-Timed, Complex, Bureaucratic Tax." *Globe and Mail,* January 4:A14.

Sjoquist, D.L., 1981. "A Median Voter Analysis of Variations in the Use of Property Taxes Among Local Governments." *Public Choice,* Vol. 36:273–286.

Skelton, O.D., 1915. "Federal Finance." *Queen's Quarterly,* 60–93.

Skelton, O.D., 1917. "Canadian War Finance." *American Economic Review,* Vol. 7 (December):816–831.

Skelton, O.D., 1918. "Federal Finance II." *Bulletin of the Department of History and Political and Economic Science,* Queen's University, No. 29. Kingston: Jackson Press (October), 1–34.

Smith, Adam, 1776. *An Enquiry Into the Wealth of Nations,* 1904 ed. by E. Cunnan. New York: Putman's Sons.

Smith, Roger S., 1979. *Tax Expenditures: An Examination of Tax Incentives and Tax Preferences in the Canadian Federal Income Tax System.* Canadian Tax Paper No. 61. Toronto: Canadian Tax Foundation.

Stager, David, 1988. *Economic Analysis and Canadian Policy.* Sixth ed. Toronto: Butterworths.

Stanfield, Honourable Robert, 1972. "Proposal for a Constant Dollar Method of Computing Income for Tax Purposes." *House of Commons Debates,* Vol. 116, No. 52, May 15, 1972:2263–2269.

Statistics Canada, 1988. *National Income and Expenditure Accounts, Annual Estimates, 1926–1986.* Catalogue 13-531 Occasional. Ottawa: Minister of Supply and Services Canada.

Stiglitz, Joseph E. and Michael J. Boskin, 1977. "Impact of Recent Developments in Public Finance Theory on Public Policy Decisions. Some Lessons from the New Public Finance." *American Economic Review, Papers and Proceedings,* Vol. 67, No. 1.

Stikeman, H.H., 1943. "Canadian Experience in Financing the War." In *Proceedings of the 36th Annual Conference of the National Tax Association,* 345–360.

Strick, J.C., 1978. *Canadian Public Finance*, Second Edition. Toronto: Holt Rinehart and Winston of Canada.

Tait, Alan A., 1988. *Value Added Tax, International Practice and Problems.* Washington, D.C.: International Monetary Fund.

Tanzi, Vito, 1970. "International Tax Burdens." In Vito Tanzi, J.B. Bradwell-Milnes and D.R. Myddelton (eds.). *Taxation: A Radical Approach.* Surrey: Institute of Economic Affairs and Union Brothers Ltd.

Taylor, K.W., 1931. "Statistics of Foreign Trade." *Statistical Contributions of Canadian Economic History*, vol. 2. Toronto: Macmillan.

Thirsk, Wayne R. and John Whalley, 1982. *Tax Policy Options in the 1980s.* Canadian Tax Paper No. 66. Toronto: Canadian Tax Foundation.

Thirsk, Wayne, 1991. "Intellectual Foundations of the VAT." In Lorraine Eden (ed.), *Retrospectives on Public Finance.* Fiscal Reform in the Developing World Series. Durham, N.C.: Duke University Press.

Timbrell, David Y., 1988. "Tax Reform: Effects on Canada's Tax Competitiveness with the United States." In Edward A. Carmichael (ed.), *Tax Reform: Perspectives on the White Paper.* Policy Study No. 4. Toronto: C.D. Howe Institute, 63–64.

Toulin, Alan, 1988. "The Ominous Rise of Canada's Federal Deficit." *Ottawa Citizen*, November 29:A9.

Updike, John, 1963. "The Blessed Man of Boston, My Grandmother's Thimble, and Fanning Island." *Pigeon Feathers and Other Stories.* A Crest reprint. Greenwich, Conn.: Fawcett Publications.

Urquhart, M.C., 1986. "New Estimates of Gross National Product, Canada, 1870–1926: Some Implications for Canadian Development." In S. Engerman and R. Gallman (eds.), *Long-Term Factors In American Economic Growth.* Chicago: University of Chicago Press.

Urquhart, M.C. and K.A.H. Buckley, 1965. *Historical Statistics of Canada.* Toronto: Macmillan Company of Canada.

Vastel, Michel, 1980. "Pour éviter une hausse des impôts, Ottawa abolirait l'indexation." *Le Devoir*, May 24:13 and 16.

Villard, Harold G. and W.W. Willoughby, 1918. *The Canadian Budgetary System.* The Institute for Government Research. New York: D. Appleton and Co.

Vogel, Robert C. and Robert P. Trost, 1979. "The Response of State Government Receipts to Economic Fluctuations and the Allocation of Counter-Cyclical Revenue Sharing Grants." *Review of Economics and Statistics*, Vol. 61 (August):389–400.

Vukelich, George, 1972. "The Effect of Inflation on Real Tax Rates." *Canadian Tax Journal*, Vol. XX, No. 4 (July–August):327–342.

White, Sir Thomas, 1921. *The Story of Canada's War Finance.* Montreal: Canadian Bank of Commerce.

Will, Robert M., 1964. *The Budget as an Economic Document.* Studies of the Royal Commission on Taxation, No. 1. Ottawa: Queen's Printer.

Will, Robert M., 1967. *Canadian Fiscal Policy 1945–63*, Studies of the Royal Commission on Taxation, No. 17. Ottawa: Queen's Printer.

Wilson, Honourable Michael H., 1986a. [Same as Budget Speech delivered Feb. 26, 1986. See Appendix E.]

Wilson, Honourable Michael H., 1986b. *Guidelines for Tax Reform in Canada*. Ottawa: Department of Finance (October).

Wilson, Honourable Michael H., 1987a. [Same as Budget Speech delivered Feb. 18, 1987. See Appendix E.]

Wilson, Honourable Michael H., 1987b. [Same as White Paper on Tax Reform, delivered June 18, 1987. See Appendix E.]

Wilson, Honourable Michael H., 1987c. *The White Paper, Tax Reform 1987*. Ottawa: Canada, Department of Finance (June 18).

Wilson, Honourable Michael H., 1987d. *Tax Reform 1987, Income Tax Reform*. Ottawa: Canada, Department of Finance (June 18).

Wilson, Honourable Michael H., 1987e. *Tax Reform 1987, Sales Tax Reform*. Ottawa: Canada, Department of Finance.

Wilson, Honourable Michael H., 1989a. [Same as Budget Speech delivered April 27, 1989. See Appendix E.]

Wilson, Honourable Michael H., 1989b. *The Goods and Services Tax*. Ottawa: Canada, Department of Finance (April 27).

Wilson, Honourable Michael H., 1989c. *The Fiscal Plan, Controlling the Public Debt*. Ottawa: Canada, Department of Finance (April 27).

Wilson, Honourable Michael H., 1989d. *Goods and Services Tax, An Overview*. Ottawa: Canada, Department of Finance (August).

Wilson, Honourable Michael H., 1989e. *Goods and Services Tax, Technical Paper*. Ottawa: Canada, Department of Finance (August).

Wilson, Honourable Michael H., 1989f. *Goods and Services Tax, Draft Legislation and Explanatory Notes*. Ottawa: Canada, Department of Finance (October).

Wilson, Honourable Michael H., 1989g. *Goods and Services Tax*. Ottawa: Canada, Department of Finance (December 19).

Winer, Stanley L., 1983. "Some Evidence on the Effect of the Separation of Spending and Taxing Decisions." *Journal of Political Economy*, Vol. 9 (February):126–140.

Winer, Stanley L. and Walter Hettich, 1991. "Debt and Tariffs: An Empirical Investigation of The Evolution of Revenue Systems." *Journal of Public Economics*, Vol. 45, No. 2:215–242.

Winer, Stanley L. and Walter Hettich, 1988. "The Structure of the Sieve: Political Economy in the Explanation of Tax Systems and Tax Reform." *Osgoode Hall Law Journal*, Vol. 26, No. 2 (Summer):409–422.

Winsor, Hugh, 1989. "Wilson Has Work Cut Out Selling Goods and Services Tax to Public." *Globe and Mail*, December 21:A9.

Wiseman, Jack, 1989. "The Political Economy of Government Revenues." In Aldo Chiancone and Ken Messere (eds.), *Changes in Revenue Structures*, Proceedings of the 42nd Congress of the International Institute of Public Finance. Detroit: Wayne State University Press, 9–20.

Witte, John F., 1985. *The Politics and Development of the Federal Income Tax*. Madison, Wisconsin: University of Wisconsin Press.

Wolfe, David A., 1985. "The Politics of the Deficit." In G. Bruce Doern (ed.), *The Politics of Economic Policy*. Toronto: University of Toronto Press, for the Royal Commission on the Economic Union and Development Prospects for Canada, 111–162.

Wolfe, David A., 1988. "Politics, The Deficit and Tax Reform." *Osgoode Hall Law Journal*, Vol. 26, No. 2 (Summer):348–366.

Young, Christopher, 1980. "Liberals are Planning Retrograde Taxation." *Ottawa Citizen*, June 5:6.

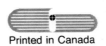

Printed in Canada